PROFESSOR LEE C. GARRISON, JR.
GRADUATE SCHOOL OF BUSINESS ADMINISTRATION
UNIVERSITY OF CALIFORNIA
LOS ANGELES, CALIFORNIA 90024

D1357095

PRENTICE-HALL INTERNATIONAL SERIES IN MANAGEMENT

Athos and Coffey	Behavior in Organizations: A Multidimensional View
Baumol	Economic Theory and Operations Analysis
Boot	Mathematical Reasoning in Economics and Management Science
Brown	Smoothing, Forecasting and Prediction of Discrete Time Series
Chambers	Accounting, Evaluation and Economic Behavior
Churchman	Prediction and Optimal Decision: Philosophical Issues of a Science of Values.
Clarkson	The Theory of Consumer Demand: A Critical Appraisal
Cyert and March	A Behavioral Theory of the Firm
Fabrycky and Torgersen	Operations Economy: Industrial Applications of Operations Research
Greenlaw, Herron, and Rawdon	Business Simulation in Industrial and University Education
Hadley and White	Analysis of Inventory Systems
Holt, Modigliani, and Simon	Planning Production, Inventories, and Work Force
Hymans	Probability Theory with Applications to Econometrics and Decision-Making
Ijiri	The Foundations of Accounting Measurement: A Mathematical, Economic, and Behavioral Inquiry
Kaufmann	Methods and Models of Operations Research
Lesourne	Economic Analysis and Industrial Management
Mantel	Cases in Managerial Decisions
Massé	Optimal Investment Decisions: Rules for Action and Criteria for Choice
McGuire	Theories of Business Behavior
Miller and Starr	Executive Decisions and Operations Research
Montgomery and Urban	Management Science in Marketing
Morris	Management Science: A Bayesian Introduction
Muth and Thompson	Industrial Scheduling
Nelson (ed.)	Marginal Cost Pricing in Practice
Nicosia	Consumer Decision Processes: Marketing and Advertising Decisions
Peters and Summers	Statistical Analysis for Business Decisions
Pfiffner and Sherwood	Administrative Organization
Simmonard	Linear Programming
Singer	Antitrust Economics: Selected Legal Cases and Economic Models
Still and Cundiff	Sales Management: Decisions, Policies, and Cases (4th ed.)
Vernon	Manager in the International Economy
Zangwill	Nonlinear Programming: A Unified Approach

PRENTICE-HALL, INC.
PRENTICE-HALL INTERNATIONAL, INC., UNITED KINGDOM AND EIRE
PRENTICE-HALL OF CANADA, LTD., CANADA
J. H. DEBUSSY, LTD., HOLLAND AND FLEMISH-SPEAKING BELGIUM
DUNOD PRESS, FRANCE
MARUZEN COMPANY, LTD., FAR EAST
HERRERO HERMANOS, SUCS., SPAIN AND LATIN AMERICA
R. OLDENBOURG VERLAG, GERMANY
ULRICO HOEPLI EDITORS, ITALY

Management Science in Marketing

DAVID B. MONTGOMERY

and

GLEN L. URBAN

of the
Alfred P. Sloan School of Management
Massachusetts Institute of Technology

Prentice-Hall, Inc., Englewood Cliffs, New Jersey

Printed in the United States of America

Library of Congress Catalog Card No.: *69-14590*

Current Printing (last digit): 10 9 8 7 6 5 4 3 2 1

Figures 2-1, 2-4, 2-5, and Table 2-2 of this book were reproduced from A. Amstutz' *Computer Simulation of Competitive Market Response* (copyright © 1967 by The Massachusetts Institute of Technology).

Prentice-Hall International, Inc., *London*
    Prentice-Hall of Australia, Pty. Ltd., *Sydney*
Prentice-Hall of Canada, Ltd., *Toronto*
    Prentice-Hall of India Private Ltd., *New Delhi*
Prentice-Hall of Japan, Inc., *Tokyo*

To our wives . . . Toby and Andrea
                    and
to our current and expected children . . . David, Scott,
            (0.60 boy + 0.40 girl) Montgomery, and
            (0.52 boy + 0.48 girl) Urban

Preface

In late 1966 the authors began developing this material for use in a new course entitled "Marketing Models" which was given the following spring at the Sloan School of Management, Massachusetts Institute of Technology. Their original intent was to develop about 100 pages of text outlining the state of the art in the application of management science to marketing. This short text was to be packaged with an extensive set of papers from the most current literature to provide a basis for the models course. Little did they suspect upon starting this project that the text would grow to nearly 400 pages by the time the material was used in the M.I.T. Summer Session Course "Management Science in Marketing" in August 1967. The interest and suggestions of the graduate students in the spring and the industrial operations researchers in the summer, coupled with suggestions from several colleagues, lead to a substantial revision during that fall and winter. The final text material grew to over 500 pages and it no longer seemed viable to package text and readings in one volume. Consequently, two volumes are being published. The first is this text and the second (yet to be published) is a companion volume of readings entitled *Applications of Management Science in Marketing*. It is hoped that users will find this arrangement more convenient.

This book is a co-authored book in the true sense of the word. Each author had a hand in writing every chapter and much time was spent in interaction between themselves and their students on the materials discussed in the text. While it would be tempting for each author to assume all credit and ascribe all errors to the other, the highly iterated nature of this material makes each author equally responsible for the contributions and errors in this text. Hopefully, the high degree of interaction has maximized the contributions and minimized the residual errors. One point can be made with assurance—that the authors learned a great deal from one another in this collaborative effort. Whatever the merits of this text, the joint product certainly exceeds that which could have been achieved by one author alone.

The purpose of this book is explicitly outlined on pages 6 and 7 of Chap. 1 and will not be reiterated. Suffice it to say here that hopefully this statement of the state of the art in the application of management science models will provide a useful base for practitioners, students, and academicians, who will soon make the contributions which will render the present material obsolete.

Since reports of applications of management science models to marketing are constantly being published (and at an accelerating rate), a cutoff date for inclusion in this text was set at October 31, 1967. Only models published before that date or in the author's hands in some written form were included in the discussion.

The objective in writing this text has not been to be encyclopedic in coverage. Thus not all applications have been reported. The applications which were selected for inclusion reflect the authors' judgments as to the quality of the models and the usefulness of such applications in the development of the substantive marketing modeling material in each chapter. Many of the models are critiqued in the text. Again, the objective has been to emphasize certain substantive issues without assuming the obligation to criticize every facet of an application.

While the models which are discussed have a considerable amount of behavioral content, it was decided that the subject of behavioral science modeling in marketing would not be exhaustively treated. This decision in no way implies a disregard for the very important contributions which the behavioral sciences have made, and will continue to make, to the modeling of market phenomena. Rather it reflects the feeling that to do an adequate job of considering the contributions of behavioral science to marketing would require a second volume. It also reflects the current state of the art in management science, which has not fully integrated behavioral science concepts and theories into its mathematical model building activities. Such integration is clearly an area of high potential for mathematical modeling, and research is called for in this area.

The authors would like to acknowledge a number of people for their support, comments, and suggestions. They would first like to thank their Sloan School colleagues John D. C. Little and Arnold E. Amstutz for being key components in a very stimulating environment. They are also indebted to their graduate students and to the participants in the M.I.T.

Summer Session on Management Science in Marketing for their patience and helpful comments on earlier versions of this material. In particular, Len Lodish and Rick Karash were very helpful.

Colleagues at several institutions made valuable suggestions for improving the manuscript. The authors are especially grateful to Ron Frank and Paul Green of Wharton, Phil Kotler of Northwestern, Jim Heskett of Harvard, and Fred Webster of Dartmouth.

Financial support for this book was supplied by the M.I.T. Summer Session Office, for which the authors would like to thank James Austin, the Director.

As every author knows, cheerful and capable typists are a crucial ingredient in the development of any manuscript. The authors would like to thank Dyanne Nielsen, Judy Mason, Carol Gearg and Leyla Uran for their typing, editing, and proofreading assistance.

Cambridge, Massachusetts
September 1, 1968

DBM
GLU

Contents

3. Advertising Decisions . . . 94

4. Pricing Decisions . . . 158

8. Implementation of Management Science in Marketing . . . 347

9. The Future of Management Science in Marketing . . . 360

1

Introduction to Management Science and Marketing

INTRODUCTION

A Marketing Dialogue in 1988

The year is 1988. The place is the office of the marketing manager of a medium-sized consumer products manufacturer. The participants in the following discussion are John, the marketing manager; Bill, the director of marketing science; Rod, Bill's assistant, who specializes in marketing research; and Scott, the sales manager for the company. The scene opens as Bill, Rod, and Scott enter John's office.

> *John:* Good morning, gentlemen. What's on the agenda for this morning?
> *Bill:* We want to take a look at the prospects for our new beef substitute.
> *John:* What do we have on that new product?
> *Rod:* We test-marketed it late in 1987 in four cities, so we have those data from last quarter.
> *John:* Let's see how it did.
> (All four gather around the remote console video display unit. John activates the console and requests it to display the sales results from the most recent test market. The system retrieves the data from random access storage and displays the information on the video device.)
> *John:* That looks good! How does it compare to the first test?
> (The console retrieves and displays the data from the first test on command from John.)

Rod: Let me check the significance of the sales increase of the most recent test over last year's test.

(Rod requests that the system test and display the likelihood that the sales increase could be a chance occurrence.)

Rod: Looks like a solid sales increase.

Bill: Good! How did the market respond to our change in price?

(Bill commands the system to display the graph of the price-quantity response based upon the most recent test data.)

John: Is that about what our other meat substitute products show?

(John calls for past price-quantity response graphs for similar products to be superimposed on the screen.)

John: Just as I suspected—this new product is a bit more responsive to price. What's the profit estimate?

(John calls for a profit estimate from the product planning model within the system.)

John: Hmm . . . $5,500,000. Looks good. Is that based upon the growth model I supplied to the model bank last week?

Bill: No. This is based upon the penetration progress other food substitutes have shown in the past as well as the information we have on the beef substitute from our test markets.

John: Let's see what mine would do.

(He reactivates the product planning model, this time using his growth model. The profit implications are displayed on the console.)

John: Well, my model predicts $5,000,000. That's close. Looks like my feelings are close to the statistical results.

Bill: Let's see if there's a better marketing strategy for this product. We must remember that these profit estimates are based on the preliminary plan we developed two weeks ago.

(Bill calls for the marketing mix generator to recommend a marketing program based upon the data and judgmental inputs which are available in the data bank's file on this product.)

Bill: There, we can increase profit by $700,000 if we allocate another sales call each week to the new product committees of the chain stores.

Scott: I don't think our salesmen will go along with that. They don't like to face those committees. The best I could do is convince them to make one additional call every other week.

John: What would happen in that case?

(The marketing mix generator is called with the new restriction on the number of calls.)

John: Well, the profit increase is still $500,000, so let's add that call policy recommendation to our marketing plan. I'm a little worried about our advertising appeals, though. Can we improve in that area?

Bill: Let's see what the response to advertising is.

(The video unit shows a graph of the predicted sales-advertising response function.)

Bill: If we changed from a taste appeal to a convenience appeal, what would the results be, John?

John: I think it would look like this.

(John takes a light pen and describes a new relationship on the video unit based upon his judgment of the effectiveness of the new appeal.)

Rod: Let me check something.

(Rod calls for a sample of past sales-advertising response curves of similar products using the convenience appeal.)

Rod: I think you are underestimating the response on the basis of past data.

John: Well, this product is different.   How much would it cost for a test of this appeal?

(Rod calls a market research evaluation model from the console.)

Rod: It looks like a meaningful test would cost about $5,000.

Bill: Wait! Hadn't we better check to see if the differences between these two advertising response functions will lead to any differences in profit?

(The marketing mix model is called for each advertising function.)

Bill: Looks sensitive to the advertising response, all right.   There's a $900,000 difference in profit.

John: I wonder what risk we'd run if we made a decision to go national with the product right now.   What are the chances of a failure with this product as it stands if we include this morning's revisions to the marketing mix?

(A risk analysis model is called on the system.)

John: Looks like a 35 per cent chance of failure.   Maybe we'd best run further tests in order to reduce the risk of failure.   What's next on the agenda this morning?

The dialogue presented in this section indicates the probable environment in which future marketing decisions will be made.   Marketing managers will be able to call upon powerful information systems to assist them in charting the course and evaluating the results of the firm's marketing efforts.   Such systems will provide the manager with advanced modeling and statistical techniques to assist him in improving his decisions.   They will also provide him with the capacity to store, retrieve, and manipulate data relevant to his decision problems.   Although the dialogue was depicted as occurring in 1988, recent developments in computer technology and marketing modeling techniques may make such systems a reality in the much nearer future.[1]

[1] See T. Hanold, "Management by Perception," *Information Systems Review* I, No. 1 (1966), pp. 6–9, or "The Pillsbury Company," Harvard Business School Case (M-255, 1967) for an example of how firms are now utilizing this computer technology in marketing decision making.

Management Science and Marketing:
The Present

In the period after World War II, a new methodology for analyzing management problems emerged. The methodology has been commonly referred to as operations research or management science. This methodology has produced models and quantitative techniques such as mathematical programming, PERT, and simulation. These new techniques have found a number of successful applications in production and finance. Marketing, however, has not experienced a parallel development. Although there is evidence of accelerating interest in the management science approach to marketing, achievements in this area remain more modest than in areas such as production and finance.

A number of factors have contributed to this relative lag in management science progress in marketing. The following six factors would seem to be the major elements in this lag:

1. *Complexity of Marketing Phenomena.* The modeling of market phenomena often requires greater complexity due to the fact that response to market stimuli tend to be highly nonlinear, to exhibit threshold effects (i.e., some minimum level of the stimulus is required for there to be any response at all), to have carry-over effects (e.g., response to this period's promotion will occur in future periods), and to decay with time in the absence of further stimulation. A further consideration is the fact that market response tends to be dependent upon many factors. This multivariate nature of marketing problems injects additional complexity into marketing decisions.

2. *Interaction Effects in Marketing Variables.* The impact of any single controllable marketing variable is difficult to determine due to interaction of the variable with the environment and with other marketing variables. For example, the impact of promotional effort may depend upon factors in the firm's environment, such as the level of economic activity, the availability of credit, and customer expectations. Interaction with other marketing variables occurs, for example, when sales results due to promotion depend upon the level of price and distribution. These interactions within the marketing mix make it difficult to uncouple the elements in the marketing mix so that they may be analyzed independently. Other management decision areas have had more success in uncoupling the component subsystems for further analysis.

3. *Competition and Marketing Decisions.* The final outcomes of

marketing decisions depend upon how competitors react. In many production and finance problems, competitive effects are negligible or considered exogenous.

4. *Measurement Problems in Marketing.* The consumer-oriented nature of marketing makes response relationships difficult, if not impossible, to observe. Recourse is often made to indirect techniques such as recall measures of advertising exposure. Production and inventory systems, on the other hand, generally require only data from physical systems within the firm. Buzzell has noted, "It is clear . . . that the development of inventory models would be far more difficult if it were necessary to rely on estimates of stocks on hand as recalled by stock clerks."[2]

5. *Instability of Marketing Relationships.* The relationships between market responses and marketing decision variables tend to be temporally instable due to changes in tastes, attitudes, expectations, etc. This factor makes continuous market measurements and the revision of decisions crucially important in marketing.

6. *Incompatibility of Marketing and Operations Research Personnel.* Initially, underlying attitudinal differences between marketing and operations research personnel formed a barrier to innovation. Marketing decision makers usually gained their experience in the sales area of the company and were not able or willing to accept or utilize quantitative techniques. Operations researchers, on the other hand, did most of their work in the production area, which is characterized by measurable and quantifiable data. The operations research people, in general, were not interested in marketing problems because of the non-quantified nature of marketing and the attitudinal incompatibility with marketing decision makers.

The underlying explanation for these factors lies in the fact that marketing deals with behavioral rather than technological phenomena.

The preceding diagnosis of the factors contributing to marketing's past lag may encourage the reader to doubt the compatibility of marketing and management science. Other factors, however, suggest accelerated progress in the future. In the first place, the profit squeeze caused by spiraling costs and increased competition is forcing firms to seek better methods for decision making. Since marketing costs are becoming a major proportion of total costs, firms will tend to focus more attention on marketing decision problems. Second, shortened product lives have

---

[2] D. Buzzell, *Mathematical Models and Marketing Management* (Boston: Division of Research, Graduate School of Business Administration, Harvard University, 1964), p. 74.

made new products of crucial importance to the firm. The staggering failure rate of these new products is leading to the acceptance of more scientific approaches to product planning. Another factor that should help management science to advance in marketing relates to the quantity and quality of marketing data available for decision purposes. Commercial and governmental data services are constantly expanding while advances in psychometric procedures, especially multidimensional scaling, promise improved quality and relevance of available market data.

In addition to these factors, which indicate greater pressures toward the acceptance of management science innovations, management science itself is maturing as a discipline. Advances in mathematical programming, such as integer programming, branch and bound methods for combinatorial problems, stochastic programming, and nonlinear programming, enable the management scientist to treat much more complex and interrelated problems than were feasible in the past. As further evidence of the maturing capability of management science to deal with marketing problems, one could cite developments in statistical decision theory, simulation techniques, and heuristic programming. The advent of the third generation computer system, with its greatly enhanced storage capabilities, speed, and software, holds great promise for implementing these new techniques in marketing. Remote consoles and graphical displays will allow considerable man-machine-data-model interaction in the future.

Finally, it is hoped that this book will contribute to the diffusion of management science methods in marketing by providing a framework for the assessment of past and potential contributions of management science to marketing problems.

Purpose of This Book

This book will attempt to present an integrated discussion of the uses of management science in analyzing and solving marketing problems. This development will begin by structuring over-all marketing problems from the point of view of the marketing manager in a firm. This structure will indicate the over-all nature of the problems and will reflect the behavioral, quantitative, and institutional aspects of marketing. Existing management science applications to marketing will be positioned in this structure. In every problem area, the scope of each work will be delineated and its relationship to other models will be outlined. The methodology of these applications will be analyzed, and advantages and disadvantages of the various approaches will be discussed.

The outcome of this analysis will be a description of the state of the art of management science in marketing. In this development of the state of the art, a number of gaps in the application of modeling techniques to marketing problems and subproblems will become apparent. These gaps may reflect an undesirable definition or understanding of particular marketing problems, an unreasonable set of assumptions, or an unsatisfactory designation of factors to be considered exogenous in the analysis. The occurrence of these gaps should not be too surprising, since the management science approach itself is very young; most of the literature in management science has been developed during the last fifteen years. The identification of the shortcomings of previous approaches is intended to define a number of opportunities for the future. It is hoped that this book will supply a base for future analytic work on marketing problems. A number of the most productive avenues for advancing the management science approach in marketing will be indicated in each chapter.

The purposes of this book are to (1) structure over-all marketing management problems from the point of view of the producer, (2) position, review, and criticize existing management science models in this structure, (3) indicate existing gaps in the application of management science in marketing, (4) assist the reader in developing his capacity to build and implement models for use in analyzing and solving marketing problems, and (5) indicate productive directions for future management science efforts in the area of marketing.

THE NATURE OF MANAGEMENT SCIENCE

Definition of Management Science

It is difficult to define and bound an area of study which is experiencing a constant development of new techniques that extend its scope and composition. Management science is such an area. Despite this difficulty, two prominent features are reflected in the name given to this area of study. "Management," in the context of the methodology, carries with it a strong implication of problem solving. Thus, management science is directed at understanding and solving management problems. The second component of the name is "science." This carries with it a strong implication of scientific methodology. This methodology can be described as:

1. Formulation of a problem
2. Development of a hypothesis for analyzing the problem
3. Measurement of relevant phenomena
4. Derivation of a solution or basis of understanding of the problem
5. Testing of the results
6. Revisions to reflect the testing of the hypothesis
7. Emergence of valid results

This is essentially the methodology used in the empirical physical sciences. In management science this methodology begins with a model to define and describe the problem (steps 1 and 2). Next the relationships within the model and the input to the model are specified and measured (step 3). A solution to the model or a specification of the explicit relationships necessary for understanding the problem is found by the application of a solution technique (step 4). The final steps in the approach are to validate the solution and model (steps 5, 6, and 7). Validity testing attempts to establish that the model represents a reasonable approximation to the system being modeled. The validity of a model may be assessed by examining the ability of the model to predict future results and the accuracy of the internal model relationships. Model testing may also include an analysis of sensitivity. Sensitivity testing is directed at determining how much the model output will change for given changes in the model input or in the values of the model parameters. The model sensitivity should correspond to the sensitivity of the real world problem environment. In this way sensitivity is related to validity, but sensitivity analysis is itself useful in developing requirements for the accuracy of model input and the estimation of the underlying model relationships.

The two central aspects of problem orientation and scientific approach lead to a definition of management science as the understanding and solution of management problems by the application of scientific methodology. It should be noted that this definition does not restrict itself to a specific enumeration of techniques. Although management science efforts up to this time have tended to be quantitative, this is not a necessary condition for work in the area of management science. There is no natural dichotomy between quantitative and nonquantitative efforts. Although behavioral science has tended to be nonquantitative, this does not imply that it does not have an important place in management science. The techniques of operations research, econometrics, mathematics, statistics, and the behavioral sciences are all relevant to management science.

The definition of management science proposed here is very broad and is intended to include all scientific research efforts directed at solving and understanding management problems. This will lead to a common, compatible field of knowledge that will encourage rigorous, productive analyses of the problems of management science.

Management Science Models

Before a discussion of the types of models used in management science, it would be useful to define what is meant by a model. A model is simply a representation of some or all of the properties of a larger system. The system is the total environment surrounding the problem, whereas the model is a description of the aspects of the system that are essential to the analysis. The representation could be physical or abstract. For example, a wooden model airplane is a physical representation of a larger system—the actual real world airplane. An alternate model would be a set of blueprints that represents the larger system. A third model might be a set of mathematical equations that represent the larger aircraft system.

In management science, four commonly used types of models can be identified:

1. Implicit models
2. Verbal models
3. Logical flow models
4. Mathematical models

Implicit models are models that are not made explicit by some communicable form of representation. All decisions that are not made on the basis of an explicit model are made on the basis of an implicit model. This exhaustive classification is based on the premise that all decisions are made by the use of a model. This is not an unacceptable proposition, since a "model" was defined in a very general sense as a representation of a larger system. With this definition it is clear that all decisions are made on the basis of a model, since some representation of the problem must be perceived before it can be solved or a decision reached. If the model is not recorded in communicable form, it is an implicit model that remains in the decision maker's cognitive structure until it is communicated and made explicit.

There are several methods of making an implicit model explicit. The first method is to communicate the model in the form of written or spoken words. This representation is a verbal model. The communication of the model is the first step in making it explicit. An example of a verbal model of pricing behavior would be, "If I change my price, my

competitor will match my price unless it would cause him to lose money."
This verbalization of an implicit model exposes the behavioral postulates
assumed in the pricing decision.

The next type of model is the logical flow model.[3]   This is an extension
of the verbal model by the use of a diagram.   The diagram makes explicit
the sequence of questions to be asked and the way in which they are
related.   In Fig. 1-1, the simple verbal competitive pricing behavior
model is described by a logical flow diagram.   This formulation of a
model is useful, since it serves to clarify the relationships between the
model's components.

The next step in model exposition is to quantify the model's components and the relationships between the components.   This leads to a
mathematical model.   In mathematical models, not only the sequence
but also the magnitude of the interrelationships is indicated.   In the
pricing example, a mathematical model to describe the simple competitive
environment is given in Fig. 1-1.   The mathematical model says that
$\bar{P}_c = P_c$, or the competitor does not change his price when $I = 0$.   This
occurs when $P_m Q_c - C_c < 0$ or when total revenue $P_m Q_c$ less total
cost C_c is negative when the competitor uses my price.   This corresponds to the verbal condition that the competitor will not change
his price if it would produce a loss.   The mathematical model
prescribes $\bar{P}_c = P_m$ when $I = 1$. $I = 1$ when $\bar{P}_c Q_c - C_c \geq 0$, i.e. when
no loss occurs when my price is used.   This corresponds to the verbal
rule that the competitor will imitate our price if it does not produce a
loss.   This simple model represents in mathematical terms how the
competitor is expected to behave if price changes.   With this model the
existing decision structure and new procedures could be tested.

Mathematical models can be described in a number of ways.   Two
useful dimensions of classification relate to methods by which the model
treats time and risk.   The first classification is divided into two subclasses:
static and dynamic, that is, those models that do not consider time effects
and those that do.   The second classification is divided into stochastic
and deterministic models.   Stochastic models consider risk or probabilistic phenomena, whereas deterministic models assume certainty of
outcomes and events.   The simple model in Fig. 1-1 is a static, deterministic model.

Implicit, verbal, and mathematical models may be used compatibly.
For example, a mathematical model may be one part of a logical flow
model that is derived from a verbal description of an implicit model.
The type of model to be used depends on the degree of explicitness

---

[3] See W. F. Massy and J. Saavas, "Logical Flow Models for Marketing Analysis,"
Journal of Marketing, Vol. XXVIII (January, 1964), pp. 32–37.

VERBAL MODEL:

"If I change my price my competitor will match my price unless it would cause him to lose money."

LOGICAL FLOW MODEL:

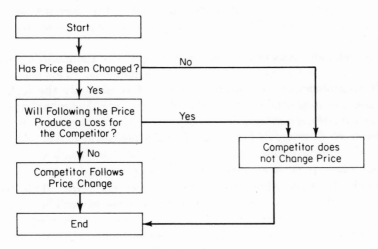

MATHEMATICAL MODEL:

$$\bar{P}_c = (1 - I)P_c + IP_m$$

$$I = \begin{cases} 0, \text{ if } P_mQ_c - C_c < 0 \\ 1, \text{ if } P_mQ_c - C_c \geq 0 \end{cases}$$

$\bar{P}_c$ = competitor's new price
P_c = competitor's old price
P_m = price of firm ("my" firm)
Q_c = quantity of sales competitor could sell at P_m
C_c = competitor's total cost of producing and selling Q_c

Figure 1-1: Simple examples of three types of models

desired in the problem or decision situation. The desired degree of explicitness depends upon the advantages that accrue to the researcher or decision maker who approaches his problems using the more formalized mathematical models. First, mathematical specification has the advantage of making assumptions explicit. This renders the assumptions more open to debate, testing, and revision. Second, mathematical models often provide a useful framework for measuring market phenomena. Finally, the language of mathematics is the richest framework in which to manipulate a model. Such manipulation may involve the optimization of policy functions or the exploration of "what if" types of questions. These and other uses of mathematical models are discussed in greater detail in a later section of this chapter.

Techniques for Analyzing Models

With the understanding that a model is an implicit or explicit representation of a larger system, it is useful to examine the techniques that can be used to analyze models.

The most general technique that can be applied is to ask questions about the effects of changing the model or the inputs to the model. These "what if" questions represent experiments on the model. The technique of experimentation applied to a model is simulation. The model itself is not a simulation. Simulation is the technique of asking "what if" questions of the model. This definition implies that simulation is the process of testing alternate input or structural relationships within a model. The limit of such testing would be enumeration and not simulation. In general, simulation is considered to be the testing of a small number of alternatives, but it is difficult to establish an exact number of trials for "small." To analyze a larger number of alternatives, but to restrict the testing to be less than enumeration, heuristic programming can be utilized. Heuristic programming techniques are based on an orderly search procedure. This procedure is guided by a heuristic or a useful rule of thumb that helps restrict the search to less than enumeration. It cannot guarantee that the best alternative will be selected, but hopefully it considers the relevant alternatives.

The three techniques of simulation, heuristic programming, and enumeration can be applied to models to generate useful information. They all involve the testing of alternatives. Enumeration examines all possibilities, whereas simulation is thought of as testing fewer than the total number of possibilities. Heuristic programming is a search procedure that is guided by a search rule that reduces the number of tests from the number in the exhaustive set to something less. For example, if a price decision was to be made, simulation might be used to generate profit forecasts for five specified alternative prices. In contrast, a heuristic search might be based on evaluating a price of ten dollars and then examining successively higher prices in one dollar increments until no more profit improvement was found. Enumeration would entail testing all possible prices so that the best outcome could be identified.

The successive trial techniques indicated in the last paragraphs are not necessarily directed at producing solutions for model problems. They explore the implications of alternatives, but they do not find the best alternative by an algorithmic procedure. Several techniques may be applied to models in an attempt to generate optimal results.

The most basic optimizing technique is calculus. If certain assumptions are met, calculus can be used to identify the optimal alternative for the model. Other algorithmic techniques are available for analysis of models. Mathematical programming is the most prominent. Mathematical programming algorithms may be divided into linear, nonlinear, integer, dynamic, and stochastic programming. The application of these techniques to marketing problems will be discussed in succeeding chapters.[4]

In addition to experimental and optimization methods, other techniques can be applied to models. Mathematical models that are characterized by probabilistic relationships can be analyzed by methods developed in probability and statistics. Statistical techniques can also be valuable in measuring and testing mathematical models. Statistical decision theory and game theory are useful methods for analyzing models that depict decision situations under conditions of risk and uncertainty, respectively.

The appropriate technique to be applied in analyzing a model will depend on the structure of the model and the purpose the model is expected to serve. One of the intents of this book is to explore the appropriateness of these techniques for models that are designed to aid in marketing decisions. It is hoped that the reader will develop facility with each technique and thereby make it a tool he can use in analyzing marketing problems. The collection of these techniques should form a tool kit that can be used to solve marketing problems and to understand marketing phenomena. The specification of this tool kit and the instruction in how it has been and can be used in marketing is the task of this book.

Uses of Management Science Models

The definition of management science developed earlier in this chapter indicates that management science is directed at understanding and solv-

---

[4] See the Index for page references to particular techniques.

ing problems. The uses of models will be discussed within this framework. Two broad classes of uses can be identified. The first relates to the understanding of problems as reflected in problem identification, definition, and exploration. The second class of uses is related to finding solutions to problems. Both these classes of uses represent attempts to extend the manager's ability to comprehend his environment and make better decisions. In general, models are designed to expand the "bounds of rationality" that limit the manager's ability to find optimal or good solutions to his problems.[5]

The class of uses related to problem identification, definition, and exploration can be subdivided into uses associated with descriptive and predictive models. See Fig. 1-2 for the classification of model uses.

I. Understanding Problems—Descriptive and Predictive Models
   A. Descriptive Models
     1. Transform data into more meaningful forms
     2. Indicate areas for search and experimentation
     3. Generate structural hypotheses for testing
     4. Provide a framework for measurement
     5. Aid in systematic thinking about problem
     6. Provide bases of discussion that will lead to common understanding of problem
   B. Predictive Models
     1. Make forecasts of future events
     2. Validate descriptive models
     3. Determine sensitivity of predictions to model parameters
II. Solving Problems—Normative Models
   A. Provide framework for structuring subjective feelings and determining their decision implications
   B. Provide a tool for the analysis of decisions
   C. Assess system implications of decisions
   D. Yield solutions to problems
   E. Determine sensitivity of decision to the model's characteristics
   F. Provide a basis for updating and controling decisions

Figure 1-2: Uses of management science models

Descriptive models are concerned with providing detailed and accurate representations of "larger systems." For example, in marketing the system may be consumer behavior. A model of the system may be used to transform a large body of detailed data relating to this system into a more understandable and meaningful form. A model of consumer behavior may be utilized to transform test market data obtained from a

---

[5] For a discussion of limits of rationality, see H. A. Simon, *Administrative Behavior* (2nd ed.; New York: Macmillan Co., 1961), pp. 80–96.

consumer panel into a more relevant form. For example, the panel data may be transformed by the model into brand switching rates or estimates of the brand loyalty characteristics of consumers. The model may indicate areas where data are needed and may lead to search for this information by experimentation or statistical studies. In the example of the consumer model, the transformed data may indicate a lack of information on psychological characteristics of the panel members and may lead to a special study to obtain this information. Consideration of the descriptive adequacy of the model may lead to the testing of alternate structural hypotheses and the generation of additional insights into the system. If an originally postulated consumer model does not accurately describe behavior, this might suggest that alternate model formulations should be developed and tested. The testing of different model structures should help the decision maker gain a better understanding of his problem situation. The model also provides a framework that is useful in specifying the variables to be measured in gathering new data and testing hypotheses.

The explicit nature of a descriptive model will provide a basis for reconciling differing opinions about the nature of the larger system. This reconciliation of ideas should lead to systematic thinking about the problem areas. All these uses are related to improved problem solving because they lead to better problem definition, specification, and understanding.

The second class of models useful in understanding problems not only describe but also forecast the system's future behavior. These predictive models may be used to generate forecasts that are useful in planning and controlling the firm's efforts. A descriptive model may be used as a predictive model simply by forecasting the model's parameters and inputs and then using the model to generate a system forecast. For example, if a descriptive consumer model is given forecasted data as inputs, the output of the model will be a transformation of the forecasted data and will provide a prediction of future consumer behavior. If this forecast does not correspond to the actual results, either the descriptive model or the method of forecasting inputs may have to be revised in order to provide a better description and prediction of system behavior. If the forecast and actual results correspond, confidence in the descriptive validity of the model will be enhanced.

Predictive models may also be used to determine the sensitivity of the model's output to the magnitudes of the variables and their structural relationships. A number of predictions can be generated by changes in the model's parameters and inputs. The magnitude of the change in the predictions can be compared to the magnitude of the parameter and input changes to measure the sensitivity of the model. If the consumer model cited as an example earlier were rerun with various psychological inputs for the consumers, the sensitivity of the output could be assessed. If the sales predictions changed greatly as the result of changes in the consumer psychological inputs, additional study would be indicated. If a model is found to be sensitive, it would then be worthwhile to determine if the sensitivity is due to the nature of the model or the system being modeled. It would be important to know if the consumer model is artificially sensitive or if the psychological state of consumers is critical to sales results.

Predictive models may also be used to answer "what if" types of questions. These conditional predictions are extremely useful in exploring the implications of alternative specifications of the marketing mix or the market impact of alternative forms of competitor retaliation. For example, the manager might have a model of his market environment. He might then use simulation to predict market response conditional upon some specific marketing mix and some particular mode of competitive response. These conditional predictions would assist him in evaluating the sales and profit implications of alternative marketing strategies.

The uses outlined in the last two paragraphs indicate that the application of descriptive and predictive models yields information and poses questions that are valuable in the identification, exploration, and understanding of management problems and the system in which they exist.

The second class of uses of models is related to normative models. Normative models attempt to specify how problems *should* be solved if some value criterion is to be optimized from the decision maker's point of view. This is in contrast to descriptive and predictive models, which indicate how a system *does* or *is* expected to operate. It might be noted, however, that descriptive-predictive aspects are generally imbedded in any normative model.

The value of normative models lies in the fact that they yield solutions or recommend decisions to solve problems. In a normative sense a model and an appropriate solution technique can be powerful tools for solving problems. The model can serve as a mechanism to structure the complex empirical and subjective considerations relating to the problem. Such a model may place the problem in a total context and explicitly identify its system implications. For example, a model of the new product decision could be used to integrate the empirical and subjective information that managers possess in the areas of demand, cost, risk, and investment. In this way, the implications of changes in one of these areas can be identified in other areas and in the decision outcome.

When this model is solved by an appropriate normative method, it will yield a solution to the problem within the limitations of the model's assumptions. Finding a solution to the new product model may require a specification of the characteristics of the marketing plan, such as price, advertising, and selling levels, as well as the details of the production commitment. If these specifications and the model's decision rules are defined, a new product solution can be found. A normative model may also be tested for sensitivity.   If the solution is very sensitive to changes in particular inputs or parameters, this would indicate the need for more accurate data concerning that variable or parameter.   Yet another useful aspect of normative models is that once they are formulated they can be used to update decisions rapidly whenever the levels of parameters are altered because of fluctuations in the environment.   In the case of new products, a model might be used to evaluate the implications of early market data and assess the desirability of changing the new product's marketing plan.   In this way a model can serve a control function.   A model could be used to monitor decision results, report exceptional deviations in the results, and recommend actions to be taken to correct the unexpected results.   The most advanced form of this usage is represented in adaptive models that not only monitor decision results, but also generate new response information by continuing experimentation.   This new information and a normative model would serve to update and improve decisions.

The comments in the previous paragraphs indicate that normative, descriptive, and predictive management science models may be useful in developing an understanding of problems and in finding solutions to management problems.   This book is designed to explore the usefulness of management science models in the functional problem area of marketing.

MANAGEMENT SCIENCE AND THE DECISION-INFORMATION SYSTEM

Management Science and the Man-information Interaction

The utility and role of management science models may be interpreted within a paradigm of the decision making system of the firm.   This total system will be depicted as a man-information interaction.   The "man" is the manager who has a problem or a decision to make.   The "information" is contained in an information system that responds to his demands and needs.   This information system attempts to translate environmental information into a more relevant form.   The manager questions the system and the system replies with information (see Fig. 1-3).

Decision—Information System

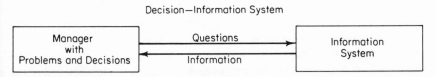

Figure 1-3: Decision-Information System

The basic concept of an information system is useful in realizing the position of models in the decision structure. The information system is made up of a number of internal components. Within the system are a data bank, a statistical methods bank, a model bank, and a display unit. These internal components interact with two external elements—the manager and the environment. The environment includes all the conditions, activities, and influences affecting the firm. These components are depicted in Fig. 1-4.

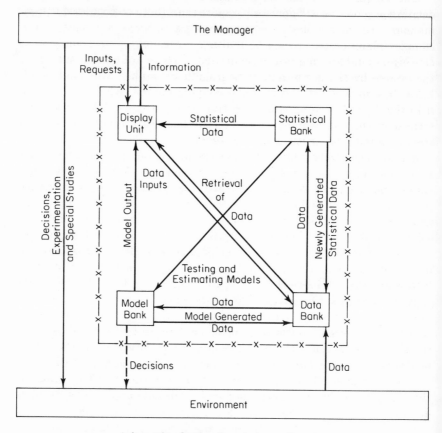

Information System Boundaries —x——x—

Figure 1-4: Information system

The environment is monitored by the information system and the resulting data are stored in a data bank. These data can be examined by the manager through the display unit after being retrieved from the data bank. A simple system depicting this retrieval function is a series of filing cabinets containing records of environmental activity. The manager can retrieve this information by instructing his secretary to find a particular file and deliver it to him. The physical file is then the display unit, and the secretary serves the retrieval function with the filing cabinet functioning as the data bank. A more complex system might be a computer-based system that displays data on a television screen in the manager's office, the retrieval being performed by a computer program searching magnetic disk records that make up the data bank.

The manager may not be interested in the raw data per se. For decision purposes he will generally require the data to be processed in some manner. In the simplest case, he may want totals or averages. More complex manipulations, such as multiple regression, cluster analysis, or contingency tables, might also be desired. These are carried out within the system by the use of a statistical methods bank. This bank would have the capability of statistically manipulating the data and displaying it in the desired form on command from the manager. The data transformed in this manner may also be sent back to the data bank to be stored for retrieval or use at a later time.

The manager may address the system with a request for information that is interpreted in terms of a particular decision. A model bank would contain management science models that are designed to solve particular problems. He can call upon one of these models to transform input data from the data bank in the hope of achieving help in understanding and solving his problem. These input data may be the original data or they may be the output of a descriptive or predictive model. The model output would be displayed and could then be stored in the data bank for future retrieval and display. If the manager is not satisfied with the retrieved, statistically manipulated, or model-generated data, he can initiate tests that will generate new data. His requests for experimentation in the external environment will generate results that will be monitored by the system and stored in the data bank. The new data may then be displayed for the manager's use in making decisions, formulating new models, and understanding his environment. With this brief outline of the information system, each component will now be analyzed in more detail.

The Data Bank

The data bank represents the system's first contact with the environment. The data bank serves as a storehouse for the information that the firm views as relevant for its decisions. A typical data bank structure is outlined in Fig. 1-5. This data bank has a data pre-processor associated

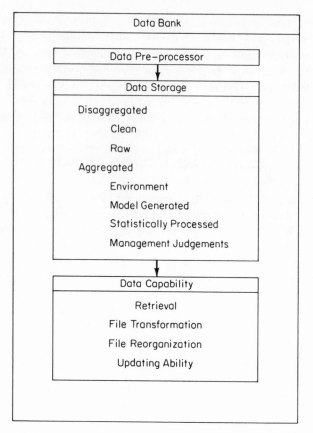

Figure 1-5: Data bank

with it. The pre-processor can be used to code and clean data. Clean data are data that are correctly recorded and organized. Since errors may occur in data during collection and preparation for processing, the data will need to be cleaned before they are in suitable form for display to management or for use in models.[6] The pre-processor may not be used to clean all data. Frequently used data will probably be cleaned as they are admitted to the bank, while other data may be directly stored and cleaned only when they are used. The cleaning activities of the data pre-processor lead to two classes of data—clean and raw.

The type of information entering the bank may be in aggregated or disaggregated form. Disaggregated data are data that are expressed in

[6] For a further discussion of data handling needs, see D. B. Montgomery, "Computer Uses in Marketing Research: A Proposal," *Journal of Marketing Research* (May, 1967), pp. 195–98.

elemental bits of information. For example, a salesman's call report generates disaggregated data if the minute details of the calls, such as person visited, time of visit, place of visit, and time of waiting, are recorded. Aggregate data are data that represent combinations of disaggregated data. In the case of call reports, the number of calls carried out by the sales force would be an example of aggregate data. The appearance of aggregate data in the data bank may reflect monitoring of this sort of aggregated data or aggregated data generated by the statistical bank, model bank, or managerial input to the system that reflects the subjective feelings and judgments of the firm's executives.

The last element of the data bank is a data processing capability. The first aspect is an output capability and is the ability to retrieve particular data on command. The next three are related to data manipulation. They are file transformation, file reorganization, and file updating. The first two reflect the need to regroup and classify data so they can be displayed in a relevant manner or so they can be used by the statistical or model bank. The last reflects the need to maintain current information in the files.

In Fig. 1-5, an outline of the desired capabilities of the data bank was given. It might be useful at this point to outline some of the relevant data that might be stored in such a bank. Figure 1-6 presents such an

---

I. Internal Corporate Records
   A. Financial and Cost Data
   B. Internal Report Data
      1. Salesmen's Call Reports
      2. Special Studies on New Product Ideas
      3. Performance Information on New Product Ideas that Have Been Implemented
      4. Life Cycle Information on Products in the Line
II. External Data
   A. Secondary Sources
      1. Government Data
      2. Commercial Data (e.g., MRCA Panel Data, Nielsen Store Audits, Brand Rating Index's Data)
   B. Primary Data
      1. Test Markets
      2. Market Experiments
      3. Studies of Corporate and Brand Images

**Figure 1-6: Data categories in a
hypothetical marketing data bank**

---

outline with a few examples. The primary dichotomy in such data relates to whether the data are obtained from records internal to the firm or whether they must be gathered by measurement external to the firm.

In the case of internal data, a further dichotomy relates to whether the data are based upon internal accounting records or whether they are generated by other reports and studies. A few examples are given in the figure. Information from any study that might be useful in the future in terms of developing market response functions would be stored in such a bank. Operationally, of course, information with a higher likelihood of use will be kept in relatively more accessible storage than data having a smaller likelihood of use. External data may also be further dichotomized into secondary and primary data. Secondary data are external data that have been gathered for purposes other than those of the firm. Examples would be government data which might be used to estimate market potentials or commercial data such as MRCA panel data, which might be used to estimate price sensitivity in various market segments. Primary external data relates to data which the firm deliberately generates in its environment. Data generated by test markets and market experiments are prime examples here. These examples are not a complete listing of all kinds of marketing data. The data bank should contain all the data relevant to the decision demands upon the system.

The Statistical Bank

Information may follow three paths to the manager in this general information system. The first is direct display, and the other two are indirect paths through the statistical or model banks. The statistical bank should contain programs that will enable the manager to test for relationships as well as estimate and test various models and market response functions. Figure 1-7 outlines some of the general capabilities that such a statistical bank should contain.[7]

The first of these is the analysis of variance and other classical parametric procedures that are helpful in analyzing the results of market experiments and exploring marketing data for useful relationships. The increasing use of experimental procedures in marketing makes the inclusion of these procedures a necessity.

Multivariate methods are especially useful in measuring and testing the multiple factor relationships that exist in marketing. Historical data from the data bank will generally serve as input to these procedures. One of the most widely used of these techniques is regression analysis, which finds many uses in estimating and testing market response functions. It is especially important that the statistical bank should have

[7] See R. E. Frank and P. E. Green, *Quantitative Methods in Marketing* (Englewood Cliffs, New Jersey: Prentice-Hall, 1967), for a basic discussion of the statistical techniques appropriate to the statistical bank.

I. Analysis of Variance and Other Parametric Procedures
II. Multivariate Procedures
   A. Regression Analysis
   B. Discriminant Analysis
   C. Factor Analysis
   D. Cluster Analysis
III. Nonparametric Statistics
   A. Cross-Classification
   B. Goodness of Fit Measures
   C. Rank Order Measures
IV. Time Series Analysis
V. Decision Theory Program
VI. Numeric Estimation Techniques

Figure 1-7: Statistical bank

complete econometric capability in terms of all the available tests of the assumptions which underlie the model. This will tend to lessen the propensity to misuse this technique of data analysis.[8] Perhaps the statistical bank itself should warn the user of potential pitfalls and recommend appropriate tests and courses of action. Such system warnings should help prevent naïve use of this method. Similar remarks apply to cluster analysis, factor analysis, discriminant analysis, and any other techniques that might be included in the statistical bank.

A nonparametric statistics subsystem plays several useful roles. In the first place, it applies to data that do not satisfy the measurement assumptions of the parametric techniques. Cross-classification procedures are especially useful for exploring relationships between sets of classificatory variables and a response measure. Tests to determine the "goodness of fit" are important in the statistical bank in order to determine the descriptive adequacy of models and standard distributions in the face of data. Rank order measures of association are relevant when the data are only measured on an ordinal scale.

Finally, time series analysis, statistical decision theory programs, and numeric estimation techniques are needed. The first is useful in analyzing the dynamics of market response or simulation output. The second, statistical decision theory, is useful in unprogrammed decision situations. However, one of the barriers to its use is the computational burden involved in problems large enough to be meaningful. A program that will perform the numerical analysis, preferably in real time from a remote console, should increase the use of this procedure by marketing managers.

---

[8] For a case in point see J. L. Livingstone and D. B. Montgomery, "The Use of Regression Equations to Predict Manpower Requirements: Critical Comments," *Management Science A*, XII (March, 1966), pp. 616–18.

The last element of the statistical bank is numeric estimation techniques. It is included to provide the manager with the ability to estimate probability models whose estimating equations contain complex functions of the model's parameters.   In general, a well-designed statistical bank should be able to estimate model parameters, specify response relationships, and test model structures.

The Model Bank

The final internal component of the decision-information system which requires discussion is the model bank.   Although the model bank is considered an internal information system element, in some cases a model in the bank may interact directly with the environment.   This could occur if the decision maker requests a model to make decisions without obtaining managerial review.   For example, a model may be used to make stock market buy and sell decisions.[9]   This type of direct model decision making is limited to repetitive decisions characterized by an accepted formal analysis procedure and the existence of accurate, measurable input data.   Even in these cases the decision-making function will be returned to the manager under new or exceptional situations.   In most marketing information systems, direct decision action by a model will probably be rare.

The three major classes of models a model bank usually would contain are outlined in Fig. 1-8, along with a few examples of representative models.   The first of these, descriptive models, is useful in understanding market phenomena.   For example, this section may contain a simulation-based model depicting the company-market interaction.   The second class of models in the bank is predictive models.   This section may contain price or competitive models designed to predict the responses that will be elicited by the firm's decisions.   The last section of the model bank will contain normative models that can be used to produce solutions for problems such as advertising budget determination or the selection of the best competitive strategy.   Each section of the bank may contain a number of models.   The purpose of the bank is to present a collection of models so that the best one can be selected when the system is attempting to help solve a manager's problem.   The "best" model is the one that answers the manager's needs at the lowest cost.   With this requirement upon the system, it is logical to place a number of models in the bank. Even if several models were directed at the same problem, it would be wise to include them if the complexity and cost of execution of each model

[9] A. E. Amstutz, "The Computer—New Partner in Investment Management," Working Paper 283-67, Alfred P. Sloan School of Management, Massachusetts Institute of Technology, 1967.

```
┌─────────────────────────────────────┐
│              Model Bank             │
├─────────────────────────────────────┤
│                                     │
│   Descriptive Models                │
│       Simulation of Market          │
│       Consumer Behavior Model       │
│   Predictive Models                 │
│       Stochastic Model of           │
│         Consumer Behavior           │
│       Model of Response to          │
│         Competitor's Price          │
│         Changes                     │
│   Normative Models                  │
│       Advertising Budget Model      │
│       Competitive Strategy Model    │
│       Price Determination Model     │
│       New Product Model             │
│       Math Programming Allocation   │
│         Model                       │
│       Optimum Marketing Mix Model   │
│                                     │
└─────────────────────────────────────┘
```

Figure 1-8: Hypothetical model bank

were different so that some particular management needs could be most efficiently satisfied by each of them.

The Man-System Interaction

This discussion of the components of the information system has now led to the point of interaction between the system and the manager. The design and specification of the system are oriented towards the manager and his needs. To design the system components such as the model bank, a clear understanding of the demands on the system is needed. The manager's demands will depend upon the relevant problems he faces and the decision structure he uses in approaching the system. The most elementary decision demands on the system will be with respect to data retrieval and an assessment of what the present marketing situation is. This may widen to a need to understand the underlying phenomena of consumer and market behavior. At the next level, the manager may desire the ability to forecast marketing events. The highest level demands on the system are problem-centered demands relating to advertising, pricing, distribution, personal selling, product planning, and competitive strategy decisions.

A manager may approach the system with a formal decision structure.

For example, his procedure may begin with problem recognition and definition and proceed through the process of generating, assessing, and selecting from alternatives to end at testing, implementation, and control of the decision.   At any point in this structure, the manager may request information and guidance from the system.   The system should be designed so that a manager may approach the system and interact with it to solve the relevant problems.   This man-system interaction will be the underlying emphasis in the development of this book.

This book will not concern itself with the entire information system. The focus of this effort is largely restricted to the model bank.   The design and implementation considerations underlying the data bank and statistical bank will not be considered.   In the following chapters, the structuring and definition of marketing problems will be used as a focus for constructing models that are oriented towards a particular information system user—the marketing manager.

PLAN OF DEVELOPMENT OF THIS BOOK

The purpose of this book is basically to describe and to provide a basis for the extension of the state of the art of the application of management science to marketing problems.   This is not a text for the study of quantitative techniques, but rather a problem-centered exposition of how the techniques, as expressed in marketing models, can be used to help make marketing decisions.   It is assumed that the reader has some familiarity with management science techniques, but the techniques will be briefly discussed as they are required in specific model developments and evaluations.

The first area of study will be the nature of market response.   In the second chapter of this book, models of market response will be presented and evaluated in the context of understanding, describing, and exploring marketing problems.   This study of marketing phenomena will be utilized in Chaps. 3 through 7.   These chapters are directed at the particular marketing problem areas of advertising, price, distribution, personal selling, and new product planning.   In each of these areas the relevant problems will be structured, analyzed, and studied from a management science point of view.   The interaction between each of the marketing variables will be considered in an evolutionary manner.   Although it would be desirable to consider all interactions under one problem heading such as marketing mix problems, pedagogic considerations led the authors to describe marketing mix effects in this evolutionary manner.

Advertising will be considered as a single variable in Chap. 3, but price and advertising multivariate problems will be discussed in Chap. 4. Distribution and personal selling variables are considered as independent variables until Chap. 7. Chapter 7 is titled "New Product Decisions" and serves as a culmination of the evolutionary exposition of the marketing mix problem. In Chap. 7, the simultaneous specification of all the marketing variables is attacked. A similar evolutionary approach is taken to competitive strategy. In the advertising chapter the elementary aspects of two firm competitive interdependency are outlined. These considerations are further developed in the pricing chapter to reflect multifirm competition and the industry marketing effects of competitive behavior. Chapter 7 integrates the marketing mix and competitive strategy within the context of new product decisions. Chapter 8 discusses the problems of implementation of the management science approach in the real world organization. The final chapter serves as a review and an opportunity for the authors to prognosticate about the future of management science in marketing.

2

Models of
Market Response

INTRODUCTION

One of the basic considerations in a management science approach to marketing is how the market responds to marketing policy variables and other elements in the market environment. An understanding of the nature of market response is a vital input to the analysis of specific marketing problems, such as those discussed in Chaps. 3 through 7 of this book. Descriptive and predictive models of market response provide a framework for organizing and advancing understanding of the complex process of market response. Recall that descriptive and predictive models are two of the three major categories of models to be incorporated in the model bank (see Fig. 1-9). This chapter will concentrate upon the analysis of certain descriptive and predictive models. The third model category, normative models, will receive more of the emphasis in Chaps. 3 through 7, where marketing decision areas are considered in some detail.

This chapter will explore the nature of market response by examining two particular types of descriptive and predictive models. Traditionally, these model types have been referred to as simulation models and stochastic models, although subsequent discussion will reveal that neither label is totally satisfactory. The discussion in this chapter will by no means exhaust the set of possible market response models, since response models are imbedded in each of the models considered in subsequent chapters. The consideration of applications of management science in marketing will be initiated with these particular types of market response models for two reasons:

1. Their importance as descriptive models of market processes
2. The subsequent pedagogical utility of certain of the concepts which are introduced in the discussion of these models

Simulation models are introduced first. After a brief discussion of the semantic problems involved in the use of the term "simulation model," attention turns to a review and analysis of some simulation models that have been applied to marketing. Then important research areas in the development of market simulations are identified. The second major section in this chapter deals with stochastic models. After existing stochastic models of brand choice and interpurchase timing are reviewed, a discussion of future research needs is presented. The final major section of this chapter examines the contrast as well as the interface between simulation and stochastic models. The chapter is followed by an appendix, which develops certain methodological considerations in stochastic modeling.

SIMULATION MODELS OF MARKET RESPONSE

Definition and Uses of Simulation Models

In this section attention will focus upon models which have historically been referred to as simulation models. These models have been characterized by a complexity of relationships which exceeds the capability of existing analytic procedures for generating model solutions. In general, these models have incorporated probabilistic components and have utilized Monté Carlo procedures as a tool for analysis.[1]

The label "simulation model" is not entirely appropriate. The technique of simulation defined in Chap. 1 can, in fact, be applied to any model—be it deterministic or probabilistic. In that sense, all marketing models may be considered "simulation models." In marketing, however, the term "simulation model" has most generally been used to describe models developed for the purpose of exploring the market response implications of a model via the technique of simulation. Thus historical usage has designated as simulation models those models for which the principal technique of analysis to be used is simulation.

---

[1] See J. M. Hammersley and D. C. Handscomb, *Monté Carlo Methods* (New York: John Wiley and Sons, 1964) for a discussion of this technique.

Simulation models have been formulated to serve two management functions: (1) planning, (2) monitoring and controlling operations. The planning role of a simulation model is quite clear. If the model constitutes a reasonable representation of the real environment, it may be used as a laboratory to examine the consequences of alternative courses of action and market events. Not only is it less expensive and risky to experiment with the model than to tinker with the firm's actual marketing operations, but it also provides a capability which cannot be duplicated in the real world environment. It gives management the opportunity to explore the joint consequences of a myriad of actions, whereas real world experimentation is limited as to the number of alternatives which may be tried. The simulation model will also yield answers in a relatively short period of time compared to real world experimentation. Given the short operating time horizon for many marketing decisions, a model is often the only practical mode of analysis if pure "seat of the pants" methods are to be avoided.

A simulation model may also be used to monitor and control operating results. Once a plan has been established, the simulation model may be used to generate a set of base line measures that can subsequently be compared to operating results. For example, the model may indicate the shifts in consumer attitudes that must be generated if sales targets are to be achieved. If survey information should indicate such shifts are not occurring, the situation will require management attention. Thus the simulation model can provide a base line for diagnosing potential problem areas. Similarly, it may provide base line information for control of such factors as sales expense.

An important fringe benefit generally accrues to the model development effort. The model's need for explicit articulation of response assumptions and market interactions forces the manager and the model builder to be very specific about their knowledge and judgment concerning market response. This process, while difficult and sometimes frustrating, very often leads to significant new understanding of the firm's market environment. It also often reveals important areas of ignorance that justify further investment in analysis and measurement.

Some Marketing Applications of Simulation Models

Marketing games

The initial applications of simulation in marketing were in the form of marketing games. These games have been used as training tools in management development programs and business school curricula. As a training tool, the marketing game may be characterized as a dynamic case study where the student or trainee is required to make explicit decisions through time and then live with the consequences of his actions. The trainee is required to adjust to changing market conditions and competitive activity. In the more complex games that require a management team to run the business, the trainee is faced with realistic human and organizational problems.

A considerable number of marketing games have been developed; however, many of these have made rather ineffective use of simulation.[2] Although it is not within the scope of this book to review and criticize the entire field of marketing games, it does seem useful to consider two of the more complex and realistic marketing games—the Carnegie Institute of Technology MATE simulation and Massachusetts Institute of Technology's TOMES.

Carnegie's MATE simulation (Marketing Analysis Training Exercise) might best be described as an aggregate simulation.[3] By an aggregate simulation is meant that individual consumers are not explicitly modeled. Rather, consumer demand is modeled in a more aggregate manner. For example, total market demand in period t is given by

$$Q_t = s_t Q_0 K^t \left(\frac{\bar{p}_t}{\bar{p}_0}\right)^{\eta_p} \left(\frac{\bar{E}_t}{as_t\bar{E}_0K}\right)^{\eta_E} \left(\frac{Y_t}{Y_0}\right)^{\eta_Y} \tag{2-1}$$

where

Q = total number of cases demanded,

s = seasonal index (where $\sum_{t=1}^{12} s_t = 12.0$),

K = growth term,

$\bar{p}$ = weighted average price,

$\bar{E}$ = total promotion expenditures in the industry,

Y = average per capita income,

t = week subscript,

0 = subscript denoting a base industry value,

η_p, η_E, η_Y = elasticity of industry demand for weighted industry price, promotion, and per capita income, respectively,[4]

a = constant.

[2] For elaboration on this point see A. E. Amstutz, "Management Games—A Potential Perverted," *Industrial Management Review*, V (Fall, 1963), pp. 29–36.

[3] A. A. Kuehn and D. L. Weiss, "Marketing Analysis Training Exercise," *Behavioral Science* (January, 1965), pp. 51–67, and K. J. Cohen, W. R. Dill, A. A. Kuehn, and P. R. Winters, the *Carnegie Tech Management Game* (Homewood, Illinois: R. D. Irwin), 1964.

[4] The elasticity of demand with respect to a given quantity such as per capita income is given by

$$\eta_Y = \frac{d(\log Q)}{d(\log Y)} = \frac{dQ/Q}{dY/Y}$$

This is just the classical economic definition of elasticity.

Once total market demand for the product is determined, it is then allocated among the competing brands.

The process of allocation of basic demand to competing brands incorporates a number of realistic market phenomena. For example, the demand for a particular brand comes from two sources. The initial component represents habitual brand purchase or brand loyalty. The remaining demand comes from what is termed the potential shifters demand. This is the potential demand that remains in the market over and above the habitual repurchases made for all brands in the market. This potential shifters demand is then allocated to brands on the basis of each brand's merchandising program vis-à-vis its competitors. The merchandising program includes product characteristics, price, retail availability, and advertising. Other phenomena which are incorporated in MATE include carry-over effects of past efforts into the future and a distribution of preferences for the various product characteristics. In sum, the MATE simulation encompasses a number of realistic and important market phenomena within the framework of aggregate market response functions.

A somewhat different approach to marketing gaming has been developed at the Massachusetts Institute of Technology.[5] This game, known as TOMES (Total Market Environment Simulation), synthesizes total demand as the sum of the demand from individual consumers in contrast to the aggregate formulation in MATE. These consumers are represented in considerable detail. For example, they form brand preferences and attitudes on the basis of experience and the receipt of both formal and informal brand communication. These attitudes and preferences interact with retailer preferences and retail availability to generate demand. This detailed modeling of the consumer provides the basis for a very realistic market research capability in the game. Since the TOMES model is based upon the simulation model developments discussed in a later section, it will not be developed in greater detail at this point.

In market gaming, the model itself defines reality for the game world. One can, of course, always question whether a particular game model is a reasonable representation of a market, but subject to passing this reasonableness test, the model itself provides the market structure, interaction between market components, response functions, and parameters. Additional questions arise when a simulation model is developed for an actual market. Problems of estimating and testing the model then arise. The model no longer defines reality; now its representation of the actual market must be tested.

[5] A. E. Amstutz and H. J. Claycamp, "The Total Market Environment Simulation," *Industrial Management Review*, Vol. 5, No. 2 (Spring, 1964), pp. 47–60.

Market simulations

Market simulation models have been used to study the dynamics of market structure and to aid management in planning its marketing strategy. This section will consider selected applications of market simulation models. The discussion of simulation applications in particular policy areas will be deferred to the appropropriate chapters. Suffice it here to indicate that subsequent chapters consider simulation applications in media selection, distribution, personal selling, and new product development.

A large-scale simulation of an industrial market has been developed by researchers at Berkeley.[6] The simulation model was designed to study the market interactions between the members of an entire marketing system—manufacturers, wholesalers, retailers, and final demand. The initial form of this model was developed by Balderson and Hoggatt. The purpose of this initial model formulation was to study the way in which market structure is affected by the costs of information and the decision rules by which market participants at each level of the model become parties to a given transaction. Experimentation with this model yielded a particularly interesting result. They found that a skew (nonsymmetric) distribution of firm size would occur simply under the impact of market pressures on identically endowed firms all employing identical decision rules. Such skew size distributions are observed in real markets. This result suggests that market factors, rather than any inherent differences in the firms themselves, may well be the prime cause of differing size between the firms. The cost of information and the nature of the decision rules were also found to be important in the final form of these distributions.

Preston and Collins used a somewhat modified form of the original Balderson and Hoggatt model to examine experimentally the extent to which small numbers of market participants lead to price-increasing and output-reducing results.[7] They also wanted to examine the market performance effects of changes in the number of market participants. In general, the results indicated that a reduction in the number of market participants would lead to price, quantity, and margin changes in the directions suggested by theory. However, it was found that large firms, and especially new market entrants, could exert a sufficiently destabilizing influence on the market to reverse these effects. Thus monopoloid results were found to depend upon entry conditions and uniformity of firm behavior.

[6] F. E. Balderson and A. C. Hoggatt, *Simulation of Market Processes* (Berkeley, California: Institute of Business and Economic Research, University of California, 1962).

[7] L. E. Preston and N. R. Collins, *Studies in a Simulated Market* (Berkeley, California: Institute of Business and Economic Research, 1966).

From a management viewpoint, probably the most detailed and successful simulation application that has been reported is the Amstutz and Claycamp model of the ethical drug market.[8] The model, certain aspects of which are discussed in the next section, provides a detailed specification of the decision processes of individual doctors. Like the TOMES simulation, this simulation synthesizes market demand by aggregating the prescription decisions of many individual, somewhat idiosyncratic, simulated doctors. This procedure of detailed specification of individual decision processes and the subsequent aggregation to the market measures of interest may be termed microanalytic simulation. This microanalytic simulation approach has also been successfully applied in a consumer product market.[9]

Microanalytic Simulation of Market Response

Microanalytic simulation models are probably the most sophisticated and complex type of simulation yet developed. Because this type of simulation modeling promises to be of increasing importance as a tool for marketing planning, it seems useful to discuss this approach in some detail. It should be noted at the outset, however, that most of the methodological comments made in this section apply equally well to more aggregate simulation models.

Recall from the earlier discussion that in a microanalytic simulation the decision processes of market elements (e.g., consumers, retailers, etc.) are modeled in considerable detail. Within each type of market element (e.g., the consumer population) there may be many individual units. A microanalytic simulation allows for differences between these individual units by giving each unit its own set of descriptive equations and parameters.

Structure of microanalytic market simulations

The development of a microanalytic simulation model begins with a specification of what the simulation is supposed to accomplish. The

---

[8] H. J. Claycamp and A. E. Amstutz, "Simulation Techniques in the Analysis of Marketing Strategy," in F. M. Bass, C. W. King, and E. A. Pessemier, eds., *Applications of the Sciences in Marketing Management* (New York: John Wiley and Sons, 1968), pp. 113–50.

[9] A. E. Amstutz, *Computer Simulation of Competitive Market Response* (Cambridge, Mass.: M.I.T. Press, 1967).

objectives developed at this stage will have far-reaching consequences in the development of the model. For example, Claycamp and Amstutz report that the management of the drug firm wanted this model to facilitate evaluation of the effectiveness of its communications mix (i.e., promotion and detail men).[10] This, in turn, had implications for model structure in terms of the extensiveness of the micromodeling of the areas which yield this information. In addition, it raised issues in the areas of estimation and measurement, data inputs, sensitivity analysis, and model validation. Thus, it is crucial that an appropriate set of broad goals be established prior to model construction, since these goals will affect nearly every aspect of the model development and can therefore result in frustrating time and cost inefficiencies if they require revision at a later stage.

This specification of objectives will provide a guide for establishing the limits of the analysis. It is important to establish the boundaries of the model since no model can hope to encompass every factor which might impinge on the market. Some aspects of the market environment must be considered exogenous to the detailed model. Thus, government decisions will generally be considered an exogenous input to the model rather than an element to be modeled in detail. For example, monetary and fiscal actions could be an important input to the model, but the process by which these decisions are reached probably would not be explicitly modeled. An exception, of course, might occur for those firms which have considerable interaction potential with the government, either through contract bidding or via antitrust action. After the system boundaries have been defined, the macromodel development process can begin. Macrostructure development involves the formulation of a conceptual framework within which are specified the key market subsystems (e.g., the firm, competitors, wholesalers, retailers, customers), the important variables in each subsystem, and the interrelations between the subsystems. Figure 2-1 presents the macrostructure of one of Amstutz's models with interrelations between the subsystems defined in terms of product and information flow.

After the major subsystems of the model have been identified, they must be described in detail. The detailed model structure for the consumer sector proposed by Amstutz is depicted in Fig. 2-2.[11] The major actions the microunit undertakes, the underlying determinants of these actions, and the controllable marketing variables associated with these actions must be developed. Amstutz's consumer first develops a perceived need for the product based on his attitudes toward the product,

[10] Claycamp and Amstutz, *op. cit.*
[11] See Amstutz, *op. cit.*, pp. 153–245.

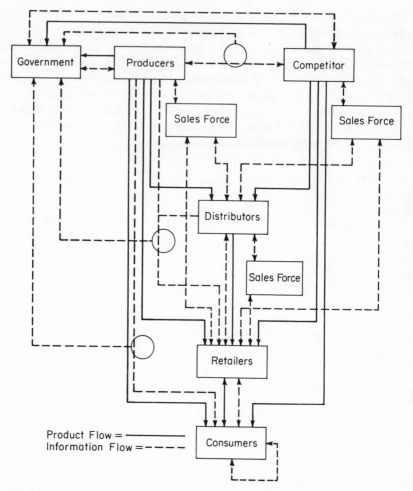

Figure 2-1: Macrostructure example*

brand, and advertising appeals, his opportunity for use, and the time since the last purchase. The level of this perceived need and his income are hypothesized as the chief determinants of the decision to shop. The selection of a retailer for the shopping trip will be dependent upon the consumer's attitudes towards retailers. The decision to purchase will depend upon the availability of the product in the retail outlet, the price of the product and competing products, the sales push at retail, and the

* Reprinted from *Computer Simulation of Competitive Market Response* by Arnold E. Amstutz by permission of The M.I.T. Press, Cambridge, Massachusetts.

consumer's attitude towards the brands available. If purchase takes place, the model allows the generation of word of mouth communication to other consumers.[12] The decisions in Fig. 2-2 are not described deterministically. Rather, a probability of shopping and purchasing is defined based on the underlying determinants. Action is generated by a Monté Carlo draw from a uniform distribution. The structure as given in Fig. 2-2 is assumed to be appropriate for all consumers in the simulation model, but the level of influence of each of the determinants and variables may differ between individual consumers.

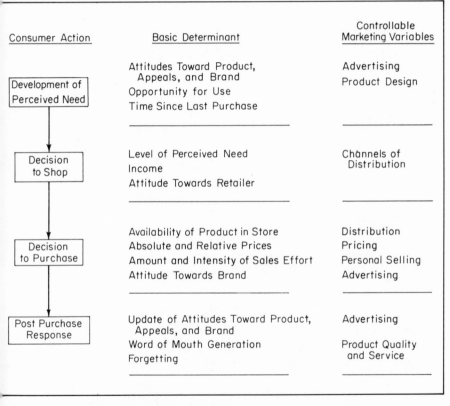

Consumer Action	Basic Determinant	Controllable Marketing Variables
Development of Perceived Need	Attitudes Toward Product, Appeals, and Brand Opportunity for Use Time Since Last Purchase	Advertising Product Design
Decision to Shop	Level of Perceived Need Income Attitude Towards Retailer	Channels of Distribution
Decision to Purchase	Availability of Product in Store Absolute and Relative Prices Amount and Intensity of Sales Effort Attitude Towards Brand	Distribution Pricing Personal Selling Advertising
Post Purchase Response	Update of Attitudes Toward Product, Appeals, and Brand Word of Mouth Generation Forgetting	Advertising Product Quality and Service

Figure 2-2: Structure of microunit consumer response in Amstutz's model

[12] The formulation also allows for word of mouth by non-buyers. See A. E. Amstutz, "Management, Computers, and Market Simulation" in D. B. Montgomery and G. L. Urban, eds., *Applications of Management Science in Marketing* (Englewood Cliffs, N.J.: Prentice-Hall, Inc., 1969) for a detailed description of the consumer model.

Management Science in Marketing

In the development of the microunit model each of the basic actions must be modeled in detail. For example, Amstutz's description of the subprocess by which advertising effects the consumer is given in Fig. 2-3.

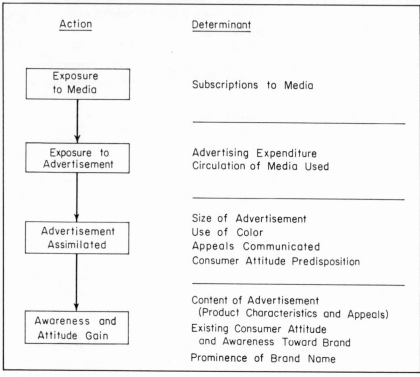

Figure 2-3: Amstutz's advertising response model*

All aspects of the consumer's decision processes must be described in a similar fashion and eventually must be expressed in mathematical equations. For example, Amstutz has proposed the following expression for the perceived need indicated in Fig. 2-2:

$$\text{PRNED}(c, b) = \left[c_1 + \frac{\text{AWARE}(c, b)}{c_2} \right] * \exp\left(-\frac{5.0 - \text{ATTBR}(c, b)}{c_4} \right)$$
$$* \text{USOPC}(c) * \text{PROWC}(c) \quad (2\text{-}2)$$

where $\text{PRNED}(c, b)$ = PeRceivedNEeD of consumer c for product of brand b. Dimension: pure number.

* Reprinted from *Computer Simulation of Competitive Market Response* by Arnold E. Amstutz by permission of The M.I.T. Press, Cambridge, Massachusetts.

c_1 = constant specifying the base value of perceived need in the absence of awareness. Dimension: pure number.

AWARE(c, b) = a binary measure of the awareness of consumer c with respect to brand b.

= 1, if aware.

= 0, if unaware.

c_2 = a constant establishing the proportionate increase in perceived need added to the base level specified by c_1 as a result of nonzero awareness of brand b for which the perceived need is being formed. Dimension: awareness scale units.

ATTBR(c, b) = the ATTitude toward BRand b by consumer c. Dimension: attitude scale units.

c_4 = a constant determining the rate of change of perceived need with increasing attitude. Dimension: attitude scale units.

USOPC(c) = USe OPportunity Coefficient. Dimension: pure number.

= $(c_5 + c_6 * \text{Descriptor } A) * (c_7 + c_8 * \text{Descriptor } B)$. Descriptor A, B, etc., are consumer population attributes determining use opportunity c_5 through c_8 are constants establishing weightings for each descriptor and normalizing the factor to a maximum value of 1.0.

PROWC(c) = PRoduct OWnership Coefficient. Dimension: pure number.

= 1, if no ownership.

$$= 0.1 * \left[\exp \left[- \frac{t - t \text{ purchase}}{c_9} \right] - 1.0 \right], \text{ if}$$

ownership.

$\leq$ 1.0, by constraint.

t = present time period. Dimension: time units.

t purchase = time period in which purchase was made. Dimension: time units.

c_9 = a constant based on average product life determining the sensitivity of the product ownership coefficient to the passage of time. Dimension: time units.

Note that Eq. (2-2) embodies the notions that perceived need increases with attitude toward a brand, with increased time since last purchase, and with increased use opportunity. Simulated microconsumer units may differ from one another by having different parameter values in Eq. (2-2). (i.e., $c_1, \ldots, c_9$). The end result of this quantification is a large set of equations that describe the important elements in a consumer's decision process.

The previous paragraphs have described the basic structure of the consumer section of the model. Similar structures and subrelationships would have to be developed for the retailer, distributor, manufacturer, and other system elements described in the macrospecifications of the model (see Fig. 2-1).

An attractive feature of microanalytic simulation is its ability to encompass very detailed and behaviorally realistic aspects of the market subsystems. In management applications of this tool, the need to provide detailed formulations of decision processes often leads management to new insights concerning the operation of its markets. This is an immediate (i.e., prior to marketing planning) benefit of the model development and may rival subsequent planning use of the model in terms of its long-range importance to management. Countervailing these advantages, the approach has certain limitations. In the first place, microanalytic simulation model development is a costly and time-consuming process. The same may be said for validation and sensitivity analysis of the model as well as for actual management use. Then too, this approach requires an enormous amount of input specification in terms of microunit response functions [e.g., Eq. (2-2)] and parameters of these functions [e.g., c_1, c_2, c_4 in Eq. (2-2)].

The drug simulation: an example of a microanalytic model

A microanalytic simulation approach was used by Claycamp and Amstutz in a model of the ethical drug market.[13] A principal goal of the model was to facilitate evaluation of one drug manufacturer's marketing communications mix (promotion and sales effort) in persuading doctors to prescribe the firm's drugs. The model utilized a simulated population of one thousand doctors. Each doctor was represented by a detailed system of equations describing his professional life, including a descriptive submodel of how he practices medicine. In the model, a patient arrives at the doctor's office with certain indications or symptoms. The

[13] H. J. Claycamp and A. E. Amstutz, *op. cit.*

doctor then analyzes these symptoms to arrive at a diagnosis of the patient's ailment. As in the real world, the simulated doctors are exposed to information about drugs through professional journals, direct mail, detail men, and one another. The latter occurs via word of mouth and medical conventions. These sources of information influence the doctor's state of knowledge about certain drugs as well as his attitudes toward them. The doctor's information and attitude state toward a drug is also conditioned by his experience in prescribing the drug for given indications. These attitudes and experiences are determinants of the brand he selects.

The model has its foundations in behavioral science theory and results. For example, the simulated doctors exhibit selective exposure, selective perception, and selective retention, just as real people do. Furthermore, they experience forgetting. Thus the model has had its genesis in scientific knowledge concerning how human beings respond.

The output of the model for each doctor is an estimate of how he would prescribe drugs in the simulated period and an estimate of his attitudes toward the various drug brands. These outputs enable aggregate conditional sales forecasts to be formed. These forecasts are conditional upon the marketing actions of the firm and its competitors.

Testing microanalytic models

The structure and relationships proposed for a microanalytic simulation must be tested before it can be confidently stated that the model is an accurate description of market response. There are three principal aspects to consider in testing a model: (1) initial testing of logic, stability, and representative behavior; (2) validity testing; (3) sensitivity testing.

Initial testing: Microanalytical simulation models are characterized by very heavy computational demands, so in almost all cases the models are represented in computer programs. The first model test is a procedure to determine if any logical errors have been made in this computer program. In complex models it is not unusual to find that initially the program is not producing the results it should. The errors are not coding errors that would be identified by the computer compiler or assembler, but rather errors due to writing statements that do not carry out the intended manipulations. For example, an unintended truncation from a floating point (decimal) number to a fixed point (integer) number may have been inadvertently specified. The test for logical errors is based upon duplicating the computer results by hand calculation for at least one set of input values. This may be a tedious process, but it is an essential one.

Stability relates to the model's performance over extended periods and perhaps over ranges of parameter values. The criterion here is that the model should exhibit reasonable behavior. For example, it should not exhibit "explosive" behavior or, say, wildly fluctuating market shares. If the model should exhibit the first of these pathologies, the model builder should be on the lookout for one or more missing negative feedback relations or perhaps for the presence of an unintentional positive feedback loop. In either case, if the model fails to pass this initial run test, it must go "back to the drawing board," since the stability test is the first "gate" through which a model must pass on its way to management implementation.

If the model passes the stability test, it should then be subjected to a Turing test for the reasonableness of its behavior. Such a test is based upon Turing's suggestion that a test of the extent to which a model captures reality can be made by determining whether a person knowledgeable in the subject being modeled can distinguish between model-generated output and output from the real system.[14]

For example, in the Amstutz and Claycamp model simulated doctors were found to practice "good medicine" as judged by doctors who examined their diagnosis and prescribing behavior in the presence of particular symptoms.

Validity testing: In theory, validity relates to the absolute truth of a model, but in practice it relates to whether or not a model is a reasonable approximation of the real process being modeled. In microanalytic simulation both the total model and the particular functional representation of its subsystems should be subjected to validity testing.

Empirical validity of either the entire model or of one of its functions is generally established by comparing the actual behavior in the real world to the model's presumption of behavior. The simplest method for making this comparison is to array (either tabularly or graphically) the actual and model results to see if they are similar. Amstutz presents such results for certain of the functions in his models.[15] For example, see Fig. 2-4. From the graph it appears that the model's functional values are reasonable approximations to the observed relationships. Although no statistical results were presented for this function, in general, statistical measures of the closeness of the representation exist. The most generally useful techniques for statistical comparison are the "goodness of fit" tests such as the chi square or the Kolmogorov-Smirnov tests and econometric procedures which yield measures of the proportion and significance of the variance in a dependent variable "explained" by a combination of other variables.[16] The results of such testing should be used to revise

---

[14] See A. M. Turing, "Computing Machinery and Intelligence," *MIND* (October, 1950), pp. 433–60.

[15] See A. E. Amstutz, *op. cit.*, pp. 385–93.

[16] See S. Siegel, *Nonparametric Statistics* (New York: McGraw-Hill, 1956), and J. Johnston, *Econometric Methods* (New York: McGraw-Hill, 1963).

Attitude Scale	Dairy Product			Frozen Food			Function Effect
	Pur-chasers	Number	Per Cent	Pur-chasers	Number	Per Cent	
+5	327	392	83	115	262	44	1.00
+4	31	51	60	21	54	39	.67
+3	50	111	45	25	98	26	.45
+2	17	51	33	6	51	12	.30
+1	15	59	25	9	72	12	.20
0	12	109	11	42	283	15	.13
−1	2	25	08	—	18	—	.10
−2	2	19	10	—	15	—	.08
−3	2	15	13	1	11	09	.05
−4	1	17	05	—	10	—	.03
−5	1	39	07	—	14	—	—
Total		888			888		

Figure 2-4a: Validity testing of a macrounit response function*

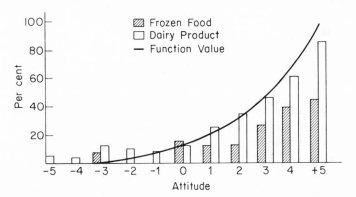

Figure 2-4b: Validity testing of a macrounit response function*

the microstructure of the model. That is, the functional forms of the equations should be refined until the best fit is obtained. The resultant output of this testing is the most accurate representation of the important parameters, functions, relations, and distributions that is feasible, given available resources.

Once refined measurement has been accomplished and the model builder believes he has a realistic, albeit abstract, representation of the real system, the major task of macromodel testing and validation begins. The

* Reprinted from *Computer Simulation of Competitive Market Response* by Arnold E. Amstutz by permission of The M.I.T. Press, Cambridge, Massachusetts.

purpose of macrotesting is to determine whether the model as a whole is a reasonable representation of the real process. The model must pass this validation test if it is to be a useful laboratory within which management may explore the consequences of strategic alternatives.

There are two general classes of methods for macrovalidation of a large-scale simulation:

1. Face or structural validation
2. Predictive validation

The first of these relates to the notion of construct validity in the social sciences. The idea is that the model representation and output are valid on their face values. For example, if management strongly believes that the model structure and the parameter values are substantially correct, then the model has face validity for management. It should be noted that face validity of a model from a manager's point of view is unlikely unless the manager has been an integral and important part of the model development process.

Predictive validation, on the other hand, requires that model output be compared to corresponding output from the real system and that the extent of agreement be determined as a measure of the predictive validity of the model. Many of the tests available to perform such analysis are of the "goodness of fit" variety. Some of these methods are discussed briefly below.[17]

In the first place, it will often be possible to use statistical methods that do not demand restrictive assumptions about the statistical distribution to test whether a simulated and an actual time series display similar amplitude and timing characteristics. An application of such an approach can be illustrated from the work of Claycamp and Amstutz on the doctor simulation.[18] They report the rank order brand share comparisons between simulation and actual output given in Table 2-1. Note that the simulated output (in this case rank order of market share) exactly matched the actual output, even though five of the ten brands experienced a shift in their brand share rank order during the year.

The question now is: "What implications about validity can be drawn from the rankings?" One statistical measure of the correlation between the ordinal measures (the brand share ranks) is the Kendall tau measure of rank order correlation.[19] In this case, the empirical rank order correlation is perfect, so the Kendall tau is +1.0. These results represent impressive model performance.

---

[17] These methods are similar to those suggested by Cohen and Cyert in K. J. Cohen and R. M. Cyert, "Computer Models in Dynamic Economics," *Quarterly Journal of Economics*, LXXV (February, 1961), pp. 112–27.

[18] Claycamp and Amstutz, *op. cit.*

[19] See Siegel, *op. cit.*

TABLE 2-1: Claycamp and Amstutz
Doctor Model Brand Share
Comparisons Actual vs. Simulated

Brand	Rank as Initialized	Year End Rank Simulated	Year End Rank Actual
A	1	1	1
B	2	3	3
C	3	4	4
D	4	2	2
E	5	6	6
F	6	5	5
G	7	7	7
H	8	8	8
I	9	9	9
J	10	10	10

Since time series are notoriously autocorrelated (e.g., display inertia) and since both the actual and the simulated brand shares began with the same rank ordering, the model builder might begin to wonder about what would be an appropriate "base" level from which to judge the significance of the "perfect" performance displayed by the simulation. One reasonable approach would be to compare the simulation model's performance to that of a naive model. In this case of suspected autocorrelation, an appropriate naive model would be one of no change or persistence in the rank orderings of the brand market shares. This "no change" brand share ranking should then be compared to the actual brand ranking in order to establish some base level for the simulation model. The Kendall tau coefficient of rank correlation between the actual year end brand share rankings and those implied by the "no change" model is +0.876. Thus the Claycamp and Amstutz model improved the rank order correlation to +1.0 from the +0.876 that a naive model would have yielded. This is in marked contrast to the somewhat implicit inference of improvement from 0 to +1.0 that a superficial examination might have indicated. Thus the model builder will want to give careful consideration to just what improvements his model yields over and above the inertia built into the real and simulated systems.

The use of rank orderings of brand shares in the above example is not totally satisfactory. The brand share data constitutes ratio scaled data, and ratio scales are the highest form of measurement.[20] Converting this data into ordinal measures sacrifices information. It is more informative to look at the actual brand share values. These values are presented in Table 2-2 for the Amstutz and Claycamp simulation.

[20] For scaling and measurement concepts, see P. Green and D. Tull, *Research for Marketing Decisions* (Englewood Cliffs, N.J.: Prentice-Hall, Inc., 1965), Chap. 7.

TABLE 2-2: Absolute Brand Share Comparison*

Identi- fication	Initialization Value	Year End Value		Magnitude of Difference (Actual vs. Simulated)	Magnitude of Difference (Actual vs. Naive)
		Simulated	Actual		
D	13.7%	15.0%	16.1%	1.1%	2.4%
E	9.7	9.1	8.7	.4	1.0
F	7.3	9.3	9.0	.3	1.7
H	5.0	3.2	2.8	.4	2.2
J	0	0	0	0	0
A	23.2	27.6	28.8	1.2	5.6
B	18.1	13.0	12.7	.3	5.4
C	15.6	13.9	14.4	.5	1.2
G	6.2	5.9	5.5	.4	.7
I	1.0	2.5	2.0	.5	1.0
	99.8%	99.5%	100.0%	5.1%	21.2%

* Reprinted from *Computer Simulation of Competitive Market Response* by Arnold E. Amstutz by permission of The M.I.T. Press, Cambridge, Massachusetts.

These results are impressive, since the magnitude of the difference between simulated and actual for the ten brands was only 5.1 per cent. Furthermore, the results are impressive in comparison to the naive no change model. The naive model would have a total year-end error (absolute values) of 21.2 per cent. Thus the simulation represented a $\dfrac{21.2 - 5.1}{21.2} \cong$ 76 per cent reduction in error when compared to the naive model. The absolute brand share data is a stronger test of validity, and, in general,

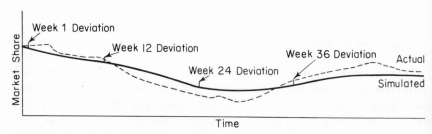

Figure 2-5: Over-time brand share deviation—time series illustration*

the most powerful scale of measurement available should be utilized in establishing validity.

* Reprinted from *Computer Simulation of Competitive Market Response* by Arnold E. Amstutz by permission of The M.I.T. Press, Cambridge, Massachusetts.

A second approach to model validation would be to examine the model output time series and compare it to the actual time series. Figure 2-5 presents an example from Amstutz and Claycamp. Although no statistics are reported, "goodness of fit" statistical measures could have been applied. If a regression of the predicted to actual results were conducted, the model could then be analyzed by testing whether the slope of this simple regression is 1.0 and the intercept zero (which are the results that would be achieved if the model time series is exact). The regression procedure provides the researcher with the ability to assess the significance of statistical deviations from a precise result. Spectral analysis may also be useful in comparing simulated and actual data.[21] Spectral analysis has the convenient property of being appropriate to the analysis of highly autocorrelated processes. It yields information on the average level of activity, deviations from this level, and the time duration of these deviations once they occur. Although a thorough discussion of this methodology is beyond the scope of this book, it should be noted that spectral analysis is likely to play an increasingly important role in the analysis of simulation experiments, since it presents a statistical basis for judging the degree of correspondence between a simulated and an actual time series.[22]

The statistical tools and procedures available for validity testing are not sufficiently well developed. Research is needed to develop practical tests for establishing validity. Existing techniques, although not completely satisfactory, should be applied and attempts should be made to compare real and simulated results, since this is the only method for gaining assurance that a microanalytical model accurately represents the mechanisms of market response.

Sensitivity analysis

The purpose of sensitivity analysis is to determine the functions, parameters, distributions, and inputs to which the model output is most sensitive. It should precede refined measurement and function validation. The reason is that sensitivity analysis can assist the model builder in allocating the scarce financial, manpower, and time resources available for measurement to those aspects of the model that make a real difference in its performance. Before turning to a more detailed considera-

---

[21] See G. S. Fishman and P. J. Kiviat, "The Analysis of Simulation-Generated Time Series," *Management Science*, XIII (March, 1967), pp. 255–557 for an application of this technique.

[22] For a further example, see M. Nerlove, "Spectral Analysis of Seasonable Adjustment Procedures," *Econometrica*, XXXII (July, 1964), pp. 241–86.

tion of sensitivity analysis, it is useful to examine the implications of the information gained from such analysis. A model may contain two types of parameters, functions, and distributions—those that are amenable to direct measurement and those that are not. If a measurable function, parameter, or distribution is found to be a crucial factor via sensitivity analysis, this suggests that the model builder undertake rather careful measurement of this factor. The implications for unmeasurable factors are twofold:

1. Refined executive judgment should be sought on subjective factors that have been identified as significant.
2. Consideration should be given to running a sensitivity analysis on these significant factors in the final runs (i.e., the runs having policy implications) so that the decision implications of estimation error in judgmental inputs can be explored.

The use of a sensitivity analysis in a microanalytic simulation model of market response has not been reported, but the potential of this type of analysis warrants its discussion. The basic considerations in sensitivity testing of microanalytic simulations are outlined below.

There are three basic methods available for performing sensitivity analysis—analytic methods, nonexperimental perturbations, and experimentation. Analytic procedures are generally only available for sensitivity analyzing functions. In these cases, the sensitivity of the response measure of interest to various parameters can often be tested by means of the derivatives of the response function with respect to the appropriate parameters. The derivative will yield an estimate of the sensitivity of the response or output variable to changes in a parameter value for any specified value of the input variables. For example, if a microunit function is $R = \bar{R}(1 - e^{-ax})$, the derivative $dR/da = \bar{R}xe^{-ax}$ would yield useful information about changes in R produced by changes in a, for a given value of x.

Although the analytical approach is usually restricted to microanalysis, other methods may be applied either to microfunctions or to the model taken as a whole. Nonexperimental perturbations involve some judgment on the part of the model builder and the managers with whom he is working concerning which factors in the model are likely to play a key role. Then he must determine the levels (i.e., explicit factor values) to test for each factor and what combination of factor levels to test. The model should then be run at each of the combinations of factor levels he has decided to analyze to see if the model output appears sensitive to the explicit values considered.

Experimentation is the most scientific form of sensitivity analysis at the macrolevel. The model builder again must decide what factors to test and at what levels. The initial difference between the experimental approach and nonexperimental perturbations lies in the fact that the experimental design chosen dictates the combinations of factor levels which must be run in the analysis. For example, a full factorial design would require that each factor be run at each of its levels in combination with all the levels of the other factors.[23] Thus if there were ten factors to be analyzed, each having two levels, the full factorial design would require $2^{10} = 1024$ separate runs of the simulation. Sensitivity analysis on this scale for a large model is generally prohibitive from a cost standpoint. However, if the model builder is willing to ignore or assume away certain or all interaction effects, an efficient sensitivity analysis may become feasible through the use of a different form of experimental design, such as a fractional factorial or a Graeco-Latin square.[24] The latter design is able to analyze changes in only four factors at a time.

The benefit of the experimental approach to sensitivity analysis is the enhanced precision with which the model builder will know the sensitivity of his model to factor levels. Experimental designs allow him to make precise probability statements concerning the results he achieves. The greatest disadvantage of this approach is the fact that experimentation can be enormously costly—particularly in the full factorial design case. Even a fractional replicate of a factorial design can be extremely costly. As an example, consider the Amstutz and Claycamp doctor model. The model consists of one thousand simulated doctors. Suppose now that the model developers wished to test the sensitivity of annual brand market shares for some product to the levels of only eight parameters or functions in the model. Further suppose that each factor is to be tested at only two levels. A full factorial design would thus require $2^8 = 256$ runs of the model. Suppose, however, that the researchers are willing to ignore certain higher order interactions and thus decide upon a one-quarter replicate or $\frac{256}{4} = 64$ runs of the model. Now if each doctor requires six seconds of computer time to practice for a year and if it is assumed that the cost of computer time is six hundred dollars per hour, the computer time costs alone will amount to

$$6 \, \frac{\text{sec}}{\text{doctor}} \times 1000 \text{ doctors} \times \frac{1}{3600} \frac{\text{hr}}{\text{sec}} \times \frac{\$600}{\text{hr}} = \$1000$$

per run. There will need to be 64 runs for a total cost of $64,000. All simulation models may not require the running of 1000 microunits as in this example, and therefore a formal approach may be feasible. Nevertheless, this example points up the potentially explosive cost situation the researcher may face if he wishes to take a formal approach to sen-

---

[23] For a treatment of experimentation and experimental designs in marketing, see S. Banks, *Experimentation in Marketing* (New York: McGraw-Hill, 1965).
[24] *Ibid.* Seymour.

sitivity analysis. Clearly, with cost possibilities such as this, the model builder will want to take full advantage of any information or insights at his disposal in designing the appropriate sensitivity analysis. In many practical instances, the costs/benefits tradeoff will tip the scales in favor of a nonexperimental perturbation of inputs and parameters.

In spite of the feasibility problems mentioned above, experimental approaches to sensitivity analysis of a model may be viable if meaningful restrictions can be placed on the size of the analysis. It seems appropriate to consider such an application in some detail, even though the model is not strictly a marketing model, because it demonstrates a sound application of sensitivity analysis. The case discussed below is Charles P. Bonini's use of a fractional factorial design to analyze a simulation model based upon the postulates contained in Cyert and March's behavioral theory of the firm.[25]

Bonini used a one-quarter replicate of a 2^8 factorial design. This design considers only first level interactions and, as noted above, this requires 64 separate runs of the model. Bonini chose to measure the effects of change in his eight factors with reference to a standard model. Thus each of the eight factors were set at two levels: a standard and an alternative value. The factors and their levels are given in Table 2-3.

TABLE 2-3: Bonini's Factor Levels*

Factor	Standard	Alternative
1. Environment	Stable	Variable
2. Market Growth	2%/Year	10%/Year
	Moderate Cycle	Irregular
3. Industrial Engineering Department	Loose	Tight
4. Contagion of Pressure	Slight	Much
5. Sensitivity to Pressure	High	Low
6. Inventory Valuation	Average Cost	LIFO
7. Sales Force Knowledge of Inventory	Knowledge	No Knowledge
8. Past vs. Present Information Used in Control of Operations	Present	Past

Bonini proposed to study the response of the model to changes in such factors as the stability of the external environment, industrial engineering standards, and method of inventory valuation.

Bonini next faced the dual measurement questions that must be answered in any analysis of a simulation model:

[25] See C. P. Bonini, *Simulation of Information and Decision Systems in the Firm* (Englewood Cliffs, N.J.: Prentice-Hall, Inc., 1963), and R. Cyert and J. March, *A Behavioral Theory of the Firm* (Englewood Cliffs, N.J.: Prentice-Hall, Inc., 1963).
* Based on C. B. Bonini, *ibid.*, p. 87.

1. What aspects of the model should be studied?
2. How should these aspects be characterized?

In answer to the first question, he chose to measure indices of price, cost, inventory, and pressure, in addition to the dollar level of sales and profits. The second was answered in three ways. The time series of these measures were characterized by their:

1. Arithmetic mean
2. Standard deviation
3. Trend

The latter was taken as the least squares regression coefficient of each variable with respect to time.

The simulation was then run the 64 times called for in the experimental design. Each run lasted 108 months or nine years, which, incidentally, represented three complete cycles in the market trend function.

The fractional factorial design ignores higher than first order interactions, but it enables the researcher to classify the results of changes as:

1. Main effects (the over-all direct effect on the measure of interest caused by the given change)
2. Interaction effects (the joint effect of two simultaneous changes)

Bonini's design also enabled him to measure the effect due to different initial conditions.[26]

In order to illustrate the results of such a fractional factorial analysis, discussion will focus upon the effects of a change in the variability of the external environment upon the arithmetic means of the variables being measured. The results of this analysis are presented in Table 2-4. First note that the main effect of their change is highly significant on each measure, reaching the 0.1 per cent level in each case. The main effect results indicate that increasing the variability of the environment has lowered the price and cost indices by 2.83 and 4.17 index points, respectively. Greater variability increased the pressure index by 5.5 index points and the inventory index went up 32.91 index points. These results were substantially anticipated. However, the somewhat surprising result is that increased variability in the external world would enhance sales and profits by about $72,180 and $63,740, respectively. From the interaction with inventory valuation, it is seen that the effect of LIFO reinforces the impact of instability in the external world. With the single exception of sensitivity to pressure, all the remaining significant interaction effects indicate that the alternative levels of all the factors serve to reinforce the impact

[26] In the parlance of experimental design, these effects are termed the block effects. See Banks, *op. cit.*

TABLE 2-4: Effects of a Change in the Variability of the External World: Highly Variable versus Stable*

	Differences in Means over 108 Periods					
	Price	Cost	Pres-sure	Inv.	Sales# $000	Profit $000
	(Index Points)					
Main Effect (Variable vs. Stable External World)	−2.83††	−4.17††	5.5††	32.91††	72.18††	63.74††
Interaction Effects with:						
Inventory Valuation Method	−1.40*	−1.47*	1.4*	20.20*	21.95*	51.83†
Contagion of Pressure					32.56†	
Sensitivity to Pressure	1.53†	1.94*			17.06*	
Sales Force Inventory Knowledge						
Fast Irregular vs. Slow Cyclical Growth			1.8*			
Loose vs. Tight I.E. Dept.		−1.88*				
Past vs. Present Data in Control				16.43*	18.55*	47.36†

Note: Only results significant at the 5 per cent level or less are included.
Sales are expressed as excess over trend or potential.
* Indicates significance at the 5 per cent level.
† Indicates significance at the one per cent level.
†† Indicates significance at the 0.1 per cent level.

of external world variability on the average values of the model measures. The interaction results for sensitivity to pressure indicate that the price- and cost-reducing impact of external world variability is diminished by a decrease in sensitivity to pressure.

For a more detailed and complete discussion of this model and its analysis, the reader is referred to Bonini's work. The purpose of the above discussion was to illustrate the use of a fractional factorial design and to introduce the measurement questions involved in such an application in sensitivity analysis. These considerations are relevant to testing marketing models and are presented in some detail to encourage their application to models of market response.

Model Revision and Maintenance

The model builder or manager who expects to undertake the development of a model "once and for all" will ultimately be sadly disillusioned. The process of model maintenance and revision must be a continuing one

* Based on C. B. Bonini, *op. cit.*, p. 120.

if the model is to be kept relevant for planning and control purposes. Markets are dynamic phenomena, and changes in market response should be expected. For example, there is constant change in competitive factors, products, and consumer tastes. The firm that wishes to utilize the planning advantages of a large-scale simulation model must organize itself to provide for a systematic updating of all aspects of the model. This step is crucial, for without it the enormous investment of time, financial resources, and human frustration that brought the model to fruition will soon come to nought as the model becomes obsolete.

Future Research Needs in Simulation

The two most pressing issues for future management science effort lie in the areas of sensitivity analysis and validation. Although some methods for performing these analyses have been discussed above, the field is far from having provided wholly satisfactory methods. It may be that new classes of statistical methods will need to be developed in order to exploit the unique aspects of simulation methodology. It seems safe to say that the potential importance of simulation models is very likely to call for the creative breakthroughs needed to improve its methodological base.

If validation procedures can be developed, the hypotheses about consumers' behavior as reflected in the model can be evaluated and an accurate understanding of market response can be gained. This understanding is an important element for the normative model building to be described later in this book.

STOCHASTIC MODELS OF CONSUMER RESPONSE

Definition and Uses of Stochastic Models

Although simulation models, especially microanalytic models, represent a very detailed and comprehensive approach to modeling market response, other methods of analysis have also been effectively used. In this section of the chapter attention will focus upon a particular class of models of consumer response.

These models represent consumer response stochastically.[27] Stochas-

---

[27] *Stochastic* is synonymous with "chance," "random," or "probabilistic."

tic models allow for a multitude of the factors that affect consumer behavior by means of response uncertainty. That is, market responses are regarded as outcomes of some probabilistic process. The impact of all factors not explicitly considered in the model is accounted for in the stochastic nature of the response. In a given model these exogenous factors might include the firm's marketing mix, competitive activity, and customer characteristics. Thus the problem of describing and predicting consumer response is reduced to the problem of specifying and estimating a probability law for the response of interest. This procedure is parsimonious in that consumer behavior may often be described by relatively simple stochastic models, whereas the adoption of a deterministic approach would require exceedingly complex models.

At this point the reader may wonder what distinction is made between the stochastic models discussed in this section and the simulation models considered in the previous section. After all, are not the simulation models also stochastic models in the sense that responses are probabilistically determined? In that sense, the two classes are identical. However, a useful distinction can be drawn in terms of some of the characteristics of these models. Stochastic models, in the sense that they are used here, are generally amenable to analysis by analytical methods, whereas simulation models require Monté Carlo procedures. A further distinction may be drawn in terms of the ability to estimate the model's parameters. Stochastic models generally have associated with them explicit statistical procedures for parameter estimation from data. This is not as universally true of simulation models, particularly models of very large systems. Additional contrasts will be drawn in a subsequent section. For present purposes, the analytic versus Monté Carlo mode of analysis is probably the most useful distinction.

Stochastic models are used as constructs for organizing and interpreting market data. The use of constructs by managers and market researchers is, of course, nothing new, even though their use may not be explicitly recognized as such. Take, for example, the case of ordinary monthly sales data. These data are aggregates of raw sales data and are used for sales comparisons between months. But consider how little information is actually conveyed by a rise or drop in sales, other than just a signal that "something has happened." These raw figures yield little idea of what has happened, where, and why; nor do they provide a very useful picture of what is likely to happen if present competitive conditions persist. A stochastic model that is a valid approximation to the market process generating sales will yield more useful insights into the behavioral dynamics of the change that has been detected and a deeper understanding of how consumers respond.

In this context stochastic models have two principal uses. They may be used (1) to test structural hypotheses, and (2) to make conditional predictions.

The use of stochastic models to test structural hypotheses is exemplified in models concerning brand loyalty, learning, and diffusion effects. In each of these applications, the stochastic model serves as the basis of market measurement and enables the parameters of market response to be explicitly identified and estimated so that the structural hypothesis may be statistically tested.

Stochastic models may be used to make conditional predictions such as the ultimate market share for a brand or the time it will take the brand to achieve its ultimate market share. The predictions depend upon market conditions remaining constant. In most actual situations, competitive conditions in the marketplace will cause the market to alter course before it ever gets to equilibrium, but these conditional predictions are nevertheless useful diagnostic indicators of where the market is heading under current conditions. Most stochastic models will yield information of this type.

In this section two basic applications of the stochastic modeling approach will be discussed. The first is an analysis of consumer brand choice processes and the second is a consideration of interpurchase timing. Both of these applications are directed at determining the best descriptor of consumer behavior as an input to marketing decision processes.

The basic methodology of stochastic modeling in marketing has not been well specified in the existing literature and as a result some confusion has arisen. A technical appendix is included at the end of this chapter in order to clarify certain methodological issues.

Stochastic Models of Brand Choice

Brand choice models attempt to describe the process of choosing one brand over another. In general, brand choice models do not concern themselves with the time of actual purchase, but rather with the choice of brand given that a purchase is to be made. Three basic types of stochastic models have been applied to the consideration of brand choice: zero-order, Markovian, and learning models. Each presumes a different consumer behavior process. Zero-order models presume that past brand choices do not affect future brand choices. Markov models assume that only the most recent purchase affects the current brand choice decision. Learning models postulate that brand choice is dependent upon the complete history of past brand purchases. Each of these approaches will be considered at the theoretical level, and empirical results will be presented to show how the theoretical process of behavior has been tested. This discussion is not intended to be an exhaustive review of stochastic models, but rather will serve to illustrate the type of work which has been done in this area.

Zero-order Models of Brand Choice

A zero-order model is one in which the response probabilities (the probability of choosing a particular brand) are not affected or altered by the particular history of responses that have been made. Consider an individual consumer in a situation in which he may make one of two alternative responses, A or B, on any given response occasion (i.e., purchase occasion). Such a situation might be a market where A represents some brand of interest and B represents an aggregate, "all other" brand. Let $P(A_t)$ represent his probability of making response A at response occasion t. Then in a zero-order model,

$$P(A_t|\{\text{some history of } A\text{'s and } B\text{'s at times } 0,$$
$$1, \ldots, t - 1\}) = P(A_t)$$

whatever the particular prior history of A's and B's may be. Note that if $P(A_t)$ does not change with time, the consumer's response process is a Bernoulli process in this case.

The early work on consumer brand and store loyalty by Brown and Cunningham contained an implicit assumption that consumer brand and store choices follow a Bernoulli process.[28] Using the purchasing records of 100 families from the *Chicago Tribune* consumer panel for the year 1951, Brown studied brand loyalty behavior toward certain frequently purchased products such as toothpaste, margarine, coffee, soap, etc. His operational measure of brand loyalty depended upon the number and pattern of purchases of different brands during the year. On the basis of his measure of brand loyalty, Brown classified households as having: undivided loyalty, divided loyalty, unstable loyalty, or no loyalty. Brown's measure of loyalty was not entirely satisfactory, but his work did reveal that consumers concentrate their purchases much more than had been previously expected.[29] Brown's work helped give impetus to

---

[28] In this instance, the term "Bernoulli process" is being used to denote both stationary binomial trials and stationary multinomial trials. The work referenced here may be found in G. Brown, "Brand Loyalty—Fact or Fiction?" *Advertising Age*, XXIII (June 9, pp. 53–65; June 30, pp. 45–47; Oct. 6, pp. 82–86; and Dec. 1, 1952, pp. 76–79), and R. M. Cunningham, "Brand Loyalty—What, Where, How Much?" *Harvard Business Review*, XXXIV (Jan.–Feb., 1956), pp. 116–128.

[29] Morrison has observed that Brown's measure of brand loyalty does not necessarily satisfy even the weakest necessary condition for a meaningful scale, the property of transitivity. See D. G. Morrison, "Stochastic Models for Time Series with Applications in Marketing," Technical Report No. 8, Joint Program in Operations Research, Stanford University. For a readable and useful treatment of measurement and scaling in marketing, see Green and Tull, *op. cit.*

subsequent empirical study of brand loyalty and consumer brand choice processes.

The definition of brand loyalty was improved in a later study by Cunningham.[30] He operationally defined brand loyalty as the proportion of total purchases within a product class that a household devotes to its favorite or most frequently purchased brand. In a subsequent study, Cunningham defined store loyalty in an analogous manner.[31] The research hypotheses in these studies centered about the postulated existence of brand or store loyalties. The null hypothesis was that brands would be purchased and stores visited on an equiprobable basis. That is, the null hypothesis was that no propensity to purchase particular brands or to shop in particular stores exists. The *Chicago Tribune* panel once again served as the data base for these studies. The results of these studies are summarized below:

1. Significant brand loyalty exists within product classes (intraclass loyalty).
2. Loyalty proneness, or the propensity to be brand loyal across product classes, does not exist.
3. Store and brand loyalty are not significantly related.
4. Purchases on deals tend to be concentrated among households having low brand loyalties.
5. Consumption and brand loyalty are unrelated.
6. A household's time in the panel does not relate to its loyalty behavior.
7. There is more store loyalty generated toward chain stores than toward specialty stores or independents.

Cunningham's results suggest that families concentrate their brand and store choices to a far greater extent than that expected under the equiprobable chance model.

A zero-order modeling approach was utilized by Frank in an analysis of consumer brand choice.[32] He postulated that consumer brand choice could be represented by a Bernoulli process in which individual consumers could differ from one another in terms of their brand choice probabilities. This assumption of differing brand choice probabilities within the consumer population is referred to as *heterogeneity*.

Frank was the first to point out the potential problem of inferring "learning" effects (changes in brand choice probabilities due to previous

[30] R. M. Cunningham, *op. cit.*
[31] R. M. Cunningham, "Customer Loyalty to Store and Brand," *Harvard Business Review*, XXXIX (Nov.–Dec., 1961), pp. 127–37.
[32] R. E. Frank, "Brand Choice as a Probability Process," *Journal of Business*, XXXV (Jan., 1962), pp. 43–56.

purchases) from brand purchase decisions aggregated from a heterogeneous consumer population.[33]   Specifically, he argued that some of the "learning" effects that had been found by Kuehn may in fact be spurious as a result of the aggregation of heterogeneous consumers whose true brand switching processes are zero-order.[34]   Kuehn's results are discussed in a later section.

Testing the zero-order hypothesis for each family via the Wald-Wolfowitz run test, Frank found that the brand choice behavior of most of the sample families was consistent with the zero-order model.   It should be noted, however, that the run test has certain limitations in this application; in spite of these limitations in statistical procedure, Frank's work raised an important issue—aggregation—with respect to inferences concerning the order of consumers' brand choice processes.[35]

Further evidence of approximately zero-order consumer choice behavior has been found by Massy and Frank.[36]   On a family-by-family basis, they developed simulated purchases of coffee, tea, and beer, assuming zero-order choice processes.   For each product class and within each product class by family, they developed 29 raw purchasing statistics such as number of brand runs, number of store runs, average length of brand runs, and average length of store runs for both the actual purchases and the simulated purchases.   These statistics for both the actual and simulated populations were then factor analyzed and their respective factor profiles were compared.   These comparisons led the authors to conclude that: (1) for coffee and tea, brand switching behavior is not distinguishable from a zero-order process, (2) for beer, brand switching seems to be a higher order process, and (3) store switching behavior for coffee, tea, and beer appears to be adequately described by a zero-order

[33] For a discussion and an example of the confounding of heterogeneity and changes in brand choice probabilities, see the technical appendix at the end of this chapter.

[34] A. A. Kuehn, "An Analysis of the Dynamics of Consumer Behavior and Its Implications for Marketing Management," unpublished Ph.D. dissertation, Graduate School of Industrial Administration, Carnegie Institute of Technology, 1958.

[35] If a family is accurately represented by a zero-order brand choice process and if its brand choice probability changes sometime during the sequence of brand purchases used for the Wald-Wolfowitz test, the test is quite likely to reject the zero-order hypothesis (even though it is true).   Another limitation is the fact that the run test is not especially powerful in rejecting the zero-order hypotheses for purchase sequences of lengths that are reasonable in consumer studies.   See L. E. Moses, "Non-Parametric Statistics for Psychological Research," *Psychology Bulletin*, XLIX (March, 1952), pp. 122–43, for some results which relate to the power of the run test.   Also see Sidney Siegel, *Non-Parametric Statistics* (New York: McGraw-Hill, 1956), pp. 144–45.

[36] W. F. Massy and R. E. Frank, "The Study of Consumer Purchase Sequences Using Factor Analysis and Simulation," *Proceedings of the Business and Economics Section of the American Statistical Association* (Dec., 1964).   The methodology employed in this paper would also be useful in validating microunit functions in a microanalytical simulation.

process. Although it is not clear how sensitive the factor profiles might be to deviations from the zero-order assumption, the method used in this study is interesting in that it attempts to explore the manner in which the underlying structure of brand and store switching behavior affects common summary statistics of brand and store choice behavior. Since the statistics are generated on a family-by-family basis, this method avoids the aggregation problem noted above.

In a later study, Massy sought to ascertain the order and stationarity of family specific brand switching in the regular coffee market.[37] The assumptions of his statistical procedures required that the families be frequent and stationary purchasers of regular coffee.[38] Only 39 out of an original sample of 800 households passed the frequency and stationarity tests. When the brand purchasing behavior of these 39 families was aggregated, the zero-order null hypothesis was rejected at a very high level of significance. However, at the individual family level, the zero-order hypothesis was tenable in a great majority of the cases, even at the relatively loose 90 per cent confidence level. Recognizing that this does not necessarily establish the validity of a zero-order switching process for regular coffee consumption, Massy notes:

> . . . If we had all the data in the world we would be surprised if the probabilities of purchasing different brands were serially independent. The real question at issue is whether the departures from a zero order process are consistently serious enough to warrant using the more complicated first order model to describe brand switching behavior.[39]

In sum, Massy's results indicate that: (1) stationarity is the exception rather than the rule, (2) consumers differ markedly in their brand choice probabilities, (3) inferences concerning the order of family specific processes from aggregate data are extremely sensitive to the assumption of homogeneity and stationarity and consequently are very tenuous, and finally, (4) a zero-order switching model seems to suffice for describing brand choice of regular coffee.

Morrison has developed statistical tests and estimation procedures for heterogeneous populations of consumers whose brand choice behavior in the short run may be described by Bernoulli trials.[40] He assumes that

---

[37] W. F. Massy, "Order and Homogeneity of Family Specific Brand-Switching Processes," *Journal of Marketing Research*, III (Feb., 1966), pp. 48–54.

[38] By stationarity is meant that the brand choice probabilities remain constant. For further elaboration of this concept see the technical appendix at the end of this chapter.

[39] Massy, *op. cit.*

[40] Donald G. Morrison, "Testing Brand Switching Models," *Journal of Marketing Research* (July, 1964), pp. 634–58. This paper is reprinted in D. B. Montgomery and G. L. Urban, eds., *Applications of Management Science in Marketing* (Englewood Cliffs, N.J.: Prentice-Hall, Inc., 1969).

each consumer, say consumer i, has some probability p_i of purchasing brand A versus all other brands on each purchase occasion and that the p_i remains constant over short sequences of purchases. The population is also assumed to be heterogeneous, which in this case means that p_i is distributed across the population of consumers. He provides statistical procedures for both arbitrary and beta distributions of p_i.

A heterogeneous zero-order model that can account for nonstationarity of the response probabilities has been proposed by Montgomery.[41] The model yields estimates of the distribution of response probability across the population of consumers, the expected equilibrium share for each alternative, the rate at which the market will approach its steady state from any disequilibrium position, and the propensity for the choice probability for a given brand to increase. These measures as well as the structural characteristics of the model are of interest in consumer product markets. Methods have been developed for estimating and testing the model. In an initial empirical test, the model was found to provide an excellent fit to Market Research Corporation of America (MRCA) National Consumer Panel data in the product class of dentifrice just before and just after the American Dental Association endorsed Crest toothpaste in August, 1960. Thus the model was found to be empirically viable in both the relatively normal pre-endorsement market and in the unstable market that followed endorsement.

The model, termed a probability diffusion model, describes the response-to-response (e.g., purchase-to-purchase) behavior of a set of heterogeneous, nonstationary consumers. Since interresponse time is not explicitly modeled, it is necessary to use an *ad hoc* segmentation criterion such as average interpurchase time in applications where real-time inferences (such as market share) as opposed to structural inferences are required.

Another heterogeneous, nonstationary zero-order model that may be applied to consumer behavior has been proposed by Ronald Howard.[42] In his model, the underlying parameters of the stochastic process that generate observable outcomes are themselves subject to change at times determined by yet another stochastic process. Hence an individual's response probability is nonstationary. The heterogeneity enters when these underlying parameters are themselves randomly distributed according to some distribution function. In essence, then, Howard's model undergoes discrete changes at randomly determined intervals. He presents an example having a Bernoulli observable process (brand purchases), a beta param-

---

[41] See D. B. Montgomery, "A Stochastic Response Model with Application to Brand Choice," forthcoming in *Management Science: Theory* and reprinted in D. B. Montgomery and G. L. Urban, eds., *Applications of Management Science in Marketing* (Englewood Cliffs, N.J.: Prentice-Hall, Inc., 1969).

[42] R. A. Howard, "Dynamic Inference," *Operations Research* (Sept.–Oct., 1965), pp. 712–33.

eter distribution, and a geometric distribution for the time between parameter changes.

Zero-order models based on the assumption that past brand choices do
not affect future brand choices provided an impetus for stochastic modeling of consumer behavior. Although the first models were simple, extensions to include heterogeneity and nonstationarity have produced sophisticated and empirically viable models of consumer response in certain
product classes.

Markov Models

Whereas zero-order models assume that brand choice is independent of
past purchases, Markov models presume that only the last brand choice
affects the current purchase.[43]

Consider the following simple first-order Markov model of brand
switching. For discussion purposes, assume a three-brand market
(brands *A*, *B*, and *C*) and define the state of a consumer by his last
brand purchase. In this example, the state of the consumer may be
defined as:

State *A* = brand *A* was purchased on the last purchase occasion
State *B* = brand *B* was purchased on the last purchase occasion
State *C* = brand *C* was purchased on the last purchase occasion.

In this model, it is postulated that all consumers may be represented by
the following first-order transition matrix:

$$
\begin{array}{c}
\text{Brand purchased at} \\
\text{occasion } t + 1
\end{array}
$$

$$
\left\{ \begin{array}{c} \text{Brand purchased} \\ \text{at occasion } t \end{array} \right\}
\begin{array}{c} \\ A \\ B \\ C \end{array}
\begin{array}{ccc}
A & B & C \\
\left[\begin{array}{ccc}
P_{A,A} & P_{A,B} & P_{A,C} \\
P_{B,A} & P_{B,B} & P_{B,C} \\
P_{C,A} & P_{C,B} & P_{C,C}
\end{array} \right]
\end{array}
$$

---

[43] Strictly speaking, this is true only of a first-order Markov process. Higher
order processes (i.e., the probability of the next event depends upon several preceding
events) may be used to describe brand choice behavior on the basis of more than
just the most recent brand purchased. For example, if the probability depends
upon the last two brands purchased, the model is termed a second-order Markov
model. In this section it is sufficient to consider only first-order models, since higher
order processes may be made equivalent to a first-order process by proper definition
of the state space.

The P_{ij}'s are the transition probabilities. They represent the probability that a consumer who purchases brand i at purchase occasion t will purchase brand j at purchase occasion $t + 1$. In this model it is required that

$$\sum_{j = A,B,C} P_{ij} = 1 \quad \text{for } i = A, B, C$$

This reflects the fact that a consumer must make a purchase of one of the three brands in the market at his next purchase occasion. This model also assumes that all consumers are characterized by the same transition matrix, that is, it assumes that consumers are homogeneous with respect to their transition (or brand-switching) matrices.

This simple Markov model may be defined to model real-time (e.g., weekly) brand purchases by specifying that the purchase occasion index t represent a basic time unit such as a week. Since some consumers will not purchase any brand of the product during a given week, the model must be further adjusted to include a "no purchase" state. For example, brand C could be defined as a dummy brand which reflects no purchase of either brand A or B. This formulation also implicitly assumes that no consumer will make more than one purchase during the time interval being used.[44]

The transition probability P_{ii} may be interpreted to be a measure of a brand's retentive or holding power, while P_{ij} is a measure of brand j's power to attract customers from brand i. From the theory of Markov chains, the expected steady-state or equilibrium distribution of consumers (i.e., expected brand shares) may be derived. A number of other interesting measures, such as the expected number of periods before an individual will try a particular brand, are available.[45]

Variants of this simple model have been proposed by a number of authors.[46] For example, Harary and Lipstein disaggregated the total consumer population into two parallel Markov models, one for families who are "hard core" loyal to one or more brands (i.e., at least one of their P_{ii} is high) and another for those families that might be termed

[44] Multiple purchases could be handled in this simple model at the cost of a greatly expanded state space. For example, one could have state A_1 = one purchase of brand A, state A_2 = two purchases of brand A,..., state A_1B_1 = one purchase of brand A and one of B,..., etc.

[45] For a more complete discussion, see F. Harary and B. Lipstein, "The Dynamics of Brand Loyalty: A Markov Approach," *Operations Research*, X (Jan.–Feb., 1962), pp. 19–40.

[46] For example, see R. B. Maffei, "Brand Preferences and Simple Markov Processes," *Operations Research*, VIII (March–Apr., 1960), pp. 210–18; J. Herniter and J. Magee, "Customer Behavior as a Markov Process," *Operations Research*, IX (Jan.–Feb., 1961), pp. 105–22; and F. Harary and B. Lipstein, *op. cit.*

switchers (i.e., all of their P_{ii} are relatively low).[47] This procedure eliminates some of the problems inherent in the homogeneity assumption, since the hard core loyals and the switchers are more likely to be internally homogeneous than the population of consumers as a whole.

Their approach requires that the Markov transition matrix be estimated separately for the hard core loyals and the switchers. This, in turn, requires an operational definition of what constitutes a hard core loyal consumer. Harary and Lipstein operationalized their model using the criterion that any consumer who devoted three-quarters or more of his total purchases in a product class to a single brand would be considered hard core loyal. Their empirical experience has shown that most product classes have from 50 to 80 per cent hard core loyal consumers.

They proposed three major types of dynamic market predictions that may be made by using the Markov model. The first was the expected steady-state or equilibrium market shares. The expected equilibrium market shares are the expected shares that the brands would have if the process of brand switching as currently estimated by the transition matrix were to be allowed to run to equilibrium. Thus these equilibrium shares provide a useful measure of the direction in which the market is heading, given the present market conditions. This may often be useful diagnostic information for the firm.

The actual predictions, of course, are highly likely to be in error. In any real market situation, the equilibrium market shares are rarely reached because competitive activity, changes in the firm's own marketing strategy, and changes in the consumer population will tend to alter the values of the transition probabilities in the Markov matrix.[48] This form of nonstationarity in no way obviates the diagnostic value of the conditional predictions which may be obtained from such a model.

The second prediction is the average time to trial. This yields information as to the average number of periods that will pass before a consumer will try a particular brand in this product class. As such, it is a measure of the attractive power of the brand. Finally, they suggest using the Markov chain model to evaluate the success of a new product introduction. The model is used to describe the evolution of brand shares, new triers, repeat buying rates, and the proportion of hard core loyal buyers for the new product.

The application of the simple Markov chain model to brand switching

[47] F. Harary and Lipstein, *op. cit.*

[48] See A. S. C. Ehrenberg, "An Appraisal of Markov Brand Switching Models," *Journal of Marketing Research*, II (Nov., 1965), pp. 347–62, and W. Massy and D. Morrison, "Comments on Ehrenberg's Appraisal of Brand Switching Models," *Journal of Marketing Research*, V (May, 1968), pp. 225–27, for further discussion of this point.

behavior involves assumptions about the order of the switching process, its stationarity over the data period, and homogeneity of transition matrices across consumers. The first (and nearly the only) analysts to examine these assumptions via statistical procedures were Styan and Smith.[49] They used the simple Markov model to analyze product switching behavior for a panel of British housewives. For the 26-week period between January and June, 1957, each housewife's purchase behavior in the laundry powder market was classified into one of the following four mutually exclusive and collectively exhaustive categories:

1. Bought detergent only in week t
2. Bought soap powder only in week t
3. Bought both detergent and soap powder in week t
4. Bought no laundry powder at all in week t

These categories define the "state space" of the Markov chain analysis.

The 26-week period enabled them to compute 25 two-period transition matrices for aggregate switching behavior. That is, a transition matrix was computed for times $t - 1$ versus t for $t = 1, 2, \ldots, 25$ (where the initial period is taken to be time 0). It should be emphasized that for any two-period transition matrix, the data for all households were aggregated which implicitly assumes homogeneity of consumers.

Using the χ^2 test developed by Anderson and Goodman, they tested the order of the Markov chain.[50] The null and alternative hypotheses were:

$H_0 =$ the data are from a zero-order process (i.e., a zero-order Markov chain)

$H_1 =$ the data are from a first-order Markov chain

Each of the 25 matrices was tested for H_0 versus H_1. It was found that H_0 could be rejected in favor of H_1 at a very high level of significance. Thus the aggregate data behaved according to a higher than zero-order Markov chain. In this case, there was not sufficient data to test the first-order hypothesis against second and higher order alternatives. Note, however, that although knowledge of this aggregate first-order behavior for this product may be useful from a marketing standpoint, it does not

[49] G. P. H. Styan and H. Smith, Jr., "Markov Chains Applied to Marketing," *Journal of Marketing Research*, I (Feb., 1964), pp. 50–55.

[50] T. W. Anderson and L. A. Goodman, "Statistical Inference About Markov Chains," *Annals of Mathematical Statistics*, XXVIII (March, 1957), pp. 89–109.

establish first-order Markov behavior on the part of the individual house-holds who enter this analysis. Recall Massy's finding (discussed earlier) that aggregation led to highly significant inferences of a first-order proc-ess, whereas disaggregation for the same sample of households tended to support the notion of zero-order or independent purchase behavior. Frank and Morrison have also warned of the danger of inferring individ-ual behavior based upon aggregate transition matrices when the models used assume homogeneity of the individuals in the sample.

The stationarity of the transition matrices over the 26-week period was also tested. In this case, the null hypothesis of stationarity could not be rejected, since the significance level of the test was relatively high (over 24 per cent). Hence, the aggregate data appear to be consistent with a stationary, first-order Markov chain.

Styan and Smith also discussed the use of the limiting distribution of market shares for the four alternatives. It was found that the market shares for these 26 weeks did not vary much from the equilibrium market shares predicted by the transition matrix formed by aggregating over all 25 of the two-period matrices. Thus this market was very close to its steady-state condition.

The methodological significance of this paper rests upon the fact that they *tested* the *assumptions* of their aggregate Markov model. Hopefully, this approach will become more common. It should be noted, however, that they were able to test only the first two assumptions mentioned at the beginning of this discussion—the order and stationarity of the choice process. Their methods did not enable them to test for homogeneity of transition probabilities across individual consumers.[51]

Two interesting new Markov models have been developed by Morri-son.[52] In previous applications of Markov models, it was always assumed that each and every consumer had the same brand switching matrix. Even when the total switching matrix is disaggregated into a loyal and a switchers matrix, previous applications have assumed identical switch-ing matrices for individuals within these segments. Morrison generalized these previous models to include the case where individual consumers may be heterogeneous with respect to their brand switching matrices in two-brand markets.

The first of Morrison's models is termed the Brand Loyal model. In this model a consumer's transition matrix is of the form:

[51] For progress on this problem in Markov models, see Morrison, *op. cit.* For progress in the measurement of heterogeneity in most classes of stochastic models, see W. F. Massy, D. B. Montgomery, and D. G. Morrison, *Stochastic Models of Consumer Behavior* (Cambridge, Mass.: The M.I.T. Press, 1969).

[52] Morrison, *op. cit.*

Brand pur-
chased at occa-
sion $t + 1$

$$
\begin{array}{c c c}
 & A & B \\
\text{Brand purchased} \quad A & p & 1 - p \\
\text{at occasion } t \quad B & kp & 1 - kp
\end{array}
$$

where brand A represents the consumer's favorite brand and where brand B represents all other brands. Heterogeneity between consumers is introduced by assuming that p is distributed across the consumer population according to some probability law. The parameter k lies between zero and one and is constant for all families. Notice that if $k = 1$, the probability of choosing brand A on purchase occasion $t + 1$ is independent of the brand purchased on occasion t. That is, for $k = 1$ the model reduces to a heterogeneous, zero-order model. The model is termed the Brand Loyal model because if p is high for a given consumer, he will be likely to purchase brand A at purchase occasion $t + 1$ even if he purchased brand B at purchase occasion t.

In contrast, the second of Morrison's models, termed the Last Purchase Loyal model, is described by a transition matrix of the form:

Brand purchased
at occasion $t + 1$

$$
\begin{array}{c c c}
 & A & B \\
\text{Brand purchased} \quad A & p & 1 - p \\
\text{at occasion } t \quad B & 1 - kp & kp
\end{array}
$$

where k is again between zero and one and p is distributed in the population of consumers. In this model if a consumer has a high p, he is relatively more likely to repeat his previous brand purchase than he is to return to brand A, as was the case in the Brand Loyal model. Thus the Brand Loyal model considers loyalty to be oriented toward a particular brand, whereas the Last Purchase Loyal model assumes that loyalty is generated toward the brand last purchased.

Morrison developed minimum chi square procedures for estimating and testing these models.[53] Empirical comparison of these models yielded interesting inferences concerning the structure of brand loyalty in a market. Using data for regular coffee purchases from the *Chicago Tribune* consumer panel, Morrison found that the Brand Loyal model was the

[53] The minimum chi square procedure yields best asymptotically normal estimates of the model's parameters as well as a chi square statistic that measures the over-all "goodness of fit" of the model to the data.

better descriptor of consumer brand choice.   Furthermore, he found that consumers were not too far from zero order in their brand purchasing behavior as indicated by values of k near one.   This is consistent with the results obtained by Frank and Massy for regular coffee.

One point can be raised concerning his empirical comparison of the Brand Loyal model and the Last Purchase Loyal model which will not alter the conclusions in this case but which may be important in other comparisons.   Morrison's comparison of these two models was based upon the magnitude of their respective chi square statistics.   The Brand Loyal model had a smaller chi square and thus was concluded to be a better fit to the data in this case.   Since these models have different degrees of freedom, one really should compare their respective chi square probability levels rather than the actual values.   A far more serious problem in his empirical results is that the purchase sequences he used overlapped. This overlap, while perhaps not invalidating the relative comparison between his models, nevertheless is likely to bias his empirical chi square statistics.   Thus one must be careful as to what is concluded in an absolute sense about the "goodness of fit" of the Brand Loyal model.

Markov models are useful as descriptors of consumer behavior, but before conditional predictions can be generated to describe the effects of changing marketing variables, these marketing variables must be linked to the transition probabilities.   For example, Telser has developed a model linking price to the transition probabilities.[54]   He used a variant of the Markov brand switching model to develop estimates of the price elasticities of branded goods.   In this type of Markov model the brand choice transition probabilities are made functions of the competitive marketing variables (e.g., prices) that prevail in the market at the time the brand choice is made.   The transition probabilities were expressed as

$a_{ii} = f_{ii}(P_{it}, P_{it}^*) =$ the conditional probability of repeating the purchase of brand i during period t as a function of P_{it} and P_{it}^*.

$a_{ki} = f_{ki}(P_{it}, P_{it}^*) =$ the conditional probability of purchasers shifting to brand i from all other brands during period t as a function of P_{it} and P_{it}^*.

where $P_{it} =$ the price of brand i during period t
$P_{it}^* =$ the average price of all other brands during period t

In this application, one would expect a_{ii} and a_{ki} to be higher when P_{it} is lower relative to P_{it}^*.   Thus in this variable Markov model, the brand

[54] L. G. Telser, "The Demand for Branded Goods as Estimated from Consumer Panel Data," *Review of Economics and Statistics*, XXXXIV (Aug., 1962), pp. 300–24.

shifting probabilities are subject to change from period to period unde the impact of competitive activity.

In order to obtain estimates, some further specifications of the func tions $f_{ii}(P_{it}, P_{it}^*)$ and $f_{ki}(P_{it}, P_{it}^*)$ are necessary. Telser chose the simples specification by making the f's linear functions of the sample period aver age prices. In particular, he let $p_{it} = P_{it} - P_{it}^*$ be the price variable an approximately specified the functions as

$$a_{ii} \simeq f_{ii}(p_{it}) = c_{ii} + b_i p_{it}$$
$$a_{ki} \simeq f_{ki}(p_{it}) = c_{ki} + b_i^* p_{it}$$

Since the magnitude of the probabilities a_{ii} and a_{ki} will vary inversely with p_{it}, both b_i and b_i^* will be negative.[55]

Telser also presented a method for estimating the transition probabil ities a_{ii} and a_{ki} from only market share data. The market share for brand i in period t is denoted by m_{it}. Starting with the relation

$$m_{it} = \sum_{j=1}^{n} m_{j,t-1} a_{ji} \quad \text{for } i = 1, \ldots, n$$

between the transition probabilities, lagged market share, and current market share and using the linear approximations for a_{ii} and a_{ki} given above, he developed an estimating equation of the form

$$m_{it} = \alpha + \beta m_{i,t-1} + \gamma p_{it} + \mu_{it} \tag{2-3}$$

where μ_{it} is the residual and the parameters α, β, and γ are functions of previously specified parameters.

Telser used MRCA National Consumer Panel data for the period from April, 1954, to March, 1957 in estimating Eq. (2-3). Using monthly mar ket share and price data, he estimated Eq. (2-3) for each of several brands in the product classes of frozen orange juice, instant coffee, and regular coffee. The multiple regression coefficients for these regressions ranged from 0.57 to 0.92, with most values over 0.70. The price elasticity esti mates derived from these fitted regressions (averaged by brands) were:

−5.7 for frozen orange juice

−5.5 for instant coffee

−4.4 for regular coffee

He also developed an equation using a relative price variable rather than $p_{it} = P_{it} - P_{it}^*$.[56]

---

[55] This will be true except when the product has a price-quality or price-snob appeal association. This is not the case for the products considered by Telser.

[56] These results are reported in Telser, *op. cit.*

Although some questions have been raised concerning the statistical properties of the estimates in this approach, the model has the advantage that it can be applied even when relatively little data (and that in aggregate form) are avaliable. This approach merits further research, since the value of stochastic models in planning and prediction will be greatly enhanced if they are able to link marketing variables to the probability processes.

Learning Models

One of the earliest attempts to develop a stochastic model of consumer behavior was Kuehn's use of a modified form of Bush and Mosteller's linear learning theory as a model of brand choice.[57] A fundamental aspect of learning models is the notion that the occurrence of a response will enhance its likelihood of occurrence in the future. In a brand switching context, this would imply that a purchase of a given brand will increase the probability that the consumer will again purchase the brand. In effect, then, learning models explicitly postulate purchase event feedback on the future response probability. The effect is accumulative, so that the probability of purchase depends not only on the last purchase or last few purchases as in a Markov model, but upon the entire purchase history.

In order to clarify Kuehn's linear learning model, consider a two-brand market. Suppose that brand A is the brand of primary interest, while brand B represents an aggregate of all other brands in the market. For a two-brand market, it is sufficient to consider as the response probability $P(A_t) = P_t$, the probability of purchasing brand A at purchase occasion t, since $P(B_t) = 1 - P(A_t)$.

Learning models assume that the actual response (purchase) made at occasion t affects the response probability at occasion $t + 1$. In particular, the linear learning model assumes that this effect is linear. This assumption is summarized in the following two linear equations:

$$P_{t+1} = \alpha_1 + \beta_1 P_t = \text{probability of choosing brand } A \text{ at purchase}$$
occasion $t + 1$ if brand A was purchased at
time t \hfill (2-4)

$$P_{t+1} = \alpha_0 + \beta_0 P_t = \text{probability of choosing brand } A \text{ at purchase}$$
occasion $t + 1$ if some other brand was pur-
chased at time t \hfill (2-5)

[57] A. A. Kuehn, *op. cit.*, and "Consumer Brand Choice—A Learning Process?" *Journal of Advertising Research*, II (Dec., 1962), pp. 10–17. For linear learning theory, see R. Bush and F. Mosteller, *Stochastic Models for Learning* (New York: John Wiley and Sons, 1955).

Equation (2-4) is known as the acceptance operator, while Eq. (2-5) is known as the rejection operator. Note that while P_{t+1} depends upon P_t and the response made at time t, P_t itself summarizes the influence of all past purchases.[58] The linear equations for P_{t+1} are depicted in Fig. 2-6.

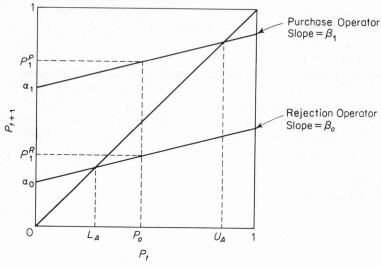

**Figure 2-6: Linear learning model*

Now consider a consumer who initially has a probability P_0 of purchasing brand A at the initial occasion ($t = 0$). That is, the consumer is at P_0 in Fig. 2-6. Now suppose that this consumer purchases brand A at $t = 0$. Since an actual purchase of brand A is assumed to enhance his probability of purchasing brand A on the next trial, the probability of his purchasing brand A at $t = 1$ may be found by reading from P_0 up to the purchase operator and then over to P_1^P. The superscript denotes the purchase of brand A on the previous trial. Similarly, if he purchased some other brand at time zero, his probability at time one would be P_1^R as read from the rejection operator. Note that the purchase of some other brand at occasion t will, in general, decrease the consumer's probability of purchasing brand A at occasion $t + 1$.

In most applications of the linear learning model, it is also assumed that $\beta = \beta_0 = \beta_1$ (i.e., the slopes of the purchase and rejection operators are equal). In this case, the influence of past purchases on the present

[58] It is interesting to note that if the probability of purchasing brand A is considered to be the state of a consumer rather than the actual brand of purchase being his state, the model is a first-order Markov process having a continuous state space.

* A. A. Kuehn, "Consumer Brand Choice—A Learning Process?" *Journal of Advertising Research*, II (December, 1962). © Advertising Research Foundation, Inc. (1962).

purchase probability are geometrically weighted, with the most recent purchase having the greatest weight.[59]

In Fig. 2-6, note that P_t and P_{t+1} are bounded by L_A and U_A. That is,

$$L_A \leq P_t \leq U_A \quad \text{and} \quad L_A \leq P_{t+1} \leq U_A$$

If $L_A > 0$ and $U_A < 1.0$, this implies that learning never goes to completion. That is, the consumer is never absolutely certain to purchase one brand or the other.

Kuehn has not directly tested or estimated the linear learning model described above in any of his published work. In his thesis, he used factorial analysis in an attempt to isolate the effects of purchases.[60] His results for past histories of four successive purchases are given in Table 2-5. The data are purchases of frozen orange juice, where brand A is Snow Crop and brand 0 is all others.

TABLE 2-5: Kuehn's Learning Model Results*

Brand Choice on Four Prior Purchases	Probability of Purchasing Brand A on the Next Trial
AAAO	0.486
AAOA	0.595
AOAA	0.665
OAAA	0.690
AAOO	0.305
AOAO	0.405
OAAA	0.414
AOOA	0.565
OAOA	0.497
OOAA	0.552
AOOO	0.154
OAOO	0.129
OOAO	0.191
OOOA	0.330

The results reported in Table 2-5 illustrate the increasing effect of the most current purchases. These results and certain others do appear to be consistent with the linear learning model of consumer brand choice. But it must be borne in mind that these results assumed that all consumers had the same P_0; thus there will be a confounding of heterogeneity with the learning effect as noted by Frank.[61]

---

[59] Note that geometric weightings are the discrete analogue of exponential weightings.

[60] Kuehn, *op. cit.*

* A. A. Kuehn, "Consumer Brand Choice—A Learning Process?" *Journal of Advertising Research*, II (December, 1962). © Advertising Research Foundation, Inc. (1962).

[61] See the technical appendix for a discussion of this confounding.

In evaluating Kuehn's work, it should be noted that although he did not directly statistically test his model, he was one of the first researchers to investigate the application of learning models to consumer behavior. Kuehn's work has served as a stimulus to more general approaches in stochastic modeling of consumer behavior.

Carman noted that little empirical evidence had been published in support of the linear learning model, and further, that the results which had been published did not directly test the linear learning hypothesis.[62] He tested the linear learning model using dentifrice purchase data from the MRCA consumer panel for the period subsequent to the American Dental Association endorsement of Crest in August, 1960.

Carman tested the special case of the linear learning model for which the "purchase operator" and the "rejection operator" have the same slope. As empirical observations for his estimation procedure, he developed weighted empirical frequencies of the probability triplet $(P_t, P_{p,t+1}, P_{r,t+1})$, where:

P_t = probability of purchasing Crest at time t,

$P_{p,t+1}$ = probability of purchasing Crest at time $t + 1$, given that a purchase of Crest was made at time t,

$P_{r,t+1}$ = probability of purchasing Crest at time $t + 1$ given that a purchase of some other brand was made at time t.

These empirical frequencies were then used to estimate the parameters of the purchase and rejection operators by least squares regressions.[63] The parameters were estimated for subgroups of the population. These subgroups were defined by the time interval between purchases and the degree of brand loyalty as exhibited in past purchase sequences. In all of the subgroups Carman found the linear learning model provided a good fit. The coefficients of determination in the regressions ranged from 0.67 to 0.99, and therefore the dentifrice data did not appear to be inconsistent with the linear learning model.[64]

Carman also examined the projected equilibrium brand shares of Crest. When the learning model was estimated on the basis of the August, 1960 to January, 1961 period, the brand share projection was approximately seventy-two per cent. However, when the learning model was estimated on the basis of the July, 1961 to June, 1962 data, the projections became

---

[62] J. M. Carman, "Brand Switching and Linear Learning Models," *Journal of Advertising Research*, VI (June, 1966), pp. 23–31.

[63] Carman derived his own set of normal equations, but he could have taken advantage of the fact that his equal slope constraint makes a dummy variable approach feasible.

[64] The coefficient of determination is the square of the multiple regression coefficient and represents the proportion of the total variance in the dependent variable which is accounted for by the linear relation to the independent variables.

more reasonable.   Then the equilibrium shares were estimated to be from 28 to 68 per cent in the subgroups.   This suggests that the learning process itself is nonstationary.   That is, α_1, α_0, and β in Eqs. (2-4) and (2-5) change over time.   This may be due to the impact of competitive reaction to the Crest success.

The efforts of Carman statistically to test Kuehn's learning model emphasizes a beneficial methodological feature of stochastic modeling. Stochastic models are in general amenable to statistical testing and therefore may be evaluated for their descriptive adequacy.   Another good methodological feature of Carman's analysis is the formulation of consumer subgroups in order to examine the effects of heterogeneity of response on the stochastic model.

A modified form of the linear learning model has been applied by Haines as a model of market behavior after innovation.[65]   The modification involved Eq. (2-5), which is the rejection or no purchase operator.   Since the model was to be of a market after innovation, it was felt that a no purchase or rejection trial should not affect the probability of a purchase on future trials.   That is, a no purchase trial with respect to the innovation does not alter the probability of a purchase on future trials.[66]   The revised rejection operator is given by

$$P_{t+1} = P_t \text{ if some other brand was purchased at time } t \quad (2\text{-}6)$$

For time series data from 34 geographic areas, Haines developed aggregate market measures in terms of his modified learning model.   The measures were asymptotic market share for the new product and the rate at which the market was approaching its asymptotic value.   The model generally was a good fit to the data with no significance level greater than 0.10.

Haines then used these empirically determined aggregate market measures as dependent variables in regressions on marketing policy variables. That is, he used the modified linear learning model to transform aggregate marketing data into two summary measures—asymptotic market share and the rate at which this asymptotic market share is approached. These summary measures were then considered as linear functions of mar-

---

[65] G. Haines, "A Theory of Market Behavior After Innovation," *Management Science*, X (July, 1964), pp. 634–58.

[66] Although this assumption appears to be reasonable prior to the first purchase of a consumer nondurable innovation, it seems less reasonable once the innovation has, in fact, been tried.   Perhaps the rejection operator should be divided into two conditional operators.   Haines' operator would be applied to no purchase trials prior to the first trial, whereas the standard form of the rejection operator would be applied once an initial purchase has been made.   It should be noted that this more realistic approach will complicate the mathematics of the process, and perhaps even render the model intractable.

keting variables. The rate of approach to equilibrium was found to relate to the amount spent on advertising during the first two months and to the prior availability of the product. The equilibrium market share, adjusted for the population in each region, related to the per capita promotional expenditures. A crucial assumption in Haines' model formulation is that there be no ready substitutes for the innovation, but he examined the potential bias that can exist when this assumption is violated.

Haines' basic approach is a sound one. He used a stochastic model of the dynamics of consumer choice behavior to estimate behavior within selected geographic segments. His model provided summary estimates of the behavioral dynamics within each segment as well as measures of "goodness of fit" of the model to the data. He then used these interpretable model parameters as the dependent variables in regressions on market decision variables. This strategy should receive increasing attention in attempts to model markets and to measure the impact of marketing policy variables.

In the above applications of the linear learning model, it is assumed that all respondents begin with the same probability of purchasing brand A. Carman, as pointed out earlier, disaggregated his sample into somewhat more homogeneous groups to minimize the possible effects of heterogeneity, but this is not entirely satisfactory. Massy has developed procedures for estimating the linear learning model when heterogeneity exists. In this formulation the initial response probability is distributed across the population of respondents.[67] He presents a minimum chi square as well as an approximate regression procedure. The former is computationally burdensome, yet it yields a single over-all measure of the linear learning hypothesis while at the same time providing best asymptotically normal estimates of the parameters. In this case, the asymptotic results are achieved as the number of respondents or households entering the analysis is increased. The approximate least squares procedure, although easy to compute, leads to difficulties in the interpretation of the properties of the estimates.

A somewhat different use of consumer "learning" is discussed by Demsetz.[68] Using an econometric model of the entire frozen orange juice industry and *Chicago Tribune* panel data from 1950 through 1957,

---

[67] W. F. Massy, "Estimation of Parameters for Linear Learning Models," Working Paper No. 78, Graduate School of Business, Stanford University, October, 1965. A more accessible version may be found in Massy, Montgomery, and Morrison, *op. cit.*, Chap. 5.

[68] H. Demsetz, "The Effect of Consumer Experience on Brand Loyalty and the Structure of Market Demand," *Econometrica*, Vol. 30, No. 1 (January, 1962), pp. 22–23.

ne investigated the following questions:

1. Is there a learning process operating in the market which depends solely on the age of that market?
2. Is the learning process a function of personal product experience?

His interest centered about the question of whether consumers learn to ignore certain artificial distinctions between brands. In the frozen orange juice market nationally advertised brands generally command a higher price than private labels, even though the private label brands are often merely a manufacturer's nationally advertised brand with a private label attached. Thus the question is whether consumers learn to ignore the artificial product distinctions generated by the advertised brand name. Frozen orange juice became widely distributed in the United States during 1948–49, just prior to the data period used in this study. Demsetz used the following model to answer question 1:

$$\frac{q_1}{q_2} = A \left(\frac{P_1}{P_2}\right)^{\alpha} (P_2)^{\beta}(t)^{\gamma} \qquad (2\text{-}7)$$

where the subscript 1 refers to nationally advertised (high-priced) brands and the subscript 2 refers to private label (low-priced) brands. Other notation is defined as:

P = the average price per ounce,
q = the number of ounces sold,
t = the number of months since January, 1950.

The remaining items (A, α, β, γ) are parameters of the functional relationship which are to be estimated from the data. In Eq. (2-7), P_2 is used as a proxy measure of the absolute price level. Demsetz's justification for the use of P_2 as a proxy variable rests on the tendency for the average prices of national and private label brands to fluctuate together (i.e., P_1 and P_2 tend to increase or decrease together). The parameter A in Eq. (2-7) is merely a scale factor, so it may be ignored in this discussion of the structural implications of the parameter estimates. The remaining three parameters may be positive, zero, or negative. Each of these is interpreted in turn. First consider γ, the exponent of t in the model. If γ is positive, this means that as the time since the introduction of frozen orange juice increases, the share of the market going to higher-priced national brands increases. Thus it would seem that promotion had led to significant market discrimination between similar products. Conversely, if γ is negative, it may be inferred that as time increases, consumers tend to learn that the private labels are equally good. A zero value of γ indicates that there is no time trend in the market in terms of the relative share between national and private label brands. That is, question 1 may be answered in the negative. For the parameter α, the exponent of the ratio of average prices of national brands to private labels, a positive value would mean the national brands' share increases as their relative price increases. Although such a price-quality association may be reasonable in certain product markets, it would be counterintuitive in the product class under study. A negative value of α would indicate that the relative market share for national brands decreases as their relative price increases. A zero value would indicate either that relative price does not have much effect in this market or that there was very little variation in the P_1/P_2 ratio for the data used to estimate α. Finally, a positive value of β would indicate that the market shifts to private labels as the general level of prices decreases. Conversely, a negative value for β indicates that as the general price level for frozen orange juice decreases, there is a shift toward the relatively expensive national brands. A zero value would indicate that the absolute price level, as measured by the proxy variable P_2, does not affect the relative market shares for these classes of brands.

Demsetz found that both α and γ were significantly negative. That is, question 1 is answered in the affirmative with the additional inference that consumers "learn" about nonessential product differences and that relative price does cause shifts between these two classes of brands. The parameter β was also found to be negative, but not significant.

In order to explore question 2, Demsetz correlated the share of purchases a given set of families devoted to advertised brands with the number of years the families in the set have been purchasing frozen orange juice. He found a significant negative correlation between the purchases devoted to national brands and the length of product market experience. Thus he answers question 2 in the affirmative.

His conclusion is that consumers are not "puppets," but that they learn to detect trivial brand differences. He believes that these results may be generalized to any low-cost, frequently purchased, relatively simple items.

Demsetz' analysis contained the implicit assumption that the relative availability of national and private labels did not change during the period of analysis.[69] This, of course, is contrary to the general pattern of development in such markets. Private labels generally appear after national brands have succeeded in developing a market. Consequently,

---

[69] By "availability" is meant whether the product is available for purchase in retail markets.

one would expect that as time increased, private labels would have been relatively more available. To the extent that consumer purchases of these two product types relates to their relative market availability, this relation will be confounded with the "learning" phenomenon identified by Demsetz. If data were available on relative availability over time, this factor should be built into the model in order to avoid this confounding of effects.

Stochastic Models of Brand Purchase Timing

The zero-order, Markov, and learning models described in the previous section directed their attention towards a description of brand choice. They did not explicitly address themselves to purchase timing. This section will examine this factor and interpurchase behavior in consumer response.

One of the first hypotheses concerning interpurchase behavior was formed by Kuehn.[70] He found an exponential decay in repurchase probability as the time between purchases increased. This was based on an analysis of orange juice brand choice data and the time between purchases. Morrison's empirical analysis of coffee did not indicate a significant change in brand loyalty as the time between purchases varied.[71] This may have been due to the fact that Kuehn used frozen orange juice data whereas Morrison used coffee data. Empirical studies by Carman which estimated the learning parameter for subgroups with different purchase frequencies also showed no decay in repurchase probability as interpurchase time increased.[72] Again, the differences in product classes used may account for these results, but in any case the Carman and Morrison results indicate that such a decay in repurchase probability is not a universally valid result in branded product markets.

Purchase timing effects can be given partial consideration in brand choice models. Recall the discussion of the simple Markov model, where it was proposed to model interpurchase time by considering the state of a consumer during some particular time interval. However, this formulation requires the use of a no purchase state. Howard has objected to the use of a somewhat artificial no purchase state in the simple Markov model. He proposed a semi-Markov chain model to overcome

---

[70] Kuehn, *op. cit.*, pp. 390–403.
[71] D. G. Morrison, "Interpurchase Time and Brand Loyalty," *Journal of Marketing Research*, III (August, 1966), pp. 289–91.
[72] Carman, *op. cit.*

this problem.[73] In the semi-Markov model, the transition probabilities representing brand choice are conditional upon a transition being made. That is, they represent the state-to-state transition probabilities that are operative whenever a choice is made. The choices occur at random times according to some probability distribution function. For example, in a brand switching application, the time between purchases would be probabilistically determined. The distribution of time to the next purchase may be a function of the current state. Thus the average time to the next purchase may be longer if the last response was response *A* than if it was response *B*. If state *A* represents a purchase of two pounds of the product and state *B* represents a purchase of one pound, the semi-Markov formulation is able to account for quantity purchased and its effect on interpurchase time. This semi-Markov model is also more amenable to conditional predictions of market share, since it accounts for different interpurchase times between successive purchases.

In its present state, the semi-Markov model is subject to certain limitations which also identify fruitful areas for future research. In the first place, the model is not able to account for heterogeneity among consumers in terms of their transition probabilities. A further theoretically desirable generalization would be to allow the distribution of interresponse time to vary over consumers. Second, there is need for development of statistical methods to render the model more empirically viable. These developments would be in the areas of tests of the assumptions and advances in estimation theory. Finally, the model may prove to place excessive burdens upon a data base when used in its most general form. That is, the general form that allows the interresponse time to be a function of the present state of the consumer may well make too great a demand on available data. It may be that sufficient data are not available for reliable estimation and testing, or it may happen that the model will require a history of responses sufficiently long to render the assumed stationarity (or constancy) of the transition probabilities and interresponse time distributions totally untenable. These empirical problems are likely to be further compounded in the heterogeneous form of the model.

Although brand choice models may be modified to include purchase timing, specialized interpurchase models may be more useful when specific predictions about sales in given periods are described. The earliest model to include specific consideration of interpurchase times was presented by A. S. C. Ehrenberg.[74] His model is outlined in Table

[73] R. A. Howard, "Stochastic Process Models of Consumer Behavior," *Journal of Advertising Research*, III (September, 1963), pp. 35–42.

[74] A. S. C. Ehrenberg, "The Pattern of Consumer Purchases," *Applied Statistics*, VIII (March, 1959), pp. 26–41.

2-6. He assumed that each individual consumer would purchase a number of units of product per time period in accordance with a Poisson distribution.[75] This, in turn, implies that the time between successive purchases for a consumer will be exponentially distributed.[76] Thus Ehrenberg's assumption of Poisson purchases incorporates random interpurchase time. It should be noted that the Poisson assumption implies that purchases occur independently of one another. Consequently, the effects of "learning" and household inventories upon subsequent purchases are assumed to be of no significant importance. The Poisson assumption will be plausible when two conditions are fulfilled, namely:

1. Successive periods of time are of equal length and are similar to each other in terms of units of measurement.
2. The time periods are not too short, so that purchases made in one period do not affect those made in another period.

These conditions are often approximately fulfilled. This model also incorporated an assumption of consumer heterogeneity. As may be seen in Table 2-6, each consumer is characterized by his own individual Poisson distribution with a mean of μ_i.

TABLE 2-6*: Ehrenberg's Stochastic Model

	Periods of Time				*Long Run Averages*	*Purchase Distribution for an Individual Consumer*
Consumers	*I*	*II*	*III*	*IV*		
1	$X_{1,I}$	$X_{1,II}$	$X_{1,III}$	$X_{1,IV}$	μ_1	Poisson with mean μ_1
2	$X_{2,I}$	$X_{2,II}$	$X_{2,III}$	$X_{2,IV}$	μ_2	Poisson with mean μ_2
.	.	.	.	.	.	.
.	.	.	.	.	.	
.	.	.	.	.	.	
N	$X_{N,I}$	$X_{N,II}$	$X_{N,III}$	$X_{N,IV}$	μ_N	Poisson with mean μ_N
Distributions (Vertically)	NEG. BIN.	NEG. BIN.	NEG. BIN.	NEG. BIN.	GAMMA	

Note: $X_{1,I}$ denotes the number of units purchased by consumer 1 during time period I.
*Adapted from Table 3 in Ehrenberg, *op. cit.*

[75] The Poisson distribution is described by $P(r) = e^{-\lambda}\lambda^r/r!$ The Poisson distribution has a single parameter λ, which is identical to both the mean and the variance of the distribution.
[76] For the basic mathematical proofs see M. Greenwood and G. U. Yule, "An Inquiry Into the Nature of Frequency-Distributions Representative of Multiple Attacks of Disease or of Repeated Accidents," *Journal of the Royal Statistical Society*, LXXXIII (1920), pp. 255–79.

If it is assumed that the distribution of the Poisson parameter in the consumer population follows a gamma distribution, then an interesting result follows for the distribution of consumer purchases during a given time period. The result may be stated as follows:

> If the number of units purchased by an individual consumer in a time period follows a Poisson distribution with parameter μ and if μ is distributed across the population of consumers according to a gamma distribution, then the distribution of consumer purchases in any time period will follow a negative binomial distribution.

That is, under the specified assumptions, the distributions of purchases $X_{1,1}$, $X_{2,1}$, . . . , $X_{N,1}$ in period I, for example, will be a negative binomial distribution. Knowledge of this distribution can be gained from the model and can be used as the basis of a prediction of the firm's sales. Ehrenberg developed his model using a chi square distribution for the Poisson parameter, but the chi square is a special case of the gamma distribution and the result holds for any gamma distribution of the parameter. The Ehrenberg model assumed stationarity, which was a limitation, but it did prove to be an empirically viable model for some product classes.

Recently, Chatfield, Ehrenberg, and Goodhardt have extended this early model in some important ways.[77] In the first place, they demonstrated that the distribution of total purchases (in a given period) for those consumers who did purchase at least once in that period may be closely approximated by a logarithmic series distribution. Thus if one is willing to ignore those consumers who do not purchase in the period, the logarithmic series distribution may be used instead of the negative binomial. This result has two practical advantages:

1. By eliminating those who do not purchase during the period, there is no problem of providing an *a priori* specification of the population of relevant purchasers.
2. The logarithmic series distribution is easier to estimate than the negative binomial.

The second development is the consideration of the joint distribution of the X's between two or more time periods. They show that since this distribution is a natural multivariate extension of the negative binomial distribution, it too arises as a consequence of the heterogeneous

---

[77] C. Chatfield, A. S. C. Ehrenberg, and G. J. Goodhardt, "Progress on a Simplified Model of Stationary Purchasing Behavior," *Journal of the Royal Statistical Society*, Series A, CXXIX (1966), pp. 317–67.

Poisson model discussed above. Their results support the notion that the negative binomial is a basic and useful distribution for modeling stationary (but random in time) purchase incidence processes. Their empirical work suggests that the negative binomial tends to fail in the tails of the distribution. This finding is attributed to a breakdown in the validity of the assumption that the distribution of μ is gamma.

There are other purchase incidence models that have been developed to aid in forecasting sales and diagnosing market responses. The Fourt and Woodlock mixed exponential model is discussed in Chap. 7 of this book. A new product purchase incidence model developed by Massy is also discussed in that chapter. For a more complete treatment of the above models as well as the basic, semi-, and nonstationary logistic model and one-element learning models, see Massy, Montgomery, and Morrison.[78]

Future Research in Stochastic Models

The stochastic models of brand choice and purchase incidence outlined in the previous sections were designed to identify the underlying process that best describes consumer purchasing behavior patterns. Although a number of viable models have been developed, there are four principal areas of stochastic modeling which deserve research effort.

The first of these relates to empirical viability and comparison between models. Most of the models discussed in this chapter have been found to be empirically viable for at least one product class, but there is a need to ascertain the descriptive efficacy of these models on new sets of data. In addition, there is a need for direct empirical comparison of models. Morrison has provided methods and results for the Brand Loyal and Last Purchase Loyal models, but more research is needed. Work should be directed toward two questions:

1. In a given product market, which model provides the best descriptive ability?
2. Is there a typology of product markets for which one type of model will tend to dominate all the other alternatives?

Second, there is a need to generalize most of the models to multi-alternative markets. The only existing multibrand models are the simple homogeneous Markov and semi-Markov models. There is a need for the development of multidimensional heterogenous Markov, diffusion, and learning models.

[78] In particular, see Chap. 8, "Models for Purchase Timing and Market Penetration," in Massy, Montgomery, and Morrison, *op. cit.*

Third, increasing attention must be given to the incorporation of random interpurchase time effects. Many of the models discussed above lacked this capability. Effort should be directed towards the development of models of purchase incidence that include consideration of heterogeneity and nonstationarity.

Finally, there is a need for research to link stochastic models to marketing variables. If the impact of variables such as price, deals, and advertising are to be considered, they must be related to the model parameters. The work of Telser and Haines described earlier represent attempts to establish such relationships. If these linkages can be made, stochastic models will not only be useful in identifying market response mechanisms and conditional predictions, but also in deriving marketing strategies.

A COMPARISON OF SIMULATION AND STOCHASTIC MODELS

In this section comparisons will be drawn between simulation and stochastic models. In addition, a heretofore untapped potential interface between these model building approaches is suggested.

The contrasts between simulation and stochastic models are presented in Fig. 2-7 in terms of the advantages and disadvantages of stochastic models vis-à-vis simulation models. Consider first the disadvantages of stochastic models. In many respects they are more difficult to implement because their complex analytic structure is not as intuitive to management as are the simple response functions which comprise the microlevel of a microanalytic simulation model. There is also less need for a direct and continuing managerial involvement in the model building process. Consequently, there tends to be less management commitment to the model. In a very real sense, it will not be "his" model in the same way a simulation model will be. Stochastic models also are not as rich in functional relations and data inputs. The influence of many factors is modeled via response uncertainty. In contrast, simulation models generally incorporate very rich representations of the process being modeled, even though the microfunctions tend to be quite simple. Another disadvantage of stochastic models is that they generally require very sophisticated mathematical and statistical techniques in their analysis. This provides a further barrier to management understanding and involvement and consequently renders implementation more difficult. Finally, stochastic models are limited to repetitive decisions and usually frequently purchased consumer product decisions. Simulation

Advantages of Stochastic Models	Disadvantages of Stochastic Models

1. Easier to apply
  a. Less programming effort
  b. Less computer time
	1. More difficult to get management to implement
	  a. Less intuitive to management
	  b. Less direct management involvement and commitment

2. Utilize available data	2. Less rich in functional relations and data inputs. Many relations modeled via response uncertainty
3. Less costly to implement	3. Highly sophisticated mathematics and statistics often required
4. Easier to validate and estimate	4. Limited to frequent and repeated purchase decisions
5. Transferable between firms and product classes	

6. Sensitivity analysis
  a. Easier
  b. Less costly
  c. Good chance it will be analytical	

Figure 2-7: Contrasts between stochastic and simulation models: relative to simulation models

models are less limited and could be used for consumer durable, industrial, and government buying analyses.

On the positive side, stochastic models are easier to apply. By virtue of their analytic properties, they require less programming effort and less computer time. Furthermore, they are easier to validate (or test) and estimate by virtue of their analytic properties. In contrast to simulation models, which tend to be highly idiosyncratic and personalistic to the firm, stochastic models are readily transferred between firms and product classes. This means that there will tend to be economies of scale in model development. It also means that the literature of stochastic models will tend to be more complete in terms of the information needed to apply this approach. Finally, stochastic models tend to be much easier to analyze for sensitivity. This again is due to their analytic properties.

Lest the reader conclude from this discussion that simulation models are the antithesis of stochastic models, it would be well to consider an interesting potential, but heretofore untapped, interface between these model building approaches. It would seem that stochastic models should have real payoff in simulation model development in terms of structural specifications and measurement and estimation. In particular, stochastic models should be of assistance to the simulation model builder in terms of specifying appropriate structural relations at the micro function level. Alternative formulations may be tested against real system data in order to ascertain which form is most appropriate. Stochastic models may also provide a measurement and estimation framework for the parameters and distributions needed at the microlevel.

The usage of simulation and stochastic models in understanding diagnosing, and predicting market response is a fertile area for management science research. This is also an important area of research since an understanding of market response and consumer behavior is essential if advances are to be made in the development of normative models that recommend solutions to specific marketing problems. The description and analysis for existing normative models will comprise the majority of the remainder of this book, but the modeling techniques and outcomes developed in this chapter will be utilized throughout this discussion of the major problem areas of marketing.

Appendix: Some Methodological Considerations in the Stochastic Modeling of Market Response

This appendix deals with three methodological questions relating to stochastic models in marketing. First, desirable properties of stochastic models in the marketing context are outlined. Then these properties are interpreted in terms of the technical characteristics of a stochastic model. In addition the statistical properties of stochastic models are considered. Finally, four technical problems in building stochastic models of consumer behavior are outlined and discussed.

Desirable Properties for Stochastic Models

In general, stochastic models of consumer behavior have been confined to product markets that are composed of frequently purchased consumer items. The reason becomes clear when it is noted that stochastic models generally require data on a sequence of several purchases for each household or individual included in the analysis. Consequently, this discussion will assume implicit concern with frequently purchased (generally branded) consumer goods.

Given this restriction, what behavior or responses should ideally be accounted for in a stochastic model? In the most general case a stochastic model should describe or account for:

1. Brand choice
2. Interpurchase timing
3. Quantity purchased
4. Store of purchase
5. The impact of marketing variables such as price, deals, advertising, in-store displays, etc.

To date, greatest attention has focused upon item 1, although some progress has been made in dealing with the other factors.

Stochastic models generally have some set (or continuum) of alternative responses. For example, a set of discrete response alternatives might be the individual brands available for the product of interest. An example of a continuous response would be the time between successive purchases. In any case, stochastic models generally have one or more response variables with two or more levels each. The actual outcome or response at any given response occasion (e.g., purchase of the product) is the result of a probabilistic process. The probability of any particular outcome is termed the response probability of that outcome.

Desirable properties for stochastic models may be segmented meaningfully into two groups: model properties and statistical properties. These properties are discussed below. At the present time no model has achieved all of these properties.[79] Nevertheless, recent work in stochastic models has greatly generalized the previous ability to model consumer behavior and, hopefully, even more rapid advances will be forthcoming.

Technical Stochastic Model Properties

Heterogeneity of consumers

On any given response occasion, consumers will tend to differ from one another in terms of their response probabilities. A model should account for this distribution of response probability or heterogeneity of the consumer population. Certain errors of inference, which may occur when a heterogeneous population of consumers is treated as homogeneous with respect to their response probabilities, are discussed below.

Nonstationarity of response probabilities

A response probability is said to be stationary if it does not change from one response occasion to the next. In some situations, this may be reasonable in the very short run. However, in most markets and in virtually all markets in the long run, consumers are likely to change their response probabilities. These changes may occur as the result of

---

[79] The model that comes closest to satisfying all these desiderata of stochastic models is W. F. Massy's Stochastic Evolutionary Adoption Model (STEAM). This model is discussed in Chap. 7.

marketing activities (e.g., price, deals, promotion), changes in family circumstances (e.g., children leaving home, the family moving to a new community), or product experience. In any case, the likelihood is high that a consumer's response probability will change, and thus a stochastic model should have the ability to detect these changes. Assuming that a process is stationary when in fact it is nonstationary may also cause erroneous inferences to be drawn. This problem is discussed below.

Measures of interest

Models generally yield market measures of interest to the researcher or the marketing manager. For example, Markov models may be used to predict expected brand shares at equilibrium and the variance about the expected brand shares at steady state. In any case, a useful model should yield interesting summary measures of market characteristics and dynamics. It might be pointed out that such measures may not be of primary interest in some cases. For example, primary interest may center upon the structural question of whether consumers exhibit learning behavior or some form of zero-order behavior in a brand market. In this case, the structural hypothesis is the focus of interest rather than the measures available from these alternative models.

Multialternative markets

Markets for frequently purchased consumer items are multibrand markets. Whenever possible, the model should encompass consumer behavior toward several of the brands in a market. In most of these markets, however, there are over one hundred different brands ranging from national and regional brands to the private labels of chain stores. Although a model may be able to encompass a very large number of brands conceptually, data requirements impose a constraint on the number of brands a model may practically include. The brands that are not explicitly modeled are generally lumped into an "all other" category. The problems involved in this procedure are discussed below under the combining-of-classes question. Note that different purchase quantities may be encompassed within a multialternative model.

Interresponse time

Unfortunately, consumers do not cooperate with model-building attempts by purchasing on a deterministic cycle (e.g., weekly or monthly).

Models that consider the sequence of outcomes on successive response occasions without explicitly considering interresponse time create certain problems. In particular, estimates of total market size or expected market share become hazardous. Some models encompass interresponse time. For example, the semi-Markov model discussed in the chapter explicitly considers these questions. In other models an *ad hoc* procedure is often used to overcome some of these problems. If interest centers upon the structure of behavior relative to a sequence of responses, this problem will not be of major importance.

Statistical Properties of Stochastic Models

Data based

If stochastic models are to be useful and empirically verifiable, they should be data based. That is, the models should relate to data that either are available or else may be obtained reasonably. It should be noted that this requirement for stochastic models does not imply a rejection of all models based upon subjective inputs. Rather, it reflects the fact that stochastic models are generally used as a framework for measuring and projecting market performance and as a test of alternative structural hypotheses concerning certain aspects of consumer behavior.

Goodness of fit

Before a set of data is interpreted in terms of a stochastic model, it is necessary to evaluate the "goodness of fit" or descriptive adequacy of the model.[80]

Parameter estimates

Stochastic models of consumer behavior generally depend upon one or more parameters that must be estimated from data in order to determine which explicit version of the basic model is appropriate or to "identify" the model. This notion is akin to identifying a particular normal distribution from the family of all normal distributions by estimating its mean and variance from sample data. Since an infinity of functions of

[80] For the use of minimum chi square measures of fit, see the papers by Morrison, *op. cit.* and Montgomery, *op. cit.* For a regression analysis approach, see Haines, *op. cit.*

the data may be proposed as estimators of any given parameter, one would prefer to have estimators that possess desirable statistical properties such as efficiency, consistency, and sufficiency.[81]

Empirical viability

It seems reasonable to require that a model be demonstrated to be empirically viable for at least one set of market data. That is, the model should be consistent with (fit) at least one set of data.

Problems in Stochastic Modeling of Consumer Behavior

Several factors complicate the life of the management scientist who seeks to build and test stochastic models of consumer behavior. They are:

1. There may be a many-to-one mapping of models into a set of data.
2. The effects of heterogeneity and nonstationarity of response probability may be confounded.
3. The stochastic process generating the response probabilities may itself undergo change.
4. There may be a combining of classes problem, which arises when an N-alternative market is collapsed into a two-alternative market.

The first factor, a many-to-one mapping of models into a set of data, reflects the fact that several alternative models may, in fact, be consistent with the data. That is, several structurally different models may prove to be plausible descriptive models of the actual outcomes that have been observed. Consequently, there is a need to develop methods which discriminate among competing models.[82] In any case, the fact that several models may be consistent with a set of data should temper enthusiasm whenever a particular model is found to be an excellent fit to the data.

The second factor is a complex problem. Many models assume that

---

[81] For a technical discussion of estimators in the context of stochastic models, see Chap. 2 in W. F. Massy, D. B. Montgomery, and D. G. Morrison, *Stochastic Models of Consumer Behavior* (Cambridge, Mass.: The M.I.T. Press, 1969).

[82] For some work along these lines, see the paper by Morrison, *op. cit.* A more extensive discussion is available in Chap. 2 of Massy, Montgomery, and Morrison, *op. cit.*

the population of consumers is homogeneous, at least with respect to their probability of making any one of the alternative responses. This assumption of homogeneity may lead the researcher to conclude that the process which generates the responses is of relatively high order (i.e., there is considerable dependence between responses) when in fact the process is of low (even zero) order. A numerical example will illustrate the difficulty. Consider a population of consumers consisting of two types. Type I consumers comprise 40 per cent of the population, and each has a probability of 0.8 of purchasing brand A rather than brand B on any given purchase occasion. Type II consumers comprise 60 per cent of the population, and each has a probability of 0.3 of purchasing brand A. This amounts to assuming that in both populations consumers choose brands according to a Bernouilli process. Some useful notation is summarized below.

$P(\text{I}) = 0.4 =$ the probability that a consumer chosen at random from the population will be a type I.

$P(\text{II}) = 0.6 =$ the probability that a consumer is type II.

$P(A_t|\text{I}) = 0.8 =$ the probability that a type I consumer buys brand A at a time t, where t indexes purchase events.

$P(A_t|\text{II}) = 0.3 =$ the probability that a type II consumer buys brand A at time t.

$P(A_t|A_{t-1}) =$ the probability that a consumer who has purchased brand A at time $t - 1$ will purchase brand A at time t.

Suppose a consumer is drawn at random from the total population. What is the probability that he will purchase brand A on purchase occasion t? It is just

$$P(A_t) = P(A_t|\text{I}) \cdot P(\text{I}) + P(A_t|\text{II}) \cdot P(\text{II})$$
$$= (0.8)(0.4) + (0.3)(0.6) \qquad \text{(A-1)}$$
$$= 0.50$$

Remember that it is not known to the analyst whether the consumer is really a type I or a type II. Now suppose that this consumer is observed over two successive purchases, say at times zero and one. What is the probability that he will purchase brand A at time one given that he purchased it at time zero? It is

$$P(A_1|A_0) = P(A_1|\text{I}) \cdot P(\text{I}|A_0) + P(A_1|\text{II}) \cdot P(\text{II}|A_0) \qquad \text{(A-2)}$$

where $P(\text{I}|A_t)$ is the probability that a consumer who purchased brand A at time t is a type I consumer. Similarly, one has $P(\text{II}|A_t)$. Since

$P(A_1|\text{I})$ and $P(A_1|\text{II})$ are already known, $P(A_1|A_0)$ may be computed if $P(\text{I}|A_0)$ and $P(\text{II}|A_0)$ can be determined. By Bayes theorem,

$$P(\text{I}|A_0) = \frac{P(A_0|\text{I}) \cdot P(\text{I})}{P(A_0|\text{I}) \cdot P(\text{I}) + P(A_0|\text{II}) \cdot P(\text{II})} = \frac{P(A_0|\text{I}) \cdot P(\text{I})}{P(A_0)}$$

$$= \frac{(0.8)(0.4)}{0.5}$$

$$= 0.64$$

$$\text{and} \quad P(\text{II}|A_0) = \frac{P(A_0|\text{II}) \cdot P(\text{II})}{P(A_0)}$$

$$= \frac{(0.3)(0.6)}{0.5}$$

$$= 0.36$$

Substituting these results in Eq. (A-2) yields

$$P(A_1|A_0) = (0.8)(0.64) + (0.3)(0.36)$$

$$= 0.62 \tag{A-3}$$

From Eqs. (A-1) and (A-3) it is seen that a purchase of brand A at time zero has seemingly increased the probability of a purchase of brand A at time one. Can the analyst infer from this that the consumer has "learned" to purchase brand A as a result of having purchased it once? The answer, of course, is no. The actual probability of the consumer's purchasing brand A at time one is independent of his purchase at time zero by the assumption upon which the probability calculations were based.

How, then, can one account for this apparent effect of the purchase at time zero on the probability of purchasing brand A at time one? The fact that the consumer (chosen at random) purchased brand A at time zero makes it likely that he is a type I consumer. Since type I consumers have a high probability of purchasing brand A and since the consumer who was chosen is rather likely to be a type I consumer, one would expect that his probability of purchasing brand A at time one would be greater than the average probability in the entire population of consumers. Thus heterogeneity in the population has created this *apparent* dependence effect.

As a further illustration, one might also compute:

$$P(A_1|B_0) = P(A_1|\text{I}) \cdot P(\text{I}|B_0) + P(A_1|\text{II}) \cdot P(\text{II}|B_0) = 0.38 \quad \text{(A-4)}$$

Using Eqs. (A-3) and (A-4), an analyst, assuming that he was dealing with a first order Markov chain model from a homogeneous population, would compute the following aggregate transition matrix:

Purchase at $t + 1$

$$
\begin{array}{cc}
 & A \quad\ \ B \\
\begin{array}{c} \text{Purchase } A \\ \text{at } t \quad\ B \end{array} &
\begin{bmatrix} 0.62 & 0.38 \\ 0.38 & 0.62 \end{bmatrix}
\end{array}
$$

He would erroneously conclude that a purchase of brand A at time enhances the probability that the brand will be purchased at time $t + 1$ It may be seen from this that such an aggregate transition matrix can exhibit only the combined effect of heterogeneity and past purchases.

If the probability mechanism that generates response probability changes over time, a true Bernoulli hypothesis may again be erroneously rejected. For example, take a type II consumer from the previous discussion. He purchases brand A with a probability of 0.3. Now suppose that his brands of purchase are observed over a sequence of 30 trials and that on the sixteenth trial (halfway through the sequence), brand A becomes his favorite. That is, he becomes a type I consumer with probability 0.8 of purchasing brand A on any given purchase occasion. Now suppose one of the standard tests of the Bernoulli hypothesis, such as the Wald-Wolfowitz run test, is applied.[83] This test assumes stationarity and will generally be misleading when applied to a nonstationary process. In the present case, one would expect the estimate of the Bernoulli parameter p to be $(0.8 + 0.3)/2 = 0.55$ for the entire series of 30 purchases. Since the true p was 0.3 for the first fifteen trials and 0.8 for the second fifteen, the series of 30 responses would be expected to "fail" this run test. That is, the Bernoulli hypothesis would be rejected. Thus the discontinuous change in the Bernoulli parameter may lead to the erroneous rejection of a true Bernoulli hypothesis. Clearly, there is a need for methods that are able to account for heterogeneity and which assume no more than short-run stationarity.[84]

The third factor, nonstationarity of the process generating the sequence of response probabilities, may even arise in models that allow the response probability itself to change. In this case, changes may take place in the process which generates changes in the response probabilities. Changes in this higher order process will generally occur more slowly than changes in response probability. But the possibility of these changes dictates that the analyst once again should strive to develop methods that assume

---

[83] See Siegel, *op. cit.*, pp. 136–45.

[84] By *short-run stationarity* is meant the notion that the response probability for an individual consumer remains constant over a few responses (e.g., purchases). An alternative label for short-run stationarity is "quasistationary" as used in Massy, Montgomery, and Morrison, *op. cit.*

only short-run stationarity—even for models that allow the response probability to change.

The fourth factor, the combining of classes problem, may arise when an N-alternative market is collapsed into a two-alternative market.[85] For example, many models consider only two brands, a brand of particular interest and an aggregate of all other brands. If this combining of all other brands into an aggregate brand is to leave the structure of the system unchanged, then a stochastic operator on the state space of the system must be of a special form.[86] This is of some importance in marketing models, since both Markov models and linear learning models involve stochastic operators. Suffice it here to say that the combining of classes problem would seem to be of second-order importance when compared to the first three factors that have been discussed.

Future stochastic models should attempt to encompass as many as possible of the desirable properties outlined earlier and overcome the problems discussed in this section. If a sound methodology is used, the value of stochastic models in testing structural hypothesis and making conditional prediction will be enhanced.

---

[85] In fact, the combining of classes problem arises whenever an N-alternative market is collapsed into an M-alternative market, where $M < N$. The case where $M = 2$ is the one generally used in marketing models.

[86] See R. Bush and F. Mosteller, *op. cit.*

3

Advertising Decisions

INTRODUCTION

Advertising and promotional expenditures have become significant in the marketing of many products. In 1966 about 16 billion dollars was spent on advertising alone. This expenditure was made because advertising performs a vital function within the over-all communication mix a firm uses to inform and convince customers of the desirability of its products. In this chapter management science techniques relevant to advertising and communication decisions will be discussed. Most of the emphasis will be placed upon advertising, but the concepts are also valid for other promotions.

The marketing manager faces many decisions in advertising. Although some of these decisions are shared with his advertising agency, he and his technical advisors should understand each decision area in order to insure the quality of the decisions. In advertising, decisions must be made with regard to the goals of the advertising expenditure, the size of the over-all budget, and the choice of media, appeals, and copy. These decisions are interrelated. For example, the media schedule cannot be determined until the budget is specified, but the effectiveness of the schedule may affect the budget necessary to achieve the specified goals. It would be desirable to specify all these decision solutions simultaneously, but this is an extremely complex problem.

To relieve the complexity, advertising decisions may be placed in a hierarchy. Figure 3-1 outlines an order of decision making, which may vary in given decision situations. For example, the budget may be established before the specific appeals are identified, but the budget decision should be made with some estimate of the probable effectiveness

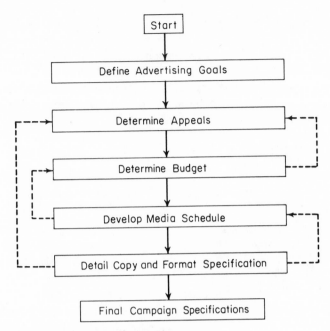

Figure 3-1: Hierarchy for advertising decisions

of the appeals to be created. Likewise, media decisions should reflect copy considerations, since the size of the ad is a factor in determining media schedules. For purposes of exposition, the hierarchy of Fig. 3-1 will be utilized in this chapter. As decisions are discussed, the interrelations between them will be developed. The dashed lines denote certain important interactions that are exceptions to this hierarchy.

DETERMINATION OF ADVERTISING GOALS

In its widest context, advertising should be viewed as an investment, and the goal of advertising should be to maximize the returns to this investment. This is the most desirable goal, but there are problems in identifying the profit effects of advertising expenditures. In an effort to express the goal of advertising in measurable terms, several alternative criteria have been suggested. In Table 3-1 a list of possible advertising goal criteria is given. The criteria are listed in order of increasing relevance to the investment decision, but this listing also is one of increasing measurement difficulty.

The ease of measurement dimension in Table 3-1 relates to the cost and methodological ease with which the criterion variable may be measured to yield an assessment of market response to advertising. For example, sales response to advertising is relatively difficult to measure, since advertising is only one of many market factors and activities of the firm which combine to determine sales. Consequently, accurate assessment of the sales response to advertising generally requires the use of advanced

TABLE 3-1: Advertising Goal Criteria

Criteria	Decision Relevance	Ease of Measurement

Exposure
   Total Exposure
   Frequency (Impact)
   Reach (Coverage)
	Low	High

Awareness		
Attitudes		
Sales		
Profits	High	Low

statistical methods, involves relatively high costs, and requires fairly long periods of time.

The criteria listed in Table 3-1 refer to a relevant segment of the total population in the market place. This segment consists of consumers who are viewed by the firm as the most likely to purchase its products, and advertising efforts should be directed towards achieving maximum results in this group. The firm may define more than one target group and may direct special advertising programs to each of them. In each target group, subsegments may also be identified that demonstrate different consumption processes or different potentials for purchase. The specifications of the target group and its subsegments are related to the wider decision of the firm's purpose in the market and the way in which it can profitably serve consumers. For example, a clothing manufacturer may identify all men over fifteen years of age as its general target group. This target group may be divided into subsegments. One subsegment may be men between 25 and 45 years of age with incomes over ten thousand dollars. In the remainder of this chapter, it will be assumed that the firm's specification of a target group is known and that the goals of advertising are measured in terms of advertising's effect on this target group. The following discussion of these goals will progress from the lower level goals (exposure) to the higher level goals (sales and profits), corresponding in order to Table 3-1.

Exposure

The three principal exposure criteria that have been proposed are total exposures, frequency (impact), and reach (coverage). Although these have been termed *exposure criteria*, a more descriptive term might be "potential" exposure. This label describes the fact that exposure measures generally reflect exposure to the medium that contains the advertisement. This is something different from actual exposure to the advertisement. For example, a subscriber to a particular issue of *Time* magazine has potential exposure to all ads in an issue. Yet he may be exposed to only a few of those ads—those on the pages which he happens to glance at or read. Special studies may be used to estimate the extent of this audience shrinkage, and the data may then be used to adjust exposure measures. In the remainder of this discussion, the term *exposure* will be used to denote either potential or adjusted exposures. Time, cost, and feasibility constraints will dictate which is used in any practical situation.

The total exposure is the sum total of the number of times any advertisement relating to the product is seen or heard by target group members in a given period. Let

A_i = number of target group members exposed to an insertion in medium i ($i = 1, 2, \ldots, I$) and

N_i = number of advertisements in medium i during the time period of interest.

The total exposure to the $N_1, \ldots, N_I$ insertions in the respective media is then given by

$$T = \sum_{i=1}^{I} A_i N_i$$

where T denotes total exposures.

A related exposure measure could be defined as the *weighted* total exposure. Let

A_{ij} = number of target group members in subsegment j exposed to an insertion in medium i ($i = 1, 2, \ldots, I$)

W_j = weight reflecting the sales potential of subsegment j ($j = 1, 2, \ldots, J$).

The weighted total exposure is then

$$WT = \sum_{j=1}^{J} \sum_{i=1}^{I} A_{ij} W_j N_i$$

where WT denotes the weighted total exposure and reflects the differing potentials between target groups.

The frequency or impact is the average number of advertisements for the product seen by each member of the target group during the given period.   If there are M individuals in the target group, the frequency is

$$F = \frac{T}{M}$$

where F denotes frequency.   Frequency is an important criterion measure whenever the sales response to the product's advertising is thought to have an "S-shaped" relationship to cumulative exposures or whenever there is a threshold number of exposures required in order to trigger the desired response (purchase) on the part of target group members.   An example of an "S-shaped" sales response to cumulative exposures is given in Fig. 3-2.   Notice that there are increasing sales returns to

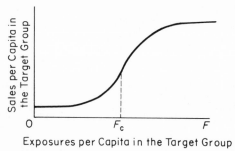

Exposures per Capita in the Target Group

**Figure 3-2: Sales response to
frequency of exposure**

cumulative exposures from $F = 0$ to $F = F_c$ and decreasing returns to F above F_c.

The final measure of exposure is reach.   The reach or coverage of advertising is defined as the total number of people exposed to at least one advertisement relating to the product in a given time period.   The three subcategories of reach can be defined as cumulative audience, net coverage, and combined coverage, where *cumulative audience* is the reach of two or more issues of a given medium, *net coverage* is the reach of a combination of single issues of two or more media, and *combined coverage* is the reach of two or more issues of two or more media.   For example, cumulative audience refers to the total number of target group members who will be exposed at least once when successive weekly insertions are made in a specific medium such as *Life* magazine.   Net coverage refers to the total number exposed at least once when insertions are made in single issues of different media, such as *Life* and *Time*.   In order to encompass both cumulative audience and net coverage, combined cover-

ge is defined as the unduplicated coverage of two or more media with
vo or more insertions in each medium. In the following discussion, the
iore general term "reach" will be used. In this over-all sense, reach is
ie number of *different* people in the target group or target group sub-
gments who are exposed one or more times to a given set of insertions.

For the case of two media, say media 1 and 2, the reach of a single
isertion in each medium will be

$$R = A_1 + A_2 - A_{12}$$

where R = the reach or number of persons exposed to one or more of
the two insertions,

A_{12} = the duplication, i.e., the number of people exposed to an
insertion in medium 1 and in medium 2,

nd A_1 and A_2 are as previously defined. Note that A_{12} measures the
xtent of overlap in exposures within the target group between the two
isertions. That is, A_{12} represents the number of target group members
who will be exposed to both ads. For insertions in three media, the reach
will be

$$R = A_1 + A_2 + A_3 - A_{12} - A_{13} - A_{23} + A_{123}$$

where A_{123} = the triplications among media 1, 2, and 3 (i.e., the
number of target group members who will be exposed
to the ads in each of the three media).

n general, for I media the expression for reach will be

$$R = \sum_{i=1}^{I} (-1)^{i-1} A(i)$$

where $A(1) = \sum_{i=1}^{I} A_i$ = total target group members in the audiences
of media $1, \ldots, I$,

$$A(2) = \sum_{i=1}^{I} \sum_{j=i+1}^{I} A_{ij} = \text{the total of all pairwise duplications of}$$
the I media,

$$A(3) = \sum_{i=1}^{I} \sum_{j=i+1}^{I} \sum_{k=j+1}^{I} A_{ijk} = \text{the total of all triplications,}$$

$$A(I) = \sum_{i=1}^{I} \sum_{j=i+1}^{I} \cdots \sum_{q=I}^{I} A_{ij\ldots pq}$$

and $i, j, k, \ldots q \leq I$.

These results follow directly from mathematical set theory.

The equation for the reach of I media requires a great deal of dat For example, for $I = 5$, it will be necessary to know (or have estimat of) the target audience overlap between each pair of media, each tripl of media, each group of four media, in addition to the overlap among a five media and their individual total audiences, in order to determine th reach of simultaneous insertions in each of these five media. Th measurement problem involved is tremendous. Fortunately, short-c estimation procedures have been found to be useful. Agostini, utilizin an extensive French study of audience duplication, triplication, and up 15-tuplication, found that the total reach for magazine insertions ma be estimated by[1]

$$R = \left\{ \frac{1}{[K \cdot A(2)/A(1)] + 1} \right\} \cdot A(1)$$

This formula was found to be an excellent approximation of reach fc French magazines when $K = 1.125$. The relation[2] is also approximatel true for American and Canadian magazines.[3] The Agostini formula i useful in estimating reach for media where data for higher than secon order replications among the media audiences is not available.

The criteria relating to exposure are relatively simple to measure since they depend only on readerships of various media, the number c insertions, and the total number in the target group. Making advertisin, decisions on the basis of exposure, however, assumes a direct relationshi, between the ultimate advertising returns—profits—and exposures t advertising.

Awareness

Exposure merely relates to the potential for having seen and noticed a particular ad. Advertising awareness, on the other hand, implies som ability to recall an advertising message. Measures of ad awareness are available commercially through such services as Starch and Gallop Robinson. These services use recall and aided recall techniques ir surveys of potential readers of ads in order to determine the extent tc which particular ads are noticed and remembered. Since awareness is somewhat closer to the ultimate sales and profit goals of advertising, it

[1] M. M. Agostini, "How to Estimate Unduplicated Audiences," *Journal of Adver tising Research*, I (March, 1961), pp. 11–14.

[2] For a theoretical discussion of this relationship, see H. J. Claycamp and C. W McClelland, "On Methods: Estimating Reach and the Magic of K," *Journal of Advertising Research*, VIII (June, 1968), pp. 44–51.

[3] J. Bower, "Net Audiences of U.S. and Canadian Magazines: Seven Tests of Agostini's Formula," *Journal of Advertising Research*, III (March, 1963), pp. 13–21.

would seem that it might be a better predictor of the sales and profit effects of advertising than exposure measures. The use of advertising awareness as a criterion is illustrated in the section on copy and format specification. In that section several studies which have linked characteristics of advertising copy and format to advertising awareness are reviewed.

Attitude

Attitude changes may be used as the criterion by which advertising performance is judged. The firm may monitor attitudes related to specific product attributes or to over-all attributes, such as brand, total product, and corporate images. Advertising may then be designed and evaluated in terms of attitude changes that the firm believes will ultimately enhance sales and profitability.

An interesting conceptual model of the progress of a consumer from unawareness through attitude changes to ultimate purchase has been given by Lavidge and Steiner.[4] They postulate the hierarchy of effects illustrated in Fig. 3-3. The consumer is seen as passing from a lack of

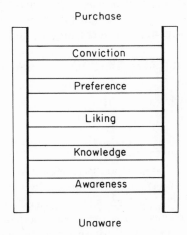

Figure 3-3: Hierarchy of effects leading to purchase

awareness about the firm's products to a state of awareness of the firm's offerings. Awareness is followed by knowledge of the product's characteristics. Advertising plays an informative role in both of these steps.

[4] R. C. Lavidge and G. A. Steiner, "A Model for Prediction Measurements of Advertising Effectiveness," *Journal of Marketing*, XXV (October, 1961), pp. 59–62.

In terms of liking, preference, and conviction, advertising plays the role of persuader. It is at these steps that attitude change would seem to be an appropriate measure of advertising effectiveness. The final step, purchase, relates to the sales criterion and is discussed in the next section of this chapter.[5]

Although considerable progress has been made in attitude measurement,[6] there are limitations in its use as a criterion of advertising performance. It is a relatively costly and time-consuming procedure and the representativeness of the sample from which attitudes are obtained is often open to question in terms of generalization to the population of potential customers. In addition, the link between attitude change and sales is not direct, since it is known that attitude change may follow a purchase rather than precede it.[7]

Sales

Several researchers have used sales as a criterion to evaluate advertising expenditures. For example, Benjamin and Maitland[8] analyzed four different models of sales response to advertising, using data from five separate advertising campaigns. Although none of the models provided a uniformly good fit to the data,[9] the best sales response to advertising relation was given by a logarithmic equation of the form

$$R = a \cdot \ln (A) + b$$

where R = sales response to A in units of product,

A = advertising expenditure,

a, b = parameters to be estimated.

This relation was initially proposed on the basis of *a priori* reasoning

---

[5] For a critical evaluation of the hierarchy of effects see K. S. Palda, "The Hypothesis of a Hierarchy of Effects: A Partial Evaluation," *Journal of Marketing Research*, III (February, 1966), pp. 13–24. Palda questions the validity of the hypothesis and suggests that advertising expenditures should be directly linked to sales.

[6] See, for example, W. C. Torgersen, *Theory and Method of Scaling* (New York: John Wiley and Sons, 1958), and P. Green and D. Tull, *Research for Marketing Decisions* (Englewood Cliffs, N.J.: Prentice-Hall, Inc., 1966).

[7] C. K. Raymond, "Must Advertising Communicate to Sell?" *Harvard Business Review* (Sept.–Oct., 1965), pp. 148–59 and Palda, *op. cit.*

[8] B. Benjamin and J. Maitland, "Operational Research and Advertising: Some Experiments in the Use of Analogies," *Operational Research Quarterly*, IX (Sept., 1958), pp. 207–17.

[9] This best-fitting form yielded a "goodness of fit" chi square value of 57.09. With seven degrees of freedom, a chi square this large means the null hypothesis that the model predictions and the data are not different from each other may be rejected at a very significant level (far in excess of the 0.01 level for which the chi square is 18.475). That is, the model predictions are significantly different from the data.

which suggested that advertising might be considered analogous to a psychological stimulus and hence might be expected to have a logarithmic relation to sales response, a relation that is common in psychophysical research.[10] The empirical results which they obtained suggested that 1) there is a threshold value of advertising expenditures (*A*) below which there is no appreciable response to advertising, and (2) saturation diminishing returns to advertising) eventually sets in.

Benjamin and Maitland have gone on to link the sales response to profit.

If   *r* = profit margin per unit of product sold
and *x* = a proposed percentage increase in advertising,

then the increment in *R* (Δ*R*) resulting from an increment in *A* (Δ*A*) will be

$$\Delta R = a \cdot \ln \frac{A + \Delta A}{A} = a \ln \left(1 + \frac{x}{100} \right)$$

and the requirement for increasing advertising by *x* per cent is

$$r \cdot a \cdot \ln \left(1 + \frac{x}{100} \right) - \frac{Ax}{100} \geq K$$

where *A* is expressed in terms of cost and *K* is a prescribed minimum increase in net revenue.

In a later paper, Benjamin, Jolly, and Maitland[11] proposed a time response function to an advertising pulse based upon an equation of the form

$$R = ae^{-bt} (1 + ct)^d$$

where   *R* = weekly sales response following a single advertising pulse,

        t = time in weeks measured from the time of the advertising pulse,

a, *b*, *c*, and *d* = parameters which must be estimated.

---

[10] For a discussion of psychophysical laws and their relation to measurement and scaling, see S. S. Stevens, "Measurement, Psychophysics, and Utility" in Churchman and Ratoosh, eds., *Measurement: Definitions and Theories* (New York: John Wiley and Sons, 1962). It might be noted that such a logarithmic relation has been found to be a good fit for message diffusion in sociological research.

[11] B. Benjamin, W. P. Jolly, and J. Maitland, "Operational Research and Advertising: Theories of Response," *Operational Research Quarterly* (December, 1960), pp. 205–18.

The model was again posited on *a priori* grounds, this time by analogy t epidemiological phenomena such as infection, incubation, and immunity This epidemic analogy to advertising response is based upon the intui tively appealing notions that:

1. Advertising is concerned with the spread or diffusion of an idea.
2. Some people may not be susceptible to the idea.
3. It takes time for an idea to take root.
4. The ideas in an ad need not be simultaneously communicated to all persons in the community; i.e., there may be word of mouth transmission of the initial message.

From their analysis of data relating to pulse advertisements the concluded that "the data suggest a response distribution over time witl a very sharp rise to a maximum and subsequent gradual decline."[12]

A significant problem in the measurement of sales response to adver tising is the likelihood that the sales response to an advertisement may continue over many periods, perhaps even years. Tull has proposed tw behavioral mechanisms that may generate such carry-over effects.[13] First, if advertising introduces consumers to the advertised product and if certain of these consumers become repeat purchasers of the produc (perhaps even hard core loyal), there will be a sales carry-over effect o advertising.[14] Second, a carry-over effect will occur if advertising impressions cumulate over time to yield sales results. That is, repeated exposures reinforce each other in inducing the consumer to purchase

An empirical study of the carry-over effects of advertising has been reported by Palda.[15] Using the Lydia Pinkham Medicine Company' annual sales and advertising expenditures for the years 1908 througl 1960, he tested many alternative models of sales response to advertising The most successful model, in terms of both goodness of fit and predictiv ability, was found to be a Koyck-type distributed lag model.[16] In it simplest form this model of sales response to advertising postulates tha sales in period t are a linear function of advertising in period t and a geometrically weighted average of all past advertising expenditures

[12] Ibid., p. 213.

[13] D. S. Tull, "The Carry-Over Effect of Advertising," *Journal of Marketing* XXIX (April, 1965), pp. 46–53.

[14] For example, see A. A. Kuehn, "How Advertising Performance Depends o Other Marketing Factors," *Journal of Advertising Research*, II (March, 1962), pp 2–10, and F. Harary and B. Lipstain, "The Dynamics of Brand Loyalty: A Markovia Approach," *Operations Research* (Jan.–Feb., 1962), pp. 19–40, and the discussion o stochastic models in Chap. 2.

[15] K. Palda, *The Measurement of Cumulative Advertising Effects* (Englewood Cliffs N.J.: Prentice-Hall, Inc., 1964).

[16] See *ibid* (Chap. 2) for a discussion of distributed lag models.

hat is,

$$S_t = \alpha + \beta A_t + \beta\lambda A_{t-1} + \beta\lambda^2 A_{t-2} + \cdots + U_t \qquad (3\text{-}1)$$

where S_t = sales in period t,

A_i = advertising in period i, $i = t, t - 1, t - 2, \ldots$,

U_t = true regression residual,

α, β, λ = parameters to be estimated,

and $\qquad\qquad\qquad 0 < \lambda < 1.$

,quation (3-1) may be transformed into

$$S_t = (1 - \lambda)\alpha + \beta A_t + \lambda S_{t-1} + U_t - \lambda U_{t-1} \qquad (3\text{-}2)$$

'he transformation from Eq. (3-1) to Eq. (3-2) is made by writing the ⅰles function for S_{t-1} as prescribed in Eq.(3-1), multiplying this by λ, nd subtracting the resulting equation from the equation for S_t defined in ,q.(3-1)

Equation (3-2) is in a form that is convenient to estimate by using ·ast squares procedures. A variant of this simple Koyck-type distrib- ∙ted lag model has been used successfully by Frank and Massy to ⅼeasure the carry-over effects of price and deals.[17] This application is ⅰscussed in Chap. 4.

When judged by the twin criteria of goodness of fit and predictive ⸱bility, Palda found the best final form of the sales response to advertising ⅼodel to be

$$S_t = 3663 + 1314 \log A_t + 0.661 S_{t-1} + 482D + 9.8T \qquad (3\text{-}3)$$

where D = a dummy variable which has the value 1 for the years 1908–1925 and the value 0 for the years 1926–1960,

T = trend measured by a year index where 1908 = 0, 1909 = 1, ... , 1960 = 52.

The variables $\log A_t$, S_{t-1}, D, and T accounted for 92 per cent of the ⅰnnual sales variation, and each had a significant regression coefficient. ⁄otice that Eq. (3-3) represents a slight modification of the simple model ⅰven by Eq. (3-2). In particular, the present model may account for ∙ecreasing returns to advertising, since it uses the logarithm of current ⸱dvertising ($\log A_t$) rather than the absolute value (A_t). The present ⅼodel also incorporates a trend variable and a dummy variable to account ⸱or certain over time effects. From Eq. (3-3) it is seen that $\lambda = 0.661$.

---

[17] Ronald Frank and William F. Massy, "Short Term Price and Dealing Effects in ∙pecialized Market Segments," *Journal of Marketing Research*, II (May, 1965), pp. 71–85.

When we recall that λ represents the annual carry-over effect of previous advertising [see Eq. (3-1)], this result is consistent with the notion that advertising had a positive carry-over effect on sales in the case of Lydia Pinkham's Vegetable Compound.

Palda has pointed out that models incorporating distributed lags tend to give an investment perspective to advertising outlays. This linkage represents the highest measure of advertising response. In this light Palda explored both the short- and the long-run marginal effects of advertising on sales as well as the corresponding advertising elasticities of sales.[18] He then went on to develop the return of the advertising investment. These results are outlined below.

For convenience, consider the simple distributed lag model given in Eq. (3-2). The short-run marginal effect of advertising on sales may be obtained by differentiating S_t with respect to A_t. Thus the short-run marginal effect is simply the coefficient β, which will be directly estimated by the application of least squares to Eq. (3-2). The long-run marginal effect may be derived by using the notion that at equilibrium there will be no tendency for sales to move away from their equilibrium level S_e. Equation (3-2) thus becomes

$$S_e = (1 - \lambda)\alpha + \beta A_t + \lambda S_e \qquad (3\text{-}4)$$

at equilibrium. If Eq. (3-4) is differentiated with respect to A_t, the long-run marginal sales effect of advertising is found to be

$$\frac{dS_e}{dA_t} = \frac{\beta}{1 - \lambda} \qquad (3\text{-}5)$$

The corresponding elasticities may be computed from

$$E_{sr} = \frac{dS_t}{dA_t} \cdot \frac{\text{avg } A_t}{\text{avg } S_t} = \beta \frac{\text{avg } A_t}{\text{avg } S_t} \qquad (3\text{-}6)$$

and

$$E_{lr} = \frac{dS_e}{dA_t} \cdot \frac{\text{avg } A_t}{\text{avg } S_t} = \frac{\beta}{1 - \lambda} \cdot \frac{\text{avg } A_t}{\text{avg } S_t} \qquad (3\text{-}7)$$

where E_{sr} = short-run advertising elasticity of sales,
E_{lr} = long-run advertising elasticity of sales,
avg A_t = average advertising for the period 1908 to 1960,
avg S_t = average sales for the period 1908 to 1960.

---

[18] Recall that an elasticity is defined as a ratio of proportional changes. Hence the advertising elasticity of sales is defined as

$$E = \frac{dS/S}{dA/A} = \frac{dS}{dA} \cdot \frac{A}{S}$$

For the Pinkham data, the short-term marginal sales per dollar of advertising was found to be $0.50. Thus in the short run, where carry-over effects were ignored, it appeared that the company was overadvertising. However, the long-term marginal sales return per dollar of advertising was $1.63. Hence, in the long run the company was not over-advertising. Notice that an entirely different managerial conclusion would have been reached regarding the level of Pinkham's advertising had the carry-over effect of advertising been ignored.

The marginal rate of return on a dollar of advertising may be found by solving for that discount rate r which equates the series of net future receipts to a dollar outlay for advertising in the present period. The unique marginal rate of return for Palda's analysis is:

$$r = \frac{c\beta + \lambda - 1}{1 - c\beta} \qquad (3\text{-}8)$$

where r = marginal rate of return per dollar of advertising.

c = the proportion of each sales dollar which contributes to profit and advertising expenditures. That is, it is the margin per dollar of sales net of all costs except advertising.

β, λ = parameters estimated from Eq. (3-2).

Although Palda's results are impressive, there is a methodological question involved in the use of a single equation model, because historically sales may have influenced the advertising budget as well as advertising having influenced sales. The presence of such a two-way influence will cause problems in the estimation of the parameters. Bass has attacked this problem directly in a simultaneous-equation regression study of advertising and sales in the cigarette industry.[19] His empirical work with data from this industry indicates that the simultaneous model is a good description of the sales effects of advertising.

The attempts to establish sales-advertising relationships have been plagued by statistical problems related to isolating the effects of advertising when sales changes may also be affected by other marketing variables, competitive actions, and environmental shifts. The problems involved in using historical data to estimate advertising response have been lucidly discussed by Quandt.[20] After reviewing the pitfalls of using

---

[19] F. M. Bass, "A Simultaneous-Equation Regression Study of Advertising and Sales—Analysis of Cigarette Data," Institute Paper No. 176, Institute for Research in the Behavioral, Economic, and Management Sciences, Purdue University, June, 1967.

[20] R. E. Quandt, "Estimating Advertising Effectiveness: Some Pitfalls in Econometric Methods," *Journal of Marketing Research* (May, 1964), pp. 51–60.

cross-sectional models, single-equation time series models, and simultane ous-equation time series models, Quandt concludes that there is a need to return to classical experimentation in order to measure the sales effec of advertising. The experimental approach is probably best able to ind cate causality in terms of advertising generating sales. However, th approach has its own particular problems, such as mortality of test unit expense, and sensitivity to the effects of the experimental variables.[21]

Du Pont has been an industry leader in the use of experimentation t measure the sales response to advertising. In one reported study, th company varied advertising by increasing its expenditures by $2\frac{1}{2}$ time normal and 4 times normal in selected market areas.[22] An interestir implication of this study was the suggestion that Du Pont consider a "in and out" advertising expenditure strategy in a trading area. That i the company should apply promotional pulses to trading areas. Befor the study a pulse-type strategy had not been considered. Note that further experiment could be used to verify or reject this implication o the study. In a further experimental study of Teflon-coated cookwar Du Pont found that its television commercials expanded the total cool ware market by 21 per cent and doubled purchases of the cookware typ promoted in its ads.[23]

Summary of Advertising Goals

In selecting the criteria to be used in setting goals for advertising, compromise is necessary between the accuracy of measurement and rele vance of the criteria in achieving the over-all objective of maximizin the profit produced by the advertising investment. If results and dec sions are not to be judged on the basis of profits, then one must explicitl or implicitly assume a relationship between the response measure (e.g., exposure, awareness, attitudes) and profits. Given a relationshi between profits and the criteria listed in Table 3-1, the over-all goal o maximizing profits can be translated into more measurable criteria, suc as reach, frequency, awareness, attitudes, or sales. For example, th goal for advertising in a target group may be to create a specified level o awareness. This is meaningful if the level of awareness goal was deter

[21] For further elaboration of the limitations of experimentation see R. E. Fran and P. E. Green, *Quantitative Methods in Marketing* (Englewood Cliffs, N.J.: Prentice Hall, Inc., 1967), pp. 51–53.

[22] R. D. Buzzell, *Mathematical Models and Marketing Management* (Boston: Ha vard University Press, 1964), pp. 157–79.

[23] J. C. Becknell, Jr. and R. W. McIsaac, "Test Marketing Cookware Coate with Teflon," *Journal of Advertising Research*, III (Sept., 1963), pp. 2–8.

nined by a consideration of the relationship of advertising to awareness,
awareness to attitudes, and attitudes to sales so as to maximize the return
on the advertising investment.

If it is assumed that the over-all goal of advertising is to maximize
profits, this goal can be expressed in terms of criteria that are more measurable. The price paid for the ease of measurement of the criterion is
difficulty in tracing the explicit effect of the criterion on advertising
profits. Ignoring the problem of linking lower level criteria to profits is
not satisfactory. It is better to attempt to make the relationships explicit
than to treat the linking relationships as implicit assumptions.[24]

CREATING ADVERTISING APPEALS

With a satisfactory set of over-all goals and subgoal criteria in mind,
the next problem is to generate the appeal that will be most effective in
achieving these goals. The creation of appeals to be used in advertising
is based upon a sound understanding of the firm's market. In particular, the behavioral characteristics of the firm's target group for this campaign must be clearly identified and understood. These characteristics
will include the psychological, sociological, and social-psychological factors affecting their behavior. Theories of buyer behavior based on
notions of perceived risk, cognitive dissonance, images, social norms,
economic utility, organization theory, and personality will be relevant
to this decision. However, it is not within the scope of this book to
discuss these theories.[25]

Management science progress in the area of appeals has lagged developments in other areas such as media selection. Perhaps this lag has existed
because the factors involved do not readily lend themselves to quantification, since the creation of appeals involves the exercise of creative intuition and behavioral science knowledge. However, management science
does offer considerable promise in the evaluation of appeals and in the
determination of the level of resources that should be allocated to the
creation of advertising campaigns.

The best example of the potential contribution of the analytical meth-

[24] See the DEMON model discussed in Chap. 7 for an application which considers
such linking relationships.

[25] This in no sense implies that behavioral science is an unimportant input to
management science. Rather, it reflects the fact that coverage of these concepts
would require a second volume, and further, it reflects the current state of the art in
management science, which has not fully integrated behavioral science concepts and
theories into its model building activities. It seems safe to predict a much closer
integration in the future.

ods of management science to the creative area of advertising is the work of Irwin Gross.[26] His analysis is concerned with the question of whether or not present expenditures for the creation and screening of advertising campaigns are appropriate. Currently, budgets for creating and screening alternative campaigns represent about three to five per cent of the total advertising media expenditure.[27] The implication of Gross' analysis is that this level of investment is substantially less than it ideally should be. This result and certain others of interest will be reviewed after presentation of the Gross model.

In analyzing the creative aspects of advertising, Gross divided his model into the following major components: (1) creating campaign alternatives, (2) pretesting to screen alternatives, (3) determining the profitability of a creation and screening plan. Each of these components is discussed below and then integrated into a decision model that determines the best expenditure for the creative aspects of advertising.

The model component dealing with the creation of appeals is primarily concerned with the relative effectiveness E of alternative campaigns. The process of creating appeals is viewed as having associated with it a distribution of relative effectiveness $f(E)$ for campaigns which might be generated. Such a distribution is illustrated in Fig. 3-4. The gener-

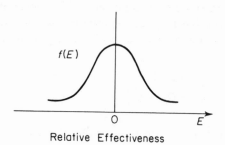

Relative Effectiveness

Figure 3-4: Distribution of relative advertising campaign effectiveness

ation of an appeal is the result of a creative effort by the personnel of an advertising agency or the sponsoring firm. This creative process is represented as a random draw from the relative effectiveness distribution. A draw represents the creation of a campaign alternative having some specific relative effectiveness. Relative effectiveness is defined as

[26] I. Gross, "An Analytical Approach to the Creative Aspects of Advertising Operations," Unpublished Ph.D. dissertation, Case Institute of Technology, November, 1967.

[27] *Ibid.*, p. 10.

the discounted present value of the increment in net profits which would accrue when one campaign is used versus another.[28]

It is convenient to take an appeal of average effectiveness as the standard of comparison for all appeals. Then, the relative effectiveness of an appeal is the difference in effectiveness between the proposed campaign appeal and an average appeal. If an appeal is average, it would have a zero relative effectiveness. If the appeal is more effective than average, it will have a positive relative effectiveness. Gross assumed that the distribution of relative effectiveness is normal with mean zero and variance σ_E^2. Fortunately, for small samples from the distribution such as one would anticipate in advertising, the decision model is not sensitive to the shape of the relative effectiveness distribution.[29] For small n, only the variance of $f(E)$ enters the decision.

The process of creating different advertising campaigns is now viewed as n independent draws from the relative effectiveness distribution. When initially drawn, the effectiveness of the appeals is not known, so the appeals must be tested to estimate their relative effectiveness.

Each of the n campaign alternatives generated in the creation of alternatives submodel would be subjected to a pretest to determine their relative effectiveness. The pretest would determine which of the n alternatives would be used. The decision rule is to choose the campaign having the highest score on the pretest. The observed pretest score of a campaign alternative may be represented as the sum of the average appeal score plus the relative appeal score plus a measurement error factor:

$$O_{ij} = \mu_0 + T_{ij} + t_{ij} \qquad j = 1,\ldots,n \qquad (3\text{-}9)$$

or $\qquad O_{ij} = O_j + t_{ij} \qquad\qquad i = 1,\ldots,r$

where O_{ij} = observed score of alternative j on the ith replication of the pretest,

μ_0 = mean pretest score for campaigns which would be generated by the process used to create campaigns,

T_{ij} = the true deviation of the jth campaign's score on the ith replication from the mean of all campaigns,

t_{ij} = deviation from the true score of alternative j introduced by random error in the testing process,

$O_j = \mu_0 + T_{ij}$ = true score on the pretest of alternative j.

If it is assumed that T and t are each normally distributed and independent

---

[28] Note that this criterion of effectiveness is similar to the discounted differential profit criterion discussed in Chap. 7, New Product Decisions.

[29] Gross, *op. cit.*, pp. 165–75.

with zero mean and respective variances σ_T^2 and σ_t^2, the observed score will be normally distributed with mean μ_0 and variance $\sigma_0^2 = \sigma_T^2 + \sigma_t^2$.
The reliability of the pretest is defined as

$$R = (1 - \sigma_t^2/\sigma_0^2)^{\frac{1}{2}} \tag{3-10}$$

Notice that $R = 1$ if σ_t^2 is zero, which implies that the measurement is perfect. Conversely, R will be very small (near zero) whenever most of the observed variation in scores is caused by random disturbances rather than true differences. The measure of reliability may be established by estimating σ_t^2 from repeated measurements on the same ad and by estimating σ_0^2 from the observed scores of a number of ads.

The validity of the pretest is also of concern. That is, to what extent does a true score on the pretest (O_j) reflect the alternative's true profit effectiveness (E_j)? Gross assumed that the true profitability and the true score were distributed as a bivariate normal distribution. This bivariate normal distribution of relative effectiveness and the true pretest score is characterized by the mean and variance of the relative effectiveness distribution, the mean and variance of the true score distribution, and the correlation between the true pretest score and the alternative's relative effectiveness. This correlation between the true score of an alternative on the pretest and its relative effectiveness provides a measure of the validity of the pretest.

The submodel that represents the creation of campaign alternatives and the submodel for pretesting the appeals must now be combined to yield the expected relative profitability of the appeal that produced the highest pretest score in the sample of n alternative campaigns which have been generated. This expectation is shown by Gross to be

$$EV(n)_{\max} = e_n \sigma_E \rho R \tag{3-11}$$

where $EV(n)_{\max}$ = expected relative profitability of the appeal that achieves the highest score on the pretest when the sample size is n,

e_n = expected value of the appeal having the greatest relative effectiveness in a sample of size n from the standardized normal distribution of relative effectiveness,

σ_E = standard deviation of the relative effectiveness distribution $f(E)$,

ρ = pretest validity—i.e., the correlation between the relative effectiveness of an appeal and its true score on the pretest,

R = reliability of the pretest.

The factor $e_n\sigma_E$ represents the expected value of the appeal having the greatest true relative effectiveness in a sample of size n from $f(E)$, which is given in Fig. 3-4. The ρ and R factors in Eq. (3-11) reflect the imperfections in the pretesting procedure. Notice that when the pretest is perfectly valid and perfectly reliable (i.e., $\rho = 1$ and $R = 1$), then $e_n\sigma_E$ represents the expected relative profitability of the appeal that achieves the highest pretest score from a sample of n. In any case, Eq. (3-11) provides the expected relative profitability when n alternative appeals have been created and screened and is based on choosing the appeal with the greatest test score.

The cost aspects of generating and screening n appeals must also be incorporated into the model. If it is assumed that the alternative campaigns are created independently and that at least one campaign will be created, the extra cost of generating n appeals rather than only one appeal is given by

$$C_n = c(n - 1) \tag{3-12}$$

where C_n = the cost of generating n appeals over and above the cost of generating one appeal,

c = the average cost of creating an advertising appeal.

Screening costs are given by the following linear equation:

$$C_{sn} = C_F + c_s n \qquad \text{for } n \geq 2 \tag{3-13}$$

where C_{sn} = cost of screening n alternatives,

C_F = fixed cost of setting up for screening,

c_s = marginal screening cost per alternative.

The complete model integrates the generation, screening, profit, and cost submodels to yield a decision concerning the optimal number of alternatives n to generate in order to maximize the profit contribution of the creative side of advertising. As n increases, the expected value of the appeal having the greatest effectiveness drawn from the standard normal distribution of effectiveness [e_n in Eq. (3-11)] increases and so does the expected relative profitability of the appeal that achieves the highest score on the pretest [$EV(n)_{max}$]. However, e_n experiences diminishing returns to n. On the other hand, from Eqs. (3-12) and (3-13), costs are seen to be a linear function of n. Hence, at some point the incremental returns to creating and testing appeals will no longer justify the incremental costs. Let

$$P_1 = 0 \tag{3-14}$$

and $$P_n = EV(n)_{max} - C_n - C_{sn} \qquad n \geq 2 \tag{3-15}$$

where P_n = the expected profit contribution of generating and screening n advertising alternatives instead of just one.

The terms on the right-hand side of Eq. (3-15) are given by Eqs. (3-11), (3-12), and (3-13), respectively. Then the optimal number of alternative appeals (n_o) is the n at which the additional profit contribution becomes negative, or the smallest n where

$$\Delta P_n = P_{n+1} - P_n < 0 \tag{3-16}$$

Once the optimum number of alternatives n_o is known, it is then possible to express the optimum creative expenditure as a proportion of the total advertising media expenditure D. If the fixed costs of screening can be ignored because they are small compared to the variable costs of generating and screening n_o alternatives, the optimal creative expenditure would be

$$d_{co} = \frac{c}{D} \qquad n_o = 1 \tag{3-17}$$

$$d_{co} = n_o p_c \qquad n_o \geq 2$$

where d_{co} = the optimum creative budget expressed as a proportion of the total media budget D,

p_c = the marginal cost per alternative of creation and screening, expressed as a proportion of the media expenditure D.

Using conservative estimates of the parameters, Gross found that the optimum creative expenditure should be about 15 per cent of the advertising media expenditure, in contrast to the 3 to 5 per cent expenditure in current practice. Furthermore, this indication of underinvestment in the creative side of advertising was not too sensitive to the parameter values used.

This model and empirical studies based upon it yield a number of significant implications for advertising decisions. Some examples are:

1. Present levels of expenditure for the creative side of advertising can be justified only if there is much less variability in profit effectiveness between advertising campaigns than is generally considered

to be the case and if there is virtually no confidence in the ability to screen alternatives.

2. From calculations based upon actual data, the results from the model were found to depend more strongly on the validity of the pretest than upon its reliability.

3. Other things being equal, the optimal size of the pretest (in terms of the number of individuals to use in the pretest) varies directly with the validity of the test. Thus, the more valid the pretest, the more justification there is for having a large pretest to increase reliability, a result that would probably not be arrived at intuitively.

When the role of management science in testing appeals and evaluating the level of resources allocated to the creative effort is understood, there will be no conflict between the creative and the research or management science aspects of this problem. Both functions are compatable; research and evaluation techniques will help to rank appeals in terms of relative effectiveness as well as perhaps to suggest new appeals. The management scientist and the behavioral scientist must both display creativity in the generation and evaluation of the appeals to be used.[30]

DETERMINATION OF THE ADVERTISING BUDGET

According to the proposed decision hierarchy in Fig. 3-1, the over-all level of commitment to the campaign should be established after the appropriate appeals for a potential campaign have been determined. Although the creation, evaluation, and selection of appropriate appeals may have required preliminary judgment as to the approximate size of the campaign, the optimal advertising budget should be determined at this stage.

The advertising budget will be optimized with respect to the goals that have been established for the campaign. Although several goal cri-

---

[30] The evaluation of appeals has received some attention in the literature. An experimental example may be found in P. L. Henderson, J. F. Hind, and S. E. Brown, "Sales Effects of Two Campaign Themes," *Journal of Advertising Research*, I (Dec., 1961), pp. 2–11. For an evaluation approach based on a probability model of appeal combinations, see E. Emmanuel, L. H. Klassen, and H. Theil, "On the Interaction of Purchasing Motives and Optimal Programming of their Activation," *Management Science*, 7, No. 1 (Oct., 1960), pp. 62–79. Another interesting possibility might be the use of microanalytic simulation models of the type described by A. E. Amstutz in *Computer Simulation of Competitive Market Response* (Cambridge, Mass.: The M.I.T. Press, 1967), pp. 153–245.

teria are available (as previously discussed), budget determination generally has a sales or profit goal as the optimization criterion. It should be once again emphasized that long-run profit maximization is the ultimate goal, even though a more measurable subgoal may be used as the explicit criterion.

A Simple Model

In the simplest case, current advertising is the only variable affecting current period sales. That is,

$$q = f(A)$$

or quantity q sold in the current period is a function of current period advertising A. Let p denote unit price, Pr denote total profit, and $C(q)$ denote the total cost of producing and marketing (exclusive of advertising) q units during the current period, the total profit may be expressed as

$$Pr = pq - A - C(q)$$
$$= pf(A) - A - C[f(A)] \qquad (3\text{-}18)$$

If $q = f(A)$ and $C(q) = C[f(A)]$ are differentiable functions and if there are decreasing returns to advertising at some level of A, then classical optimization procedures may be used to solve Eq. (3-18) for the profit maximizing budget level of advertising. If variables other than advertising affect demand, a multivariate version of this simple model may be developed.[31]

Dynamic Models

If the advertising decision made in the present period will have an impact on sales and profits in future periods, the budget problem becomes more complex, since it takes on dynamic aspects. A simple model for determining an advertising budget in the presence of carry-over effects is given by Julian Simon.[32] He assumes that revenues realized in future periods due to an advertising expenditure in the present period will decrease by a constant rate per period into the indefinite future. In addition, there will be sales revenue realized in the present period even if the present advertising budget is zero. This is because previous advertising has carry-over effects on present period sales. If b denotes the retention rate of sales revenue per period (i.e., $b = 1 -$ [constant rate of

[31] For price as a codeterminant of demand, see Chap. 4.

[32] J. Simon, "A Simple Model for Determining Advertising Appropriations," *Journal of Marketing Research* (Aug., 1965), p. 285-92.

revenue decline per future period]) and i denotes the firm's cost of capital, the discounted present value in period t of all present and future revenues generated by an advertising expenditure of A_t in period t is given by

$$PV(A_t) = \left[\frac{1}{1 - b\left(\dfrac{1}{1+i}\right)} \right] [\Delta R(A_t)]$$

where $\Delta R(A_t)$ represents the incremental net sales revenue generated in the present period (period t) by the expenditure of A_t for advertising. The sales revenue is the net of incremental gross revenue and all costs except advertising. Profit from advertising in the present period is given by

$$Pr = PV(A_t) - A_t$$

The profit maximizing rule is to continue advertising in period t until the increase in $PV(A_t)$ due to ΔA_t is just equal to ΔA_t. It should be noted that this model concentrates upon a single-period budget decision.

A more general formulation would look at the effect of advertising decisions in each of a number of future periods and determine the optimum on the basis of the dynamic effects of the series of decisions. Nerlove and Arrow[33] attack this problem by allowing dynamic advertising effects to accumulate in a storage variable called "goodwill." This goodwill is assumed to depreciate at a fixed rate, and advertising plays the role of replenishing it to the desired level. Sales are assumed to be a function of the level of goodwill, so the problem is to determine the optimum level of goodwill over time. Then the optimum yearly advertising rate is equal to the depreciation of the goodwill or, in other words, the amount of advertising necessary to build the goodwill to the desired level. To determine the optimum level of goodwill, the classical calculus model is applied with enough assumptions to assure that the necessary conditions for the optimum are also sufficient. An interesting finding which results from the study is that in the *special* case of

1. Constant marginal costs of production
2. A demand function that is linear in its logarithm
3. A stationary environment
4. Exogeneous competition

the optimal advertising budget is a constant percentage of sales. This is a rule of thumb which has often been used by business and which has been criticized for "putting the cart before the horse" in the sense that

---

[33] M. Nerlove and K. J. Arrow, "Optimal Advertising Policy Under Dynamic Conditions," *Economica*, XXIX (May, 1962), pp. 129–42.

advertising is supposed to be a determinant of sales, not vice versa.   It is interesting that it proves to be optimal in this special case.

The investment aspects of the Palda's distributed lag model discussed earlier may be viewed in a manner similar to the Nerlove and Arrow approach.[34]   Suppose that current period sales S_t are a linear function of accumulated advertising capital a_t^*.   The accumulated advertising capital corresponds to the store of goodwill in the Nerlove and Arrow model. This capital has accumulated via past advertising expenditures and depreciates over time at the rate r per period.   These relations may be expressed as

$$S_t = a + ba_t^* \tag{3-19}$$

and
$$a_t^* = (1 - r)a_{t-1}^* + A_t \tag{3-20}$$

where A_t is the expenditure for advertising during the present period. Now if Eq. (3-19) is multiplied by $1 - r$, lagged one period, and the result is subtracted from Eq. (3-19), the result will be

$$S_t = ar + b[a_t^* - (1 - r)a_{t-1}^*] + (1 - r)S_{t-1} \tag{3-21}$$

and substitution of (3-20) in (3-21) gives

$$S_t = ar + bA_t + (1 - r)S_{t-1}$$

But notice that Eq. (3-21) is identical to the original distributed lag model given in Eq. (3-2).   Thus the distributed lag model views advertising as an investment, rather than as an expense.   Also note that the rate of depreciation r is equivalent to $1 - \lambda$ in the distributed lag formulation.

Another dynamic investment approach to advertising was taken by Telser in a study of sales response to advertising expenditure for the three leading brands of cigarettes between 1912 and 1939.[35]   His sales model was developed in terms of a variable Markov brand switching model which he estimated by least squares.[36]   In his analysis, as in that of Nerlove and Arrow and Palda, advertising was viewed as an accumulation of capital (good-will) that was subject to depreciation over time.   Using the model as a basis for analysis, he estimated that the rate of depreciation on cigarette advertising capital was between 15 and 20 per cent per year.   He was also able to obtain the marginal rate of return on advertising capital expenditures.   The marginal rate of return for Lucky Strike was 15 per cent.   In the case of Camels, he found a negative marginal

[34] See Palda, *op. cit.*, pp. 17–18.

[35] L. G. Telser, "Advertising and Cigarettes," *Journal of Political Economy*, (Oct., 1962), pp. 471–99.

[36] See Chap. 2, Models of Market Response, for a discussion of a similar variable Markov application.

rate of return of -6.8 per cent, which was interpreted to mean that consumers were being oversupplied with Camel advertising.

The procedure of incorporating interperiod effects into a store of goodwill or advertising capital is one of a number of alternative dynamic formulations. Forrester has investigated some dynamic advertising effects by considering advertising as a mechanism to borrow sales from future periods.[37] He gives particular attention to amplified production fluctuations and their related costs that may result from this borrowing effect. In spite of a rather limited view of the functions of advertising, this work raises the important issue of the total system impact of the level and timing of advertising expenditures. In any given situation the demand creation functions of advertising and its timing must be balanced against any diseconomies that the advertising plan may create in other areas of the firm if policies that are profitable to the entire firm are to be pursued.

Vidale and Wolfe have considered dynamic advertising effects in a model that is based upon experimental evidence.[38] In their studies for several major industrial concerns, they found that the rate of change in sales may be related to advertising expenditures in terms of the following differential equation:

$$\frac{dS}{dt} = [rA(M - S)/M] - \lambda S \qquad (3\text{-}22)$$

where S = rate of sales at time t,

r = response constant (sales generated per dollar of advertising expenditure when $S = 0$),

A = rate of advertising expenditure at time t,

M = saturation level (the maximum sales that can be practically achieved via a given campaign),

λ = sales decay constant (the proportion of sales lost per time interval when $A = 0$).

Strictly speaking, S and A should have a time subscript. The parameters r, M, and λ are taken as constant for a given product and campaign. It might be noted that λ is measured by observing sales declines in areas where A has been set at zero for measurement purposes.

Equation (3-22) may be solved to yield the rate of advertising necessary to maintain sales at a constant level $\left(\dfrac{dS}{dt} = 0\right)$ or at a specified

[37] J. W. Forrester, "Advertising: A Problem in Industrial Dynamics," *Harvard Business Review*, XXVII (March–April, 1959), pp. 100–111.

[38] M. L. Vidale and H. B. Wolfe, "An Operations Research Study of Sales Response to Advertising," *Operations Research* (June, 1957), pp. 370–81.

growth rate $\left(\dfrac{dS}{dt} = k\right)$. For example, to increase sales by k units per period, the advertising for this period would have to be

$$A = \frac{(k + \lambda S)M}{(M - S)r}$$

Vidale and Wolfe also present sales results for a constant advertising expenditure for a period of length T and for a pulse campaign. (A pulse is a short, intense advertising campaign.) For the constant campaign of length T, integration of Eq. (3-22) yields

$$S(t) = \left[\frac{M}{1 + \dfrac{\lambda M}{rA}}\right] (1 - e^{-[(rA/M)+\lambda]t}) + S_0 e^{-[(rA/M)+\lambda]t}$$

$$\hspace{8cm} \textit{for } t < T \quad (3\text{-}23)$$

and $\bar{S}(t) = S(T)e^{-\lambda(t-T)}$ \hspace{3cm} \textit{for } t > T

where S_0 is the rate of sales at $t = 0$, the start of the campaign. The total additional sales generated by this campaign may be obtained from

$$\int_0^T S(t)\, dt + \int_T^\infty \bar{S}(t)\, dt \hspace{3cm} (3\text{-}24)$$

where the integrands in Eq. (3-24) correspond to the appropriate functions in Eq. (3-23). For a pulse campaign, if there is no saturation, the total additional sales generated are

$$\frac{M - S_0}{\lambda} (1 - e^{-rA/M}) \hspace{3cm} (3\text{-}25)$$

where S_0 now denotes the sales rate just prior to the pulse campaign. If Eq. (3-22) can be integrated for a particular campaign, a pulse or continuous campaign, the resulting sales equation may then be optimized. Vidale and Wolfe present an investment approach to advertising for the case of a pulse campaign. For many potential campaigns, the integration of Eq. (3-22) may be analytically intractable. Numerical integration may be of help in these instances.[39] Numeric methods may also be necessary when one is optimizing the resulting equation relating sales to advertising.[40]

---

[39] See, for instance, H. F. Buckner, "Numerical Methods for Integral Equations," in J. Todd, ed., *Survey of Numerical Analysis* (New York: McGraw-Hill, 1962), pp. 439–67.

[40] See D. J. Wilde and C. S. Beightler, *Foundations of Optimization*, (Englewood Cliffs, N.J.: Prentice-Hall, Inc., 1967).

Competitive Models

The models described above are rather powerful if the relationship between sales and advertising can be estimated, if the equation for optimality can be solved, and if a sufficiency check is feasible. Even if these conditions are satisfied, these models suffer another limitation: they do not explicitly consider competitive effects. In most marketing situations it would be desirable to incorporate competitive effects.

The simplest advertising model that incorporates competitive effects is the one in which advertising does not affect total industry demand but does affect a firm's market share. In this model, relative advertising expenditures are assumed to determine the share of market gained by each of the N firms in the industry. Thus market share for firm j may be expressed as

$$MS_j = \frac{A_j}{\sum_{j=1}^{N} A_j} \tag{3-26}$$

where MS_j = market share of firm,
A_j = advertising expenditures of firm j.

This simple model may be extended to account for differential sales effectiveness per dollar of advertising between the firms by multiplying each term by a constant or by raising each advertising term to a constant exponent. This yields

$$MS_j = \frac{e_j A_j}{\sum_{j=1}^{N} e_j A_j} \quad \text{or} \quad MS_j = \frac{A_j^{\epsilon_j}}{\sum_{j=1}^{N} A_j^{\epsilon_j}} \tag{3-27}$$

where e_j and ϵ_j represent the sensitivity of the firm's market share to changes in the level of advertising expenditures. The ϵ_j are similar to but not identical with the economist's concept of elasticity.[41] The ϵ_j exponents are measures of competitive sensitivity that reflect the fact that a change in the level of advertising for each firm may have a different effect on market share at different levels of a firm's advertising. A firm's sales may be determined simply by multiplying the total industry sales by the appropriate MS_j. Thus a firm's sales are a function of its own and its competitors' advertising budgets.

[41] The advertising elasticity of market share is the percentage of change in market share divided by the percentage of change in advertising.

The determination of an optimum advertising budget is now complicated by the fact that the payoff to advertising expenditures depends not
only upon how the market responds to the firm's advertising, but also
upon how competing firms will react. To begin to attack this problem,
the first step is to construct a table describing the firm's return to advertising expenditures for each of the competitors' possible reactions. The
market share terms given in Eq. (3-27) may be used in the calculation of
the net profits to the firm for each budget level it is considering and for
each competitive response it wishes to analyze.

An example of such a payoff table is given in Table 3-2 for the case of

**TABLE 3-2: Payoff to the
Firm's Advertising Budget**

	P_{ij}	Competitor's Advertising Budget ($ in 000's)		
		100	*200*	*300*
The Firm's Advertising	100	400	200	150
Budget ($ in 000's)	200	390	225	200
	300	350	300	250

P_{ij} = profit contribution to the firm when the firm expends level i on advertising and the competitor expends level j ($ in 000's).

a single competitor. Suppose that the payoffs are measured in terms of
profit contribution net of advertising expenditures.[42] To specify the best
advertising level, some decision criterion must be specified. If the firm
knew what its competitor was going to do, it could then choose its best
alternative. This is rarely the case. However, if the firm could ascribe
a subjective probability to each of the competitor's possible actions, a
logical decision rule would be to choose the strategy that yields the
greatest expected net profit contribution to the firm. When the firm is
able to make these subjective probability assessments for each action
available to the competitor, the analysis of the competitive situation is
made under conditions of risk. If the firm's state of knowledge about
competitive action is such that it cannot make such assessments, the
firm is faced with a decision under uncertainty. The analysis of competitive advertising decisions is pursued below both under conditions of
uncertainty and under risk.

---

[42] If the utility for money is linear for the firm over the range being considered,
then a dollar measure on the payoffs is appropriate.

Competitive Models under Uncertainty

A number of alternative decision criteria are available for decision under conditions of uncertainty. These criteria will be described and then a game theory model utilizing them will be discussed.

The maximin criterion

If the decision maker is pessimistic or if he places high value on security, he might use the maximin criterion to establish his advertising budget. The maximin approach first examines the worst outcome that could result for each of the alternative budget levels. For Table 3-2 these worst outcomes are (in units of $1,000):

Firm's Advertising Budget	*Worst Possible Outcome*
100	150
200	200
300	250

Now the pessimist or the security maximizer would choose that budget level that guarantees him the greatest payoff in the most adverse circumstances. In this example, a budget level of $300,000 will yield the greatest payoff under the worst circumstances. Hence the decision maker can guarantee himself a payoff no less than $250,000 if he allocates $300,000 as the advertising budget. The major limitations of this decision criterion are its extreme conservatism and the fact that it ignores all information in the payoff matrix except the worst outcomes for each decision (or strategy).

The maximax criterion

At the opposite extreme is the optimist or the gambler. This type of decision maker will probably choose to use a maximax criterion. That is, he will choose that strategy (budget level of advertising) that has the greatest possible reward associated with it, regardless of how the competitor responds. In the example, a budget level of $100,000 has the highest payoff in the matrix, $400,000. Thus the maximax criterion would require $100,000 in advertising, in contrast to the maximin criterion, which specified $300,000. The problem with this criterion is that it allows the best payoffs to blind the decision maker to potential dangers in a strategy.

Hurwicz α criterion

As a compromise between the extreme pessimism of the maximin criterion and the extreme optimism of the maximax criterion, Hurwicz proposed the "α criterion." The α criterion is a weighted combination of the maximin and the maximax strategies. Formally, this is

$$\alpha \text{ criterion for strategy } i = (1 - \alpha)(\text{best payoff to strategy } i)$$
$$+ (\alpha)(\text{worst payoff to strategy } i) \quad (3\text{-}28)$$

where $\quad 0 \leq \alpha \leq 1,$

α = an index of the pessimism of the decision maker,

and $1 - \alpha$ = an index of the optimism of the decision maker.

The decision rule is to choose the strategy having the highest α criterion. Suppose the decision maker in the example is rather venturesome and thus weights the worst outcome by $\frac{1}{4}$ and the best outcome by $\frac{3}{4}$. The α criterion values for the alternative budget levels specified in Table 3-2 will be:

Strategy	α Criterion Value
100	$(\frac{3}{4})(400) + (\frac{1}{4})(150) = 337.50$
200	$(\frac{3}{4})(390) + (\frac{1}{4})(200) = 342.50$
300	$(\frac{3}{4})(350) + (\frac{1}{4})(250) = 325.00$

Notice that in this case a budget level of $200,000 would be chosen, in contrast to $100,000 for a maximax criterion and $300,000 for a maximin criterion. It should be noted that this criterion also considers only the extreme payoffs to a strategy.

The Laplace criterion

A criterion that does consider payoffs other than the extreme payoffs to a strategy is the Laplace criterion. This criterion takes the position that since the decision maker does not have sufficient information to ascribe probabilities to the likelihood of each of the competitor's countermoves, each move should be considered equally likely. In the present case, this would mean that the competitor would be considered equally likely to spend $100,000, $200,000, or $300,000 on advertising. The decision rule now is to choose the strategy having the highest expected payoff, where the probabilities are computed on the basis of the equally likely assumption. The results for the payoff matrix in Table 3-2 are:

Strategy	Laplace Expected Payoff
100	$(\frac{1}{3})(400) + (\frac{1}{3})(200) + (\frac{1}{3})(150) = (\frac{1}{3})(750) = 250$
200	$(\frac{1}{3})(390) + (\frac{1}{3})(225) + (\frac{1}{3})(200) = (\frac{1}{3})(815) = 271\frac{2}{3}$
300	$(\frac{1}{3})(350) + (\frac{1}{3})(300) + (\frac{1}{3})(250) = (\frac{1}{3})(900) = 300$

Under the Laplace criterion, the budget would again be set at $300,000, just as it would be under the maximin criterion. Notice that the ranking and choice that this criterion yields are equivalent to those which would be obtained by simply summing the payoffs to a strategy across all competitive countermoves.

The minimax regret criterion

The minimax regret criterion is designed to protect the decision maker from excessive costs of mistakes. In psychological terms, it reflects a desire on the part of a decision maker to minimize his post-decision regret or dissatisfaction at not having done as well as he might. For decision makers whose organizational career development is at stake the minimax regret criterion may well have strong personal appeal.

The minimax regret criterion requires that the payoffs in Table 3-2 first be transformed into a regret matrix as in Table 3-3. To illustrate

TABLE 3-3: Regret Matrix for the Firm's Advertising Budget

		Competitor's Advertising Budget (in 000's)		
	R_{ij}	*100*	*200*	*300*
Firm's Advertising Budget	100	0	100	100
(in 000's)	200	10	75	50
	300	50	0	0

the development of the regret matrix, consider the case of the competitor spending $200,000 for advertising. In this case, the firm would earn a payoff of $300,000 if it spends $300,000 on advertising. This strategy is optimal against a competitive expenditure of $200,000. If the firm had spent only $200,000 on advertising, its payoff would have been $225,000, which means an opportunity loss of $300,000 − $225,000 = $75,000. Thus the entry in the regret matrix for the firm spending $200,000 against a competitive expenditure of $200,000 is $75,000. More generally, the method of determining the entries in the regret matrix is to take a cell value in the payoff matrix (P_{ij}) and subtract it from the maximum payoff in the *j*th column. Thus the regret for the *ij*th entry is

$$R_{ij} = \max_j P_{ij} - P_{ij}$$

The decision criterion now is to choose that budget level which minimizes the maximum regret. From Table 3-2 the maximum regret for each strategy is:

Strategy	Maximum Regret
$100	100
$200	75
$300	50

Hence, the minimax regret criterion would choose a budget level of $300,000, since it has the smallest maximum regret. It should be noted that the minimax regret criterion ignores all but the extreme values of regret and consequently is subject to the same type of limitation as the maximin strategy.

Game theory models

The preceding discussion of choice criteria has implicitly ignored the decision strategy to be employed by an intelligent competitor. Game theory may yield useful insights into appropriate strategies when the firm is able to make certain assumptions about how the competitor views the market situation and how he will formulate his own strategy for advertising budget determination.

Suppose the payoff table in Table 3-2 is considered to be the payoffs to the firm from promotional competition with the competitor. Further suppose that the total market is nonresponsive to advertising, but that each firm's share of the total market is reflected by its relative advertising expenditures. The example thus becomes a two-person constant sum game, since the total rewards available to the two firms are fixed and what one firm gains the other loses. Now, if it is further assumed that both firms view the same total and individual payoff matrices, the strategy decisions of both firms may be considered in a game theory framework.

One of the prime concerns of a game theory analysis is whether or not a stable competitive equilibrium exists. An equilibrium exists when all participants in the game are in a position where it does not behoove any of them to change their strategies. To understand the equilibrium notion, further consider the constant sum game described in Table 3-4. The first matrix describes the payoffs to firm one and the second describes the payoffs to firm two. The game is a constant sum game, since the sum of the rewards each firm receives is constant and equal to $500,000 in this example. Now assume that each firm uses the maximin criterion in determining its budget level. This would lead firm one to establish a level of $300,000. Firm two also finds that $300,000 is the best level. This strategy pair is also an equilibrium pair, since neither firm can improve its payoff by changing its advertising level when it is assumed that the competitor will not change his advertising level. Since neither firm has an incentive to move from the $300,000 level, an equilibrium exists.[43] Most game theory models are directed at identifying the

TABLE 3-4: Two-person Constant Sum Game Solution to Advertising Budget Determination

	Payoff to firm 1	Firm 2's Advertising Budget ($ in 000's)				
		100	200	300	Row Min.	Maximin
Firm 1's Advertising Budget	100	400	200	150	150	
($ in 000's)	200	390	225	200	200	
	300	350	300	250	250	X

	Payoff to firm 2	Firm 1's Advertising Budget ($ in 000's)				
		100	200	300	Row Min.	Maximin
Firm 2's Advertising Budget	100	100	110	150	100	
	200	300	275	200	200	
	300	350	300	250	250	X

existence of such equilibria and the characteristics of the market at equilibrium.

The first game theory applications to advertising were developed by Friedman.[44] He was concerned with promotional competition between two competitors in n geographic areas. Attention was focused upon the final demand in each geographic region which would be allocated to the competitors on the basis of their respective advertising shares. Sales in each area that are not influenced by advertising are ignored. The total

---

[43] In this case an equilibrium exists for a pure strategy on the part of the firms— i.e., they will always use $300,000. Many games only yield equilibrium solutions when the players randomize between their strategies. For a discussion see W. J. Baumol, *Economic Theory and Operations Analysis*, 2nd ed. (Englewood Cliffs, N.J.: Prentice-Hall, Inc., 1965), Chap. 23 and the consideration of competitive models discussed in Chap. 4, Pricing Decisions, of this text.

[44] L. Friedman, "Game Theory Models in the Allocation of Advertising Expenditures," *Operations Research*, VI (Sept.–Oct., 1958), pp. 699–709.

advertising-influenced sales of each competitor are assumed to be

$$S_A = \sum_{i=1}^{n} \left(\frac{X_i}{X_i + Y_i} \right) s_i \quad \text{for firm } A \qquad (3\text{-}29)$$

and

$$S_B = \sum_{i=1}^{n} \left(\frac{Y_i}{X_i + Y_i} \right) s_i \quad \text{for firm } B \qquad (3\text{-}30)$$

where s_i = total potential sales influenced by advertising in area i,
   X_i = company A's advertising expenditure in area i,
   Y_i = company B's advertising expenditures in area i.

This formulation assumes that an advertising dollar is equally effective for both advertisers. In terms of Eq. (3-27), this implies that $e_A = e_B = 1$ or $\epsilon_A = \epsilon_B = 1$. Each competitor is also assumed to have a budget constraint. Since the total sales influenced by advertising $\left(S = \sum_{i=1}^{n} s_i \right)$ are constant in this case, the problem becomes a two-person constant sum game. Now in order to make the model amenable to game theory analysis define $D = S_A - S_B$ as the difference between firm A's sales and firm B's sales. Since the total market is fixed, sales gained by firm A are lost by firm B and vice-versa. Thus firm A will want to allocate its promotional budget over areas so as to maximize the difference D, and firm B will seek to minimize this difference. The criterion function is thus

$$D = \sum_{i=1}^{n} \left(\frac{X_i - Y_i}{X_i + Y_i} \right) s_i \qquad (3\text{-}31)$$

subject to the budget restrictions

$$\bar{A} = \sum_{i=1}^{n} X_i$$

where $\bar{A}$ = firm A's advertising budget

and

$$\bar{B} = \sum_{i=1}^{n} Y_i$$

where $\bar{B}$ = firm B's advertising budget.

Friedman shows that the equilibrium allocation of funds to areas, if it is assumed that firm A is trying to maximize Eq. (3-31) while firm B is imultaneously trying to minimize it, will be

$$X_i = \bar{A} \left(\frac{s_i}{S} \right) \qquad i = 1, \ldots, n \qquad (3\text{-}32)$$

$$Y_i = \bar{B} \left(\frac{s_i}{S} \right) \qquad i = 1, \ldots, n$$

That is, the optimal allocation of funds to each area by each competitor should be proportional to the sales potential in each area. It is interesting that this maximin equilibrium solution is a common advertising allocation practice in many companies. If both companies use their optimum strategies, the difference in sales from Eq. (3-31) will be

$$D = \left(\frac{\bar{A} - \bar{B}}{\bar{A} + \bar{B}} \right) S \qquad (3\text{-}33)$$

and firm A's total sales will be

$$S_A = \left(\frac{\bar{A}}{\bar{A} + \bar{B}} \right) S \qquad (3\text{-}34)$$

These results may now be incorporated in a model for budget determination. Let the total costs of producing and selling an amount S_A be

$$TC = C_1 + C_2 S_A \qquad (3\text{-}35)$$

where TC = total costs exclusive of advertising,
$\quad C_1$ = fixed costs,
$\quad C_2$ = variable production and selling costs per unit.

Then if C_3 equals the gross return per unit of sale, the total profit Pr as a function of firm A's advertising budget will be given by

$$Pr = C_3 S_A - C_1 - C_2 S_A - \bar{A} \qquad (3\text{-}36)$$

Maximizing Eq. (3-36) with respect to $\bar{A}$ after substituting Eq. (3-34) for S_A yields the optimal advertising budget for firm A when both firms A and B allocate optimally to each geographic region. The optimal budget is given by

$$\bar{A}_{\max} = \sqrt{(C_3 - C_2)S\bar{B}} - \bar{B} \qquad (3\text{-}37)$$

Thus the optimal advertising budget for firm A is a function of the total sales potential which may be influenced by advertising, S, the competitor's budget $\bar{B}$, and the profit contribution per unit of sale $C_3 - C_2$.[45]

---

[45] Friedman also explored other models of advertising budget determination in the game theory context. For example, he studied firm A's optimal strategy when firm B does not use its optimal strategy. For the results of these analyses the reader is referred to Friedman, *ibid.*

There have been various other applications of game theory to adver tising. For example, Mills extended Friedman's models by considering constant sum games with more than two competitors.[46] He also used a more realistic market share term that is similar in form to that described in Eq. (3-27). A variable sum game approach was taken by Baligh and Richartz.[47] Shakun has been concerned with developing game models for coupled markets,[48] that is, for markets in which there are product line interdependencies. The effects of product interdependency and multiple control variables in competitive models will be discussed in Chap. 4 Pricing Decisions.

Competitive Models under Risk: Decision Theory

Statistical decision theory offers an alternative method of formulating the budget decision problem.[49] The probabilistic nature of both competitive and market response can be encompassed within this framework Assuming constant marginal utility for money (at least in the relevant range of operation), the Bayesian criterion dictates choice of that level of advertising which generates the greatest expected value of profits.[50] The states of nature in this case represent the joint occurrence of some particular market and competitive responses. In order to compute the expected value of some level of advertising A, the conditional probability for each state of nature, given the level of advertising A, is needed. In the Bayesian framework, these probabilities may be objectively based upon past data or upon subjective estimates of the likelihood of various outcomes (i.e., joint occurrences of particular market and competitive responses). In addition to the probability of each outcome, given the level of advertising A, the value (profits net of advertising A) of each outcome for the level A must also be estimated by objective or subjective procedures. These values are then multiplied by their respective proba-

---

[46] H. D. Mills, "A Study in Promotional Competition," in Bass, et al., eds., *Mathematical Models and Methods in Marketing* (Homewood, III: R. D. Irwin, Inc., 1961), pp. 271–88.

[47] H. H. Baligh and L. E. Richartz, "Variable-Sum Game Models of Marketing Problems," *Journal of Marketing Research*, IV (May, 1967), pp. 173–83.

[48] M. F. Shakun, "Advertising Expenditures in Coupled Markets—A Game Theory Approach," *Management Science B*, XI (Feb., 1965), pp. B-42–B-47 and "A Dynamic Model for Competitive Marketing in Coupled Markets," *Management Science B*, XII (Aug., 1966), pp. B-525–B-530.

[49] See P. E. Green, "Bayesian Decision Theory in Advertising," *Journal of Advertising Research*, II (Dec., 1962), pp. 33–42, for additional Bayesian concepts related to advertising.

[50] If the marginal utility of money is not constant, monetary terms should be transformed into utilities, and the criterion becomes maximum expected utility.

>ilities and summed over all outcomes to yield the expected payoff to the evel of advertising A. This procedure is repeated for each budget level under consideration, and the one generating the greatest expected value s chosen. This procedure develops the best budget level (in terms of expected profits) among the budget levels being considered. A global optimum (the best possible) budget will be chosen whenever the global optimum lies in the set of candidate budgets. Whenever it does not, the procedure yields a suboptimum budget level.

As an example of the application of decision theory to the establishment of an advertising budget, again consider the firm whose payoffs are represented in Table 3-2. Suppose now that the decision maker is willing to ascribe judgmental (or subjective) probabilities to his competitor's alternative budget levels. He now faces a budget decision under risk rather than uncertainty. If he believes that the competitor will spend $100,000, $200,000, and $300,000 with probabilities $\frac{1}{4}$, $\frac{1}{2}$, $\frac{1}{4}$, respectively, then his expected payoff for each level of his budget will be:

Budget		*Expected Payoff*
100	$(\frac{1}{4})(400) + (\frac{1}{2})(200) + (\frac{1}{4})(150)$	$= 237\frac{1}{2}$
200	$(\frac{1}{4})(390) + (\frac{1}{2})(225) + (\frac{1}{4})(200)$	$= 260$
300	$(\frac{1}{4})(350) + (\frac{1}{2})(300) + (\frac{1}{4})(250)$	$= 300$

Thus if the decision maker believes that the competitor will establish his budget level with these probabilities, his optimal decision is to spend $300,000 on advertising.

Stochastic Models

Stochastic models of consumer behavior can also be useful in advertising budget determination. A model using the concepts developed in the linear learning model of consumer behavior has been proposed by A. Kuehn.[51] He conceptualizes sales as made up of three segments: sales due to habit, sales due to product characteristics, and sales due to advertising interacting with the product characteristics. Only the third segment is affected by the advertising expenditure. This advertising-dependent section of the total sales function is contingent upon the industry growth rate, upon the lags between placing the advertising and achieving results, and upon the relative advertising market share effects. The cumulative profit function resulting from this sales function is quad-

[51] A. A. Kuehn, "A Model for Budgeting Advertising," in Frank M. Bass, et al., eds., *Mathematical Models and Methods in Marketing, op. cit.*, pp. 315–48.

ratic with respect to the firm's advertising and may be optimized by classical methods. The model can be used to construct a competitive payoff matrix, and the game theory concepts previously indicated can be utilized to find the best advertising budget.

The potential gain from utilizing stochastic consumer models in the budget determination decision is great. Research should be directed at linking the parameters of the stochastic consumer models to controllable marketing variables.[52] Linking the effects of the advertising budget to the models would be helpful in the optimum determination of the advertising expenditure.

Adaptive Models

An adaptive model is based on a decision procedure that is continually updated with new information. This information is generated by observing the results of the model's last decision and the outcomes of carefully designed experiments. It is then fed back to the model, where the decision, and perhaps the decision model parameters themselves, are updated. Thus the adaptive model is continually "learning" about its environment.

John D. C. Little has developed a model for the adaptive control of advertising expenditures.[53] The macroelements and their sequencing in the model are outlined in Fig. 3-5. The sequence of application of these macroelements will be discussed briefly, and then the units will be considered in somewhat greater detail. The application of the model begins with a determination of the profit-maximizing level of expenditures for advertising, given a model of sales response to advertising. Since it is unlikely that the parameters of the sales response function will be known with much precision and since it is likely that the response may change over time, an experiment is designed to measure the sales response to advertising during the next period. The third element entails the implementation of the advertising expenditures and the sales experiment during the period. Element four represents the market's sales and profit response to the firm's expenditure policy and measurement activities. The sales results are then fed back into element five, which adjusts the parameters of the sales model in the light of the information gained from

[52] For example, see the research by Haines, *op. cit.*, discussed in Chap. 2. For an example of a descriptive stochastic model which includes the effects of advertising, see B. Lipstein, "A Mathematical Model of Consumer Behavior," *Journal of Marketing Research*, II (Aug., 1965), pp. 259–65.

[53] J. D. C. Little, "A Model of Adaptive Control of Promotional Spending," *Operations Research*, XIV (Nov.–Dec., 1966), pp. 175–97. This paper is reproduced in David B. Montgomery and Glen L. Urban, eds., *Applications of Management Science in Marketing* (Englewood Cliffs, N.J.: Prentice-Hall, Inc., 1969).

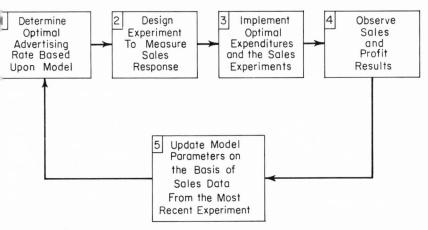

Figure 3-5: Adaptive model for advertising control

he sales experiment. The cycle then repeats itself as the optimal dvertising budget is established for the next period, the updated paramter values being used.

The first element in the adaptive model is composed·of the sales and rofit models, which are given by:

$$s = \alpha + \beta x - \gamma x^2 \qquad (3\text{-}38)$$

and
$$Pr = ms - x - c \qquad (3\text{-}39)$$

where s = sales rate (dollars per household per year),
Pr = profit rate (dollars per household per year),
x = promotion rate (dollars per household per year),
c = fixed cost rate (dollars per household per year),
m = gross margin per unit,
α, β, γ = parameters.

The model assumes a simple quadratic sales response to advertising that xhibits diminishing returns. A graphical example of the general shape f the response function is given in Fig. 3-6. Using Eq. (3-38) in Eq. 3-39), by the usual calculus procedures the profit maximizing level of romotional expenditures x^* may be found to be

$$x^* = \frac{(m\beta - 1)}{2m\gamma} \qquad (3\text{-}40)$$

This budget is the profit maximizing level, given current estimates of the parameters.

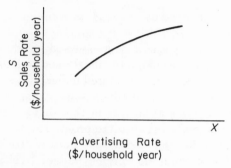

Figure 3-6: Sales response to advertising in the adaptive model

If the parameters of the sales response function were constant ove
time, a large one-time expenditure on measurement would probably b
justified. However, it is highly likely that competitive activity, eco
nomic shifts, changes in advertising quality, and product changes wi
cause these parameters to change over time. Consequently, a large one
time investment in measurement seems unattractive. A continuin
series of smaller experiments would enable the firm to increase the pre
cision of its parameter estimates as well as to monitor changes in th
response function which occur over time. Thus a program of continu
ous market experimentation would seem viable, particularly when th
sales response function exhibits changes over time.

Little formulates a relatively simple change mechanism for the model'
response parameters by postulating random changes in α and β over time
In this model, γ is taken to be a known constant. A sensitivity analysi
found that this latter assumption may not be too serious for the suc
cessful operation of the adaptive model. He then formulates an experi
ment to gather information about α and β.[54] Information is gathere
by operating n markets at $\Delta/2$ less than the optimal rate x^* and n
markets at $\Delta/2$ more than x^*, where Δ is a design parameter of th
experiment.

The experiment is designed to choose n and Δ to minimize the sum o
two losses: (1) the loss in profits due to lack of perfect information on β
(2) the profit loss due to the measurement process, since the test area
levels will probably be at nonoptimal levels. The information gaine
from the sales response to the chosen level of x and the experiments is the
used to update the estimates of the sales response parameters, and th
cycle begins anew. The updating procedure uses exponential smoothin
and Bayesian methods. It should be evident at this point that since th

---

[54] Strictly speaking, information is only needed on β, since α does not enter deci
sions in the model. See Little, *ibid.*

sales response parameters are viewed as random variables, the profit function given in Eq. (3-39) is itself a random variable. Thus the profit maximizing rule is really maximizing expected profit.

In order to compare the adaptive model to other budget determination rules, a simulated market was structured under an assumption of random changes in the sales response to advertising parameters. The effectiveness of a budget determination rule in this simulated environment was taken to be the difference between the profits realized by using the decision rule and the profits that could have been realized if the parameters were perfectly known and the optimal budget level established. This effectiveness of a budget decision rule versus a perfect decision rule was termed the loss rate and was used to contrast the adaptive rule to certain fixed budget rules. In this simulated environment the adaptive model for setting the advertising budget was generally found to yield a smaller loss rate than constant budget level decision rules. In addition, the adaptive model had a surprisingly low absolute loss rate, which tended to have a magnitude in the range of 0.7 to 5 per cent of the optimum advertising budget level.

Little's adaptive formulation has much to recommend it. The adaptive model is particularly useful in that it will sense and react to changes in market response to advertising. It is also useful in sharpening the determination of the optimum budget even if the market parameters do not change. If the market is stable, the adaptive model will improve the estimates of the response parameters. Furthermore, the notion of continuous market experimentation to monitor market change is attractive even if it is not imbedded in an adaptive model framework. Too often experiments are performed on a one-shot basis when a better approach might be to set up a procedure for continuous monitoring. This notion clearly has significant implications for the design of marketing information systems.

In its present state, Little's adaptive model has certain limitations. For example, it ignores the possibility of carry-over effects. In addition, competitive effects are only partially and implicitly encompassed. Current period competitive effects are not incorporated at all. For planning periods of several months duration (which will be necessary in order to carry out the experimental measurements), this may be a serious shortcoming. In addition, it ignores the interdependencies in the marketing mix of the firm. That is, it ignores the profit consequences of interactions between price, distribution, product, and advertising. An attack on this latter problem has been made by Little in an extension of the adaptive model to multiple control variables.[55]

[55] J. D. C. Little, "A Multivariate Adaptive Control Model," Alfred P. Sloan School of Management, Working Paper 211-66, Massachusetts Institute of Technology, August 18, 1966.

Little's formulation utilizes a simple calculus model to perform the actual budget optimization. It would be interesting to incorporate in an adaptive framework the more sophisticated models discussed earlier in this section. If these extensions proved feasible, many of the current limitations would be overcome. In any case, adaptive models appear to be an especially fruitful area for research in marketing.

The Advertising Budget as Part of the Marketing Mix

Most of the models indicated above make budget determination recommendations based on the assumption that advertising is the only variable. This is an assumption that is usually not true. Price, channels of distribution, and personal selling effort are a few of the other variables important in the over-all marketing program. Advertising is part of a marketing mix and should be determined simultaneously with other elements of the mix. For example, if price were changed, the optimal advertising level might change, and vice versa. These marketing mix considerations and efforts to obtain the optimum mix will be discussed in the chapters to follow on pricing and new products. Advertising may also be linked to the total marketing program when a product line is offered by the firm, in which case product interdependencies may be important. Consideration of these product interdependency effects will be deferred to the pricing and new product chapters.

Summary of Models of Budget Determination

Models designed to determine advertising budgets have been based on the use of sales or profits as the goal of advertising. The first attempts to find the best budget used the marginal principles of the simple single variable calculus model. This approach has been extended to include dynamic, competitive, and risk effects, although these extensions have not been simultaneously considered in solving the advertising budget problem. Stochastic consumer models have been proposed for use in budget determination, since these models are capable of mapping the effects of advertising into the consumer behavior process. If advertising can be linked to the basic parameters of consumer models, some of the problems of measuring aggregate sales response to advertising may be overcome. The most productive modeling approach to budget etermination seems to be in the area of adaptive processes. The pdating advantage of adaptive models will be particularly valuable in arketing environments subject to significant changes over time.

SPECIFICATION OF THE MEDIA SCHEDULE

Introduction to Media Scheduling

After the optimum budget has been determined, the next problem in he proposed advertising decision hierarchy is the selection of the media ɔ be used in the campaign. If the results of considering media produce nexpected opportunities or identify significantly different responses to dvertising from those anticipated, the budget decision would have to be eviewed. This review may lead to an iterative consideration of the udget and media decisions.

In media selection decisions must be made concerning the allocation of he budget between radio, television, magazines, newspapers, and outdoor dvertising. In each of these media, decisions must be made concerning he number of insertions in each medium, the timing of the insertions, and ome preliminary designation of the kind of insertion (e.g., full page olor or half page black and white magazine insertions). The output f the media decision is a schedule of number, frequency, and kind of nsertions in the media to be utilized. The problem is to determine a nedia schedule that will optimize the effect of the advertising budget llocation.

The first question to be resolved is what is the "effect" of the adverising. What criteria will be used to measure the effects? Earlier in his chapter several criteria were listed (see Table 3-1), and it was stressed hat the use of each of them required assumptions concerning how it was inked to the over-all goal of profit maximization. The choice of criteria or the media selection problem is the same. The exposure criteria are elatively easy to measure but are removed from sales and profit results. teach and frequency are possible exposure criteria, but each has differnt market implications. They cannot be maximized simultaneously by ne campaign.[56] Reach tends to assure that everyone receives at least ne message, whereas frequency is concerned with generating the greatest umber of exposures for each person in the target group. Reach may ɔe more appropriate during early stages of the campaign, when a mini-

---

[56] A. M. Lee, "Decision Rules for Media Scheduling: Static Campaigns," *Opertional Research Quarterly*, Vol. XIII (Sept., 1962), pp. 229–41.

mal awareness in all segments of audience is desired. Frequency may be more appropriate in later stages of the campaign, when repeated exposures are needed to move people closer to the purchase state.

Instead of being concerned with reach or frequency, media could be selected to maximize total exposure. In this case, the reach and frequency are replaced by an over-all criterion, which reflects the total exposure potential in the target market. The most desirable criterion short of profit would be sales results of the media schedule.

Using the profit criterion, the media problem is to find the profit maximizing media schedule. This poses a complex problem. First, the media insertions must be linked to sales results. With this linkage and with unit production cost functions (perhaps nonlinear), the profit result of the media schedule can be calculated. The sales results of the campaign are caused by a number of complex factors. The sales response to each medium will probably change in a nonlinear manner as the number of insertions increases. This nonlinearity will be compounded by the carry-over effects of past insertions. In addition to replication over time, duplication between media in a given time period will affect the response relationships, as will the tendency for target group members to forget insertions with the passage of time. The sales response to media insertions may also be different for subsegments of the target group (e.g., geographic areas, income class, etc.). Even further complexity is introduced by the fact that sales responses may also depend upon competitor's choice of media.

The complexity of the sales response relationship is not the only barrier to simple solution of the media problem. The nature of insertions and media cost structures pose additional difficulties. For example, media insertions are necessarily integer values. One cannot purchase a fraction of a billboard facing or part of a full-page ad without changing the nature of the ad's sales response. Furthermore, media discount policies are such that media costs per insertion are not constant. In fact, the cost per insertion, which reflects the medium's cumulative discount policy, is usually a discontinuous function of the number of insertions. The costs may be further complicated if the firm is placing ads for a number of its products in the same medium. The cost per insertion is then interdependent with media selections for other products in the firm's line.

If all the factors and complexities noted above were considered in resolving the media problem, a comprehensive solution would be produced. If this general problem were then solved, the output would be an optimum media schedule.

This general formulation being used as a reference, the past efforts to solve the media selection problem can be analyzed and placed in perspective. Three basic approaches to the media problem have been made: simulation, heuristic programming, and mathematical programming.

Simulation of Media Schedules

The most comprehensive and detailed approach to analyzing the media selection problem is to utilize simulation. A microanalytic simulation approach has been proposed by the Simulmatics Corporation.[57] In their model, a given media proposal is analyzed in detail. Each microunit (individual) is potentially exposed to each insertion in the media schedule over a time period. Actual exposure of a microunit to an insertion is probabilistically determined, where the probability is a function of the microunit's socioeconomic and demographic characteristics. The 2944 simulated microunits have media habits and socioeconomic and demographic characteristics that are representative of the national market. The output of the simulation is a summation of the exposure experienced by each of the 2944 microunits. The large number of microunits and the detail used in specifying each microunit allow the generation of a comprehensive specification of the exposure effects of a given media combination. The results of the campaign can be measured by the cumulative reach over time, the frequency of exposure over time, the total exposure, the audience profile, and the costs for each of these results.

Media simulations could encompass the factors of replication, forgetting, media interaction, duplication, cost discounts, and nonlinear response to integer media insertions.[58] Although a richness of output is obtained and all the desirable features of a media schedule are encompassed, there are two problems with this microanalytic simulation approach. First, the results of the campaign are in terms of exposure (e.g., reach, frequency, total exposure), so the relation to profit must be assumed.[59] The second limitation of the Simulmatics simulation model is that it does not solve the media problem. It only evaluates given media schedules. If enough schedules are tested, information relevant to selecting a near optimum schedule would be generated. However, the number of trials would be tremendous. The costs of the simulation approach expand very rapidly if it is used as a tool to search for the best media schedule. Given a reasonable set of alternative media schedules, microanalytic simulation can be used to generate comprehensive data concerning the outcome of each campaign. Hence it is an evaluative procedure that may assist the decision maker in determining a satisfactory, but not optimum, media schedule.

[57] *Simulmatics Media-Mix: General Description and Technical Description* (New York: The Simulmatics Corporation), Oct., 1962.

[58] The microanalytic simulation approach advocated by Amstutz would be appropriate here. See A. E. Amstutz, *op. cit.*

[59] The more detailed approach used by Amstutz includes actual purchase responses and consequently relates more directly to profit effects. The major limitation here is the cost of evaluating a single media schedule, let alone several alternatives. See A. E. Amstutz, *op. cit.*

Beale, Hughes, and Broadbent have proposed a media simulation model that yields information useful in improving media schedules.[60] This model yields marginal rates of return for altering the schedule from the proposed media selections. This is a useful method of generating new test alternatives, but it does not overcome the basic nonoptimal character of media simulation models.

Heuristic Programming Models for Media Selection

A number of attempts to specify the best media schedule have been based on heuristic procedures. A heuristic procedure is one that is useful in determining better solutions to a problem. Heuristic programming leads to good solutions, but it cannot guarantee that the optimal solution has been found.

Heuristic programming is the application of a heuristic rule to a mathematical model in an ordered fashion. Several British authors have done substantive work in building models of the media problem and developing heuristic rules to generate good solutions. Lee and Burkart were the first authors to formulate mathematically the media problem in a meaningful fashion.[61] They clearly differentiated between the exposure criteria of impact (frequency) and coverage (reach) and developed mathematical relationships for them. In Lee and Burkart's first paper the maximization of the impact (frequency) of the campaign was attempted by a heuristic rule of purchasing advertisements in an inverse proportion of the square of the cost per thousand. The maximation of coverage (reach) was attempted under the assumption that the square of the proportion of the target group readership for a media divided by the cost for an insertion was equal for all media:

$$\frac{A_1^2}{C_1} = \frac{A_2^2}{C_2} = \cdots = \frac{A_i^2}{C_i} = \cdots = \frac{A_n^2}{C_n} \qquad (3\text{-}40)$$

where A_i = proportion of target group reading media i,

$\quad C_i$ = cost of one insertion in media i (all media assumed to have a common insertion unit—e.g., full page ad).

They showed that there is an equivalence between impact and coverage maximazation under this assumption. The conditions for this equivalence are not usually fulfilled, however.

[60] E. M. L. Beale, P. A. B. Hughes, and S. R. Broadbent, "A Computer Assessment of Media Schedules," *Operational Research Quarterly*, Vol. XVII, No. 4 (Dec., 1966), pp. 381–411.

[61] A. M. Lee and A. J. Burkart, "Some Optimization Problems in Advertising Media," *Operation Research Quarterly*, XI (Sept., 1960), pp. 113–22.

Later in the research and in the next paper, Lee showed that it is enerally impossible to maximize the coverage (reach) and impact (frequency) simultaneously.[62] His analysis further stressed the differences etween the two criteria and explored the implications of maximizing nem separately. Lee suggested that a meaningful alternative would be o maximize one criterion subject to a restriction on the other.

Taylor proposed a graphical, heuristic procedure to derive solutions o the problems Lee and Burkart formulated.[63] The procedure was ased on first determining the optimum size of ads for each medium and hen specifying the number of insertions. The criterion function is a ombination of coverage and impact and represents a compromise etween the two criteria. The magnitude of the compromise is specied by a managerial decision regarding the relative weights to be given o coverage and impact. The number of insertions is determined by a raphical procedure which attempts to determine the point where the narginal returns to the last insertion are equal to the cost of the insertion for each medium. The output of the procedure is the number of ds to place in each medium and the size of each insertion.

D. M. Ellis modified Lee and Burkhart's problem formulation to nclude a more complete probabilistic response function by assuming different probabilities of exposure for different people in the target group.[64] Ie also found a mathematical algorithm to solve the problem. His algoithm is based on a marginal response versus marginal cost calculation, vhere the marginal efficiency measure is a function of the log of the narginal response magnitude.

Lee has also developed an approach that considers the dynamics of nedia problems.[65] The criterion for this formulation is awareness, which s characterized by recall of the advertisement. Lee postulates a mathenatical rule of forgetting in which the proportion of people who saw an nsertion on day r and remember it on day d is hypothesized to be:

$$mq^{d-r} \tag{3-41}$$

where $q < 1$ and m and q are memory parameters.

Total awareness is defined to be proportional to total exposure. The otal proportion of the readership of medium i who are aware of the

[62] A. M. Lee, "Decision Rules for Media Scheduling: Static Campaigns," *Operation Research Quarterly*, XIII (Sept., 1962), pp. 229–41.

[63] C. J. Taylor, "Some Developments in the Theory and Application of Media scheduling Methods," *Operational Research Quarterly*, XIV (Sept., 1963), pp. 291–305.

[64] D. M. Ellis, "Building Up a Sequence of Optimum Media Schedules," *Operational Research Quarterly*, Vol. XVII, No. 4 (Dec., 1966), pp. 413–24.

[65] A. M. Lee, "Decision Rules for Media Scheduling: Dynamic Campaigns," *Operational Research Quarterly*, XII (Dec., 1963), pp. 365–72.

insertion during d is

$$AU_i(d) = \sum_{r=1}^{d} A_i m q^{d-r} (1 - P_i) P_i^{r-1} Z_i \qquad (3\text{-}42)$$

where A_i = proportion of target group reading medium i,
   P_i = probability of not reading insertion in medium i,
   Z_i = size of insertions in medium i,
   $AU_i(d)$ = awareness units associated with medium i on day d.

The criterion function is the total awareness on each day:

$$TAU(d) = \sum_{i=1}^{n} AU_i(d) \qquad (3\text{-}43)$$

Lee formulated the problem as one of determining the schedule that will maintain at least a specified TAU for each day of the campaign at a minimum cost. The minimization may be done subject to constraints on the level of coverage and impact. Although Lee does not directly solve the problem, he suggests approaches that could be used to derive solutions.

This series of papers by British authors was a comprehensive mathematical exploration of the problems surrounding media selection. They explicitly defined the criteria and the relationship among them.[66] Although they did not explicitly link the criteria to profit, they indicated response relationships that could be used to do this. Their procedures were heuristic and led to good solutions, but in general they could not be termed optimal.

During the time of the British work, an American advertising agency developed a heuristic model for media selection. Created by Young and Rubicam, the "High Assay Media Model" develops a media schedule based on purchasing media one unit at a time in each period.[67] The first media insertion purchased is the one with the lowest cost per prospect reached. The criterion appears to be related to reach (coverage). After the first purchase, the media exposure values are revised for duplication, and if there is a media discount schedule, the costs for the next insertion are changed. This cycle is then repeated. Marginal insertions are placed until a target exposure value has been reached for that period.

[66] See O. B. Mevik and N. Vinding in "Two Dimensions of Media Selection: Coverage and Frequency," *Journal of Advertising Research*, VI (March, 1966), pp. 29–35 for a discussion of the effect of changing from a basic criterion of coverage (reach) to one of frequency and total exposure.
[67] This description is adapted from W. T. Moran, "Practical Media Models— What Must They Look Like?" *Proceedings of the Eighth Annual Conference of the Advertising Research Foundation* (New York: Advertising Research Foundation, 1963), pp. 578–94.

This marginal approach is repeated for each time period so that the output is a media schedule that meets target exposure requirements which have been set for each period. The determination of the target exposure values is presumably the result of demand considerations which incorporate the effects of the number of potential customers in the population, purchase cycles for the product, and brand switching rates. The media schedule is specified so as to meet the target exposure criteria at the least cost.

A similar heuristic for a media schedule has been indicated by Kuehn.[68] The heuristic places insertions one at a time in the medium having the highest incremental consumer impact per dollar at the current stage of the analysis.

The heuristic procedures outlined here allow considerable flexibility in comprehending the complexities of the media selection problem. They can consider the factors of inter- and intramedia replication, forgetting, nonlinear response, and the integer nature of the problem. On the whole, they will generate reasonably good solutions.

Mathematical Programming
Approaches to the Media Problem

A number of attempts have been made to derive optimal media schedules by the use of mathematical programming. Since the chronological development of mathematical programming in media selection has been somewhat inconsistent, the models will be presented in order of their increasing relevance and sophistication.

The application of the simple linear programming model to the media problem requires a number of very restrictive conditions. Suppose, first, that the problem is reduced from one of determining a schedule of placement of insertions to one of specifying only the number of insertions to be placed in each medium in a given time period. Then a series of assumptions can make the linear programming model applicable. Assume that:

1. The measure of effectiveness will be total exposure.
2. Responses to media insertions are constant.
3. Costs of media insertions are constant.
4. There are no intermedia interaction effects.
5. The number of insertions is a continuous variable (i.e., it may take on fractional values).

[68] A. A. Kuehn, "Models for Budgeting Advertising" in Peter Langhoff, ed., *Models, Measurement, and Marketing* (Englewood Cliffs, N.J.: Prentice-Hall, Inc., 1955), pp. 135–36.

With this set of assumptions and the problem reduction, the media problem[69] is to

maximize: Total exposure $= \sum_{i=1}^{I} R_i X_i$ (3-44)

subject to $\sum_{i=1}^{I} C_i X_i \leq B$

$$X_i \leq L_i$$
$$X_i \geq 0 \qquad \text{for } i = 1, 2, \ldots, I$$

where X_i = the number of insertions in medium i,
C_i = the cost per insertion in medium i,
B = the total advertising budget available,
L_i = the physical limit of insertions in medium i,
R_i = the rated exposure value of a single insertion in medium i.

This formulation can be solved by linear programming computational routines. In fact, this simple model can be solved without them or a computer. First, each R_i is divided by C_i to get the rated exposure value per dollar. Then the solution is simply to select the medium with greatest rated exposure value per dollar (R_i/C_i) and purchase as much as possible in that medium (the limit being B or L_i). If the budget is not expended, purchase L_i in the medium and then purchase as much as possible of the medium with the next highest rated exposure value per dollar. The result is optimal, but it represents concentration of the budget in one or a few media. Since this is intuitively implausible, users of the model were led to specify lower limits for the number of insertions in each medium X_i. These artificial constraints were added on the basis of judgment. One could still solve the problem without a computer or linear programming, following the procedure outlined above but satisfying the lower limits first. After the lower limits were bought, the remaining budget would be expended on the medium with the highest rated exposure value per dollar R_i/C_i. This would be carried to the

[69] The following references discuss the simple LP model: F. M. Bass and R. T. Lonsdale, "An Exploration of Linear Programming in Media Selection," *Journal of Marketing Research*, III (May, 1966), pp. 179–87; R. D. Buzzell, Chap. 5 in *Mathematical Models and Marketing Management*, (Boston: Graduate School of Business Administration, Harvard University, 1964); C. L. Wilson, "Use of Linear Programming to Optimize Media Schedules in Advertising," *Proceedings of the 46th National Conference of the American Marketing Association*, Henry Gomez, ed., 1963, pp. 178–91; R. L. Day, "Linear Programming in Media Selection," *Journal of Advertising Research*, II (June, 1963), pp. 40–44; J. F. Engel and M. R. Warshaw, "Allocating Advertising Dollars by Linear Programming," *Journal of Advertising Research*, IV (Sept., 1964), pp. 42–48.

pper limit of this medium L_i or until the budget is expended. If the
budget is not expended, insertions are purchased up to the limit of the
budget in the remaining media in increasing order of rated exposure
value per dollar.

The counterintuitive nature of the solution to the simple model is
argely due to the assumption that the rated exposure values are con-
tant. If the R_i are nonlinear, this conflict need not appear. Special
cases of nonlinear R_i can be solved by linear programming. The procedure is termed piecewise-linear programming and is appropriate if the
$R = f(x_i)$ function is concave (e.g., no increasing returns). This is based
upon splitting the nonlinear problem into an equivalent linear problem.[70]

Suppose that the total rated exposures relate to X_i as shown in
Fig. 3-7. This equation is not concave, but a concave piecewise linear

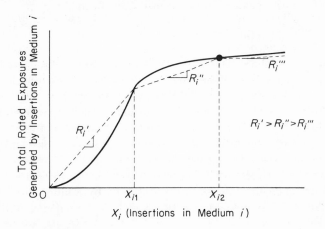

**Figure 3-7: A concave piecewise
linear approximation to a noncon-
cave response function**

approximation to this nonlinear function may be formed (as shown in
Fig. 3-7). The linear segments must form a concave function before
linear programming routines will guarantee an optimum. If the function is not concave, the solution found by the linear programming routine
will not guarantee that the global optimum has been found.

The piecewise linear equation for the response in Fig. 3-7 can be

[70] The following references discuss the piecewise extension: D. B. Brown and M. R.
Warshaw, "Media Selection by Linear Programming," *Journal of Marketing Research*,
II (Feb., 1965), pp. 83–88; M. L. Godfrey, "Media Selection by Mathematical Pro-
gramming," Talk before the Metropolitan New York Chapter of the Institute of
Management Sciences, Oct. 10, 1962.

written as

$$R_i X_i = R_i' X_i' + R_i''(X_i'' - X_{i1}) + R_i'''(X_i''' - X_{i2})$$

where the following constraints must be met:

$$0 \leq X_i' \leq X_{i1}$$
$$X_{i1} < X_i'' \leq X_{i2}$$
$$X_{i2} < X_i'''$$

The ability to form these piecewise approximations to the nonlinear response function allows the problem to be solved by linear programming routines.

The scheduling aspects of the problem can be added to the linear programming models by adding a time subscript to each X_i and defining the total exposure as the sum of $R_{it} X_{it}$ over each medium i and over time t.[71] This does not, however, include the dynamic carry-over effects of replication and forgetting. A similar procedure can be used to add preliminary copy considerations to the model. The X_{it} could be subscripted by a j to reflect size or color characteristics of the insertions. Alternatively, each i could index the choice of a particular medium-copy combination. For example, X_{1t} might be a four-color, full page ad in *Life* during time t, whereas X_{2t} might be a black and white full page ad in the same magazine during time t.

The choice of criterion for the linear programming model is generally fixed as total exposure. This can be softened by adding constraints on reach, following Alec Lee's suggestion which was cited in his discussion of media selection.[72]

Another formulation of the linear programming model directed at overcoming the criterion limitations is based on setting goals for the reach and frequency for market segments and finding the media schedule which best satisfies the set of exposure goals.[73] This form of linear programming is called goal programming. It is based upon minimizing an objective function which is the weighted sum of the deviations from the set of goals. The deviations are weighted so that some goals can be given precedence over others. The constraints in this programming

---

[71] See S. Stasch, "Linear Programming and Space-Time Considerations," *Journal of Advertising Research*, IV (Dec., 1965), pp. 40–47.

[72] For an alternative method see W. I. Zangwill, "Media Selection by Decision Programming," *Journal of Advertising Research*, V (Sept., 1965), pp. 30–36.

[73] A. Charnes, W. W. Cooper, J. K. DeVoe, D. B. Learner, and W. Reinecke, "A Goal Programming Model for Media Planning," *Management Science*, XIV, No. 8 (April, 1968), pp. 423–30, and A. Charnes, W. W. Cooper, D. B. Learner, and E. F. Snow, "Note on an Application of a Goal Programming Model for Media Planning," *Management Science*, XIV, No. 8 (April, 1968), pp. 431–36.

model entail reach and frequency goals which are established for various market segments in particular time periods. The model is, of course, subject to additional constraints (e.g., budget) as in other L.P. models. The goal-programming model provides a useful extension to previous L.P. models in that it considers the distribution of the proportion of each segment which is exposed a given number of times. Thus it allows people in any segment to experience differential exposure to ads. Of course, persons in different segments may also be differentially exposed.

The model is subject to several limitations. First, the method used to consider duplication is relatively simple. Charnes et al. assume that the distributions of the proportion of the audience segment exposed to particular insertions are independent. That is, the joint frequency of a reader's exposure value to two media is the product of the frequency function of the two media (e.g. if the probability of reading *Life* is .6 and the probability of reading *Time* is .5, the probability of reading *Time* and *Life* is .3). This is a strong assumption and although it is mathematically convenient, it should be empirically validated since behaviorally there is little a priori support for the notion of independence. A second limitation of the goal programming formulation is that it does not explicitly consider the integer nature of insertions. The model uses a rounding off procedure to specify the integer number of insertions.

In addition to these theoretical limitations there is a major structural drawback of the goal programming. It is that the model is completely dependent upon the goals that are set. The model fulfills a set of exogenously defined goals, but does not maximize the effectiveness of the campaign unless the exposure goals are optimal with respect to higher order criteria such as sales and profits. Optimally determining the goal levels is not a trivial task.

Basic linear programming routines discussed in this section allow the number of insertions to be fractional. This can be theoretically overcome by integer programming.[74] However, the computational effectiveness of these algorithms is generally poor and it is not presently feasible to consider the use of integer programming for most media problems. Developments in combinatorial programming may be forthcoming that will make this procedure more feasible.

The linear programming model described in Eq. (3-44), when placed in its extended form, is basically reasonable and yields optimal media schedules. The greatest disadvantages are (1) the inability to deal with the integer nature of insertions, (2) the restrictive nature of the criterion of total exposure or deviation from exposure goals and (3) the inability to comprehend the dynamic and cumulative effects of forgetting and intermedia replication.

[74] Zangwill, op. cit.

These three limitations can be overcome by the use of other mathematical programming models.   Little and Lodish have developed a mathematical programming model called MEDIAC.[75]   The model uses sales
as the criterion for the media schedule.   The sales results of a schedule
are defined as the sum of the sales in each of a number of market segment
over a number of time periods.   The sales in each segment depend upon
the number of people in the segment, their sales potential, and the level
of advertising exposure in the segment.   That is,

$$\text{SALES} = \sum_{i=1}^{S} \sum_{t=1}^{T} n_i p_{it} f(y_{it}) \qquad (3\text{-}45)$$

where n_i = number of people in market segment i,

$\quad p_{it}$ = per capita sales potential of market segment i in time
period t,

$\quad y_{it}$ = exposure value per capita in segment i during period t,

$\quad f(y_{it})$ = proportion of the per capita sales potential that will be
gained in segment i during time period t when the exposure value per capita is y_{it}.

The function $f(y_{it})$ is taken to be a nonlinear function that exhibits diminishing returns to exposure value per capita y_{it}.

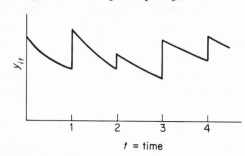

**Figure 3-8: Exposure value per
capita over time**

The per capita exposure value y_{it} is subject to change over time.   For
example, its level may increase because of further exposure to advertising.
On the other hand, past exposures are eventually forgotten, and thus the
exposure level may decrease.   A typical pattern of y_{it} over time is given
in Fig. 3-8.   The discontinuities at times 1, 3, and 4 reflect exposure of
the market segment to the company's advertising at those points in time.

---

[75] J. D. C. Little and L. M. Lodish, "A Media Selection Model and its Optimization
by Dynamic Programming," *Industrial Management Review*, VIII (Fall, 1966), pp.
15–24.

The reduction in y_{it} between periods 1 and 2 reflects forgetting of past exposure to the company's advertising. This over time accumulation and depletion of exposure is conceptually analogous to the formulations discussed earlier, which considered advertising as a depreciable investment.

The increase in the per capita exposure value y_{it} in segment i during time period t due a schedule of media insertions is given by

$$Inc = \sum_{j=1}^{M} e_j k_{ijt} x_{jt} \qquad (3\text{-}46)$$

where Inc = increase in per capita exposure value in segment i during time t,

e_j = exposure value conveyed by one exposure in vehicle j,

x_{jt} = number of insertions in media vehicle j in time period t,

k_{ijt} = exposure efficiency in segment i of an insertion in media vehicle j during time period t.

The exposure efficiency factor in Eq. (3-46) is the expected number of exposures per person produced in market segment i by one insertion in media vehicle j at time t. It is based on the seasonal trend, the media's audience in the subsegment, and the probability of a person in the subsegment being exposed to the insertion. That is,

$$k_{ijt} = h_j g_{ij} s_{jt} \qquad (3\text{-}47)$$

where h_j = probability of exposure to an ad in vehicle j, given that a person is in the audience of the vehicle,

g_{ij} = fraction of people in market segment i who are in the audience of vehicle j (average value over a year),

s_{jt} = seasonal index of audience size for vehicle j.

The efficiency (k_{ijt}), the number of insertions in the media in the period x_{it}, and the exposure value e_j determine the added exposure value due to new insertions as indicated in Eq. (3-46). The exposure value at time t is the exposure value at $t-1$ discounted for forgetting plus the added exposure value of the period t media schedule:

$$y_{it} = \alpha y_{i,t-1} + \sum_{j=1}^{M} e_j k_{ijt} x_{jt}$$

where α is the fraction of y_{it} retained from one period to the next. This exposure value per capital is a principal determinant of sales [see Eq. (3-45)] and reflects the sales effects of a media schedule. The mathematical programming problem in the MEDIAC model is to maximize the total sales over the planning period subject to budget and media restrictions. This is equivalent to profit maximization if the variable unit costs of production are assumed to be constant.   Little and Lodish have developed several computational techniques for finding solutions to the mathematical programming problem posed by the model.   Dynamic, piecewise linear, and heuristic programming have been utilized as solution techniques.

Although the Little and Lodish formulation may face computational limitations, it comes the closest to solving the general media problem. Their model includes considerations of accumulation of insertions and forgetting over time, as well as intermedia replications in target group subsegments.   This is done by making sales a function of the cumulative exposure level of target subsegments.   The number of media, the timing of the insertions, and the retention rate determine the cumulative exposure level.   The computational limit of the dynamic programming formulation of the model requires that the number of subsegments must usually be restricted to two or less.   Piecewise linear programming routines have been able to comprehend a relevant number of subsegments (e.g., 20), but the disadvantage of this technique is that it yields non-integer values of the number of insertions.   A heuristic program has been developed to include the subsegment and integer effects, and it has proved to be a very efficient method of generating solutions to the Little and Lodish model.   The heuristic procedure does not guarantee that the optimum solution has been found, but experiments have shown that the heuristic came within one per cent of the optimum in five test cases.

The greatest limitation of the Little and Lodish model discussed above is its inability to consider explicitly the duplication of media within subsegments.   This is due to the fact that exposures are summed across subsegments without explicit recognition of exposure duplication that may occur for people in the same subsegment.[76]   This limitation is not severe, however, if the number of target group subsegments is large.   The greatest advantages of the model are its ability to comprehend the relevant media considerations and its explicit linking of exposures to the higher order goals of sales and profits.

Summary of Media Selection Models

A good deal of progress has been recorded since the work of Lee, Taylor, and Burkart and the early linear programming formulations

---

[76] Little and Lodish are conducting research in an effort to overcome this limitation by considering the statistical characteristics of the exposure value distribution in market segments.   See J. D. C. Little and L. M. Lodish, "A Media Selection Calculus," *Operations Research*, forthcoming, and reproduced in D. B. Montgomery and G. L. Urban, (Eds.) *Applications of Management Science in Marketing* (Englewood Cliffs, N.J.: Prentice-Hall, Inc., 1969).

of the media problem. Models have been developed to consider the dynamic carry-over, nonlinear, noninteger, and scheduling effects in media selection. In addition, a capability has been developed to link lower level characteristics, e.g., exposure, to higher order goals such as sales and profits.

However, two factors are not satisfactorily encompassed by the present media scheduling models. The first is the discount structure that exists in media today. It is not uncommon for volume cumulative discounts to be granted to customers after a given size of purchase in a medium is made. This gives rise to a total cost curve in the given medium as depicted in Fig. 3-9. Sharp discontinuities occur at the point where

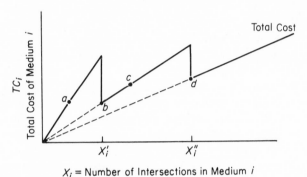

X_i = Number of Intersections in Medium *i*

Figure 3-9: Typical media discount structure

discounts are granted. This is because tne discount is a cumulative one that applies for all insertions, not just the ones in excess of a given amount. For example, in Fig. 3-9, if more than X_i' insertions are placed in medium *i*, the cost per insertion drops for all the insertions X_i'. If more than X_i'' are placed, the cost per insertion is further lowered. An examination of Fig. 3-9 will indicate that a rational business would not actually experience this cost function. For example, if the firm were moving up the cost function, when it reached point *a* it would be wise to immediately shift to point *b*, since this would entail no additional costs and more insertions would be gained. The same reasoning would lead the cost function to be adjusted by a horizontal segment between points *c* and *d*. The total cost function facing the firm placing insertions in medium *i* would be as shown in Fig. 3-10.

This discount structure has not been incorporated in any existing comprehensive media scheduling model. The difficulty revolves around the fact that the cumulative discount changes not only the cost per insertion for future placements but also the cost per insertion of all placements. One case of discounting has been encompassed in the

media model developed by Ellis.[77]   His model attacks the special case
of the static, one-period, media selection problem.   The cost discounts
are included by examining a marginal exposure/cost ratio of each insertion.   Examination of Fig. 3-9 indicates that the marginal cost per
insertion is zero between points a and b.   This means that the marginal
value/cost ratio is infinity and hence will enter the solution.   Ellis'
algorithm is based on locating the insertion N with the greatest marginal
value.   If this value is greater than the marginal value of the previous
insertion in this media, the two insertions are considered as one, and the

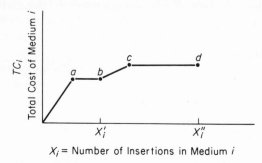

X_i = Number of Insertions in Medium i

**Figure 3-10: Firm's view of discount
structure**

average of their marginal returns is used as the measure of the combined
marginal value.   This grouping could include up to N insertions and
would be continued as long as the marginal value of the $(N - 1)$st
insertion was less than the marginal value of the Nth insertion.   The
procedure allows the discount structure to be considered, since the cumulative changes in the cost and value per insertion are explicitly considered.
Ellis' algorithm will locate the best selection of media in the one period
problem in the presence of cost discounts.

Unfortunately, there are two aspects of Ellis' model that inhibit general applications.   First, he has assumed the probability of readership
to be independent in each media, so the duplication is merely the product
of the probabilities of exposure to each of the two media.   In addition to
the limitations in considering duplication, the extension of his static
model to the dynamic problem of media scheduling is infeasible.   In the
multiperiod case, his algorithm would not be appropriate because of the
expanding complexity produced by the combinatorial problems of media
scheduling.

The inability to consider the discount structure is a significant problem
when a firm is deriving a schedule for a product line.   When multi-

[77] Ellis, *op. cit.*, pp. 422–24.

product scheduling is undertaken, the volume discounts generated may be very significant. None of the media models developed up to this time can realistically encompass the discount structure and the more complex multiproduct effects on discounts.

The second factor that has not been considered by existing models is the competitive factor. It may be meaningful to build competitive media effects into media scheduling models. For example, should a company match its competitor's insertion levels in certain media or should it try to use media not utilized by its competition? Competitive effects in media schedules might be considered by making the media response function dependent upon the media decision of competitors. Perhaps game theory notions would be relevant in encompassing competitive interdependencies.[78]

Although the discount and competitive problems of media selection remain, media selection has probably received more management science research effort than any other single marketing problem. The development followed several paths, but it can be concluded that four techniques are relevant:

1. Simulation models to evaluate the details of a given plan
2. Heuristic procedures to develop a good media schedule
3. Extended linear programming models to specify optimal plans when the exposure criteria are appropriate and dynamic carry-over effects are not important
4. Dynamic programming models to specify optimal solutions when the computational problems are not overburdening

The best technique and model will vary with the particular firm utilizing it. Having a number of the models available on an interactive time-sharing system may provide the ideal arrangement. The manager could then use his intuition and combinations of the models to solve the media selection problem.

SPECIFICATION OF COPY AND FORMAT

The solution to the media problem is a schedule of insertions in various media. The copy to be used in these insertions must be deter-

---

[78] For an approach in an analogous context see the discussion of Baligh and Richartz in Chap. 5.

mined. Copy is made up of two parts—content and format. The content refers to what the insertion communicates to the viewer. Content includes the design of the photographic, artistic, and written sections of the insertion. This will be directly related to the appeals selected earlier in the decision hierarchy. In fact, the appeals decision probably was made with some preliminary copy content in mind. The problem is how to design the final copy content. Although statistical techniques can be useful in testing alternate copy content, the essential problem of design is a creative one. Buzzell has reported that the quality of the message content and the presentation (as measured by Schwerin) are important factors in explaining changes in market share.[79]

With the content in mind, the detailed format decision must be made. The format is concerned with the physical details of the insertion such as size, color, bleed (white page margins), and exact positioning in media (e.g., time of day for television insertion). When the media problem is solved as outlined in the last section, a preliminary specification of copy has been determined. This is necessary because the number of insertions X_{ijt} referred not only to a particular media i and time t but also to a copy parameter j. This parameter could be page size or use of color in the case of magazine media. These parameters refer to the preliminary format of the copy. A number of other format characteristics must be specified. In magazines, for instance, the number of colors to be used, position in the magazine, the use of the left or right page, headline layout, and use of bleed must be determined.

The format variables should be determined so as to present the content or appeal in the most effective way. The over-all copy effectiveness will be related to the effect it has on the buyer's attitudes and predisposition to purchase the product. The effect can be maximized by developing the best copy possible and making sure it is seen. This second function is partially dependent upon the format of the insertion. The format should be designed to attract the attention of the reader so that full impact of the copy appeal will be felt. The attracting power

[79] R. D. Buzzell, "Predicting Short-Term Changes in Market Strategy as a Function of Advertising Strategy," *Journal of Marketing Research*, I (Aug., 1964), pp. 27–31. This article stimulated considerable controversy, which is contained in the following comments and replies:

J. E. Fothergill and A. S. C. Ehrenberg, "The Schwerin Analyses of Advertising Effectiveness," *Journal of Marketing Research*, II (Aug., 1965), pp. 298–306, and "Concluding Comments on the Schwerin Analyses of Advertising Effectiveness," *Journal of Marketing Research*, II (Nov., 1965), pp. 413–14.

R. D. Buzzell, M. Kolin, and M. P. Murphy, "Television Commercial Test Scores and Short-Term Changes in Market Shares," *Journal of Marketing Research*, II (Aug., 1965), pp. 307–13.

M. P. Murphy and R. D. Buzzell, "A Further Clarification," *Journal of Marketing Research*, II (Nov., 1965), pp. 415–16.

of the insertion could be measured by the number of times an ad is seen. If the parameters of format can be linked to the attention generating power of the ad, decisions concerning the best format may be made. This linking has been attempted by regressions of the attention-gathering power of an ad to format parameters. Twedt used the parameters of size of insertion, size of illustration, and number of colors in a regression of readership results of 137 advertisements in *The American Builder*.[80] These three variables accounted for about fifty per cent of the variation in the criterion variable of ad readership. Yamanaka did a similar study for Japanese newspapers and explained eighty per cent of the variance in readership.[81] The most comprehensive format regression study has been the one carried out by Diamond.[82] The regression is based on Starch readership data and about one thousand *Life* magazine advertisements. The regression model was tested on an additional 43 ads, and it was found to explain about seventy per cent of the variance in the number of people seeing (noting) the ad. The author then placed the model on an on-line time-sharing computer system. The interactive model called ADFORS (*AD*vertisement *FOR*mat *S*election) can be used to estimate Starch scores for a particular advertisement or to design a format for a given ad. In the design mode ADFORS considers the readership and cost aspects in selecting the best format. These regression approaches are based upon an available store of past readership data. For media where data are available, the regression model can help design formats that will be most effective in calling attention to the insertion's appeal.

A word is in order on the interaction between advertisement format decision aids such as ADFORS and the media models discussed in the section on "Specification of the Media Schedule." Procedures such as ADFORS and the other regression studies are capable of supplying necessary market response input to the media models. For example, the effectiveness coefficients for black and white and for color ads may be estimated, as well as the effectiveness of various sizes (half page, full page, three-page gatefold, etc.). These coefficients then enter the media model as input data. Thus the decision hierarchy is not an inviolable sequence, but rather is a useful framework in which to discuss advertising decisions.

[80] D. W. Twedt, "A Multiple Factor Analysis of Advertising Readership," *Journal of Applied Psychology*, XXXVI (June, 1952), pp. 207–15.

[81] J. Yamanaka, "A Method of Prediction of Readership Score," *Journal of Advertising Research*, II (March, 1962), pp. 18–23.

[82] D. S. Diamond, "A Quantitative Approach to Magazine Advertisement Format Selection," Sloan School Working Paper No. 277–67 and *Journal of Marketing Research* (forthcoming). This paper is reproduced in D. B. Montgomery and G. L. Urban, *Applications of Management Science in Marketing* (Englewood Cliffs, N.J.: Prentice-Hall, Inc., 1969).

A NOTE ON OTHER PROMOTIONS

This chapter has directed itself exclusively to the subject of advertising, but advertising is only one of the elements in the total promotional mix. Personal selling is an element of the mix and is considered in Chap. 6. Price-deal promotions are considered in Chap. 4. Promotions such as service, credit, and guarantee are considered as product variables and are discussed in Chap. 7.

Packaging is not considered elsewhere, but the tools outlined in this chapter are directly applicable to the packaging decision. The total allocation of funds to packaging must be determined in a manner similar to the advertising budget. It could be considered as a separate budget or as one media channel in the allocation of the combined advertising and packaging budget. Package design is similar to selection of advertising appeals and copy specification. The design is constrained, however, by the physical package characteristics necessary for product protection. If the package itself has physical utility (e.g., aerosol cans) the package should be considered an integral product characteristic.

Point of purchase displays are another promotional technique. They may also be analyzed by considering them as media in the advertising decision. Similarly, the distribution of free samples could be considered a media channel with a particular copy. The copy is the sample physical good. The relative effectiveness of these promotions should be reflected in the funds allocated to them in the media selection decision.

SUMMARY OF MANAGEMENT SCIENCE AND ADVERTISING DECISIONS

In this chapter, advertising decisions have been analyzed within a hierarchical framework. The first decision was to identify advertising goals, objectives, and measurement criteria. The profit generated by advertising was suggested as the ultimate goal, but the necessity of transforming this goal into measurable criteria was recognized. The measurable criteria of reach, frequency, awareness, or attitudes are suitable subgoals, if they are determined by linking them to sales and the ultimate goal of long-run profit maximization. With the profit goal in mind, the next step is to create the best appeals for the advertising. Creativity is essential at this step. Management science procedures can help evaluate the relative effectiveness of appeals, and can assist in determining the level of resources to allocate to the creative process. With the best appeal in mind, the next decision is to determine the best advertising budget by considering sales response and competitive effects of advertising.

After the advertising budget has been specified, it must be allocated among the possible media. The determination of the best media schedule can be approached by simulation, heuristic programming, extended linear programming, and dynamic programming models. The criterion used for allocation may be related to exposure, awareness, or sales. In each case, the criterion must be implicitly or explicitly related to the over-all goal of profit maximization. After the media schedule has been specified, the detailed copy and format decision must be made. Regression models and interactive computer-aided format models were discussed as decision aids at this stage.

It can be anticipated that future research will widen the role of management science in advertising. Research is needed to gain a better understanding of the advertising process. It is especially important to link the more measurable criteria to higher order goals. If a more exact understanding of relationships can be identified, management science will yield more meaningful advertising recommendations.

The second area of research is in the area of model building. More comprehensive models of budget and media decisions should be built. In particular, dynamic and competitive effects should be more clearly integrated into the decision frameworks. Attention should also be directed at developing a series of advertising models that can be placed in a model bank. These models should be designed to give the user the desired recommendations or information at a minimum cost. For example, a media simulation may be appropriate for detailed evaluations, while a piecewise linear programming model might be used to generate a rough specification of the best media schedule.

Along with the development of better models, more powerful solution techniques can be expected. These new techniques will remove many of the computational limitations of present models and thereby allow the models to consider more of the relevant aspects of advertising problems.

The last future development that can be expected is the availability of better data. As more companies become interested in detailed advertising information, this demand will be met. The availability of additional information should make management science models more effective in serving as tools for advertising decision makers.

4

Pricing
Decisions

INTRODUCTION

The discussion of the use of management science models to solve pricing problems begins with a discussion of pricing goals and heuristic pricing decision rules. Attention is then focused upon a statement of the classical economic pricing model. This statement is based on calculus, so multivariate extensions can be made. The place of price in the total marketing program will then be discussed along two dimensions. The first is the place of price in the mix of controllable marketing variables, and the second is the multiproduct nature of product line pricing. After normative models have been proposed, competitive effects and some of the problems of measuring demand relationships will be analyzed. In this demand measurement section, techniques are discussed that are relevant not only to pricing response but also to advertising and other marketing variables. The chapter will close with a statement of the state of the art of management science in pricing decisions.

Pricing Goals

Price determination has long been a primary concern of economists. At the microeconomic level, their analysis has centered around the use of price to achieve profit maximization under various market structures. In contrast to theory, actual pricing decisions in general have not been based

158

)n the pure marginal economic principles.[1]   For example, a common pric-
ng procedure has been the use of break-even analysis.   Break-even anal-
sis is based on testing a proposed price to determine how much must be
old before the firm will break even (i.e., profit = 0).   The equation for
he break-even condition is

$$TR - TC = 0 \qquad\qquad (4\text{-}1)$$

or

$$p \cdot q_b - (c \cdot q_b + FC) = 0$$

Solving gives

$$q_b = \frac{FC}{(p - c)}$$

where TR = total revenue,
$\quad\ TC$ = total cost,
$\qquad p$ = price to be tested,
$\qquad c$ = variable unit cost,
$\qquad q_b$ = quantity required to break even,
$\quad FC$ = fixed cost.

When the break-even quantity has been calculated, it is compared to
the forecast of sales.   If the forecasted sales volume exceeds the break-
even sales by a "satisfactory" margin, the price is accepted.   The satisfactory margin is set by managers to reflect the buffer needed in view of
the risks present in the market and their forecast of demand.   This simple
model is often preferred by firms because of its ease in use and its implicit
consideration of risk.   It might be noted that these risk aspects are not
included in the basic economic model; it is not surprising, therefore, to
find that firms have accepted the break-even approach.

Other methods of pricing have been developed to reflect other goal
structures.   In some firms, prices are set to yield a target rate of return
on investment.   The price level is set so that the profits generated by an
efficient long-run average rate of plant utilization are such as to produce
a desired, or target, return on investment.   The goal here is production
based on and aimed at a minimum financial objective.   Another common
goal is based on the competitive market structure.   Some firms set prices
to increase or maintain market share.   The use of market share as a
short-run goal is not necessarily consistent with long-run profit maximization, and it represents a departure from the economic model.   In oligopolistic market structures, pricing goals may be to stabilize industry
prices or to price to meet competition.

[1] R. F. Lanzillotti, "Pricing Objectives in Large Companies," *American Economic Review*, XLVIII (Dec., 1958), pp. 921–40.

The goals of pricing seem to be based on three considerations: (1) risk (2) profit, and (3) competition. These goals reflect a knowledge that the pricing decision is a complex one and that some goal structure appropriate to the long-run success of the firm should be selected. Firms would probably like to have the ability simultaneously to include the profit, risk and competitive effects of pricing within the framework of the long-run goal of profit maximization. Before examining management science's possible normative contributions to this area, some of the descriptive modeling efforts in the area of pricing will be examined. This exposure to "real world" procedures will supply a healthy background for the normative model building approaches outlined in later sections of this chapter.

Heuristic Approaches to the Pricing Decision

The overwhelming complexity of the pricing decision faced by most businessmen has forced them to develop useful and satisfactory rules of thumb, or heuristics, for determining prices. The most commonly used heuristic is to price at some percentage above cost, but other, more elaborate heuristics are in use. Management scientists have constructed descriptive models of the decision procedure in attempts to identify the heuristics used by executives. If the model is accurate in replicating and predicting the executive's price decisions, the model is assumed to be a valid representation of the decision maker's pricing heuristics. Although descriptive models seem to be a useful and necessary first step, attention should ultimately be given to normative procedures that build upon these descriptive models.

The pioneering management science work in identifying heuristic pricing procedures was carried out by Cyert, March, and Moore, who developed a descriptive model of pricing behavior in a department store.[2] The heuristic procedure followed by the store in determining prices was based on two goals: a sales volume goal and a markup objective. These are not compatible goals. A high markup may mean less sales volume, and higher sales may be obtained by a lower markup. These goals were not aimed at the normative criterion of profit maximization but were heuristic goals that yielded satisfactory results.

In the department store studies by Cyert, March, and Moore, pricing was carried out in three stages: (1) normal pricing, (2) sales pricing, and (3) markdown pricing. The regular prices were determined by

[2] R. M. Cyert and J. G. March, *A Behavioral Theory of the Firm* (Englewood Cliffs, N.J.: Prentice-Hall, Inc., 1963), pp. 128–48.

applying a standard industry margin or by pricing at the manufacturer's suggested price level. The normal pricing heuristic reflected a tacit agreement between competitors to establish similar initial prices.

Sale pricing was used when the sales volume goal was not being achieved. Two heuristic rules were used in sale pricing:

1. If the normal price falls at one of the levels listed below, establish the indicated sale price.

Normal Price	Sale Price
1.00	0.85
1.95	1.65
2.50	2.10
2.95	2.45
3.50	2.90
3.95	3.30
4.95	3.90
5.00	3.90

2. (a) Reduce normal prices not encompassed by rule 1 by at least 15 per cent if the normal price is less than or equal to three dollars and by at least $16\frac{2}{3}$ per cent if the normal price is greater than three dollars.

(b) All sale prices must end in a 0 or 5.

(c) No sale price can fall at a normal price line value.

(d) Always choose .90 over .85 in the cents part of the price.

With these rules a logical flow diagram and mathematical model were used to describe the complete heuristic routine. If sale pricing did not successfully achieve the sales volume goal, a markdown procedure for pricing was initiated.[3] The general pricing rule was to reduce the price by at least $\frac{1}{3}$ and end the price with .85.

The hypothesized models were tested for validity. In the test cases the models correctly predicted to the penny 188 out of 197 of the normal prices, 36 out of 58 sale prices, and 140 out of 159 markdown prices. These test results indicated that the model was a good description of the actual pricing procedure used in that particular department store. The procedure was not a normative one of profit maximization, but rather one made up of a number of heuristic rules that had produced satisfactory results in the past.

Morgenroth and Howard conducted another study of a heuristic

---

[3] See Cyert, March, and Moore, *op. cit.*, for a flow diagram of the sale-pricing and markdown procedure.

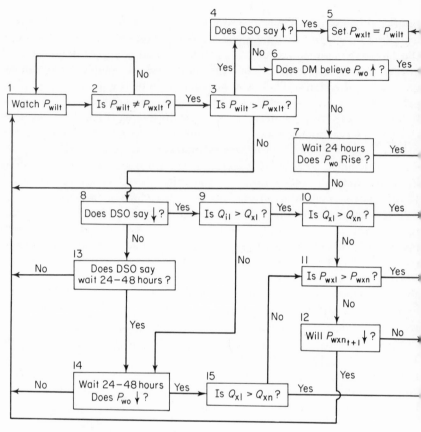

Symbols:

P = price
w = wholesale
x = our company
o = other major competitors in local market
i = initiator
t = time, at present
Q = quantity, i.e., sales volume in physical terms
l = local market wherein price change is being considered
n = nearby market with funnel influences
DSO = District Sales Office (District Sales Manager)
↑ = raise price
↓ = drop price
DM = decision maker

Figure 4-1: Descriptive model of a particular pricing decision process

Source: John A. Howard and William M. Morgenroth, "Information Processing Model of Executive Decisions," *Management Science, 14* (March 1968), p. 419. By permission of the publisher and authors.

pricing procedure.[4] They describe a rather simple procedure followed by a large company facing an oligopolistic market structure. Although the model is simple, executives of the firm had felt prior to the model development that their pricing procedure was a complex and unprogrammable decision. The basic heuristic rule of the model is to follow price increases by competitors if the district sales office agrees, and to follow competitive price decreases if sales decrease. Figure 4-1 presents the descriptive pricing model. The procedure begins by watching the price of major wholesalers in a local market (see box 1). If the price does not change, no action is taken. If the price increases, it is followed if the district sales office agrees to the price change (see boxes 3, 4, 5). If the district sales office disagrees, the price decision maker can overrule the district sales office and raise the price if he thinks other competitors will increase their prices (see boxes 3, 4, 6, 5). If the decision maker feels others will not raise their price, a holding period is enforced (see box 7) and the price is increased if other competitors' prices rise. If the prices do not increase, no action is taken (return to box 1). In the case where the initial competitive price decreases, the district sales office is contacted (boxes 2, 8, 13), competitors' sales are observed (box 9), waiting periods are utilized (box 14), and procedures are instituted to prevent the price cut from spreading to adjacent areas (boxes 15, 10, 11, 12). Tests of the model showed that its structure and decision output closely corresponded with 31 actual decisions. Thus, Morgenroth and Howard's model appears to be a reasonable description of the heuristic procedure used by the company.

The Pricing Problem

The firm would like to set prices at a level that will achieve long-run success. For the purpose of developing normative management science models, the long-run goal will be specified as profit maximization. Explicit recognition must be made of the complexities that surround the setting of prices to achieve this goal. It should be recognized that price is only one of the variables which the company controls to achieve long-run profits. The multivariate nature of the environment of price decisions must be considered along with the risk and competitive aspects of pricing.

[4] W. M. Morgenroth, "A Method for Understanding Price Determinants," *Journal of Marketing Research*, I (Aug., 1964), pp. 17–27, and J. A. Howard and W. M. Morgenroth, "Information Processing Model of Executive Decisions," *Management Science: Theory*, XIV, No. 7 (March, 1968), pp. 416–428. This reading is reprinted in D. B. Montgomery and G. L. Urban, eds., *Applications of Management Science in Marketing* (Englewood Cliffs, N.J.: Prentice-Hall, Inc., 1969).

THE CLASSICAL ECONOMIC
MODEL

The classical economic model of price determination is a univariate model linking price and quantity sold.   Under certain assumptions, the classical model may be solved to yield the price that will maximize profits to the firm.   Suppose that

$$q = F(p) \tag{4-2}$$

$$TC = C(q) + FC \tag{4-3}$$

$$TR = p \cdot q \tag{4-4}$$

where q = quantity sold,
   p = price per unit,
   TC = total costs,
   $C(q)$ = total variable cost as a function of q,
   FC = fixed costs,
   TR = total revenue from the sale for q units at a price of p per unit.

and it is assumed that the functions $F(p)$ and $C(q)$ are at least twice differentiable with respect to p and q, respectively.   If Eq. (4-2) can be solved for p in terms of q, then this inverse function of $F(p)$ will be denoted by

$$p = f(q) \tag{4-5}$$

If the product is offered at price p, Eq. (4-2) indicates that an amount $q = F(p)$ will be sold.   Conversely, one may use Eq. (4-5) to determine the selling price of q units of the product.   For estimation purposes in an empirical situation, Eqs. (4-2) and (4-5) are not strictly interchangeable, since a regression of price on quantity and a regression of quantity on price do not in general produce the same response estimates when applied to the same data base.

The criterion for setting price in this classic model is to maximize profits.   Using the definition of profit and Eqs. (4-3), (4-4), and (4-5), we can express the profit function as

$$Pr = TR - TC = p \cdot q - C(q) - FC = [f(q)]q - C(q) - FC$$

$$= R(q) - C(q) - FC \tag{4-6}$$

where $R(q) = [f(q)]q = p \cdot q = TR$ = total revenue as a function of q.

he first order optimality condition then is

$$\frac{dPr}{dq} = \frac{dR(q)}{dq} - \frac{dC(q)}{dq} = 0 \tag{4-7}$$

where $\dfrac{dR(q)}{dq}$ = the marginal revenue generated by the qth unit of sales,

$\dfrac{dC(q)}{dq}$ = the marginal cost of the qth unit.

'he well-known rule that marginal revenue equals marginal cost for rofit maximization is clear from Eq. (4-7). The solution of Eq. (4-7) ill locate the profit maximizing quantity (q^*). The optimum price

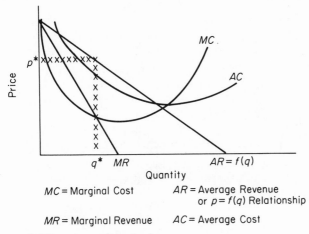

MC = Marginal Cost   AR = Average Revenue
or $p = f(q)$ Relationship

MR = Marginal Revenue   AC = Average Cost

Figure 4-2: Economic model of price determination

p^*) is then found from Eq. (4-5) with $p^* = f(q^*)$. A second-order test of ptimality is necessary to ascertain that a maximum rather than a ninimum has been located.[5] The condition is

$$\frac{d^2R(q)}{dq^2} - \frac{d^2C(q)}{dq^2} < 0 \tag{4-8}$$

t $q = q^*$. The calculus conditions are displayed for a monopoly market tructure in Fig. 4-2. The first-order condition requires that marginal

---

[5] This is especially important if the demand function $q = F(p)$ is not simple, such s in the case when quality is judged by the price level itself. These kinds of psycho-ogical pricing phenomena can cause the demand function to be discontinuous or to ave a positive slope.

cost MC be equal to marginal revenue MR, and the second-order condition requires that the slope of the marginal cost function be greater than the slope of the marginal revenue curve. The intersection of the marginal cost and marginal revenue curves determines the optimum quantity q^*. The optimum price corresponding to q^* is found by the average revenue relationship $[p = f(q)]$. This price maximizes the firm's profit, given the demand and cost functions Eqs. (4-2) and (4-3), if it is assumed that price is the only relevant variable.

PRICE AND THE FIRM'S TOTAL MARKETING PLAN

There are two major aspects of the interaction between price and the firm's total marketing plan: (1) price as an element in the marketing mix and (2) demand interdependencies within the firm's product line. In the first case, the price level a firm sets is not the only element in its marketing mix. The expenditures for personal selling, distribution, and promotion interact with price. For example, high expenditures on these three variables may enable a firm to charge higher prices to maximize profit as a function of price. Thus, the optimum level of price requires consideration of the interrelation between all the controllable variables in the firm's total marketing mix. Second, product complementarity or substitutability will also influence the optimum price levels for the multiproduct firm.

Price and Advertising in the Marketing Mix

From a normative standpoint, the firm should consider the interactions between its advertising and pricing decisions. For example, a high price and a large advertising expenditure may be as effective as a low price and a small advertising expenditure. Table 4-1 presents a hypothetical price and advertising marketing program and the associated sales and profits. It is important to note that the best price level is dependent upon the advertising level chosen. With no advertising expenditures, the best price ($55) yields a profit of $12,500. If an advertising level of $40,000 were established, an examination of the profit tabulation indicates that the best price would be $60. This marketing mix yields a profit of $20,000. Table 4-1 also indicates the effects of the advertising level of $8100. At this level, the best profit is $24,650. This mix is better than the price of $60 with $40,000 spent

or advertising. This example indicates the interaction between the
variables of price and advertising. Marketing decisions should include
considerations of such marketing mix effects.

**TABLE 4-1: Hypothetical Market-
ing Mix Effects**

Price	Advertising	Sales	Total Revenue	Total Cost	Fixed Cost	Profit
40	0	6,000	240,000	60,000	190,000	−10,000
50	0	5,000	250,000	50,000	190,000	10,000
55	0	4,500	247,500	45,000	190,000	12,500
60	0	4,000	240,000	40,000	190,000	10,000
65	0	3,500	227,500	35,000	190,000	2,500
70	0	3,000	210,000	30,000	190,000	−10,000
40	8,100	6,450	258,000	72,000	190,000	−4,600
50	8,100	5,450	272,500	62,600	190,000	19,900
55	8,100	4,950	272,250	57,500	190,000	24,650
60	8,100	4,450	267,000	52,600	190,000	24,400
65	8,100	3,950	256,750	47,600	190,000	19,150
70	8,100	3,450	241,300	42,600	190,000	8,700
40	40,000	7,000	280,000	110,000	190,000	−20,000
50	40,000	6,000	300,000	100,000	190,000	10,000
55	40,000	5,500	302,500	95,000	190,000	17,500
60	40,000	5,000	300,000	90,000	190,000	20,000
65	40,000	4,500	292,500	85,000	190,000	17,500
70	40,000	4,000	280,000	80,000	190,000	10,000

Determination of the optimum price and advertising combination is a
problem in multivariate optimization.[6] The general profit equation is

$$Pr = p \cdot q - C(q) - A - FC$$
$$= p \cdot F(p, A) - C[F(p, A)] - A - FC$$
$$= R(p, A) - \hat{C}(p, A) - A - FC \qquad (4-9)$$

where Pr = profit,
$q = F(p, A)$ = quantity sold,
p = price per unit,
A = advertising expenditures,
$C = C(q)$ = total variable costs,
FC = fixed costs,
$R(p, A) = p \cdot F(p, A)$ = total revenue at price p and advertising expenditure A,
$\hat{C} = C[F(p, A)]$ = total variable costs at price p and
advertising expenditure A.

[6] See P. Kotler, "Marketing Mix Decisions for New Products," *Journal of Marketing Research*, I (Feb., 1964), pp. 43–49, for an example.

If the functions can be identified, the maximum profit conditions may be specified by the application of multivariate calculus. For example the functions in Table 4-1 can be explicitly identified. The sales function is

$$q = 10,000 + 5A^{0.5} - 100p \qquad (4\text{-}10)$$

and the cost function is

$$TC = 10q + A + 190,000$$
$$= (100,000 + 50A^{0.5} - 1,000p) + A + 190,000 \qquad (4\text{-}11)$$

The profit equation for Table 4-1 is

$$Pr = p \cdot q - TC = 10,000p + 5pA^{0.5} - 100p^2 - 290,000$$
$$- 50A^{0.5} + 1,000p - A \qquad (4\text{-}12)$$

Given differentiable sales and cost functions, an optimum may be identified by differentiating Eq. (4-9) with respect to p and A to yield the following two equations:

$$\frac{\partial Pr}{\partial p} = \frac{\partial R(p, A)}{\partial p} - \frac{\partial \hat{C}(p, A)}{\partial p} = 0 \qquad (4\text{-}13)$$

$$\frac{\partial Pr}{\partial A} = \frac{\partial R(p, A)}{\partial A} - \frac{\partial \hat{C}(p, A)}{\partial A} - 1 = 0 \qquad (4\text{-}14)$$

If these equations can be solved simultaneously, the solutions will identify the points (p, A) that may maximize profits. The points specified may include maximums, minimums, or flat points of the function. To identify the maximum point or points, second-order conditions must be checked. These second-order conditions assure that the curvature of the function is strictly concave (i.e., decreasing returns) at the point (p, A).

For a two-variable problem, the sufficiency conditions for relative maximum profit are

$$\frac{\partial^2 Pr}{\partial p^2} < 0 \qquad (4\text{-}15)$$

$$\begin{vmatrix} \dfrac{\partial^2 Pr}{\partial p^2} & \dfrac{\partial^2 Pr}{\partial p\,\partial A} \\[2mm] \dfrac{\partial^2 Pr}{\partial A\,\partial p} & \dfrac{\partial^2 Pr}{\partial A^2} \end{vmatrix} > 0 \qquad (4\text{-}16)$$

where Eq. (4-16) is a determinant, and the condition can be restated as

$$\left[\frac{\partial^2 Pr}{\partial p^2} \cdot \frac{\partial^2 Pr}{\partial A^2} - \frac{\partial^2 Pr}{\partial A\,\partial p} \cdot \frac{\partial^2 Pr}{\partial p\,\partial A} \right] > 0 \qquad (4\text{-}17)$$

'he points found by the solution of Eqs. (4-13) and (4-14) must be
ubstituted in Eqs. (4-15) and (4-16) to see if they satisfy the sufficiency
onditions. When more than one point satisfies the necessary and suffi-
ient conditions, this reflects the occurrence of relative maxima. The
reatest relative maximum is called the maximum maximorum and may
·e located by substituting the relative maximum points (p, A) into the
·rofit Eq. (4-9) and then selecting the point (p^*, A^*) producing the
reatest profit.

This procedure can be applied to the example developed in Table 4-1
nd described by Eqs. (4-10), (4-11), and (4-12). The necessary condi-
ions for the maximum are

$$\frac{\partial Pr}{\partial p} = 10{,}000 + 5A^{0.5} - 200p + 1000 = 0$$

$$\frac{\partial Pr}{\partial A} = 2.5pA^{-0.5} - 25A^{-0.5} - 1 = 0$$

;olving these equations simultaneously yields the unique solution of

$$p^* = 58$$
$$A^* = 14{,}400$$

The profit associated with this marketing mix is $26,000. This is
;reater than any of the values depicted in Table 4-1. A check of the
·ufficiency conditions will prove this to be the optimum marketing mix.

$$\frac{\partial Pr}{\partial p^2} = -200 \qquad\qquad (4\text{-}19)$$

$$\frac{\partial Pr}{\partial p\,\partial A} = 2.5A^{-0.5}$$

$$\frac{\partial Pr}{\partial A^2} = -1.25pA^{-1.5} + 12.5A^{-1.5}$$

$$\frac{\partial Pr}{\partial A\,\partial p} = 2.5A^{-0.5}$$

First, Eq. (4-15) indicates that $\partial^2 Pr/\partial p^2$ must be less than zero. In
this example, $\partial^2 Pr/\partial p^2 = -200$, so this part of the test is satisfied.
The second part of the test is based on the value of the determinant in
Eq. (4-17). In the example, the determinant obtained by substituting
the proposed optimum values in the second-order differentials Eq. (4-19)

yields the determinant

$$\begin{vmatrix} -200 & 2.5A^{-0.5} \\ 2.5A^{-0.5} & (-1.25pA^{-1.5} + 12.5A^{-1.5}) \end{vmatrix}$$

$$= \begin{vmatrix} -200 & 2.5(14{,}400)^{-0.5} \\ 2.5(14{,}400)^{-0.5} & [-1.25(58)(14{,}400)^{-1.5} + 12.5(14{,}400)^{-1.5}] \end{vmatrix}$$

The value of this determinant is calculated by Eq. (4-17) and is 0.017 Since this value is greater than zero, the sufficiency test is complete and the point $p^* = 58$ and $A^* = 14{,}400$ is the unique maximum of the profit equation (4-12).

This two-variable maximization was outlined under the assumption that competition is exogenous or behaves in some expected fashion that underlies the input functions. The only way the model as outlined above could include dynamic competitive effects is to constrain the prices to be considered. Competitive retaliation might be considered as constraining the range of possible prices. In addition to competitive constraints, other price restrictions may be present. Government regulation or pressures may limit the freedom to establish prices; the financial policies of the firm may limit advertising expenditure. If such constraints are present, the calculus model will have to be expanded by Lagrangean analysis.[7] The constraints would be placed into Lagrangean forms so that the problem could then be considered an unconstrained maximization. If the price must be less than a value L, $p \leq L$, the equality form of the constraint would be $p + S^2 = L$, where S is a new unconstrained slack variable. S^2 is used in the equation so that S may take on both positive and negative values (i.e., S is unconstrained) while maintaining the inequality. The Lagrangean form of the constraint is

$$p + S^2 - L = 0 \qquad (4\text{-}20)$$

and the function to be maximized is

$$Pr(p, A) + \lambda(p + S^2 - L) \qquad (4\text{-}21)$$

where λ is termed the Lagrange multiplier. The unconstrained maximization of Eq. (4-21) with respect to p, A, S^2, and λ will result in the values of p and A that will yield the maximum profit subject to the price constraint. Additional constraints may be handled in a similar fashion by adding one slack variable and one Lagrange multiplier per constraint. A slack variable S^2 is not required if the constraint is already an equality.

In addition to advertising effects, price determination should also

[7] See C. R. Carr and C. W. Howe, *Quantitative Decision Procedures in Management and Economics* (New York: McGraw-Hill Book Company, 1964), pp. 248–52.

flect price interaction with other elements of the marketing mix.
hannels of distribution, for example, may affect price decisions. The
rice established for middlemen has to reflect the expected functions
f the middleman and his policies in setting the final retail price. Price
lso interacts with personal selling intensity. These additional market-
g mix aspects will be considered in the product decisions chapter.

Pricing Decisions and the Product Line

The interaction between pricing decisions and the total marketing
rogram appears in the area of marketing mix decisions, but additional
omplexities may have to be considered when the firm offers more than
ne product. In this case, interactions between the pricing decisions
or each product may be present.

The multiproduct nature of most firms makes consideration of product
nterdependency an important aspect of pricing. This further complicates
he pricing decision whenever there are significant complementarity or
ubstitution effects within the firm's product line. Complementarity is
positive demand interaction between two products in the firm's product
ne. That is, as demand increases (decreases) for one product, it is
kely to increase (decrease) for the other. An example would be the
omplementarity between Sears Roebuck's appliances and their appliance
ervice contracts. Increased sales of appliances are likely to be asso-
iated with increased sales of the corresponding service contracts. Sub-
titution effects in the product line occur whenever the firm's products
ompete with each other. The automobile manufacturers provide a
rime example here. A customer who buys a Mustang is not likely to
e a good prospect for a Galaxy in the near future, and vice versa.
ince the firm has as its over-all goal the maximization of profits across
he entire product line, complementarity and substitution effects are
mportant aspects of the pricing of individual products in the line.

If these interdependencies could be identified in a mathematical form,
he demand equation could be adjusted to reflect this fact. The sales
unction cited in the previous example might be adjusted to reflect inter-
ctions by adding an interaction effect. For example, the equation
night be changed from

$$q_1 = 10,000 + 5A^{0.5} - 100p_1$$

to

$$q_1 = 10,000 + 5A^{0.5} - 100p_1 + 10p_2 \qquad (4\text{-}22)$$

where p_1 is the price of product one and p_2 is the price of product two (the interrelated product). The new equation indicates that the sale of product one are increased as the price of product two increases. Thi is a substitution effect. It implies that as the price of product tw increases the quantity of product two sold decreases, and product one i substituted for it. In theory, finding the best price for a product in th product line is a multivariate problem that could be attacked by calculu. The general formulation then is given by[8]

$$q_1 = f_1(p_1, p_2, \ldots, p_n; A_1, A_2, \ldots, A_m) \qquad (4\text{-}23)$$

$$\cdot$$
$$\cdot$$
$$\cdot$$

$$q_n = f_n(p_1, p_2, \ldots, p_n; A_1, A_2, \ldots, A_m)$$

where p_1 = the unit price of product i ($i = 1, \ldots, n$),
A_j = cost of nonprice offer variant j ($j = 1, \ldots, m$).

The A's may be nonprice items such as advertising, personal selling inten sity, package design, etc.

The total cost to the firm of selling $q_1, q_2, \ldots, q_n$ units of its product, may be expressed in functional form as

$$C = C(q_1, q_2, \ldots, q_n; A_1, A_2, \ldots, A_m) \qquad (4\text{-}24)$$

The firm's profit function is then

$$Pr = \sum_{i=1}^{n} p_i q_i - C \qquad (4\text{-}25)$$

To find the optimum profit, the profit function would have to be partially differentiated with respect to each variable. The differentiated equa tions, when set equal to zero and solved simultaneously, would theo retically identify the prices which satisfy the necessary conditions fo optimality. The complexity of such a set of partial differential equa tions is such that solution for the optimal price and nonprice mix for th product line is analytically intractable in all but the simplest cases Even when solutions to the necessary condition have been obtained there remains the complex problem of testing for sufficiency of each o these solutions. Thus this multiproduct, total marketing mix form o model would seem to have its greatest use as a framework for analyzing broad marketing and policy implications.

---

[8] See B. R. Holdren, *The Structure of a Retail Market and the Market Behavior o Retail Units* (Englewood Cliffs, N.J.: Prentice-Hall, Inc., 1960), pp. 125–33 for a mor detailed analysis of this formulation.

An empirical example of product line interdependency has been ana-
zed by Urban.[9] He formulated a demand equation that was a function
' the prices and promotional variables of the other products in the
roduct line. The interdependent demand equation for each of three
roducts in the subject firm's line was of the form

$$q_1 = a_1 P_{1I}^{EPI1} F_{1I}^{EFI1} P_{2I}^{CP12} F_{2I}^{CF12} P_{3I}^{CP13} F_{3I}^{CF13} (MS_1) \qquad (4\text{-}26)$$

where q_1 = brand sales of product one ("our" brand),

a_1 = constant,

P_{jI} = industry average price for product j,

$EPI1$ = industry price elasticity for product one

$$= \frac{\partial q_1}{q_1} \bigg/ \frac{\partial P_{1I}}{P_{1I}},$$

F_{jI} = industry total number of package facings on the
store shelf for product j,

$EFI1$ = industry shelf facing elasticity for product one

$$= \frac{\partial q_1}{q_1} \bigg/ \frac{\partial F_{1I}}{F_{1I}}$$

$CPjM$ = cross price elasticity between product j and M,
$j \neq M$

$$= \frac{\partial q_j}{q_j} \bigg/ \frac{\partial P_{MI}}{P_{MI}},$$

$CFjM$ = cross shelf facing elasticity between product j and
M, $j \neq M$

$$= \frac{\partial q_j}{q_j} \bigg/ \frac{\partial F_{MI}}{F_{MI}}$$

MS_1 = observed brand share of our brand in industry one
(see Chap. 7 for more detail concerning this term).

The exponents in this form are the direct and cross elasticities with
espect to the decision variables. The cross price elasticity represents
he proportional change in the quantity of product j that results from a
roportionate change in the price of product M. This form could be
xtended to other variables by adding the price or promotion levels of
ther products to the chain, each raised to the appropriate cross elas-
icity, or by adding promotional variables other than the number of
helf-facings.

The elasticities and cross elasticities in Eq. (4-26) were estimated by

---

[9] G. L. Urban, "A Mathematical Modeling Approach to Product Line Decisions,"
Journal of Marketing Research (forthcoming, February 1969). This paper is repro-
uced in D. B. Montgomery and G. L. Urban (eds.) *Applications of Management in
Marketing* (Englewood Cliffs, N.J.: Prentice-Hall, Inc., 1969).

a linear regression of the log of observed industry sales (q_1/MS_1) an the log of the price and facing observations. The data used in th analysis were 100 test market store audits of the sales, prices, and facin for all brands in three product classes of a type of frequently purchase consumer goods. The regression results are given in Table 4-2. Th

TABLE 4-2: Industry Elasticities and Cross Elasticities

	Product One $j = 1$	Product Two $j = 2$	Product Three $j = 3$
$EPIj$	−3.525	−1.584	−1.529
	(−3.79)**	(−1.95)*	(−2.56)**
$EFIj$	−0.071	0.812	0.350
	(−0.36)	(3.9)**	(1.78)*
$CPj1$		−0.284	0.861
		(−0.30)	(0.78)
$CFj1$		−0.09	0.071
		(−0.45)	(0.31)
$CPj2$	−1.332		−0.548
	(−1.69)		(−0.59)
$CFj2$	0.936		0.475
	(4.75)**		(2.04)*
$CPj3$	−0.222	−0.324	
	(−0.43)	(−0.62)	
$CFj3$	−0.304	0.120	
	(−1.83)*	(0.74)	
R^2	0.448**	0.292**	0.252**
$F(6, 88)$	11.9	6.0	4.9

$CPiN > 0 \Rightarrow$ substitutes $CFiN > 0 \Rightarrow$ complements
$CPiN < 0 \Rightarrow$ complements $CFiN < 0 \Rightarrow$ substitutes

( ) = t statistic for regression coefficient (elasticity) for 88 degrees of freedom
  * = significant at least at the 5 per cent level—one tail test for direct elasticities and two tail for cross elasticities
 ** = significant at least at the 1 per cent level—one tail test for direct elasticities and two tail for cross elasticities

table indicates that the interactions among the three products at th industry level are primarily ones of complementarity. That is, generall the most significant cross price elasticities are negative and the cros facing elasticities are positive. But further analysis based on splittin the industry parameters into our brand (us) and its competitors (them indicated a more complex interdependency pattern. The new estima tions indicated that the "our" brands were substitutes for the "their" brands from different product classes and generally complements to "our

ands from different product classes.[10]   This is the type of product line
ituation that is most desirable.   Our products help each other and
ompete with brands of other firms in related product classes.

The estimated direct and cross elasticities were used in a model that
attempted to maximize the total product line profit for "our" firm as a
unction of the price and facings of each of our products.   After the
otal product line profit function was described [see Eq. (4-25)], an inter-
ctive on-line computer search routine was used to find the best price
nd facings level for each product.   The interactive search recommended
lower price for brand one and a higher price for brands two and three.[11]
The maximization routine recommended that the product line facing
allotment be reallocated so that product two receive more facings and
product one and three receive fewer facings.   The total product line
rofit was estimated to be increased over 50 per cent by these changes.

Two additional applications of management science to product line
ricing problems have been presented by Hess.[12]   He describes two cases
f new products replacing existing products and examines the possibility
f changing the price of the old products in an effort to increase total firm
rofit.   In one case a new product called "cheap" was replacing an old
roduct called "dear."   Both products performed equally well in service,
ut cheap was priced lower.   However, a customer would have to
undergo a one-time fixed cost to convert to cheap.   The rate of conversion
f dear buyers to cheap was linear in the first five periods of the new
roduct's life.   At this point in time there was a suggestion that the
rice of dear be changed.   The price change was measured by the price
ifferential between dear and cheap.   The response to the price differ-
ntial was estimated under the assumption that the slope of the rate of
onversion curve (the rate at which dear customers converted to cheap)
as proportional to either the price differential, the square of the price
ifferential, or the cube of the price differential.   In all three of these
ases a higher price for dear was found to yield higher total firm profits.
t was recommended that the price of the old product be increased,
ssuming that competitors would follow the price increase.

[10] An interesting asymmetric interdependency was discovered between two of our
rands.   Product three exhibited substitution effects with our brand two when brand
wo's price was changed, but product two was complementary with respect to our
rand three's price changes.   The asymmetry was statistically significant.   See
Urban, *op. cit.*

[11] If the asymmetric relationship between brands two and three is considered, the
rice of product three should be decreased for maximum profits for the product line.

[12] S. W. Hess, "The Use of Models in Marketing Timing Decision," *Operations
Research*, XV (July–Aug., 1967) pp. 720–37.   This paper is reproduced in D. B.
Montgomery and G. L. Urban (eds.), *Applications of Management Science in Marketing*
Englewood Cliffs, N.J.: Prentice-Hall, Inc., 1969).

The second case related to a new product called "modern" whic was a modified form of an old product called "ancient." Because mode had a lower price, ancient would ultimately be replaced. The proble was complicated by the fact that wholesalers and retailers held stoc of ancient and they would have to be accommodated as the lower-pric modern was introduced. Three alternatives were considered:

1. Reduce the price of ancient to modern's price at some time T and compensate the middlemen for the devaluation of their ancient inventories with free quantities of modern.
2. Recall all ancient remaining in the wholesaler and retailer channels at some time θ.
3. Do nothing and accept returns of ancient and credit middlemen at the wholesale price.

To decide which alternative to select, a model was developed to descril the sales pattern and total profit of the firm for the two products. Fe example, for the first alternative the profit is the profit generated befor the price cut (before T) plus the profit accruing after the price cu (after T) less the costs of free stocks of modern. The profit from time to time T is the profit of selling modern less the costs of returned ancien

$$\text{Profit} \Big|_0^T = \int_0^T (p' - c_v' - c_f')S_{mw}' \, dt$$
$$- \int_0^T (p + c_f - c_s)S_{wm} \, dt \quad (4\text{-}27)$$

where p' = wholesale price of modern,
c_v' = variable manufacturing cost of modern,
c_f' = freight cost for modern,
S_{mw}' = sales per month of modern to wholesalers at time t,
p = wholesale price of ancient,
c_f = freight cost for ancient,
c_s = salvage value of returned ancient,
S_{wm} = amount of ancient returned to manufacturer per month at time t.

The cost of free goods to compensate the channel members after a decreas in the price of ancient (i.e., after T) is

$$CFG = (c_v' + c_f')\alpha[I_r(T) + I_w(T)] \quad (4\text{-}28)$$

where $I_r(T)$ = inventories of ancient at retail at time T,
$I_w(T)$ = inventories of ancient at wholesale at time T,
α = units of free modern to be given per unit of ancient to equalize inventory value change.

inally, the profit after the price cut is

$$\text{Profit}\Big|_T^\infty = (p' - c_v' - c_f') \left\{ \int_T^\infty S_{mw}' \, dt \right.$$
$$\left. - \beta\alpha[I_r(T) + I_w(T)] \right\} \quad (4\text{-}29)$$

here β is the fraction of the free goods that will cannibalize future ales of modern. The β coefficient in Eq. (4-29) reflects the fact that ιe free supplies of modern may reduce the profit generating sales of ιodern that would have occurred in the future.

When Eq. (4-28) is subtracted from the sum of Eqs. (4-27) and (4-29) ιe total profit is specified as a function of the single control variable T, ιe time at which ancient's price is to be reduced to modern's price. nivariate calculus procedures yield

$$kS_{wm}(T) = S_{rc}(T) \quad (4\text{-}30)$$

s the necessary condition for maximum product line (ancient and mod-rn) profits, where the constant k is

$$k = -1 + \frac{(p + c_f - c_s)}{\alpha[\beta p' + (1 - \beta)(c_v' + c_f')]} \quad (4\text{-}31)$$

nd $S_{rc}(T)$ = sales of ancient from retailers to consumers at time T. 'he sufficient condition for maximizing profits with respect to T is given y

$$k\left[\frac{dS_{wm}(T)}{dT}\right] > \frac{dS_{rc}(T)}{dT} \quad (4\text{-}32)$$

'rom Eq. (4-30) it is seen that the best time to change ancient's price ιust come at a point in time when the sales of ancient to consumers ιst equals k times the returns of ancient from wholesalers to the manu-ιcturer. If returns from wholesalers never reach the level of $1/k$ times ales to consumers, the model indicates that ancient's price should ever be reduced. For any time T' which satisfies Eq. (4-30), the ιfficient condition Eq. (4-32) must be examined. If the rate of change ι consumer sales of ancient at this time T' is less than k times the rate f change in wholesaler's returns at time T', then T' will be the best time t which to lower ancient's price, given the goal of maximizing the product ιne profits.

The analysis of the alternative that would recall all ancient is similar ο that of the price cut, except that cost of the free goods is higher. The ιest time for recall θ is described by the same necessary condition as ̇q. (4-30), except that a different constant is present.

Using estimates of retail sales and returns of ancient from wholesalers

which were available prior to the introduction of modern, Hess applie
the calculus model to the ancient-modern case.   His prior assumptior
were that retail sales of ancient would be proportional to the outstandir
inventory and that ancient returns would increase until they becam
asymptotically proportional to the outstanding inventory within approx
mately 12 months, after which returns would be about two-thirds a
great.   These prior assumptions allowed him to examine the necessar
and sufficient conditions for maximum profit.   In the case of the price cu
alternative, he found that the best time for the cut would be ten montl
after modern's introduction.   This recommendation was important, sinc
management had considered reducing ancient's price *immediately* whe
modern was introduced.   In fact, Hess' analysis indicated that reducin
the price at introduction would have been the worst time for a price reduc
tion.   The price reduction was found to be a better alternative tha
calling back all the ancient or doing nothing, given parameter estimate
which were available prior to the introduction of modern.

Given the decision to delay a price cut based upon prior estimates, th
model suggested that the firm monitor retail sales and returns in order t
ascertain, on the basis of actual market response, when it might b
appropriate to cut ancient's price, wait and recall it later, or do nothing
Upon implementing the model's recommendation to delay a price cut
the firm was surprised to find that promotion of modern stimulated th
sales of ancient and returns never materialized.   Thus the decision t
retain ancient and not to cut its price was a good one.   The compan
still produces both products.

Both the Hess and Urban models indicate the importance of examinin
product interdependency and the effects of price and marketing variable
on this interdependency.   The area of product line decisions and market
ing variable specification is a fertile area for research.

COMPETITIVE MODEL:

The preceding section of this chapter described the complexities o
price-nonprice interaction for a product and the complexities of pric
interdependencies within a firm's product line.   In addition to thes
intrafirm interdependencies, external competitive interaction should als
be considered.   The producer of a product (with the exception of a
monopolist) is vitally concerned with the competitive strategy to b
employed in marketing his product.   The manufacturer is interested ir
how competitors will react to his marketing effort.   If there currently i
no competition, he will be concerned with the time of entrance of poten

ial competitors and how he may affect it. If competition already exists, he firm must establish levels for the elements of the marketing mix with he realization that competitors will react to these actions.

In the economist's world of pure competition, there is a very large number of firms offering a homogeneous product, in which case the market dictates price and producers can only vary the quantity to be produced. In the more realistic case of oligopoly, where there are only a few rival firms, the quantities sold by a firm are dependent both on its own price and on the price of other firms in the industry. For this case, economists have proposed the concept of a kinked demand curve to help analyze price-quantity relationships (see Fig. 4-3). It is hypothesized that a

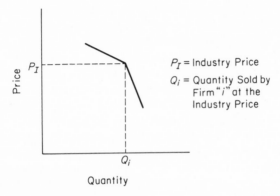

P_I = Industry Price

Q_i = Quantity Sold by Firm "i" at the Industry Price

Figure 4-3: Oligopoly demand curve

kink exists at the current industry price P_I. This kink will exist if other firms in the industry follow price decreases so the firm initiating the price cut will not gain the sales it might have expected. Conversely, if the firm raises its price others may not follow, and it will lose more sales than it anticipated. It is important to realize that much of the interdependence among the firms in the industry is generated by the decision rules that competitors use to adjust or adapt to other firms' marketing decisions. A kink in the response curve is produced when competitors follow price decreases, but not price increases.

The firm may choose from a number of other competitive strategies. It might follow the price of the "leader" of the industry. Alternatively, the firm might choose not to react to the price of other firms, but rather to adjust its marketing effort on the basis of changes in its own market share or profit level. The selection of the best strategy depends upon how other firms in the industry will react to market changes. If the firm knew the strategies of the other firms in the industry, it could choose the best counterstrategy. The consideration of competitive strateg and pricing can be approached by examining a payoff matrix that pre scribes the outcomes of all combinations of prices that the firm wishe to consider in the market. This type of payoff matrix is depicted in th advertising chapter in Table 3-2. The risk and uncertainty criteria tha may be used in reaching a decision when faced with a payoff matrix wer also discussed in Chap. 3. In this section certain of these criteria will b applied and analyzed in the context of the competitive pricing decision First extended game theory models employing randomized strategie and games in which the total rewards to the players are not constant wil be analyzed. Then Bayesian models for competitive pricing will b discussed. This section will close with a comparative discussion of gam theory and Bayesian approaches in the area of bidding models.

Game Theory Models

The use of game theory models in analyzing situations in which the total reward to the players is constant was demonstrated in the adver tising chapter, and an example of a pure strategy equilibrium pair wa presented. This type of analysis is equally valid for pricing decision when the game rewards can be considered fixed. The example in Chap. was special, however, in that an equilibrium was generated by each firm using one advertising level continuously over time. In general, a con stant sum game will not always yield a pure strategy equilibrium. But there is another way in which an equilibrium may occur. This is by the competitors using a "mixed strategy." A mixed strategy is based upon selecting one alternative at one time and another alternative at another where the selection at any particular time is based on a specified proba bility. The probability is constant and reflects the long-run relative frequency with which the player will select a particular decision. To make the concept of a mixed strategy more clear, an example of a "loss leader" pricing game is presented.

If two retailers are competing for a fixed number of customers, they may play a constant sum game in selecting a loss leader. A loss leader is a product selected for a very large price reduction even to the extent of a loss on that product. The reason for using a loss leader is to attract people to the store. If it is assumed that the profit per customer is constant, the profit payoffs will be directly proportional to the number of customers attracted to the store. If the number of people to visit the two stores is fixed (e.g., by geographical considerations) and the cost of loss leading each item is the same, the game is a two-person constant sum game. A hypothetical example is given in Table 4-3. Retailer one can

TABLE 4-3: Two-person Constant Sum Pricing Game

Retailer Two's Leader

Payoff to 2 / Payoff to 1	1-Steak -	2-Butter -
Retailer One's Leader / 1-Chicken -	500 / 400	400 / 500
2-Coffee -	300 / 600	600 / 300

loss lead either chicken or coffee, and retailer two can lead steak or butter in this example. The payoffs are the number of people shopping at the store in the time period of interest. The differences in the payoffs reflect the different relative preferences of consumers with respect to the stores and to the item used as a loss leader.

If retailer one is conservative and attempts to obtain the greatest payoff assuming the strongest play is made by his opponent, the maximin strategy, he would use chicken as a loss leader. If retailer two also used the maximin criterion, he would use butter as a loss leader. The resulting pair would not be an equilibrium pair, since player two could see a way of improving his position, assuming his competitor did not change his strategy. Retailer two could increase his payoff one hundred units by changing to steak, assuming firm one remained with chicken. This force destroys the possibility of a maximin equilibrium for this game if competitors must always play the same alternative or, in other words, display a pure strategy.

Although pure strategies will not yield an equilibrium, a strategy based on randomizing the item to be led each time period will produce an equilibrium. This randomized manner of play is called a "mixed strategy." If firm one plays a mixed strategy against firm two's steak, the expected payoff would be

$$V_{11} = P_1(400) + (1 - P_1)(600) \qquad (4\text{-}33)$$

where P_1 = proportion of time strategy one is played by firm one,
V_{11} = payoff of firm one's using a mixed strategy against his competitor's pure strategy one.

The expected payoff against firm two's strategy of butter is

$$V_{12} = P_1(500) + (1 - P_1)(300) \qquad (4\text{-}34)$$

This payoff set is graphically shown in Fig. 4-4. The maximin strategy is to find the point where the minimum payoff is a maximum. The crossed line in Fig. 4-4 shows the minimum payoffs against the competitor's best decision. The highest minimum payoff is at point D. Here $P_1^* = 0.75$ and the expected maximin payoff is 450 in this case. The mixed strategy pairs will be an equilibrium. If there are more than two alternatives, the problem of finding the mixed equilibrium strategy is

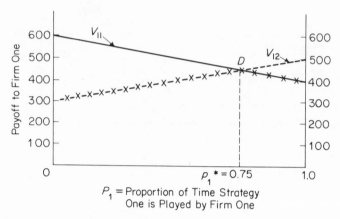

Figure 4-4: **Mixed strategy payoff**

more difficult, and linear programming must be utilized. But a two-person constant sum game will always have an equilibrium maximin strategy pair.[13]

The limitations of this game formulation stem from the fact that it allows only two competitors and requires the total rewards received by the firms to be constant. If the game is not constant sum or if there are more than two firms competing, the analysis may not yield a maximin equilibrium strategy.

In order to explore the problems a non-constant sum game may present in selecting competitive prices, consider a situation where the total rewards change as different strategies are employed. For example, if all firms lower prices, the total rewards to all competitors may decrease. A good example of this phenomenon is presented in the gasoline industry. The payoff to any one firm obtained by reducing prices is very large, but it is almost certain to be followed by competitors. Successive price cuts can lead the industry to a very low price and profit level.[14] Figure 4-5 is a hypothetical matrix that could explain the self-

[13] R. D. Luce and H. Raiffa, *Games and Decisions* (New York: John Wiley and Sons, 1964), pp. 71–73.

[14] See R. Cassady, Jr., "Price Warfare—A Form of Business Rivalry," in R. Cox, W. Alderman, and S. Shapiro, eds., *Theory in Marketing* (Homewood, Illinois: Irwin, 1964), pp. 355–79.

destructive rivalry of two firms. If both firms one and two are currently charging a price of 40 and firm one lowers his price to 30, he would get a reward of 1500. This is firm one's maximax strategy. Firm two would have his payoff reduced to 100, so he would certainly follow the reduction and may even reduce his price to 20 and obtain a reward of

Firm Two's Price

Payoff to Firm One \ Payoff to Firm Two		10	20	30	40	50
Firm One's Price	10	200 / 200	100 / 700	100 / 1000	100 / 1300	100 / 1000
	20	700 / 100	400 / 400	100 / 1200	100 / 1400	100 / 1100
	30	1000 / 100	1200 / 100	600 / 600	100 / 1500	100 / 1200
	40	1300 / 100	1400 / 100	1500 / 100	800 / 800	100 / 1300
	50	1000 / 100	1100 / 100	1200 / 100	1300 / 100	700 / 700

Figure 4-5: Self-destructive game

1200. This process could continue until both firms are charging a price of ten. There is no incentive to stop the price spiral until both firms realize the destructive nature of the process. If the firms colluded, they probably would establish a price of 40, since there the total rewards of the game are a maximum and the reward to each firm would be acceptable, given that they intend to cooperate. Tacit collusion resulting from the realization of the nature of the game might also lead to price stability. Formulating the game payoff table might be just as effective in producing this realization as an actual war and therefore might serve a useful function by preventing price wars.

The usual zero-sum strategies are not reasonable for this example.[15] For instance, if both players used the most conservative strategy (the maximin strategy), the game would be played at a price of ten and payoff

---

[15] See Chap. 3 for a brief discussion of game theoretic strategies in the context of advertising decisions.

of 200.   The worst returns for firm one are

Firm One's Price	Lowest Payoff Using This Price Strategy
10	200
20	100
30	100
40	100
50	100

The largest of the worst results for firm one would be associated with a price of ten.   A similar analysis would indicate that firm two's maximin strategy would also be to establish a price of ten.   Intuitively, this does not seem to be a good way for either of the firms to behave.   This inconsistency dramatizes the dangers of applying zero-sum game rules to non-zero sum games.   Not all non-constant sum games will produce such perverse results, but the appropriateness of rules derived from constant sum games should be analyzed in each case.   In many non-constant sum games a reasonable equilibrium may exist.   In the self-destructive game in Fig. 4-5, there is no equilibrium, so the game theory analysis does not directly solve the strategy problem.

An interesting non-constant sum game theory approach has been proposed by Krishnan and Gupta.[16]   They developed a two-firm model for the analysis of the two marketing mix elements of price and advertising within the game theory context.   The competitive effect is described by

$$MS_i = \frac{e_i A_i}{e_1 A_1 + e_2 A_2} + k(P_1 + P_2 - 2P_i) \qquad (4\text{-}35)$$

where MS_i = market share of firm i,
  A_i = advertising expenditure by firm i,
  e_i = effectiveness of firm i's advertising,
  P_i = price of firm i,
  k = price response constant.

The advertising term is similar to the forms indicated in the advertising chapter.   The price effects in the model are based on the assumption that market share is linearly related to the difference in prices.   These two relationships are used to describe the market share effects of marketing mixes by each firm.   The market share results are translated into profit payoffs on the assumption that total industry sales are fixed.   This assumption may not be realistic in view of the nature of price and advertising effects outlined in this book, but it may be an acceptable research

[16] K. S. Krishnan and S. K. Gupta, "Mathematical Models for a Duopolistic Market," *Management Science*, XIII (March, 1967), pp. 568–83.

hypothesis for the model. Although the industry sales are fixed, the game is a non-constant sum game, since the payoffs are measured in terms of profit and both price and advertising affect profit through total revenue and costs. The equilibrium solutions of the game are defined by the solutions to the set of partial differentials of each firm's profit function. The solution describes a point where each firm is in an optimal position, given that the other firm does not change its strategy. Since the solution of the game theory model is based on the use of multivariate calculus, the form of the reward function must be differentiable and must lead to a solvable set of partial differential equations. Krishnan and Gupta examine the existence of possible equilibria and derive the necessary conditions for an equilibrium. They examine the conditions under which a nonboundary equilibrium exists and the sensitivity of the nonboundary equilibrium under various advertising and price responses [e and k, respectively, in Eq. (4-35)]. For example, when both firms have equal promotional effectiveness [when $e_1 = e_2$ in (4-35)] and when the price response coefficient times the difference in unit manufacturing costs of the firms is less than $\frac{1}{9}$, the equilibrium prices are equal and the equilibrium promotional outlay of any competitor is proportional to his marginal unit profit.

Although Krishnan and Gupta define the necessary conditions for an equilibrium, they do not describe a mechanism that would lead firms to this equilibrium. If some mechanism does not adaptively lead to the equilibrium, it must be assumed that each competitor carries out the same analysis and that they simultaneously arrive at the equilibrium.

Shakun has developed a game theory model that sheds light on the path towards an equilibrium as well as considering dynamic and product interdependency effects.[17] Although this model deals primarily with advertising as a controllable variable, Shakun's model is discussed here because of its non-zero sum nature, and its consideration of equilibria and product line effects. The model postulates an exponential industry sales response to advertising and does not assume that total industry sales are given, as did Krishnan and Gupta. The sales response is

$$y_{in} = c_i(1 - e^{-\alpha_i x_{in}}) \qquad (4\text{-}36)$$

where y_{in} = industry sales of product i in period n,

c_i = saturation level of sales for product i,

$\alpha_i = a_i/c_i$,

a_i = slope of sales response curve at the origin ($x_i = 0$),

x_{in} = "effective" advertising expenditure on product i in period n for the total industry.

---

[17] M. F. Shakun, "A Dynamic Model for Competitive Marketing in Coupled Markets," *Management Science*, XII (Aug., 1966), pp. 525–29.

Effective advertising dollars include considerations of the dynamic (carry-over) effects of advertising as well as advertising interdependencies between products. The total industry effective advertising expenditure on product i in period n is given by

$$x_{in} = \beta_i \left[\sum_h x_{hin} - \sum_{\substack{j \\ i \neq j}} k_{ij} \sum_h x_{hjn} \right] + (1 - \beta_i)x_{i,n-1} \quad (4\text{-}37)$$

where x_{hin} = advertising expenditure of firm h on product i in period n,

k_{ij} = coupling coefficient which indicates the effect of advertising expenditures for product j upon the "effective" advertising for product i,

β_i = smoothing constant weighting current period and the preceding period's "effective" advertising for product i.

The first term in Eq. (4-37) reflects the impact of current period promotional effort. It is the sum of total industry advertising for product i and the gain (loss) in advertising effectiveness resulting from advertising expenditures on other products. If $k_{ij} > 0$, advertising expenditures on product j will detract from sales of product i. Conversely, if $k_{ij} < 0$, expenditures on j will enhance the sales of i. For example, if $k_{ij} < 0$, $x_{hjn} > 0$ will increase x_{in} in Eq. (4-37), which in turn will enhance the sales of product i given in Eq. (4-36). The exponential smoothing of current period effort with the preceding period's "effective" advertising in Eq. (4-37) encompasses the phenomenon of the carry-over of advertising effects.

The share of the total market for product i that will be obtained by firm h in period n is based upon its relative advertising expenditure for product i in period n and its share of the product i market in the previous period. That is,

$$\phi_{hin} = \frac{x_{hin}\phi_{hi,n-1}}{\sum_h x_{hin}\phi_{hi,n-1}} \quad (4\text{-}38)$$

where ϕ_{hin} = firm h's share of the product i market in period n.

Firm h's profits (weighted) on all of its products over the next $T + 1$ periods is then given by

$$P_{ht} = \sum_{i=1}^{I} \sum_{n=t}^{t+T} w_{hn}(m_{hi}\phi_{hin}y_{in} - x_{hin}) \quad (4\text{-}39)$$

where P_{ht} = the weighted profit to firm h at time t of the profit stream earned on the entire product line over the next $T + 1$ periods,

w_{hn} = weight assigned by firm h to profits received in period n. These weights may reflect long versus short-term profits preferences as well as the usual discounting,

m_{hi} = unit profit margin of product i for company h,

ϕ_{hin} = see Eq. (4-38),

y_{in} = see Eq. (4-36).

To find an equilibrium solution to this non-constant sum game, Eq. (4-39) must first be partially differentiated for each firm with respect to its level of advertising for each product in each period. This will result in a set of $H \cdot I \cdot (T + 1)$ nonlinear equations, where H denotes the number of firms in the market and I denotes the number of different products in the market. The necessary condition for an equilibrium is given by those x_{hin} which satisfy these $H \cdot I \cdot (T + 1)$ nonlinear equations when each of these equations is set equal to zero.

The solution of these $H \cdot I \cdot (T + 1)$ nonlinear equations requires the use of iterative techniques. A number of solutions satisfying the necessary conditions may be found. Thus sufficiency tests and tests for the maximum maximorum (i.e., the greatest maximum) must be carried out. Shakun proposes that an equilibrium be found by a step-by-step procedure in which each firm sets its next period advertising so as to maximize its profit [see Eq. (4-39)], assuming that his competitor will not change his advertising. Shakun presents an example where this procedure leads to an equilibrium. This is encouraging, since the decision rules for each firm are intuitively appealing and the method prescribes a mechanism for reaching the equilibrium. Although it is difficult to be sure that the best equilibrium has been found since multiple equilibria are possible, the approach is appealing.

The discussion of game theory models presented in this chapter indicates the flexibility of these models in considering industry, dynamic, marketing mix, and product interdependency effects. These models seek to identify competitive equilibria, but Shakun's approach indicates that these models may also be useful in describing the decision rules firms might use to reach a maximin equilibrium.

Bayesian Decision Theory

If the decision maker is willing to ascribe subjective probabilities to each alternative response which competition is likely to exhibit, Bayesian decision theory will provide a useful framework for analyzing decisions under competitive conditions.   Thus the Bayesian approach transforms a case of decisions under uncertainty to that of decisions under risk via the mechanism of subjective (or judgmental) probabilities.

In the Bayesian approach, the possible competitive reactions to various price levels are defined and a probability of occurrence is associated with each of them.   When these probabilities are multiplied by the profit payoffs of establishing the respective price levels, the expected value of the payoff is generated.   The selected price is the one that yields the greatest expected profit.   This procedure was illustrated in Chap. 3, Advertising Decisions.

Bayesian analysis has sufficient flexibility to represent very complex payoff and outcome situations.   The remainder of this section will consider an application of the Bayesian approach to a pricing decision. This example, presented by Green, will illustrate the flexibility of the approach.[18]   The analysis concerned the price for a product called Kromel.   Kromel was available to four market segments, but was being sold in only three.   In the fourth segment, called *A*, no penetration had been made and a product called Verlon held the sales in that segment. The purpose of the analysis was to determine whether it would be wise to lower the price of Kromel so that segment *A* could be penetrated and additional profits could be earned.   Two competitive dimensions were considered.   The first was the possibility that Verlon producers would match a price cut in Kromel.   The second was the possibility that competitive manufacturers of Kromel would cut the price of Kromel if market segment *A* was not penetrated.   In this dimension the possible effects of competitors' adding capacity, given various market prices, was also included.

Estimates of subjective probabilities of penetration and of the various competitive actions were described in a decision tree, which identified 400 possible outcomes.   A portion of Green's decision tree is presented in Fig. 4-6.   The tree begins at the current price of one dollar and investigates the possibility of penetrating segment *A* in that year and the extent of penetration if it occurs.   If market segment *A* is not penetrated at a price of one dollar, then the possibility of competitive Kromel manufacturers reducing their price in the first year is examined.   In each case there is the possibility of Verlon producers fully matching or half matching any price change.   In each circumstance the probabilities of penetrating segment *A* in the next year are described.   If the segment is not penetrated, the possible sales stimulation effect of the price cut in other segments is considered.

---

[18] P. E. Green, "Bayesian Decision Theory in Pricing Strategy," *Journal of Marketing*, XXVII (Jan., 1963), pp. 5–15.

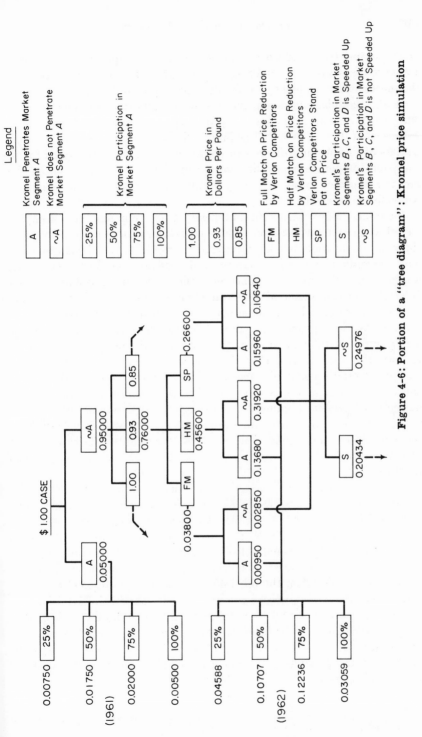

Figure 4-6: Portion of a "tree diagram": Kromel price simulation

Green, *ibid.*, p. 7.

189

The tree branch of $1.00 is only one example of the four basic price alternatives ($1.00, .93, .85, and .80) that were considered. Each price would branch in a manner similar to Fig. 4-6.

The probabilities at each branch were estimated by sales personnel, but this may not have been the best source of subjective input, since sales people are usually overly optimistic. After the subjective inputs were specified, the marginal and conditional outcomes described in the tree were combined to produce joint probabilities. For example, in Fig. 4-6 the marginal probability of penetrating segment A was 5 per cent and the conditional probability of achieving 25 per cent of the market, given that it was penetrated, was 15 per cent, so the joint probability of penetrating and achieving a 25 per cent market share was 0.75 per cent (5 per cent $\times$ 15 per cent).

The decision tree format described 400 outcomes and their probabilities of occurrence. The selection of the best price alternative was based on the total compounded profit the pricing policy generated over five years and was calculated by the following equation:

$$CCN(X_k) = \sum_{j=1}^{n} p_j \cdot \sum_{i=1}^{m} \{(1 + r)^{m-i} T[(D_{ij} - Z_{ij})(K_{ij}M_{ij})]\} \quad (4\text{-}40)$$

$$Z_{ij} = \phi(K_{ij}M_{ij})$$

where $CCN(X_k)$ = expected value of firm's profit at the end of m years compounded at rate r and generated by net profits under each price strategy X_k ($k = 1, \ldots, 4$),

p_j = probability assigned to the jth outcome ($j = 1, 2, \ldots, n$),

r = interest rate per annum, expressed decimally,

T = ratio of net to gross profits of firm's Kromel operation (assumed constant in the study),

D_{ij} = Kromel price in $/pound in the ith year ($i = 1, 2, \ldots, m$) for the jth outcome,

Z_{ij} = cost in $/pound of firm's Kromel resin in the ith year for the jth outcome (this cost is a function of the amount of Kromel pounds sold by the firm),

ϕ = function of,

K_{ij} = firm's over-all market share of Kromel industry sales (in pounds) in the ith year for the jth outcome (expressed decimally),

M_{ij} = Kromel industry poundage (summed over all four market segments) in the ith year for the jth outcome.

When the calculations in Eq. (4-40) were carried out it was found that the price of $.80 had the greatest expected profit. Since this was the lowest alternative tested, it would have been interesting to examine even lower prices to see if they would improve the expected profit results.

Green investigated the sensitivity of the model to several of the inputs. He found that the results were sensitive to the assumptions about the probabilities of competitors increasing their capacity when faced with high Kromel prices. When this factor was removed, the best price was $.85 and the total profit estimate dropped 21.5 per cent. Other sensitivity testing indicated that the price recommendation was not sensitive to the cost of capital [r in Eq. (4-40)] or the forecast of total industry sales [M_{ij} in Eq. (4-40)].

The Bayesian analysis is capable of encompassing intricate competitive behavior and is an appropriate technique for competitive analysis when subjective probabilities can be estimated for alternative outcomes.

Stochastic Bidding Model

In pricing situations where competitors submit sealed bids, such as in construction and aerospace marketing, special purpose models have been developed. In this type of pricing problem the profit generated by the pricing strategy depends upon the bid price and the cost of fulfilling the bid. Given that the objective of the firm is to maximize profits, Churchman, Ackoff, and Arnoff have developed a model to specify bids so that the expected value of profit is maximized.[19] The expected value of profit is

$$E(Pr) = [\text{PROB}(p)] \cdot (p - C) \tag{4-41}$$

where $E(Pr)$ = expected value of profit,
         p = bid or price,
   $\text{PROB}(p)$ = probability of winning the contract at bid (or price) p,
         C = estimated cost of fulfilling contract.

If the probability of winning the contract, $\text{PROB}(p)$, could be determined for each possible bid p, the price or bid corresponding to the maximum expected value of profit could be found. The probability of winning the bid is the probability of submitting a bid lower than all other competitors. If contractors form their bids independently, the probability of being lower than all bids is the product of the probabilities of being lower than each of them:

[19] C. W. Churchman, R. L. Ackoff, and E. L. Arnoff, *Introduction to Operations Research* (New York: John Wiley and Sons, Inc., 1957), pp. 559–73.

$$\text{PROB}(p) = \text{PROB}(p)_1 \cdot \text{PROB}(p)_2 \cdots \text{PROB}(p)_j \cdots$$
$$\text{PROB}(p)_n \quad (4\text{-}42)$$

where $\text{PROB}(p)_j$ = probability of submitting a bid p that is lower
    than competitor j's bid.

The probability of submitting a bid lower than competitor j may be
determined by an analysis of competitor j's past bidding behavior, if he
is expected to continue to behave in this manner. It might be noted
that the probability may change to reflect the past success of the competitor in bidding. For example, if he has been successful recently and
is reaching capacity, he might bid higher prices. If he has been unsuccessful in the past, lower prices might reflect a need to maintain at least
a minimum level of production. In the absence of useful past data or if
the changes just discussed would make use of his past bidding behavior
suspect, subjective probability distributions may be utilized. In any
case, the distributions for competitors might appear as in Fig. 4-7.

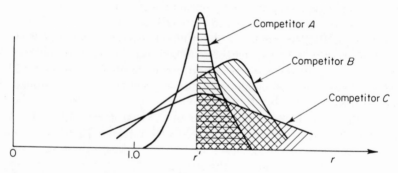

where p = bid or price,
    c = cost,
    r = ratio of bid to cost estimate = p/c,
    r' = firm's contemplated bid divided by the estimated
       cost = p'/c.

**Figure 4-7: Competitor bidding
distributions**

In Fig. 4-7 the competitor's bidding distributions have been developed
for the ratio of the competitor's bid to the cost estimate c. The use of
c normalizes the distribution so that competitors can be compared on the
same scale, no matter what their past bids p and costs c have been. If
the firm makes the bid $p' = r'c$ (as noted in the figure), the probability
of winning the bid from any given competitor is the area in the upper

tail $(r > r')$ of the appropriate distribution in the figure. These probabilities are then inserted into Eq. (4-42) in order to determine the probability that the firm will win the contract with a bid of $p' = r'c$. This probability is then used in Eq. (4-41) in order to determine the expected profit from a bid of p. The decision rule then is to choose that bid p which maximizes the expected profits.

If the number of bidders n in Eq. (4-42) is not known, the probability of being lower than bidder j is conditional upon the probability that j will bid. In this case, the probability of being lower than bidder j is

$$\text{PROB}(p)_j = 1 - \text{PROB}(j) \cdot \text{PROB}(p|j) \qquad (4\text{-}43)$$

where $\quad \text{PROB}(j) = $ probability competitor j will bid,
$\quad \text{PROB}(p|j) = $ probability that competitor j bids at a price $\leq p$ if he makes a bid.

The probabilities of Eq. (4-43) when placed in Eq. (4-42) define the probability of winning the contract, which in turn is used in Eq. (4-41) to define the expected profit. If specific distributions of the probability of being lower than a competitor $[\text{PROB}(p)_j]$ and the probability of a number of bidders could be determined, explicit expressions of the expected profit could be specified.[20] Whenever the resulting expressions are analytically intractable, trial and error search procedures could be used to determine the optimum bidding price so as to maximize the expected profit.

A stochastic bidding model similar to the one developed by Churchman, Ackoff, and Arnoff has been applied by Edelman at RCA.[21] Edelman's model was based on selecting the bid with the highest expected profit, where profit is defined as the incremental profit. That is, the profit generated if the bid is won minus the loss in profits if it is not won. The model is based on a payoff matrix arraying the alternative bids for RCA against possible competitive bids. The payoffs to each RCA-competitive bidding pair are determined on the basis of the relative bids. Figure 4-8 depicts the change in the probability of RCA's winning the contract for various differentials in the competitive bids. When the probability of winning is multiplied times the value of the contract, the payoff for the particular bid pair is determined. Next, the prior probabilities of the competitor's choosing a particular bid must be subjectively estimated. When these priors are applied to each of the payoffs for a particular RCA

[20] *Ibid.*
[21] F. Edelman, "Art and Science of Competitive Bidding," *Harvard Business Review*, XXXIII (July–Aug., 1965), pp. 53–66. This paper is reproduced in D. B. Montgomery and G. L. Urban (eds.), *Applications of Management Science in Marketing* (Englewood Cliffs, N.J.; Prentice Hall, Inc., 1969).

bid, the expected payoff of this bid is determined. After this expected value has been calculated for each bid, the bid with the highest expected value would be selected.

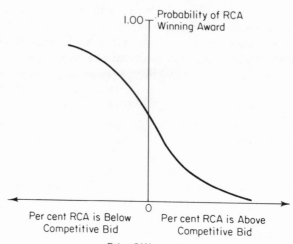

Figure 4-8: Probability of winning
at different price differentials*

Edelman has analyzed the sensitivity of this model and found that it is more sensitive to the distribution of prior probabilities of competitors using specific prices than to the slope or intercept of the probability of the winning function (see Fig. 4-8). The validity of the model was also examined. In seven tests, the model improved upon the perform-

TABLE 4-4: Seven Tests of the RCA
Bidding Model*

Test	Bid without Model	Bid with Model	Lowest Competitive Bid	Bid without Model: Per Cent under (over) Lowest Competitive Bid	Bid with Model: Per Cent under Lowest Competitive Bid
1	44.53	46.00	46.49	4.2	1.1
2	47.36	42.68	42.93	(10.3)	0.6
3	62.73	59.04	60.76	(3.2)	2.8
4	47.72	51.05	53.38	10.6	4.4
5	50.18	42.80	44.16	(13.7)	3.1
6	60.39	54.61	55.10	(9.6)	0.9
7	39.73	39.73	40.47	1.8	1.8

Franz Edelman, "Art and Science of Competitive Bidding," *Harvard Business Review*, XXXIII (July–August 1965), pp. 56 and 60.

ance of the usual bidding procedure (see Table 4-4). The measure of performance was the percentage by which the bid was below the lowest competitive bid. The model submitted the winning bids in all cases, was an average of two per cent below the next competitive bid, and generated at least as much profit in all cases as the existing procedure. In these tests the model made a positive contribution to improved decision making, since it increased profits by using the same input information available to the standard decision procedure.

The bidding situation can also be attacked from the game theory point of view.[22] In a bidding game in which both players know the value of the contract V, the only pure strategy equilibrium is when both firms bid V. If mixed strategies are appropriate, then any randomized strategy that assigns a zero probability to bids exceeding V is maximin for each player.[23] If the value of the game is not known with certainty, but rather each competitor believes that the value will be drawn from some distribution, the same conclusions are valid, except that they would be based on the expected value of the contract value $[E(V)]$.

An interesting case develops when one bidder has more information about the value of the bid than the other. Wilson has analyzed this asymmetric information state within the framework of equilibrium game theory strategies.[24] In Wilson's analysis one party knows the exact value of the contract. In this game situation the party with the perfect information will play a pure strategy and the competitor will play a randomized strategy. Wilson derives the expressions for the payoff to each player, partially differentiates them with respect to the player's bid, equates the set of equations to zero, and proposes that solutions be found by numeric methods. In a simple example of asymmetric information Wilson shows that the expected return to the party with perfect information was 8.5 times the expected return of the party with imperfect information at the game equilibrium. This implies that it would be potentially very valuable to institute an information system to gain information about the value of the object of the bidding.

Lavalle has attacked the problem of asymmetric information from a Bayesian point of view.[25] He formulates expressions for the expected returns for each player, given various levels of information about the game value and the competitor's bids. The information levels are reflected in the distributions of the game value and conditional estimates

[22] See H. J. Griesmer and M. Shubik, "Toward A Study of Bidding Processes I, II, III," *Naval Research Logistics Quarterly*, X, Nos. 1, 2, and 3 (1963).

[23] *Ibid.*

[24] R. B. Wilson, "Competitive Bidding with Asymmetric Information," *Management Science*, XIII (July, 1967), pp. 816–20.

[25] I. H. Lavalle, "A Bayesian Approach to an Individual Player's Choice of Bid in Competitive Sealed Auctions, " *Management Science*, XIII (March, 1967), pp. 584–97.

of the competitor's behavior. When the value of the game is distributed as a gamma-1 density function and the competitor's bid is described by a beta density, the expected value of perfect information can be calculated. This value would represent the maximum amount a firm would pay for information about the game or the competitor. Whereas the game theory analysis indicated a positive value of information, the Bayesian analysis yielded a specific value of information that would represent an upper bound for the costs of an information system to aid in bidding.

Summary of Competitive Pricing Models

This section has explored the game theory and Bayesian approaches to analyzing competitive effects. Beginning with the concept of a simple payoff table, game theoretic approaches to mixed strategy, non-zero sum, and equilibrium considerations were developed. The game theory approach emphasized the existence and stability of competitive equilibria, but the need for the specification of the mechanism to reach such equilibria was indicated. Whereas the game theory approach assumes uncertainty, Bayesian analysis operates in a risk environment where subjective probabilities can be established for outcomes. The flexibility of this approach and its utilization of business judgment are desirable features. The Bayesian analysis usually does not explicitly consider the interestedness of competitors. That is, the Bayesian analysis against nature is the same as against a competitor. Lavalle has suggested that this can be encompassed in the Bayesian analysis if the distributions over competitive states reflect second-guessing or higher orders of outguessing the opponents' strategy.[26]

Another approach to including game strategy concepts within the context of Bayesian analysis would be to define one competitive alternative as playing the maximin game solution. Then prior probabilities of the opponent using the game theory rules and of his not using game strategy could be prescribed. The strategy of the competitor not using the game rules could be broken down in the usual manner into substrategies with prior probabilities for each substrategy. After this breakdown of competitors' strategies has been accomplished, the usual expected value criterion could be applied to select the strategy for the firm to employ. In both the game theory and Bayesian approaches good decisions are based on an understanding of competitors and the payoffs for alternative market situations. This knowledge can be gained from an informa-

[26] *Op. cit.*, p. 585.

ion system. The competitive advantages for the firm with better
information indicated by Wilson and Lavalle support the necessity for
competitive decisions to be based on a sound information system.

ESTIMATING DEMAND
RELATIONSHIPS

In order to apply the models discussed in this chapter, the firm
generally must have knowledge of demand relationships in its market
environment. For purposes of discussion, consider the deceptively simple price-quantity relationship. This relationship, also known as a
demand schedule, represents the quantity of a product that would be
demanded at various price levels. At any point in time, however, the
firm generally knows only the quantity that is demanded at its present
price. A single data point, of course, is insufficient to determine even
the simplest demand schedule. Subjective estimates of the demand
equation $q = F(p)$ may be made, but managers often prefer to have
empirical market data to integrate with their subjective judgments prior
to reaching a price decision.

Three basic approaches are available for obtaining empirical information about the price-quantity relationship: questionnaires, regression
analysis, and experimentation. These approaches, as well as their limitations, are discussed below. They are also relevant to the estimation
of the effects of other demand determinants such as advertising and
personal selling.

Questionnaire Methods

Various questionnaire approaches have been used to estimate price
sensitivity. Customers may simply be asked how much they would
purchase of a particular product (or brand) at a number of alternative
prices. In the case of a new product, customers may be given a choice
between the new product and some amount of cash, the amount being
varied between customers in order to estimate the price sensitivity of the
new product. Somewhat more subtle approaches are available. For
example, the interviewer may ask the consumer about the price difference between competing products and brands. If many consumers are
aware of the difference, relatively higher price sensitivity may be pre-
sumed than if few consumers are aware of the difference.

The questionnaire method has serious limitations. A number of some what heroic assumptions must be made in this approach. In general, i must be assumed that:

1. Consumers can perceive how they would react to different price changes.
2. Consumers will honestly and accurately report these perceptions.
3. Consumers' perceptions in the interview situation are reliable predictors of their future market behavior.

Clearly, all three assumptions are suspect, and any given questionnaire procedure should attempt to minimize the probable violation of these assumptions.

Regression Analysis

If data on past market response to price are available, the firm may attempt to measure the market's sensitivity to price. Suppose for the moment that demand for the firm's product can be specified as

$$q_i = a p_i^b p_j^c z^d \qquad (4\text{-}44)$$

where q_i = demand for firm i's product,

p_i = price of firm i's product,

p_j = price of firm j's product,

z = disposable income,

a = scaling factor,

b = price elasticity for firm i,

c = cross competitive price elasticity of firm i's demand with firm j's price,

d = income elasticity of firm i's demand.

Now if natural logarithms are taken on both sides of Eq. (4-44), a standard regression format is obtained as

$$\ln (q_i) = a + b \cdot \ln (p_i) + c \cdot \ln (p_j) + d \cdot \ln (z) \qquad (4\text{-}45)$$

The coefficients in Eq. (4-45) would generally be expected to have values in the following regions:

$$\begin{aligned} b &\leq 0 \\ c &\geq 0 \qquad (4\text{-}46) \\ d &\geq 0 \end{aligned}$$

Since b is the price elasticity of firm i's demand, it represents the proportionate change in demand for its product that may be expected from a hange in its price. Its expected negative sign represents the fact that emand changes and price changes will tend to move in opposite direcons. Similar arguments apply to c and d.

Regression is also useful in accessing the time pattern of response. Iassy and Frank have examined dynamic sales response relationships or price and dealing (price off) activity in a frequently purchased conumer product category.[27] The regression was based on the equation escribing the market share of a brand:

$$MS_t' = a_0 + a_1 P_t' + a_2 P_{t-1}' + a_3 P_{t-2}' + a_4 D_t' + a_5 D_{t-1}'$$
$$+ a_6 D_{t-2}' + a_7 PD_t' + a_8 ES_t' + a_9 ES_{t-1}'$$
$$+ \lambda MS_{t-1}' + v_t \tag{4-47}$$

where MS_t' = log of market share of brand in week t,

P_t' = log of relative price index in week t (brand price/ average price),

D_t' = log of relative deal index in week t,

PD_t' = log of proportion of market sales that occurred under a deal in week t,

ES_t' = log of expected market share in week t,

= past average market share of those families buying in week t,

v_t = error term,

a_i = constant $(i = 0, \ldots, 9)$,

λ = distributed lag coefficient.

he presence of MS_{t-1} on the right-hand side of Eq. (4-47) indicates that is equation is a distributed lag model similar in form to the one used y Palda to investigate the cumulative effects of advertising [see Eq. 3-1) through Eq. (3-3)]. This equation assumes that after three eeks (where the current week is the first week) the effects of both relative rice and deals decay to zero according to an exponential having the arameter λ.

Massy and Frank estimated Eq. (4-47) using consumer panel data. hey found that in week one (the current week) the price and deal fects were as anticipated. That is, a decrease in price would increase aarket share, whereas an increase in dealing would increase market aare. They also found that for price, the carry-over effect in weeks vo and three negated a portion of the sales advantage gained by a curnt period price cut. Lagged competitive price reaction was thought account for this effect. For dealing, however, the carry-over effects ato weeks two and three from a current period deal were both found to

[27] W. F. Massy and R. E. Frank, "Short Term Price and Dealing Effects in Selected larket Segments," *Journal of Marketing Research*, II (May, 1965), pp. 171–85.

be positive, which implies that dealing in the current period will enhanc
sales in future periods. Finally, they found very few carry-over effect
for either price or dealing after three weeks.

The Massy and Frank model illustrates the usefulness of regressior
but there are pitfalls in the approach. For example, if an importan
demand determinant has been left out of the model, errors will be intro
duced into the estimates of the coefficients in the regression. In Ec
(4-44) this will cause the elasticity estimates to be in error. If bot
supply and demand are changing in time, the manager is faced with
simultaneous equations problem which leads to more complex estimatio
procedures.[28] It may, of course, no longer even be possible to estimat
the demand coefficients, because the demand relationship is confounde
by the supply relationship. Many other theoretical, statistical problem
such as heteroscedasticity, autocorrelation, multicollinearity, and erroi
in variables must be considered in order to make proper application c
regression.[29] Although a discussion of these problems is beyond the scop
of the present book, there is a need for marketing researchers to procee
with caution in order to avoid inappropriate applications of the regressio
model. This caution is especially important in view of the ready avai
ability of regression programs and their deceptively simple underlyin
models.

Experimentation

Experimental approaches find increasing application in marketing
In the area of price policy, both laboratory and field experimentation hav
been used. Pessemier[30] has been the principal advocate of the use of th
experimental approach in determining a demand schedule. He has use
simulated shopping trips, where prices are varied, as the basis for estimat
ing the demand schedule. This approach is subject to the criticism tha
laboratory experiments are not duplications of real world situations, bu
Pessemier's approach is an interesting one which should receive furthe
research effort.

Field pricing experiments have also found increasing use. This i
particularly true in supermarkets and department stores, where exper
mentation is relatively easy. The use of sophisticated methods such a
factorial designs and covariance analysis has greatly enhanced the utilit

---

[28] See J. Johnson, *Econometric Methods* (New York: McGraw-Hill, 1963), pɪ
231–92, for a discussion of these problems.

[29] *Ibid.*, Chaps. 6, 7, and 8.

[30] E. A. Pessemier, "An Experimental Method for Estimating Demand," *Journ*
of Business, XXXIII, (Oct., 1960), pp. 373–83.

nd accuracy of experimental results.[31]   However, there are three prin-
ipal problems in price experimentation:

1. *Cost.*   The method is generally expensive.
2. *Competitive retaliation.*   Competitors will attempt to disrupt
an experiment if they learn of it.   Increased promotion or a special
sale on their part may greatly disrupt an experimental program.
3. *Governmental constraints.*   Federal legislation limits the ability
of a firm to vary its price in different areas and to different classes
of customers, even on an experimental basis.[32]

Future developments in the use of experimentation, regression, and
uestionnaire techniques should improve the marketing manager's ability
o obtain reasonably good estimates of the price-quantity relationship.
These estimates of the firm's demand function will provide useful input
o analytical pricing models.

MANAGEMENT SCIENCE AND PRICING DECISIONS

Although businessmen have found the classical economic approach
nsufficient as a model for pricing decisions, management science developments have overcome many of its deficiencies.   The multivariate effects
f the firm's total marketing program and of the pricing decision have
been attacked by the use of multivariate calculus.   This approach is
estricted in the kinds of relationships it can comprehend.   However, it
an specify an optimum marketing mix if the demand relationships are
differentiable and yield a set of partial derivative equations that can be
solved.

Product interdependencies also complicate pricing decisions.   Two
empirical product line models were presented to indicate the potential
or encompassing this complexity in pricing and marketing mix decisions.

Competitive effects have been analyzed by the use of game theory,
Bayesian, and stochastic models.   The multivariate and competitive
effects have been combined in two-person variable sum game models
and in Bayesian models.   Research should continue this type of model-
ng.   Specifically, models should be expanded to consider general multivariate demand relationships and competition among more than two
firms.

[31] S. Banks, *Experimentation in Marketing* (New York: McGraw-Hill, 1965).
[32] See M. C. Howard, *Legal Aspects of Marketing* (New York: McGraw-Hill, 1964).

The normative models discussed in this chapter will require increasingly accurate estimates of the sales-price relationship. The use of questionnaires, regression, and experimental techniques may yield acceptable results, but these techniques must be improved. With developments in measurement techniques and improvements in the ability of models to consider marketing mix, product line, and competitive effects, management science will be prepared to supply marketing managers with more practical normative models to aid in the pricing decision.

5

Distribution
Decisions

INTRODUCTION

At this point in the exposition of the management science approach to marketing, the management decision areas of advertising and pricing have been examined. These decisions were initially analyzed as single-variable problems. Then the multivariate marketing mix effects of price and advertising were investigated. A third element in the marketing mix—distribution—will be analyzed in this chapter. It will be treated as a separate entity; however, its part in the optimal marketing mix will be considered in the new product chapter.

Distribution refers to the activities that occur between the time a product is manufactured and the time it is bought by the customer. Some of these activities are associated with the physical movement of the goods from the manufacturer to the customer, whereas others are associated functional marketing tasks. Although distribution problems have traditionally been categorized as logistics and channels of distribution problems, this separation will not be explicit in this chapter. The distribution activities of the firm will be considered in the context of an integrated distribution system.

The discussion of distribution problems will begin with an examination of the nature of distribution systems. The following section will focus on the underlying functions performed by a distribution system. In the third section, the specific decision problems involved in the design of a distribution system will be analyzed. The final section will review the state of the art of management science in distribution.

THE NATURE OF DISTRIBUTION
SYSTEM*

A manufacturer places a number of demands on his distribution sys
tem. For example, he would like to have his product in ample supply
at the point and time of potential purchase. In addition, he would like
to have it presented with the proper level of sales effort, promotion, and
service. A manufacturer could establish his own system, thus assuring
himself greater control over how the product will be presented. How
ever, the establishment of a vertically integrated distribution system
may be quite expensive and inefficient. These functions may generally
be performed more effectively by intermediaries who gain economies
of scale by performing the functions for a number of manufacturers
Therefore, the manufacturer's first and most basic distribution problem
is to decide if he should use intermediaries or middlemen in his distribu
tion system, and if so, what type of middlemen to use. The outcome
of this decision depends upon the firm's marketing plans and upon the
functions the system must perform, and at times upon the availability
of appropriate middlemen.

The marketing-oriented firm designs its products to fit the needs of
a particular group or groups of potential customers. The distribution
system must efficiently implement this market planning. The manufacturer may find it desirable to present the product differently to
different market segments, so the marketing plan is generally broken down
into subplans that reflect the heterogeneity of the market. Some dimensions of such a market-segment program are the availability of the product to potential customers, sales appeals, sales effort required of the
channel, point-of-purchase promotional requirements, reputation of the
final seller, and level of service available to the customer. The manufacturer would like to establish a distribution system that will achieve
the optimal marketing program in each market segment so that he will
generate the maximum profit. The system should include middlemen
whenever they can increase the manufacturer's profitability by performing distribution functions at a lower cost without deleterious effects on
the performance of the necessary marketing functions.

A hypothetical distribution system is depicted in Fig. 5-1. In this
example, the manufacturer has identified three relevant market segments, each of which is to be served by a different channel structure.
Each segment is to receive a particular market exposure designed to
optimize the profits of the manufacturer. The market exposure received
by segment j may be expressed as a vector $\mathbf{M}_j$, which represents the

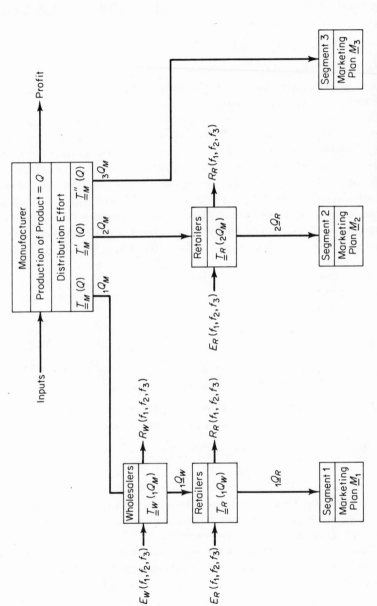

Figure 5-1: A hypothetical channel system

firm's marketing plan for segment j. This marketing plan may be expressed as

$$\mathbf{M}_j = (M_{1j}, M_{2j}, \ldots, M_{ij}, \ldots, M_{nj})$$

where M_{ij} = marketing variable i as presented to segment j.

Examples of the marketing variables indexed by i would be the price at the point of purchase, credit terms, the quality of sales effort, and the local advertising exposure.

As indicated in the figure, the firm plans to market the product to each segment via a different channel structure. Segment one receives the product through a channel composed of both retailers and wholesalers. The second segment also purchases directly from the retailers; however, these retailers are supplied directly by the manufacturer. Finally, the third segment purchases directly from the manufacturer.

In each of these alternative distribution structures, the channel members expend effort in the performance of needed market functions. In general terms these functions may be defined as

f_1 = availability,
f_2 = information,
f_3 = demand creation.

The nature of these functions is obvious from their names and they will be discussed in detail in the next section of this chapter. The effort expended by channel members on these three general channel functions is represented in the figure by the expression

$E_h(f_1, f_2, f_3)$ = effort expended by channel member h with respect
to the channel functions f_1, f_2, and f_3

where $h = M$ denotes the manufacturer's effort,
$h = W$ denotes the wholesaler's effort,
$h = R$ denotes the retailer's effort.

By performing these functions, the channel member earns a reward $R_h(f_1, f_2, f_3)$ that is dependent upon his degree of performance of the possible functions.[1]

The application of effort by channel members has the effect of altering the product. For example, the effort expended by the retailer changes the product from the viewpoint of the customer by making it available

---

[1] The proper rewarding of channel members induces them to participate in the channel and to perform their functions well. In an interorganizational context this represents an extension of the March and Simon intraorganization concepts of rewards, participation, and performance. See J. March and H. Simon, *Organizations* (New York: John Wiley and Sons, 1958).

for purchase.[2]   Symbolically, this change in the product may be expressed as a transformation of the product:

$$_jQ_h = T_h(_jQ_{h-1})$$

where $_jQ_h$ = the vector of physical and marketing properties of the product as it leaves channel member h in the channel system serving segment j,

and T_h = the transformation matrix applied to the product by channel member h through his effort $E_h(f_1, f_2, f_3)$.   The elements of this matrix are taken to be arbitrary functions in this discussion.

The final transformation in each channel results in the product as presented to each segment.   The $_jQ_h$ submitted to each segment will have the designated marketing plan M_j associated with it in a properly designed distribution system.   The use of different channels for each segment, as depicted in the example, might be necessitated by: (1) the need for accomplishing different segment marketing plans M_j, (2) the availability, willingness, and ability of channel members to serve particular segments, and (3) the compensation R_h required by channel members if they are to perform the desired functions.   Normatively, the manufacturer attempts to design a distribution structure that maximizes his profits.   This example has presented an abstract outline of such a marketing channel system.

FUNCTIONS OF DISTRIBUTION

Availability Functions

The first function a distribution system can perform is related to the physical availability of products, i.e., the activities necessary to place the product before the customer.   Availability has two aspects— time and place.   The product should be available at the time of purchase and at the physical location of purchase.   To generate this time and place utility, physical outlets must be identified, inventories must be established, orders must be filled, and the goods must be transported to the purchaser.

Some of these functions can be demonstrated in a simple model

[2] The input, transformation, and return approach to channels of distribution was first proposed by Stanley Stasch in *A Method of Diagramatically Analyzing the Stability of the Economic Structure of Channels of Distribution*, (Unpublished Ph.D. dissertation, Northwestern University, 1964).

developed by Baligh and Richartz[3] (see Fig. 5-2). This model uses a hypothetical firm which produces a product, carries inventories, and fills orders. The order-filling activity could be extended to include transportation and other availability functions. The firm has the capability to produce at a mean rate E_{MP} of q units per time period and to distribute at a mean rate E_{MD} of e units per time period, where the E's again denote

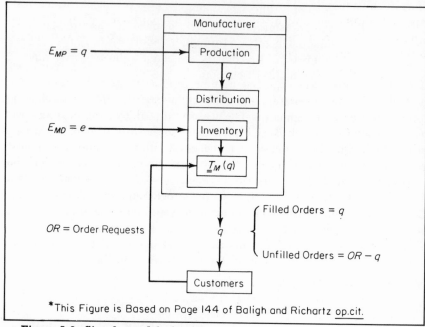

*This Figure is Based on Page 144 of Baligh and Richartz op.cit.

Figure 5-2: Simple model of availability functions of a manufacturer*

effort. The production system is represented by an exponential distribution (with mean $1/q$) of the time between the production of successive items. Similarly, the distribution system has an exponential distribution (with mean $1/e$) of service time between filling orders. The distribution system receives goods from the production sector of the company and stores them as inventory until they are needed. Goods are drawn from the inventory as orders OR are received. The order-filling functions are represented as a distribution transformation $T_M(q)$. It is assumed that the receipt of orders is characterized by a random process. If an order arrives and the inventory is not empty, the order is filled and shipped to

[3] H. H. Baligh and Z. E. Richartz, *Vertical Market Structures* (Boston: Allyn and Bacon, Inc., 1967), pp. 128–81. The following discussion is based upon their work.
* This figure is based on page 144 of Baligh and Richartz, *op. cit.*

he customer. If an order is received and no goods are in the inventory,
he order is unfilled and assumed to be lost.

This model can be used to investigate the manufacturer's availability
ecision and the possible role of intermediaries in the distribution sys-
em. If it is assumed that the order arrival rate may be described by a
'oisson process with a mean of OR, the optimum level of distribution
ffort e can be found. The best level is the one that produces the greatest
xpected profits per unit of time. Since the expected arrival of orders
s fixed by the arrival rate OR, the maximization of profit is equivalent
o the minimization of cost in this model.

The first cost to consider is the cost of production. If a unit cost
of C_1 is assumed, the expected cost of production for the firm is C_1
nultiplied by the average production rate, or $C_1 q$. The second cost
s the expected cost of holding the inventory. This is the holding cost
er unit time C_2 multiplied by the average amount of inventory held per
unit time. Queuing theory can be used to determine the average amount of inventory.[4] The average inventory per period is
$q^2/[OR(OR - q)]$ and the inventory carrying cost is $C_2 q^2/[OR(OR - q)]$.
f the cost of carrying the product during production is to be considered,
he total expected holding cost is increased by C_2 and is equal to

$$C_2\left[1 + \frac{q^2}{OR(OR - q)}\right] \tag{5-1}$$

and it is assumed that $OR > q$.

The third cost to be considered is the cost of maintaining the order-
illing or distribution transformation capability. If C_3 is the unit cost
of maintaining the transformation facility, the expected total fixed
osts of maintaining the facility is $C_3 e$. The fourth cost is the cost of
illing each order. If C_4 is the cost per unit time of handling an order,
he total order-handling cost is C_4 multiplied by the average time an
order spends in the order-filling facility multiplied by the average number of orders arriving at the facility. The average time an order spends in
he system is $1/(e - OR)$, and the average number of orders is OR, so
he total expected cost of the order filling is

$$C_4\left(\frac{OR}{e - OR}\right)$$

and it is assumed that $e > OR$.

The fifth cost is the shortage cost due to an inability to fill an order.

---

[4] See C. McMillan and R. F. Gonzales, *Systems Analysis* (Homewood, Ill.: Irwin,
1965), pp. 122–45, for a discussion of basic queuing theory concepts and proofs for the
referenced relationships.

If the cost per unit of an unfilled order is C_5, the total expected shortag
cost is C_5 multiplied by the amount of time the inventory is empt$_\text{i}$
multiplied by the average order arrival rate during the time period, o

$$C_5 \left(1 - \frac{q}{OR} \right) (OR) = C_5(OR - q).$$

Finally, there is a cost associated with holding current period produc
tion to service current period demand. This cost represents the fac
that even when current period production services current period deman$_\text{i}$
[as opposed to going into the interperiod inventory, whose costs ar$_\text{i}$
accounted for by Eq. (5-1)], the firm must still bear the cost of holding
those products for some time during the unit period. Since an averag$_\text{i}$
of $1/e$ units of time is required to fill an order in the distribution secto$_\text{i}$
of the company, the expected costs of this current period holding activit$_\text{y}$
will be the average order rate times the average service time per orde
times the holding cost per unit of product per unit of time. That is

$$C_2 \left(\frac{OR}{e} \right)$$

The total cost per unit time for the firm is now

$$TC = C_1 q + C_2 \left[1 + \frac{q^2}{OR(OR - q)} \right] + C_3 e + C_4 \left(\frac{OR}{e - OR} \right)$$
$$+ C_5(OR - q) + C_2 \left(\frac{OR}{e} \right) \tag{5-2}$$

The one distribution decision that the manufacturer has at his contro$_\text{i}$
is the capacity of the transformation or order-filling facility e. If Eq
(5-2) were differentiated and set equal to zero, the optimum e could b$_\text{e}$
identified and the minimum total cost could be specified. The manu
facturer would use a middleman to carry out these availability function$_\text{s}$
of inventory, order filling, and transportation only if the total cos$_\text{t}$
could thereby be reduced.

The simple queuing model of Baligh and Richartz has been used t$_\text{o}$
display the relationship between the production and distribution sector$_\text{s}$
within the firm. Middlemen could even play a role in production b$_\text{y}$
receiving an incomplete product and completing its production befor$_\text{e}$
further distributing it.[5] The middleman will be used to carry out functions if such use increases the efficiency of distribution and the manu-

[5] See Baligh and Richartz, *op. cit.* pp. 153–81, for extensions of this model t$_\text{o}$
include the "degree of completeness" of production and intermediaries. Also see L. P
Bucklin, "Postponement, Speculation and the Structure of Distribution Channels,"
Journal of Marketing Research (Feb. 1965), pp. 26–32.

acturer's profits while allowing the intermediary systems to earn a profit or carrying out these functions.[6]

Information Functions

The availability functions described in the last section were developed on the assumption that transactions had been arranged between the manufacturer and his customers. These transactions reflect an exchange or two-way flow of information between the producer and the customer. The producer must transmit information to his customers concerning the availability and attributes of his product offerings. In turn, the customers provide information about such items as new potential markets, problems in his market offerings, and competitive activity. For example, the information may be bids and offers or perhaps the exchange of product information and the promise of purchase. The information gained from the customers may also be market research information that will be useful in making future marketing decisions. It is important to bear in mind this two-way flow of information in a channel system.

If the manufacturer were to contact each customer, he would have to exchange n bits of information, where n is the number of customers. If each customer communication were carried out at a cost of b per contact, the total information cost would be b multiplied by n or bn. A middleman might be able to carry out this function more efficiently. To understand the economies gained by the use of middlemen, the aggregate intermediary structure must be investigated.

An industry of m sellers and n customers would have to carry out nm information exchanges. If there were one middleman who pooled these information exchanges so that producers only contacted him and he in turn contacted consumers, the total number of exchanges would be reduced to $n + m$. The m suppliers would be linked to the middleman, and he would then be linked to the n customers. The existence of the middleman will depend in part on the unit cost of information transfer. The total cost without a middleman would be bnm, where b is cost per information exchange of one seller to one customer. The total cost of information with one middleman would be $\bar{b}(n + m)$, where $\bar{b}$ is the cost per information exchange of the middleman and one customer or supplier. Since the middleman must now relay all the information from each of the suppliers to each of the customers and vice versa, b may not equal $\bar{b}$. The value of b relative to $\bar{b}$ will depend on the economies of scale involved in the information transmission. The middleman will reduce the total

[6] See Baligh and Richartz, *op. cit.*, pp. 146–50, for a discussion of the vertical market structure implied by the queuing model discussed here.

costs of information exchange if

$$bnm \geq \bar{b}(n + m) \tag{5-3}$$

where $b, \bar{b}, n, m > 0$.

As n and m become larger, the value of b versus $\bar{b}$ becomes less significan in the inequality. For example, if there are five producers and ter consumers, bnm is greater than $\bar{b}(n + m)$ even if $\bar{b}$ is 3.33 times b.

For the case of $b = \bar{b}$, Balderston has analyzed the place of the middle man in the distribution information network.[7] With constant anc equal costs per information exchange, condition (5-3) reduces to

$$nm > n + m \tag{5-4}$$

where both $n > 2$ and $m > 2$.

That is, there must be at least two sellers and two buyers before a middle-man performs the information function more efficiently. In cases where condition (5-4) holds, the wholesaler will reduce the total costs and earr profits. These profits will encourage entry into the middleman industry The equilibrium number of middlemen will occur when the total informa-tion costs with and without the intermediaries are equal. The total information costs with more than one middleman would be $bw(n + m)$, where w is the number of middlemen, and b is assumed to be constant. This formulation assumes that each wholesaler carries out the same information exchanges. The maximum number of wholesalers w^* will occur when

$$bnm = bw(n + m) \tag{5-5}$$

or
$$w^* = \frac{nm}{n + m}$$

The equilibrium number of intermediaries would not be as indicated in Eq. (5-5) if middlemen service different subsegments of the network or if the cost of information b were not constant and equal for all middle-men. The condition would also be more complex if multiple products were offered by the producers.[8]

Even if the conditions for Eq. (5-5) were satisfied, the achievement of w^* would depend upon the entry conditions in the intermediary industry. New firms may be able to enter only by offering incentives to existing firms. The effects of these types of rebates on the equilibrium have been

---

[7] F. E. Balderston, "Communication Networks in Intermediate Markets," *Man-agement Science*, IV (Jan., 1958), pp. 154–71. The comments in this and the preceding paragraphs are based on his work.

[8] See *ibid.*, pp. 163–67, for a discussion of these complexities.

studied by Baligh and Richartz.[9] The entrance of new firms may also be affected by the fixed costs of establishing a middleman business. In order to induce an intermediary or, for that matter, a producer, to invest in facilities, an acceptable rate of return must be assured.

The consideration of equilibrium in the industry clarifies the nature of the information function in distribution and again indicates that the middleman will exist only if he carries out a distribution function more efficiently than the manufacturer. As well as increasing over-all information efficiency, an individual manufacturer must gain a savings from the use of a middleman. Without a middleman, each individual manufacturer would have information costs of bn. If bn were greater than the charge levied by the middleman for carrying out the function, the manufacturer would use the middleman. If the costs with a middleman $[(m + n)b]$ were distributed equally among manufacturers, each manufacturer would pay $(m + n)b/m$. Now, the manufacturer would use a middleman to carry out the information function if

$$bn > \frac{(m + n)b}{m}$$

This inequality can be expressed as

$$mn > m + n$$

which is the same as the condition obtained in Eq. (5-4) from considerations of the total industry structure.

Demand Creation Functions

Demand creation aspects are present to some degree in the performance of both the availability and information functions. If the product is not available, there can be no sales, so availability is certainly a necessary part of the demand creation efforts directed at sales results. If the product is out of stock and delivery delay is an important factor in the decision to buy, the customer may be reluctant to purchase. Similarly, the execution of the information function uses the content of the information to exert demand creation influence. Although these factors have been discussed, the previous sections did not explicitly consider other possible demand aspects of distribution. The demand creation function

[9] See H. H. Baligh and L. E. Richartz, "An Analysis of Vertical Market Structures," *Management Science*, X (July, 1964), pp. 667–89, for a discussion of equilibrium in the face of market imperfections.

can be separated into three areas:

1. Service
2. Customer efficiency
3. Persuasion

Service is the first aspect of demand creation during distribution. The ability and willingness of the seller to provide service for the product is an important determinant for many customers. This service may be in the form of repair and maintenance facilities, return and exchange privileges, the extension of financial credit, or rapid delivery. The level of service is specified in the manufacturer's marketing plan, but he may call upon middlemen to carry out this function when he designs the total distribution system.

Customer efficiency relates to the reduction in the amount of effort expended by customers to purchase products to fill their needs. This may be dependent on the distribution parameters of retail location and the assortment available at each outlet. The use of channels of distribution that display the product at convenient physical locations will be a demand stimulus. The internal layout of the store will be another factor affecting shopping efficiency. The extensiveness of distribution will also be a factor in increasing sales, but it will have to be balanced against the cost of additional distribution outlets.

The use of distribution intermediaries can also improve customer efficiency by making an assortment of goods available at one location or from one source. For example, a consumer may save time by shopping at a retail store that stocks the assortment of goods he is interested in purchasing. Industrial buyers often prefer to purchase from sources that maintain complete selections. The pooling of products by intermediaries exerts a demand creation effect on the manufacturer's product when it is made available at a convenient location or from a convenient source and is stocked or presented with a relevant collection of other goods.

The persuasion functions of distribution are necessary to convince customers of the desirable features of the product and to encourage purchase. Convincing information must reach the customer, and his questions concerning the product should be answered. One of the manufacturer's available methods of performing the persuasion function is to place a sales force in the field to contact each customer. For some consumer goods, this is done in door-to-door sales efforts. In industrial product markets, the use of a manufacturer's sales force to carry out the persuasion function is common. For many product distribution systems, however, direct selling force methods may not be the most efficient way to carry out the persuasion effort. Intermediaries often may more efficiently carry out the function by using a sales force within the channel. Retailers' use of clerks to aid in selling products is an example of the execution of the persuasion function by an intermediary. If the outlet carries competing products, persuasion effort in this channel may be less effective than the manufacturer desires, since the intermediary's representative may not have a commitment to any one brand. Although this reduces the sales pressure on the manufacturer's brand, the availability of a selection of competing products may be a positive factor for a customer shopping at a particular outlet. The manufacturer must balance these factors in designing his distribution system.

In Chap. 3 it was indicated that persuasion functions may be carried out by the use of advertising. Although manufacturers could reach all customers with directly placed advertising, channel members may be more effective in carrying out parts of the advertising program. This is especially true in convincing the consumer to make the effort to examine the actual product.

In addition to advertising and sales effort, the reputation of the intermediary can be an important demand creation aspect of a channel. The intermediary's reputation may be a very persuasive factor in achieving sales of the product at the final point of purchase. These factors will be reflected in the past performance of the store and in its physical appearance. A modern, well-designed retail store may have a good reputation and an environment consistent with the psychological and sociological characteristics of the customers. In industrial markets, the reputation of the manufacturer's representative and his personal relations with customers' buyers influence demand.

The demand creation functions of distribution have been discussed under the classifications of service, customer efficiency, and persuasion. These functions are vital to the efficient marketing of the product and may be carried out by either the middlemen or the manufacturer. In actual practice, each stage of the channel generally contributes to the performance of the demand creation function. The efforts of all channel members should be complementary and should be designed so as to optimize channel performance.

Summary of Distribution Functions

This section has analyzed the functions of distribution as defined in the areas of availability, information, and demand creation. This development did not concern itself with the decision of who should carry out the function, but rather with the over-all nature of the functions of distribution and the possible role middlemen could play in performing the functions.   The next task is to structure the decision aspects of the manufacturer's distribution system design and to explore the possible solution techniques available to help in making these decisions.

SPECIFIC DISTRIBUTION DECISIONS

Distribution Decision Procedure

The over-all distribution problem from the manufacturer's point of view is to design a distribution system that presents the desired marketing profile to customers and maximizes the firm's profit.   This is a complex decision, and it will be analyzed in a series of steps with appropriate feedback loops.   This decision structure is indicated in Fig. 5-3.

The decision procedure begins with the specification of the desired endpoint or point-of-purchase marketing mix for the product.   This includes a detailed specification of the best combination of controllable marketing variables such as advertising, price, etc. and is based on an understanding of market behavior and response.   With this marketing plan in mind, the manufacturer must decide what channels of distribution to utilize.   The output of this decision is the selection of the middleman institutions to be used in reaching each market segment.   Figure 5-1 illustrates this process.   It might be noted that the channel selection process is often one of mutual seeking out.   That is, channel intermediaries may seek out manufacturers as well.   The selection of a set of institutions may not be sufficient to design the system.   The selected intermediaries may be unable or unwilling to carry out the desired functions at the specified reward structure.   If this is true, the manufacturer could attempt to create the desired performance by integrating the middleman functions into his company, by persuading the middleman to cooperate by bargaining with intermediaries, or by changing the reward structure for these middlemen (e.g., higher margins).   If these efforts cannot be effectively carried out, the manufacturer would have to change his marketing plans and repeat the selection decision.

After the selection of the channels of distribution, the detailed facilities decisions must be made.   The number, size, and location of each type of middleman must be specified.   The output of this decision is an indication of the desired level of distribution facilities.   If any of the indicated middlemen do not exist or are unwilling to carry out the desired functions, efforts must be made to create them or to bargain with them to achieve the desired plan.   If these agreements cannot be profitably reached, the local marketing plans and perhaps the over-all marketing mix

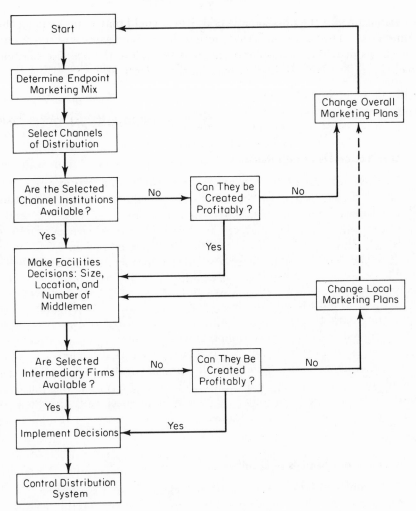

**Figure 5-3: Distribution decision
flow diagram**

would have to be changed and the facilities level again specified. Given
that all the middlemen exist and are willing to perform the required
functions, the plan is implemented. After implementation, the channel
must be controlled to assure that the specified marketing plan is correctly
carried out and to signal when it is time to adjust the marketing mix
and/or the channel structure to changed market conditions.

The decisions outlined in Fig. 5-3 will be discussed in the following
sections of this chapter. Solution techniques will be outlined and existing management approaches to distribution will be developed.

Determination of Endpoint Marketing Mix

The basic decision underlying the determination of the distribution system is the specification of the marketing mix for the firm's product. This decision includes the final selling price, the level of advertising, the characteristics of the product, and the degree of distribution effort. The intensity of distribution effort would be expressed in terms of the level of availability, the degree of market communication, and the amount of demand creation activity established for the product. For example, the distribution variables might include the delivery rate, credit availability, repair service capability, sales effort, promotion, point-of-purchase display, and market feedback to the firm.

The determination of the best marketing mix to be presented to each market segment is a multivariate decision problem similar to the optimal price and advertising decision discussed in Chap. 4. To solve the problem, a sales response function to the marketing variables would have to be generated for each segment. These responses and the costs associated with them would provide the bases for a profit model to determine the optimum marketing mix. The optimum marketing mix problem will be considered in Chap. 7 in conjunction with the analysis of new products. In the remainder of this chapter, it will be assumed that the best levels for the marketing variables have been determined. Although some of the models developed in this chapter would be useful in specifying the best marketing plan for the product, they are more specifically designed to aid in making distribution decisions.

Selection of Channels of Distribution

The problem of the selection of the channels of distribution for a manufacturer has been described in an earlier section of this chapter. The problem is to determine the intermediary institutions to be utilized in establishing a desired marketing plan in designated market segments. This is a complex problem, since the firm may visualize a number of segments in its market, thus producing an intricate interrelated system of channels. The selection problem is further complicated when the firm sells a number of products and may therefore gain economies of scale by utilizing the same channels of distribution for more than one product. The selection problem will be approached by exploring management science techniques that may be used to aid in the normative designation of channel members. The considerations of implementing this normative plan in an environment of independent intermediaries where bargaining and feedback adjustments are necessary will also be discussed.

The determination of the middlemen to utilize in the channel ideally should be made on the basis of profit considerations. Artle and Berglund have analyzed a single-channel decision with profit and cost as criteria.[10] The decision they considered was the choice between a direct sales force channel and the use of a wholesaler to aid in the distribution of the manufacturer's goods. They constructed a hypothetical example of an industry with two wholesalers and ten customers and developed a cost comparison of the wholesale and direct sales force systems. The costs included salaries, imputed costs for the time of each call, transportation costs, and ordering costs. In their example, the wholesaler reduced total distribution costs when the direct sales force and wholesaler's calling force were assumed to be equally effective. It is probable that this assumption does not usually hold true in actual practice. Since the direct sales force is not selling as many products, it may be able to make more frequent calls and should be able to generate more sales for the manufacturer. If this were true, cost could not be an appropriate criterion. Profit would be more desirable as a criterion, since the additional effectiveness would be measured in terms of added profit. For example, if the direct sales force generated more profits for the manufacturer by making more calls and selling more goods on each call, a direct channel would be preferable to the use of wholesalers. The greater profits could result even if the costs of the direct sales force were greater than the wholesaler costs.

Artle and Berglund developed an example to show that the channel choice is sensitive to the relative sales effectiveness of each channel. The indifference states between the direct sales and wholesaler choice would be those in which either alternative is equally attractive, that is, when either choice would produce equal profit. The model is based on defining the indifference states by an equation that is dependent upon the number of calls and average order size produced by each type of sales force. A pair of values for the number of calls and average order size for wholesalers will fall on a specific indifference or isoprofit line. If the direct sales force is estimated to be more effective, so that its pair of values fall on a higher isoprofit curve, it would be selected over the wholesaler.

This analysis is beneficial, since it indicates the profit implications of each channel choice and the differential performance required for one channel to be chosen over the other. The analysis does not consider the fact that the wholesaler's effectiveness (number of calls and average order size) might be changed by modifying the reward given to the

[10] R. Artle and S. Berglund, "A Note on Manufacturers' Choice of Distribution Channels," *Management Science* (July, 1959), pp. 460–71.

middleman, but it does include considerations of the demand creation function of channels of distribution.

. The profit approach to selection of channels of distribution outlined in the last paragraphs can be generalized to include more complex

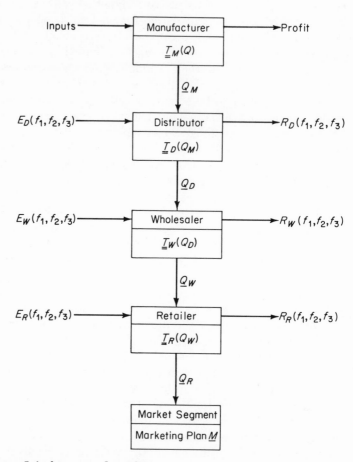

**Figure 5-4: A proposed market
segment channel**

channel structures.   The model structure presented earlier in this chapter provides the basis for such extensions (see Fig. 5-1).   For discussion purposes a single market segment channel is depicted in Fig. 5-4.   Recall that each middleman applies effort E with respect to the distribution unctions of availability f_1, information f_2, and demand creation f_3. This effort is called forth by a reward $R(f_1, f_2, f_3)$ that the intermediary gains from carrying out his functions. These rewards could be provided by a margin or markup in the selling price of the good. The effort expended by the middleman transforms the product $[\mathbf{T(Q)}]$. The transformation may be in adding time and place utility to the product or in making the product more attractive by the application of selling effort. The transformed product proceeds down the channel until it reaches the final market segment customer. The channel is required to meet the manufacturer's market segment plan.

The model can be used in the selection of channels if the channel can be optimized with respect to the reward functions to be established for each middleman and if alternate channel structures can be proposed and compared. The first demand on the model is to determine the optimum functions and rewards for each member in a proposed channel. If the effort, transformation, and reward functions can be made explicit, dynamic programming can be used to determine the maximum profit gained by the manufacturer from a given channel structure. For example, if the wholesaler receives the product $\mathbf{Q}_D$, he could transform it by accumulating an inventory of the product. If his reward (margin) were increased, he could be encouraged to stock more of the product and therefore to reduce the required inventory at the next distribution level. The retailer could also carry out this inventory function. The margin required by the retailer might be less than that of the wholesaler, so that the channel could accomplish the endpoint marketing plan at lower cost and thereby increase the manufacturer's profit.

In real channels, the functions cannot be so easily separated. The input is usually in the form of a specific reward that will generate effort $f(f_1, f_2, f_3)$ from a particular middleman. The effort transforms the product by changing the accumulated level of availability f_1, information f_2, and demand creation f_3. The channel reward structure should be established in such a way that it maximizes the manufacturer's profit subject to the constraint of achieving the market plan. A recursive model which assumes that the manufacturer receives the market revenue (final selling price times quantity sold) and then compensates or rewards each middleman r_i may serve as the basis of a solution to the channel selection problem. This is reasonable, since the manufacturer could carry out all the channel functions and is therefore suffering an opportunity loss by delegating functions to the middleman and allowing them to take part of the revenue generated in the market segment by the marketing plan. The solution to this model will specify how the functions should be split between the manufacturer and the intermediaries.

The technical recursion is

$$\text{Profit}_i(\mathbf{Q}_i) = \max_{r_i \in R_i} [G_i(\mathbf{Q}_i, r_i) + \text{Profit}_{i+1}(\mathbf{Q}_{i+1})]$$

where

$$\text{Profit}_4(\mathbf{Q}_4) = \max_{r_4 \in R_4} G_4(\mathbf{Q}_4, r_4)$$

Subject to

$$\mathbf{T}_4(\mathbf{Q}_4) = \mathbf{Q}_5 = \mathbf{M}$$

where Profit_1 = total profit gained by the manufacturer from sales of the product through the channel structure.

Profit_i = profit gained by the manufacturer at intermediary level i where $i = 2$ represents the distributor, $i = 3$ represents the wholesaler, and $i = 4$ represents the retailer. This will be a cost or negative profit, since the manufacturer is viewed as paying or rewarding the channel members for performing a prescribed set of distribution functions.

$\mathbf{Q}_i$ = the vector representing the state of the product as it enters the ith stage of the channel as expressed in the level of accomplishment of the marketing plan.

$\mathbf{Q}_5$ = state of product when submitted to the market segment. This is given by the segment marketing plan $\mathbf{M}$.

r_i = reward given by manufacturer to intermediary i, $i = 2, 3, 4$, for carrying out effort with respect to functions f_1, f_2, f_3.

R_i = total set of possible rewards that could be supplied to middlemen for carrying out distribution functions.

$G_i(\mathbf{Q}_i, r_i)$ = cost of carrying out transformation in channel when $i \neq 1$.

= profit earned by manufacturer when $i = 1$. Profit is based on valuing sales at their endpoint price and includes the costs (r_i) of the manufacturer performing his own distribution functions.

The use of the backward induction procedures of dynamic programming and this recursion relationship will yield the maximum profits for the manufacturer and the optimal assignment of distribution activities to intermediaries. If the structure of the channel were changed by removing a middleman, the model could be rerun and it would generate

ie best profit level for the new channel. Likewise, at each level in the
iannel, alternate types of middlemen could be tested. For example,
ie retail level could be tested with the use of discount stores or depart-
ient stores. The new total profit for the channel would supply the
·levant information needed to select the best channel structure. The
iodel could also supply information about the opportunity costs of alter-
ate endpoint marketing mixes **M**. If the model were rerun for various
I, the profit and channel structure implications could be estimated.

Although this embryonic model formulation is theoretically attractive,
has a number of practical limitations. The first is computational.
'he number of calculations necessary to analyze a proposed channel
iay be large, and the computational aspects of the dynamic program-
iing technique become burdensome when a number of market segments
re involved and when a number of channel structures are to be tested.
' the market segments are themselves interdependent, the complexity
icreases further. The second limitation is related to the structure of
ie firm's particular distribution problem. The model is useful in ana-
·zing the channel of distribution decision for one product when there
re only a few market segments, but if the number of segments is increased
nd if multiproduct channels are to be designed, the number of theoreti-
al and computational problems increases. The third limitation is the
ifficulty inherent in the specification of valid transformation and cost
inctions **T** and **G**. The last limitation of this selection model formula-
on is that it does not consider the risk aspects of the channel.[11] Fluctua-
ons resulting from changes in market demand may build up in a channel.
t may be preferable for the manufacturer to carry out more of the dis-
·ibution functions to reduce the channel demand fluctuations, even if the
rm's profit is lessened.

The risk aspects of channels of distribution have been analyzed by
ay Forrester by the use of industrial dynamics.[12] Forrester shows how
hanges in market demand can produce amplified fluctuations in the
emand of intermediaries and the manufacturer. The magnitude of the
uctuation is dependent upon the inventories and ordering rules of inter-
iediaries, the delays in processing and filling orders, the number of
iiddlemen, and the methods of sales forecasting applied by the manu-
icturer and intermediaries. Industrial dynamics and its associated com-
uter language, DYNAMO, are useful in simulating the amplification and
isk effects in a channel of distribution. There are a number of methods
hat may be used to reduce the fluctuations. The most relevant to this

[11] For considerations of the stochastic aspects of dynamic programming, see
t. Howard, *Dynamic Programming and Markov Processes* (Cambridge, Mass.: The
I.I.T. Press, 1960).
[12] J. Forrester, *Industrial Dynamics* (Cambridge, Mass.: The M.I.T. Press, 1961).

discussion is the reduction of risk by elimination of an intermediary level in the channel. If reducing the number of intermediaries reduces fluctuation and risk, it may be desirable to do so even if the manufacturer's total profit decreases.[13] The decision would have to be reached by balancing the reduction in risk with the reduction in total firm profits that results from altering the channel of distribution.

The analysis of the selection process up to this point has concerned itself with a normative designation of the channel structure and rewards. This idealized system may be desirable for the manufacturer, but intermediaries may be unable or unwilling to carry out the designated role. The middleman industry also operates on a profit maximization system and the manufacturer's requests may not be compatible with its goals. The model described in Fig. 5-4 did include the compensations that would be necessary to entice intermediaries to carry out functions, but this may be too superficial. The manufacturer may have to bargain and apply selling effort directly to the intermediary. If this persuasion effort or bargaining is not successful, the manufacturer will have to reconsider his normative structure in the light of the new information. This feedback aspect of the selection of channels of distribution will probably be necessary, since intermediaries operate as independent firms. The feedback procedure first leads to efforts to achieve the desired middleman ability and willingness (see Fig. 5-3). If the channel can be adjusted in a profitable fashion, this change is undertaken and the firm continues to consider the facilities aspects of distribution. If the desired changes cannot be accomplished, the manufacturer must readjust his endpoint marketing plans and goals and again repeat the normative channel selection procedure. This procedure is continued until a satisfactory channel system and marketing plan evolve.

Distribution Facilities Decisions

With a designation of the types of middlemen a manufacturer intends to use in his channel of distribution, the next problem is to determine the

---

[13] This would be true if the manufacturer's utility for money is nonlinear in the operating region or if goals other than profit (e.g., stabilization of jobs for the company's employees) are important considerations.

[14] This raises the issue of what might be termed "interorganization management." For a related discussion, see J. L. Heskett and R. H. Ballou, "Logistical Planning in Interorganizational Systems," *Proceedings of the Academy of Management*, 1966, pp 124–36. For models of intermediary behavior see A. E. Amstutz, *Computer Simulation of Competitive Market Response* (Cambridge, Mass: The M.I.T. Press, 1967) Chaps. 9 and 10, and G. S. Schussel, "Sales Forecasting with the Aid of a Human Behavior Simulator," *Management Science*, XIII, No. 10 (June, 1967), pp. B-593-B-611.

umber, size, and location of the distribution facilities. If the manu-
acturer carries out all the distribution functions, the problem is one of
eciding where to build or contract for distribution facilities. If the
niddleman institutions chosen are independent firms, the problem is to
ecide what intermediaries to choose and how to create the desired facili-
ies capability within the chosen intermediary firms, if the facilities are
ot as desired. (See Fig. 5-3 for the relation of the facilities decisions
vith the total distribution decision.)

Facilities decisions have been approached by two basic methods. The
irst approach is based on minimizing the total cost of distribution. The
econd approach is based on maximization of the firm's profits that are
roduced when distribution is effectively carried out. The second
pproach includes consideration of the demand aspects of distribution and
ttempts to optimize not only the profit earned by carrying out physical
listribution of goods but also the total profits of the firm. The cost
ninimization approach to facilities decisions has received considerable
esearch effort. The cost minimization technique generally assumes
lemand to be fixed or exogeneous and will be described only briefly in
his book. The profit maximization approach has not received the
esearch it deserves, but the existing models will be described in some
letail, since they are particularly relevant to marketing.

Cost minimization approaches to the facilities decision

The first cost minimization approaches were related to single plant
or warehouse location. Bowman developed a cost function for distribut-
ng goods based on fixed warehouse costs and transportation costs that
varied with the area served by the facility.[15] The function was then
lifferentiated and solved to find the optimal size of area for a facility
o serve. The assumption of this method is that demand is fixed and uni-
ormly distributed over the geographic area. Thus, for the Bowman
model to be appropriate, demand must be approximately uniformly
listributed rather than located at specific points (e.g., cities) in an area.

Early attempts to minimize the costs of transporting goods from one
plant or warehouse to a number of given demand points were based on the
center of gravity method. The method was used because of the logical
appeal of the analogy to physical systems. The quantity demanded at
each point is weighted by the cost per mile of reaching it, and the weighted
demands are treated as mass centers. The center of gravity of the system

[15] E. H. Bowman and J. B. Stewart, "A Model for Scale of Operations," *Journal of Marketing*, XX (Jan., 1956), pp. 242–47, and E. H. Bowman, "Scale of Operation—An Empirical Study," *Operations Research*, VI (May–June, 1958), pp. 320–28.

is found by applying the principles of mechanics.[16] The difficulty with this approach is that, in general, it does not specify the lowest cost location. If the total cost function is differentiated with respect to the coordinates of the proposed warehouse and these equations are solved it will not yield the center of gravity, except in special cases.[17] A simple example will demonstrate the limitations of the center of gravity approach. Consider two demand centers a distance d apart and having total demands M_1 and M_2, respectively. Further, let the cost per unit of the product shipped a unit distance be given by C. Then the total cost of shipping to these demand centers will be

$$TC = C[xM_1 + (d - x)M_2]$$
$$= C[x(M_1 - M_2) + dM_2]$$

where TC = total shipping costs to satisfy demands M_1 and M_2,
     x = distance of warehouse from M_1 along a straight line connecting M_1 and M_2.

If this total cost is differentiated with respect to x and set equal to zero the result is

$$C(M_1 - M_2) = 0$$

which is uninformative as to the optimal value of x (i.e., the optimal location of the warehouse). Since the calculus did not prove useful, the optimum x, if it exists, must lie at one of the extreme values of $x = 0$ or $x = d$. If $M_1 > M_2$, the optimal x is zero. If $M_1 < M_2$, the optimum is $x = d$. For $M_1 = M_2$, the extreme location selected for the warehouse will have no effect on cost. These cost minimization solutions are entirely different from the center of gravity solution which would set

$$x = \left(\frac{M_2}{M_1 + M_2}\right) d$$

The logical appeal of the center of gravity method is strong, but it does not in general minimize distribution cost.

The center of gravity analogy has been generalized from the single facility case to the multifacility case.[18] These approaches use cost func-

[16] E. W. Smykay, D. J. Bowersox, and F. H. Mossman, *Physical Distribution Management* (New York: The Macmillan Company, 1961), pp. 176–201.

[17] R. C. Vergin and J. D. Rogers, "An Algorithm and Computational Procedure for Locating Economic Facilities," *Management Science*, XIII (Feb., 1967), pp. 240–54.

[18] L. Copper, "Location-Allocation Problems," *Operations Research*, XI (May-June, 1963), pp. 331–43, and F. E. Maranzana, "On the Location of Supply Points to Minimize Transport Costs," *Operational Research Quarterly*, XV (Sept., 1964), pp. 261–70.

ions similar to the center of gravity forms, but they find the best location
y heuristic procedures rather than solving directly for the center of
ravity.

The costs considered in the distribution facilities models outlined
bove included warehouse fixed costs and transportation costs but not
ventory costs and considerations. Inventories can be used to gain
conomies of scale in transporting larger quantities, but this gain must be
alanced against the additional storage charges and working capital costs
f the inventory. Magee has outlined these considerations and empha-
ized that the cost minimization should entail all the cost elements in the
hysical distribution system.[19] Magee proposes to minimize the total
osts of inventory and transportation. Minimization of this function by
he univariate calculus model yields the optimum size of order.[20]

The concepts of inventory costs and multiple distribution facilities
an be integrated within the framework of mathematical programming.
The programming problem is:

$$\text{Minimize total cost} = \sum_{ijk} C_{ijk}(x_{ijk}) + \sum_{j} F_j I_j$$

subject to
$$\sum_{ij} x_{ijk} = Q_k$$

where $x_{ijk} \geq 0$ and $I_j = 0, 1$.

x_{ijk} = quantity of goods shipped by factory i via wholesaler
j to retailer $k(i = 1, \ldots, m; j = 1, \ldots, n; k = 1, \ldots, q)$.

$C_{ijk}(x_{ijk})$ = cost function for distributing x_{ijk}. This includes transport and inventory costs and is not necessarily linear
over x_{ijk}.

F_j = fixed costs for warehouse j.

I_j = integer of zero or one indicating usage of facility j if
$I_j = 1$ and no usage if $I_j = 0$.

Q_k = demand requirements (assumed to be fixed).

This is a mixed integer programming problem (i.e., x_{ijk} is noninteger and
I_j is integer). This form is designed to determine the optimum number
f facilities to utilize, given a set of m potential plant locations, n wholesalers, and q retailers. It also specifies the optimum assignment of
customers to warehouses and warehouses to factories.

[19] J. F. Magee, "Logistics of Distribution," *Harvard Business Review*, XXXVIII
(July–Aug., 1960), pp. 89–101.

[20] It should be noted that the optimum order size developed here differs from the
standard economic ordering quantity (EOQ) presented in most discussions in that it
minimizes transportation costs as well as inventory costs.

The first attempt to solve the problem was by Baumol and Wolfe. They did not consider fixed costs (i.e. $F_j = 0$), so the problem became nonlinear programming problem. This assumption is reasonable if th manufacturer does not own the wholesale warehouse, but rather utilize intermediaries to carry out the wholesale functions and therefore accrue no fixed warehousing costs. The growth in mathematical programmin technology led to attempts to solve the general facilities problem wit fixed costs. Balinski formulated it as a mixed integer programmin problem,[22] whereas Chuang and Smith used dynamic programming. Manne considered an iterative search routine based on an algorithm o movement in the direction of steepest assent.[24] Efroymson and Ra applied branch and bound techniques to derive solutions to the facilitie selection and cost minimization problem.[25] Each of these mode examines slightly different problems, but they are all relevant to th general facilities problem.

Although the programming efforts described above were theoreticall attractive, they proved to be computationally unsatisfactory in som situations. For this reason and because of a felt need for greater flexibi ity, heuristic procedures for facilities location were developed. Kueh and Hamburger developed the first heuristic model.[26] Their model wa designed to determine the best number and location of warehouses for manufacturer who owns his own distribution system. The objectiv was to minimize the total cost of distribution. An interesting aspec of this model is the inclusion of a demand creation factor in the costs the factor is delivery delay, and it was treated as an opportunity cos to the manufacturer and measured by lost sales and profits resultin from poor delivery service times.[27] The heuristic used to minimize th total distribution was based on first defining a set of trial locations an then adding, removing, or shifting warehouses one at a time until n further cost reductions can be gained by this procedure.

The Kuehn and Hamburger heuristic program is indicated in Fig. 5-5

[21] W. J. Baumol and P. Wolfe, "A Warehouse Location Problem," *Operation Research*, VI (March–April, 1958), pp. 252–63.

[22] M. L. Balinski, "Integer Programming: Methods, Uses, Computation," *Man agement Science*, XII (Nov., 1965), pp. 286–93.

[23] Y. H. Chuang and W. G. Smith, "A Dynamic Programming Model for Combine Production Distribution and Storage," *Journal of Industrial Engineering*, (Jan., 1966) pp. 7–13.

[24] A. S. Manne, "Plant Location Under Economies of Scale-Decentralization an Computation," *Management Science*, XI (Nov., 1964), pp. 213–35.

[25] M. A. Efroymson and T. L. Ray, "A Branch-Bound Algorithm for Plant Loca tion," *Operations Research*, XIV (May–June, 1966), pp. 361–68.

[26] A. A. Kuehn and M. J. Hamburger, "A Heuristic Program for Locating Ware houses," *Management Science*, IX (July, 1963), pp. 643–66.

[27] See L. P. Bucklin, "Postponement, Speculation, and the Structure of Distribu tion Channels," *Journal of Marketing Research*, II (Feb., 1965), pp. 26–31, for a dis cussion of this opportunity cost approach.

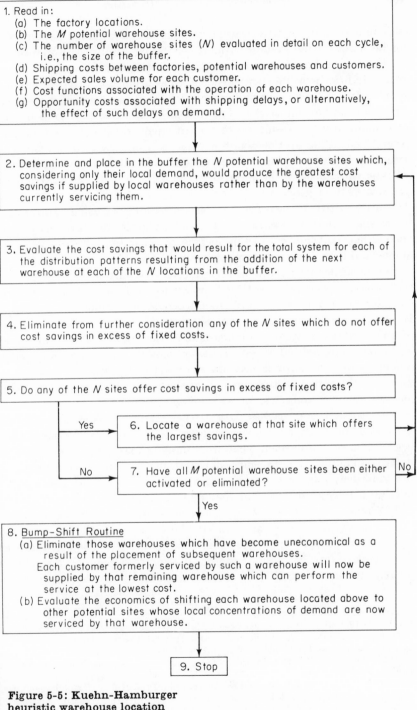

1. Read in:
   (a) The factory locations.
   (b) The *M* potential warehouse sites.
   (c) The number of warehouse sites (*N*) evaluated in detail on each cycle, i.e., the size of the buffer.
   (d) Shipping costs between factories, potential warehouses and customers.
   (e) Expected sales volume for each customer.
   (f) Cost functions associated with the operation of each warehouse.
   (g) Opportunity costs associated with shipping delays, or alternatively, the effect of such delays on demand.

2. Determine and place in the buffer the *N* potential warehouse sites which, considering only their local demand, would produce the greatest cost savings if supplied by local warehouses rather than by the warehouses currently servicing them.

3. Evaluate the cost savings that would result for the total system for each of the distribution patterns resulting from the addition of the next warehouse at each of the *N* locations in the buffer.

4. Eliminate from further consideration any of the *N* sites which do not offer cost savings in excess of fixed costs.

5. Do any of the *N* sites offer cost savings in excess of fixed costs?

   Yes → 6. Locate a warehouse at that site which offers the largest savings.

   No → 7. Have all *M* potential warehouse sites been either activated or eliminated? No

   Yes

8. Bump-Shift Routine
   (a) Eliminate those warehouses which have become uneconomical as a result of the placement of subsequent warehouses.
       Each customer formerly serviced by such a warehouse will now be supplied by that remaining warehouse which can perform the service at the lowest cost.
   (b) Evaluate the economics of shifting each warehouse located above to other potential sites whose local concentrations of demand are now serviced by that warehouse.

9. Stop

Figure 5-5: Kuehn-Hamburger heuristic warehouse location program

Source: Kuehn and Hamburger, *op. cit.*, p. 647.   By permission of the publisher and authors.

The main program locates warehouses one at a time until no additions can be made to the system without increasing total distribution costs. The bump and shift routine receives a list of the potential warehouse sites with an indication as to whether each site has been activated or eliminated by the main program. The bump and shift program serves two functions. First, it examines all of the activated sites to see if any have become uneconomical as a result of the addition of subsequent warehouses. Second, it evaluates the possibility of shifting a warehouse to other potential sites whose local demand concentrations are now being serviced by that warehouse. The inputs needed by the heuristic program are outlined in the figure.

Other heuristic procedures have been developed by using various rules for finding lower cost locations. Feldman, Lehrer, and Ray have developed a heuristic procedure that begins by including all possible warehouses and then dropping them one by one until no further cost reduction is gained, while at the same time preserving the current location pattern that produces the least cost.[28] This model also has the advantage of considering economies of scale associated with the size of the warehouse. Hammond has developed a transshipment model to minimize the cost of a distribution system and a heuristic procedure to remove warehouses with low volume.[29] L. Cooper has proposed a number of alternate models based on heuristic procedures of successive approximation, random specification of destination, subset analysis, and alternate allocation-location specifications.[30]

The heuristic approaches outlined here have considerable flexibility and have proven capable of specifying good solutions in practice. However, advances in mathematical programming may make the previously described analytical approaches computationally more feasible and therefore relatively more attractive. Both of these approaches deal with the over-all facilities problem, but they do so at an aggregated level.

In some situations a very detailed representation of the distribution system is desired. For example, simulation may be the only realistic method for incorporating exceedingly complex distribution factors such as transportation costs.[31] In order to analyze a detailed distribution model, simulation must generally be used.[32] It has the capability of

[28] E. Feldman, F. Lehrer, and T. L. Ray, "Warehouse Location Under Continuous Economies of Scale," *Management Science*, XII (May, 1966), pp. 670–84.

[29] R. A. Hammond, "Reducing Fixed and Variable Costs of Distribution," *Management Technology*, III (Dec., 1963), pp. 119–27.

[30] L. Cooper, "Heuristic Methods for Location-Allocation Problems," *SIAM Review* (Jan., 1964), pp. 37–53.

[31] H. N. Shycon and R. B. Maffei, "Remarks on the Kuehn-Hamburger Paper," *Management Science*, IX (July, 1963), pp. 643–44.

[32] H. N. Shycon and R. B. Maffei, "Simulation—A Tool for Better Distribution," *Harvard Business Review*, XVIII (Nov.–Dec., 1960), pp. 65–75.

considering specific factors, such as the types of products by customer types, by the size of the orders, and by the location of customers. The technique can encompass specific details of warehouses, factories, transportation costs, customer assignment, and delivery requirements.[33]

The simulation approach is useful in analyzing alternative distribution systems. In this role the computational requirements for most distribution simulation models restrict evaluation to a few alternatives. The question is what alternatives should be chosen for analysis. A promising approach would be to generate alternatives for simulation evaluation by using mathematical or heuristic programming on a simpler version of the model. In this way, the different cost minimization approaches could be used compatibly to specify and describe in detail the distribution facilities plan that minimizes total cost of distribution.

Profit maximization approaches to facilities decisions

The cost minimization approaches to facility location outlined in the previous section did not fully consider the demand creation aspects of facilities location. Some of the cost minimization models have an implicit constraint that represents the service level required by the market, or an objective function that includes an opportunity cost term associated with poor service. However, these modifications are not the best method of incorporating the demand creation aspects of distribution. These aspects are best measured in sales results, which are then related to over-all company profit. Since total firm profit was the criterion for the choice of the channels of distribution, it would be consistent to use it as the criterion for solving the facilities problem. The facilities decision is the physical implementation of the channels decision, so to retain the optimizing nature of distribution decisions, facilities should be determined so as to maximize profits.

The desirability of maximizing profits through plant location has been stressed by Greenhut.[34] His analysis emphasizes the fact that location may be affected not only by costs but also by competition and market demand conditions. Greenhut examines the implications of spatial effects upon market structure, input factor prices, and firm behavior. This approach has also been explored by Churchill.[35] He proposes a

---

[33] See M. L. Gerson and R. B. Maffei, "Technical Characteristic of Distribution Simulators," *Management Science*, X (Oct., 1963), pp. 62–69. It should be noted that Kuehn and Hamburger's approach also incorporated many of these features.

[34] M. L. Greenhut, *Microeconomics and the Space Economy* (Chicago: Scott Foresman and Company, 1963).

[35] G. A. Churchill, Jr., "Production Technology, Imperfect Competition and the Theory of Location: A Theoretical Approach," *Southern Economic Journal*, XXXIV (July, 1967), pp. 86–100.

plant location analysis based on profit maximization and explicitly considers the adjustment of price in determining the maximum profit produced at a location. When this approach is used, the minimum cost location may not be chosen, because both costs and marketing variables (price) are considered. The approaches of Greenhut and Churchill have not considered multiplant firms or the facilities problems of the distribution channel, but they do reflect a first attempt at profit maximization in facilities location.

Profit maximization within the distribution channel is important in cases where the distribution channel is to carry out demand creation functions. Earlier in this chapter the demand creation functions were grouped into three classes: (1) service, (2) customer efficiency, and (3) persuasion. Each of these functions can be affected by the selection of the number, size, and location of facilities.

One aspect of the service function of the distribution channel may be expressed in terms of delivery time. More rapid delivery may be a demand creation factor that could increase sales. The delivery time will depend upon the availability of the desired products. Availability is affected by the distance to the distribution outlet, which is dependent upon the number and location of outlets and the inventories maintained at these outlets. The sales aspects of service as measured by delivery time can be included in facilities decision models. Recall that the Kuehn and Hamburger heuristic programming approach incorporated this demand creation aspect as an opportunity cost. Another example is given by Mossman and Morton, who have directly included delivery time effects in the center of gravity approach to the location of a single facility given a number of point demands.[36] In their formulation, they assume demand to be related to delivery time by the expression

$$q = aq_0e^{-\alpha t/t_0} \qquad (5\text{-}6)$$

where t = delivery time,
         q = quantity ordered with delivery time t,
         q_0 = quantity ordered with delivery time t_0,
         α, a = constants.

Then, with the added assumption that the delivery time t is proportional to the distance from the facility, they use calculus to find the optimum single facility location, given the demand relationship in Eq. (5-6) and given that the demand occurs at given points.

The delivery time may not be related only to the distance from the consumer to the distribution outlet. The delay in filling an order may be

[36] F. H. Mossman and N. Morton, *Logistics of Distribution Systems* (Boston: Allyn and Bacon, Inc., 1965), pp. 247–56.

related to the inventory of that good at the distribution facility. The inventory level established at each facility is related to the size of the facility. Hanssman has attacked this facility size problem by modeling the inventory problem for a distribution system when the criterion is profit.[37] Hanssman links delivery time to sales and profits. Although Hanssman does not mathematically state the relationship of delivery time to sales, his graph indicated that sales are a nonlinear decreasing function of delivery time. With this relationship, he describes the expected profit that will result from an expected weekly demand that is normally distributed, an inventory target level, and a given facilities location. He then maximizes this equation to find the optimal inventory size and delivery time. The model is extended to production decisions and to a multilevel distribution system for a multiproduct firm. It is not within the scope of this chapter to discuss the details of the inventory decision, but it is important to note that these decisions can affect the facilities decision and that the methodology of encompassing the demand creation and inventory aspects of distribution has profit maximization as its objective.

Another service factor related to delivery time appears when the customer purchases the goods at a retail outlet. The customer must be serviced by a clerk who completes and records the sale and receives payment. If the customer is not willing to be delayed and he must wait, this will have an adverse effect on sales. Queuing theory may be used to analyze the effects of the service by clerks.[38] For example, Stokes and Mintz have developed a model to determine the number of clerks to place on a selling floor.[39] Five variables are defined and expressed as probability distributions: (1) the number of customers arriving per time period, (2) the amount of sales time required by a customer, (3) the number of items purchased per sales contact, (4) the profit generated by the sales, and (5) the amount of time a customer is willing to wait before leaving without purchasing. These distributions are combined by a Monte Carlo analysis which draws successive samples from the distributions to produce an aggregate profit distribution. With a model of this type, different numbers of clerks or service facilities could be tested until the most profitable level of service facilities is found.

In addition to the use of service as a demand creation factor, increasing

[37] F. Hanssman, "Optimal Inventory Location and Control in Production and Distribution," *Operations Research*, VII (July–Aug., 1959), pp. 483–98.

[38] D. Y. Barrer, "Queuing with Impatient Customers and Indifferent Clerks" and "Queuing with Impatient Customers and Ordered Service," *Operations Research*, V (Oct., 1957), pp. 644–56.

[39] C. J. Stokes and P. Mintz, "How Many Clerks on a Floor?" *Journal of Marketing Research*, II (Nov., 1965), pp. 388–93.

consumer efficiency may positively affect sales. Earlier in this chapter, the location and assortment of goods at an outlet were cited as factors influencing sales. The layout of the outlet may also be a determinant of consumer efficiency. For example, the layout of a retail store may affect the total sales in that store. The efficiency of the traffic flow in a retail store can be examined by management science techniques as in the model for traffic flow in a supermarket developed by Farley and Ring.[40] It examines the demand creation effects of store layout by studying the traffic flow in the supermarket. The dependent variable of the model is a first-order Markov matrix that describes the probabilities of a customer's moving from one area of the supermarket to another. These transition probabilities are established by four independent variables, which describe the forces exerted on a consumer facing a routing choice and the basic tendencies of consumers to follow the store perimeter and to move in a circular fashion. The mathematical expressions describing these variables are based on loose analogies to physical laws. A linear regression procedure is used to relate the independent variables to the dependent Markov transition probabilities.

The proposed model was tested by attempting to replicate observed store traffic flows and by predicting new traffic flows. In five tests, the model explained between 61 and 74 per cent of the past flows and 60 to 74 per cent of the newly observed flows. The stochastic formulation appears to yield acceptable predictions of store traffic patterns. With this model, layouts and merchandising policies could be tested to determine the best traffic flow in a store.

Store layout could also be analyzed by queuing theory. The number of check-out counters would be important in determining the amount of time a customer must wait for check-out service.[41] This analysis would be similar to the model used to determine the number of clerks to have in a store, which was discussed earlier.

The consumer efficiency aspects of distribution may be an important factor in determining the number of distribution outlets. Retail stores that are conveniently located will reduce the total effort expended by consumers to purchase goods and services. The density of outlets in an area will depend on these demand creation aspects as well as on the costs of distribution.

An interesting analysis encompassing these considerations has been developed by Hartung and Fisher.[42] They developed a model to aid in

[40] J. U. Farley and L. W. Ring, "A Stochastic Model of Supermarket Traffic Flow," *Operations Research* (July, 1966), pp. 555–67.

[41] See C. McMillan and R. F. Gonzalez, *Systems Analysis* (Homewood, Ill.: Irwin, 1965), pp. 166–85, for a discussion of simulation of multichannel queuing systems.

[42] P. H. Hartung and J. L. Fisher, "Brand Switching and Mathematical Programming in Market Expansion," *Management Science*, XI (Aug., 1965), pp. 231–43.

the facilities decision for gasoline stations. The model explores the sales effects of the density of outlets in an area. The most interesting finding is that the sales of each station of a brand are not independent. This implies that the change in total sales resulting from adding one more station in an area may not be merely the sales of that station.

Hartung and Fisher's model begins by postulating a theoretical model for gasoline purchases. They propose a brand switching model to explain consumer behavior. The basic relationship is

$$X_{t+1} = aX_t + bMS_t$$

where
X_t = market share of brand A in time period t,
MS_t = market share of all competitive brands in time period t (Note: $X_t + MS_t = 1$),
a = probability of repurchase of brand A if customer purchased brand A in the last period,
b = probability of switching to brand A if customer purchased a competitor's brand in the last period,
$0 < a, b, < 1$.

This is a first-order Markov process, and if a and b are constant over time, it will converge to[43]

$$X = aX + bMS$$

or
$$X = aX + b(1 - X)$$

where X is the steady state market share for brand A.

Solving for X gives

$$X = \frac{b}{1 - a + b}$$

The transition probabilities (a, b) are now hypothesized to be proportional to the relative number of outlets the brand has in the market:

$$a = K_1\left(\frac{P}{N + P}\right) \quad \text{and} \quad b = K_2\left(\frac{P}{N + P}\right)$$

where
P = number of outlets carrying brand A,
N = number of outlets carrying competitive brands,
K_1, K_2 = constants.

Reexpressing the steady state market share under this hypothesis yields

$$X = \frac{K_2 P}{N + (1 + K_2 - K_1)P}$$

[43] See J. G. Kemeny, H. Mirkil, J. L. Snell, and G. L. Thompson, *Finite Mathematical Structures* (Englewood Cliffs, N.J.: Prentice-Hall, Inc., 1959), p. 394.

If S = sales of brand A and T = total sales of all brands, this equation becomes

$$X = \frac{S}{T} = \frac{K_2 P}{N + (1 + K_2 - K_1)P} \tag{5-7}$$

or

$$\frac{S}{P} = \frac{K_2 T}{N + (1 + K_2 - K_1)P}$$

S/P is the average sales per outlet and the equation implies, given K_1, K_2, and T, that the average sales per outlet depends upon the number of outlets P carrying brand A and the number N carrying other brands. If $(1 + K_2 - K_1)$ is negative and the number of competitive locations are given, the average sales S/P for each of brand A's outlets would increase as the number of stations in the area is increased. Conversely, if $(1 + K_2 - K_1)$ is positive, more brand A stations will decrease the average sales of all of brand A's stations. The factor $(1 + K_2 - K_1)$ reflects the interdependency between distribution outlets for a given brand.

To estimate the values of K_1 and K_2, Hartung and Fisher reexpressed Eq. (5-7) by defining two variables:

$$\hat{N} = \frac{T}{N + P}$$

$$\hat{S} = \frac{S}{P}$$

where $\hat{N}$ is the average sales per outlet for the total industry and $\hat{S}$ is the average sales per station for brand A. With these new terms, Eq. (5-7) can be written as

$$\frac{\hat{S}}{\hat{N}} = K_2 + (K_1 - K_2)X \tag{5-8}$$

The term $\hat{S}/\hat{N}$ represents the company's average sales per outlet as a proportion of the total industry average sales per outlet. Using Eq. (5-8), a linear regression of actual sales data in the Pittsburgh standard metropolitan area yielded values of $K_1 = 4.44$ and $K_2 = 0.64$ and explained over 64 per cent of the variation in the data. It is interesting to note that $(1 + K_2 - K_1) = 1 + 0.64 - 4.44 = -2.8$, so that by Eq. (5-7), the average sales per station would increase as new stations were added. This is true, however, only for the range of the data used in estimation (brand A market share < 20 per cent). It is reasonable to assume that the linear relationship would not be true outside this range and that diminishing returns would eventually occur.

The empirical economies of scale of additional facilities in an area might be explained by two facts. The first explanation reflects the consumer efficiency gained by the use of gasoline credit cards. If consumers tend to obtain credit cards for the most convenient brand in an area (this may be the brand with the largest number of stations in the area), then increasing the number of outlets of a brand will increase the number of credit card holders and therefore will supply a mechanism to explain why the average sales of all of the brand's outlets would increase by adding a new station. Another explanation is that the promotional aspects of displaying a brand name more frequently in an area might lead to increased sales to stations with the same brand name as the new station.

The model's result at this point is an equation relating total company sales to the number of outlets in the area. This can be seen by multiplying both sides of Eq. (5-7) by T:

$$S = \frac{K_2 P T}{N + (1 + K_2 - K_1)P}$$

The total profit generated by the system of outlets would be the sum of the total of the profit for each area. The profit for each market area would be the profit per unit of sales times the quantity sold. The total profit, when discounted and summed over a specified number of years, would provide an objective function for the facilities decision. This total discounted profit would be maximized, subject to the capital constraints on the company. The result would be the optimum number of stations to build and areas in which to build them. Hartung and Fisher provide a mathematical programming model of these considerations. In summary, the results of Hartung and Fisher's model illustrates the importance of the demand creation effects of distribution.

The facilities location problem may also be affected by the selling or persuasion effects of facilities locations. A model which considers most of the demand creation aspects of distribution (service, efficiency, persuasion) has been developed by Hlavac and Little.[44] This model is concerned with the facilities decision for auto dealerships. In this model the demand creation functions carried out during distribution are represented by an auto dealer's "pull." This pull reflects the distance that the consumer must travel to reach the dealer, the brand preference of the buyer, and the characteristics of the dealer, such as his promotional

[44] T. E. Hlavac, Jr., and J. D. C. Little, "A Geographic Model of an Automobile Market," Alfred P. Sloan School of Management Working Paper No. 180-66 (Massachusetts Institute of Technology, 1966).

policies. The pull of a dealer is used to define the probability of a buyer's purchasing at a particular dealer. The probability of buying at a dealer is the pull he exerts relative to the total pull exerted by all dealers. This probability is modified to reflect the geographic effect of location by the use of a factor that reflects a hypothesis that pull decays exponentially with distance.[45] The sales of a dealer are then

$$S(j) = \sum_{i=1}^{s} N(i)P(i, j)$$

where $S(j)$ = sales of dealer j,
$N(i)$ = potential number of buyers in market segment i,
$i = 1, 2, \ldots, s$,
$P(i, j)$ = probability of buyer in market segment i purchasing from dealer j (adjusted for geographic effects).

To estimate the parameters of the model, empirical data based on 47,670 purchases were analyzed. The data were fitted by a maximum likelihood procedure, and the resulting predictions were excellent. Thus the model was a good description of the sales effects of distribution facilities decisions.

A particularly interesting aspect of the Hlavac and Little model was that they made it operational on a man-model interactive basis. That is, as an aid in determining improved facilities locations, they developed an interactive computer program that can be used by a marketing manager to explore the sales results of changing the dealership pattern. Using a remote input console and a time-shared computer system, the manager can propose new dealerships and locations and immediately see the model-predicted results. This flexible system is extremely useful, since it puts the decision maker directly in contact with the model. A manager having interactive access to such a descriptive-predictive model may be able to generate substantial improvements in distribution facilities decisions.

The models described in this section have attempted to include a number of the demand creation aspects of distribution, but none of them has dealt with the total distribution system. What is needed are efforts to include the complexities of transportation, inventory, and capital costs, as well as the demand creation aspects of service, consumer efficiency, and persuasion in management science models to maximize the profits resulting from facilities decisions.

----

[45] The assumption that an outlet's pull decreases with distance was first formulated by W. J. Reilly. See W. J. Reilly, *The Law of Retail Gravitation*, 1st ed. (Austin, Texas: University of Texas, 1931).

Bargaining and the Selection of Facilities

The previous sections of this chapter attacked the problem of determining the number, size, and location of distribution facilities. This analysis was done normatively on the assumption that the desired facilities would be available or could be created. This assumption would be violated if there were not facilities of the desired size available or if the intermediary firms who control the facilities were not willing to make them available•at the proposed level of cooperation and reward. The normative analysis would also be insufficient if more than one facility were available to fill the desired position. In this case, a selection would have to be made.

The inavailability of facilities leads to a choice between creating the facilities or bargaining with existing intermediaries to obtain the desired facility usage. The bargaining may be in the form of granting privileges to middlemen in exchange for the facility service. For example, the intermediary may be willing to carry out the desired availability, information, and demand creation functions in an area if he is given the privilege of returning unsold merchandise. Another method that may be used to gain the desired facilities capability is to convince the intermediary of the advantages of stocking the product and carrying out the desired distribution functions. This persuasion of middlemen would be carried out by the manufacturer's sales force. If the bargaining is unsuccessful or the facilities cannot be created, the firm's local marketing plans will have to be adapted. If these failures are widespread, they may lead to a revision of the firm's over-all marketing plans and a reevaluation of the channels of distribution. (See Fig. 5-3 for these feedback relationships.)

The converse of this problem occurs when there is more than one facility that would fill the normative specification of the facilities plan. In this case, a selection problem must be solved. At this level, the selection decision may be considerably more detailed than the over-all channel or facilities decision. This may be reflected in a detailed list of factors that might differentiate the facilities. These may not all be directly implied in profit considerations but rather in intangible factors such as reliability, flexibility, and personal relations within the community. Terry and Walson have prepared a framework for making distribution decisions of this type.[46] They propose that all the factors that might be important to the selection problem be listed. They are then combined in a "tree"

[46] W. M. Terry and R. B. Walson, "A Systems Approach for the Selection of Distribution Channels" (unpublished M. S. thesis, Massachusetts Institute of Technology, 1967).

structure which logically describes how the factors interrelate. For example, in Fig. 5-6, the relationships between a number of detailed facilities considerations are related to an over-all factor of sales effectiveness.

With this tree in mind, the subfactors are weighted to reflect the relative value of each factor.[47] The weights can be obtained by questioning executives with regard to the importance of these factors in outlet success.

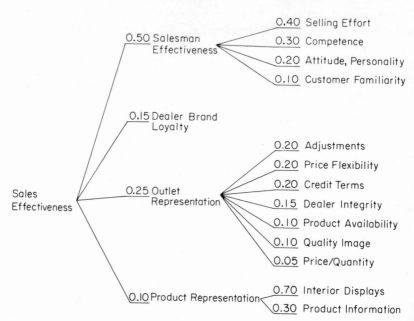

Figure 5-6: Some facilities selection factors*

Care must be taken to normalize the weights so that the weights associated with the branches of the tree always sum to one at each node.

The sales effectiveness may be only one of the branches of a large tree, but the same tree and weighting procedures could be used to describe more intricate factor listings. After the weights have been established for each branch, the factors associated with the ends of the tree branches are scored for each possible selection alternative. The scores are combined and weighted by the values described in the tree to produce an over-all score. The alternative with the greatest score is then selected to fill the facility requirement.

[47] See Chap. 7 of this book for additional factor scoring considerations.
* Terry and Walson, *op. cit.*, p. 38.

The contribution of this model is in the structure it lends to a problem characterized by a large number of factors. The procedure allows the decision maker to structure his feelings into a useful form and explore the implications of his judgments. One limitation of the Terry and Walson procedure is that it does not account for interactions between the factors. See the discussion of the Freimer and Simon approach to interrelated factors in Chap. 7 with regard to screening new products.

The output of the bargaining feedback and selective procedure is a specification of the exact intermediaries to utilize in fulfilling the facilities plan designated to implement the over-all channels of distribution decision.

Control of the Distribution System

After the decisions concerning channels and facilities have been made, steps must be taken to assure that these decisions remain appropriate. Several factors may necessitate updating of the decisions. The marketing plans of the firm may change in response to changing consumer desires, and therefore may lead to consideration of a new distribution system. If it is desirable to expose a segment to a new marketing mix, the channel of distribution might have to be altered or new facilities might have to be selected.

An information system would be valuable in sensing and monitoring changes in the distribution system. Information receptors should be placed at the critical points in the system to monitor the performance characteristics of middlemen. For example, it would be useful to have a company salesman inspect the final display of the product to determine whether it fulfills the endpoint marketing plan. If it does not, the firm should reexamine its channel's performance to determine why the distribution goals are not being achieved. The firm may find it wise to monitor changes in consumer tastes and response by developing a series of continuing experiments to generate new response information. For example, an experiment to determine the effectiveness of alternate retailers (e.g., hardware store vs. department store) would indicate if consumer preference was changing with respect to these channel members. The input to the information system may be recycled through the channel selection or facilities planning model to update these decisions. This adaptive procedure is important if a firm is to maintain an efficient distribution system.[48]

---

[48] J. D. C. Little, "A Model for the Adaptive Control of Promotional Spending," *Operations Research*, XIV (Nov.–Dec., 1966), pp. 1067–97.

SUMMARY OF MANAGEMENT
SCIENCE IN DISTRIBUTION DECISIONS

This chapter began by investigating the nature of channels of distribution and the distribution activities related to the functions of availability, information, and demand creation. The understanding of these functions and the nature of the firm's market response are the necessary input to determine the firm's endpoint marketing plans. The development of explicit models to find the best marketing mix for the product was deferred until Chap. 7. For the purposes of this chapter, it was assumed that the optimal marketing mix was given. With the endpoint marketing mix in mind, a sequential structure of distribution decisions was proposed. The first decision was to determine the intermediary institutions to utilize in achieving the desired marketing plan in the relevant market segments. This specification of the channel of distribution was designed to maximize the manufacturer's profit. Very little management science effort has been directed toward the channels decision. A preliminary model was developed in this chapter, but additional research is needed to overcome its computational limitations and to extend it to include multiproduct channels and risk considerations within the channel. If the designated normative channel was not compatible with the goals of the middleman institutions structure, the manufacturer was led to bargain, to create his own channel, or to revise his marketing plans.

With a given channel structure, the next distribution decision was the facilities decision. Although most effort has been directed toward cost minimization in distribution, several profit-centered facilities models were discussed. It would be desirable to make facilities decisions on the basis of profit so that the demand creation aspects of distribution could be explicitly considered. If the desired facilities were not available, bargaining or an adjustment of local marketing plans was required. More than one available facility indicated the necessity for a selection decision. After specifying the channel and its facilities, adaptive procedures were proposed to control and modify the distribution system.

6

Personal
Selling Decisions

In the previous three chapters of this book the marketing mix elements of advertising, price, and distribution have been considered. The next marketing mix element to be considered is personal selling. In spite of the fact that it is the largest single item in the marketing budgets of most firms, personal selling continues to be an elusive and poorly understood element of the marketing program. Only a small number of analytical or management science efforts have been reported during the past fifteen years. However, developments in marketing information systems and in the technical aspects of management science can be expected to expand both the need for and potential of management science approaches in this important marketing decision area. Thus the time is ripe for an accelerated application and development of management science models in this rather neglected area of marketing management.

In this chapter attention will focus upon sales force decisions. The major decision areas are structured in Fig. 6-1. The first step in the decision process is to recognize the role of personal selling in the firm's total marketing program and to establish goals or criteria for use in sales force decision making. Once the criteria for the evaluation of decision alternatives have been specified, a resource commitment to the personal selling effort must be established. This total resource commitment involves setting the sales budget and determining the size of the sales force.

After a preliminary budget has been established, the problem of allocat ing the sales resources must be attacked.   The sales effort must be allo cated along three dimensions: (1) customers, (2) sales territories, and (3 time (i.e., scheduling effort).   The allocation decision very often has a significant interaction with the budget and size of sales force decisions For example, at the allocation stage, the firm might discover that sales

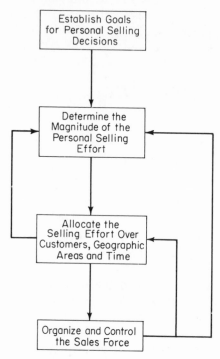

Figure 6-1: Personal selling decisions

response is greater than expected so that profits can be enhanced by allo cating more resources to personal selling.   Conversely, a need to prune the personal selling effort might be identified.   The commitment of resources to personal selling is generally made with some preliminary allocation in mind.   This initial resource commitment may be updated in the light of the optimal or nearly optimal customer and territory allo cations.   It would be theoretically attractive to allocate the sales force resources simultaneously across customers, territories, and time, but in actual practice firms usually allocate sequentially across the dimensions.

After budget and allocation decisions have been considered, a number of organizational decisions must be made.   For example, the number of levels in the sales organization must be determined and control units must be defined. Another organizational decision is related to motivation of the sales force. Although the average compensation of each salesman may have been estimated at the budget decision level, the specifics of the compensation plan must be determined. The details of selection, training, and assignment of salesmen to control units must also be developed. The final organizational aspect to be considered in this chapter is the control procedure that should be developed in support of the selling program. In order to improve its sales performance in the future and discover potential problem areas, the firm will want to provide for continuous evaluation and control of its personal selling effort. The information obtained by these activities should then be fed back into all the decision points in order to assist the firm in adapting to changing market conditions.

Each of the decisions described in Fig. 6-1 will be considered in this chapter. The goal hierarchy that is present in sales decisions will be outlined, but most of the attention will be directed at the budget and allocation decisions. The chapter closes with a discussion of some selected organizational aspects of personal selling management.

PERSONAL SELLING GOALS

In most firms, personal selling is a vital element in the firm's communications with its markets. As an element in the total marketing mix and more particularly in that subset of the marketing program called the communication mix, personal selling would seem to play at least three distinct roles: (1) disseminating factual information, (2) presenting persuasive information, and (3) rendering service. The salesman's informational function operates in two directions. He communicates to the market information about the technical characteristics, prices, service aspects, and availability of his firm's product offerings. The opposite information flow is the transmittal of market information back to the firm. The salesman is often in a good position to detect problems developing in the firm's competitive position, to identify potential areas for new products, and to recommend service policies that would better fulfill customers' needs. The presentation of persuasive information is the personal selling role most often associated with the salesman. In his persuasive role he marshals evidence in the social-psychological environment of the salesman-customer interaction in an effort to influence the customer to purchase the product and service offerings of his firm. Service is the third important function of the salesman in many selling situations. For example, the salesman may be able to assist the customer in solving some problem related to the firm's product line. The advice given by Xerox salesmen concerning paper flow in the customer's office is a case in point. Expediting orders and setting up point-of-sale displays are further examples of service functions performed by salesmen.

The three communication functions of personal selling discussed in the previous paragraph closely parallel the functions of distribution discussed in the last chapter. In fact, personal selling may be viewed as one aspect of a firm's channels of distribution. The persuasive and service functions of the salesman are part of the demand creation aspects of the channel system. Likewise, the information function of channels may be carried out by the manufacturer's own salesmen. The sales force may even be called upon to carry out the availability function of distribution. For example, in the food industry the salesman often stocks the shelves for the grocer and removes any product that is too old to sell.

The use of a direct sales force by a manufacturer generally reflects the result of his analysis of the relative merits of alternative channels. In such a case, the use of a direct sales force may have been found to yield the most profitable methods to fulfill the availability, information, and demand-creation functions of distribution.

Another interaction between personal selling and channels of distribution is the use of a sales force to convince middlemen to carry out the desired distribution functions. This selling within the channel may be necessary in order to implement the total distribution plan. Personal selling effort may convince a middleman to stock the product (availability function) and support the product with the desired service and promotional effort (demand-creation function). The sales force may also provide information feedback to the manufacturer from the middlemen and the ultimate market.

Thus, the sales force functions as part of the firm's distribution system and transmits appeals and product information as part of the firm's total communication mix. These two functions were discussed in greater detail in the distribution and advertising chapters, and they comprise the principal objectives of personal selling effort. The ultimate goal of the firm's personal selling effort is to fulfill these functions in the most profitable manner.

As in other decision areas, profit is the primary goal. This goal may be translated into lower level goals in a meaningful fashion. For example, a goal for the sales manager may be to maximize sales subject to a fixed sales force budget constraint. This is consistent with profit maximization if the size of the sales force and other constraints have been calculated to generate a maximum return for the firm.

SIZE OF PERSONAL SELLING
EFFORT

The Theory of Optimal Sales Force Size Determination

The budget for personal selling represents the financial resources the firm intends to commit to personal selling effort during the budget period. This budget will depend upon both the size of the sales force and the firm's salesman compensation and selling expense plan. If the budget were specified, the sales force size could be obtained by dividing the budget by the estimated average compensation and sales expense per man. If the number of salesmen were determined first, the budget would be specified by the total compensation that each man receives plus their associated selling costs. These transformations are deceptively simple. The proposed compensation per salesman will affect the quality of salesmen the firm can attract. This quality will affect the sales response to selling effort and therefore will also affect the optimal sales budget and again the number of salesmen. Whether the budget or sales force size decision is made first, it will have to be made with an implicit compensation decision and salesman quality level in mind. It may be necessary to specify the budget and sales force size under a number of over-all compensation-quality conditions until the decision converges to the best budget and number of salesmen.

The best sales force is simply the one that helps to maximize the firm's profits. If all other marketing variables (e.g., price, advertising, etc.) are specified, and if there are no carry-over or competitive effects due to personal selling expenditures, the problem is to maximize

$$Pr = pQ(PS) - TC(Q) - C(PS) \qquad (6\text{-}1)$$

where Pr = profit,
           p = selling price per unit of product,
      PS = the level of personal selling effort,
  $Q(PS)$ = number of units sold as a function of personal selling effort, given that the effort is allocated optimally,
  $TC(Q)$ = total costs of producing and merchandising Q units, exclusive of personal selling costs,
  $C(PS)$ = total costs of personal selling effort as a function of PS, the level of personal selling effort.

In this equation the variable PS could be measured by the number of salesmen of a specified quality level. The quality level would be associated with some average compensation level that would allow budget estimates $C(PS)$ to be generated. The details of the compensation plans for selling effort will be discussed in the final section of this chapter, but the compensation implication is clear at the resource commitment stage. In fact, in some cases it might be useful to make the sales response $Q(PS)$ a function of the number of salesmen and the level of compensation.

Equation (6-1) would be much more complex if the interaction effects between selling and the other marketing variables were considered. The equation would become a multivariate one, and the modeling and solution procedures for multivariate models given in Chap. 4 would be appropriate. Budget determination would also be more difficult if competitive interdependencies were to be included in the decision. In this case, the competitive Bayesian and Game Theory models discussed in the price and advertising chapters would be useful. Since these modeling concepts have been outlined in the earlier chapters, this chapter will treat the size of sales effort decision as an independent decision. Under these conditions, finding the optimal size of sales force would be relatively simple if the sales response function to selling effort $Q(PS)$ were known, since then the one variable model could be optimized by calculus if $Q(PS)$ were differentiable.[1] The cost functions $C(PS)$ and $TC(Q)$ would also have to be known and differentiable, but the primary difficulty is involved in identifying $Q(PS)$.

The discussion of the determination of the optimal size of sales force will center upon the estimation of the sales response to selling effort. It is, of course, possible to specify the sales response by the subjective judgments of the firm's managers, but this should be relied upon only after empirical estimation procedures have been exhausted. Although the measurement techniques are presented in the context of the personal selling decision, it should be realized that they are also useful in estimating the response to other marketing variables.

Estimating Sales Response to Personal Selling Effort

Three basic management science approaches to the estimation of sales response to personal selling can be identified: (1) analysis of historical data, (2) field experimentation, and (3) simulation. Each of these approaches will be discussed, and examples of the application of these techniques to the size of sales effort decision will be presented.

---

[1] See Pricing Decisions, Chap. 4 of this book for a discussion of the simple calculus model.

Analysis of historical data

Perhaps the most accessible data are contained in the historical records of the firm's past sales effort. If the future responses to sales effort can be expected to be similar to those in the past, estimation based on this data base may shed some light on the sales effects of personal selling effort that may be expected in the future.

To demonstrate a historical data-based approach to the size of sales force decision, the modeling work done by Semlow will be discussed.[2] His estimation procedure requires that the firm possess a good measure of the sales potential of each territory as well as historical sales performance records of salesmen in territories of different sales potential. The performance criterion in each sales territory is taken as the dollar sales per one per cent of the total market potential. It is generally found that territories having greater sales potential also have more, but not proportionately more, sales. A representative result is shown in Fig. 6-2, where

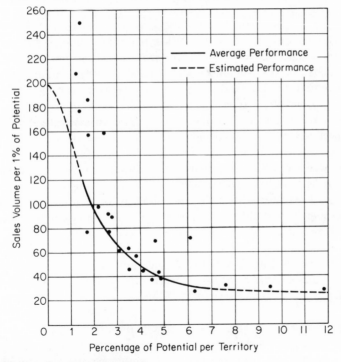

Figure 6-2: Sales potential per
territory and sales volume per one
per cent of potential*

[2] See W. J. Semlow, "How Many Salesmen Do You Need?" *Harvard Business Review*, XXXVIII (May–June, 1959), pp. 126–32.

* *Ibid.,* p. 129.

each point represents a territory. From the figure it is seen that sales per one per cent of market potential decline as the size (measured in terms of market potential) of sales territories increases. This figure represents the historical pattern of sales response to selling effort in the firm's sales territories.

This response relationship can be useful in determining the sales force size. If maintenance of salesmen in the field were cost-free and if motivational considerations were ignored, the above analysis would suggest that the firm might do well to have many salesmen, each of whom has a territory having only a small fraction of the total market potential. However, consideration of the field maintenance costs led Semlow to suggest the following simple marginal rule for adding salesmen:

$$S\bar{p} - C > 0 \qquad (6\text{-}2)$$

where S = sales volume of each additional salesman,
$\bar{p}$ = expected profit margin per unit on this sales volume,
C = cost of maintaining this salesman in the field.

This is essentially a restatement of the necessary condition for an optimum; i.e., the first differential of the profit function (6-1) must be zero. The data for $\bar{p}$ and C should be fairly accessible from company records.

The validity of the results depends on the accuracy of the response estimation procedure. The dollar sales per one per cent of market potential information discussed above may be used to estimate sales results, if it is assumed that

1. All salesmen, including those to be added, are homogeneous in terms of their sales performance.
2. A good measure of territory potential is available.
3. Competitive conditions are relatively equal in all sales territories.
4. The firm has sufficient salesmen to provide a sound basis for analysis.
5. The firm is not dominant in the industry and a substantial increase in sales will not lead to destructive competitive retaliation.
6. The firm will assign territories of equal potential to its salesmen.

In addition, Semlow's historical analysis implicitly assumes that intensity of past sales effort accounts for the observed relationship. Other factors, such as travel requirements and cumulative past territorial effort, are confounded with the intensity of coverage. Furthermore, the analysis implicitly assumes that the type of salesmen currently in the field is the correct one. Perhaps a higher salary would attract a better average quality of salesman and therefore change the optimal size of the sales orce. The analysis could be extended by repeating the sales response estimation and sales force size determination for several compensation/ salesman quality cases. If the desired compensation/salesman quality levels can be identified in the current sales force, this analysis may be based upon historical data. If not, judgmental inputs will be required. Using this approach, the firm would choose that quality/compensation and size combination that generates the greatest profit. Under these assumptions and keeping these considerations in mind, the firm may use the analysis of historical data depicted in Fig. 6-2 to estimate total sales for a given size of sales force. The rule given in Eq. (6-2) may then be used to determine the profit-maximizing size of the sales force.

Another interesting historical estimation procedure and management science approach to personal selling decisions is the Waid, Clark, and Ackoff study of the General Electric Lamp Division.[3] It presents an example of the usefulness of historical analysis. Before the study the division was about to undergo a reorganization, which at first appeared to require a substantial increase in the size of the sales force. Before making this commitment, management decided to request an Operations Research study of the problem. Assuming the intuitively attractive S-shaped response function for cumulative sales volume versus sales time spent with a customer, the research team concluded that the division was presently over-allocating calls to customers. That is, the company was operating in the saturation region of the response curve. Consequently, the General Electric Lamp Division was able to reduce the average number of calls per customer and thereby handle the increased sales call load entailed in the reorganization without having to hire additional salesmen. Sales results, taken eighteen months after the study recommendations were implemented, were substantially the same as results anticipated by the study. Furthermore, it was estimated that the savings in the first year were twenty-five times greater than the cost of the study.

The authors recognized in their recommendations that the sales response to a reduction in the number of sales calls might exhibit a considerable lag. Consequently, the research team recommended that General Electric monitor sales response via call reports in order to detect any lagged deterioration in market position resulting from the recommended reduction in calls. The coming era of marketing information systems should render this type of monitoring much more feasible in the future than it has been in the past and therefore improve the historically based response estimates.

[3] C. Waid, D. F. Clark, and R. L. Ackoff, "Allocation of Sales Effort in the Lamp Division of General Electric Company," *Operations Research*, IV (Dec., 1956), pp. 629–47.

In summary, there are several general limitations in the analysis of historical data. First, it is difficult, if not impossible, to establish causality.[4] The confounding of a multitude of forces in the past data may lead to the assumption of spurious relationships or may altogether obscure the causal relations. Furthermore, the results of historical analysis are relevant only to the past operating range. Finally, the important factors and relations must remain stable over time in order to make extrapolation appropriate. Fortunately, there quite often is a fair degree of inertia or autocorrelation in market factors and relationships so that historical data analysis may yield useful estimates of sales response.

Field experimentation

The causal relation between number of salesmen and sales response often can be best determined by experimental procedures. Different sales intensities may be applied to different sales areas according to an experimental design. If the experiment is well designed and executed it should yield information relevant to the optimal size of the sales force.

Estimation of the responses to sales effort based on a controlled field experimental design has been reported by Brown, Hulswit, and Kettelle. The researchers specified that salesmen allocate various levels of effort— high, medium, and low—to three groups of accounts. The objective was to ascertain which level of effort had the greatest market impact.

After the experimental results were obtained, the best levels of effort were designated, and a model which indicated the optimal number of salesmen was developed on the basis of the recommended sales allocation to the groups. The modeling aspects of this study will be reviewed in the allocation section of this chapter, but the measurement aspects of the experimental approach are relevant to the current topic.

The Brown, Hulswit, and Kettelle study is subject to certain limitations because of the design of the experimental procedure. The largest accounts were assigned the greatest effort, while the salesmen were allowed to choose which accounts would receive the medium and low sales effort. Both of these factors violate the random assignment assumptions necessary for good experimental design and contribute to an overstatement of the market response to sales effort. Moreover, the procedure assumes that customers and salesmen are perfectly substitutable (i.e., it ignores heterogeneity).

---

[4] For an interesting discussion of the development of causal inferences outside of experiments, see H. M. Blalock, *Causal Inferences in Nonexperimental Research* (Chapel Hill, N.C.; University of North Carolina Press, 1961).

[5] A. A. Brown, F. T. Hulswit, and J. D. Kettelle, "A Study of Sales Operations," *Operations Research* (June, 1956), pp. 296–308.

Field experimentation, in general, has other limitations. It tends to
e a costly and time-consuming activity and, in many instances, historical
ata, field surveys, or subjective judgments may provide better data for
ecisions in terms of a costs/benefits tradeoff. In addition, changes in the
ize of sales force for experimental purposes involves changing the number
nd perhaps location of people. Altering these control variable levels is
ot as easy as in other areas of marketing. In view of these limitations,
; may be expected that field experimentation is likely to enter the sales
orce size decision only indirectly through the more readily controlled
reas of allocation, such as call frequency and scheduling.

Simulation

The third principal approach to estimating the sales response to selling
ffort is simulation. Simulation models provide a framework within
vhich the manager or researcher can identify improved levels of personal
elling. Given a valid model of the market, simulation enables its user
o ask "what if?" types of questions. For instance, he may interrogate
he model concerning market response to X salesmen, $X + 1$ salesmen,
tc. In this way, the manager or researcher can generate alternatives
nd choose the best one. This will probably represent a good solution
o the size of effort problem. This analysis assumes that a good market
nodel exists. For example, if the firm has developed a microanalytic
imulation (such as those employed by Amstutz) that examines in detail
he interaction between the salesman, the product, and the customer,
nformation regarding the number and type of salesmen the firm should
mploy could be generated.[6]

In spite of their considerable potential, few market simulation ap-
roaches to sales force decisions have been reported. The discussion
elow will consider two special-purpose sales simulators that have been
leveloped. One is the simulation developed by Stokes and Mintz,
vhich had as its objective the determination of the number of clerks to
ssign to a floor in a department store.[7] This Monté Carlo queuing
nodel was discussed in Chap. 5. The use of stochastic variables to
epresent the arrival of customers, the service time, the incremental value
of sales, and the amount of time a customer is willing to wait for service
nabled profits to be imputed to alternate sales force sizes.

The second published report of a simulation approach to selling

---

[6] See A. E. Amstutz, *Computer Simulation of Competitive Market Response* (Cam-
ridge, Mass.: The M.I.T. Press, 1967) for specific models which are appropriate here.

[7] C. J. Stokes and P. Mintz, "How Many Clerks on a Floor?" *Journal of Marketing
Research*, II (Nov., 1955), pp. 388–93.

decisions deals with the service aspect of personal selling. Service is a important factor in the computer market, business equipment mark (e.g., Xerox), and major household appliance markets (e.g., Sears service A firm which assumes the responsibility to service all its machines as pa of its sales agreement is faced with the need for a plan for the develop ment of its service function. An interesting example of a simulatic approach to this problem is given by Hespos.[8] A field survey indicate that customers differed considerably in their service expectations. Co sequently, the use of a simple "first-in/first-out" priority rule led to mo customer dissatisfaction than was necessary. From data on the distr bution of customer service expectations, the distribution of the occu rence of service calls, and the distribution of service time requirements, simulation was performed which helped identify the best (or at least, good) combination of call scheduling rules and size of the service sta The model was also useful in identifying future service needs by enablin management to identify the best operating posture for various futu levels of machines in the field.

These model approaches indicate the potential of the simulation tech nique in personal selling. The technique is useful, but it requires a vali model of the market-salesman interaction. There is a need for a soun model of the customer-salesman interpersonal communication proces If this sort of model could be developed and validated, it would becom the essential element of a heterogeneous microanalytical simulation tha could be used to estimate the sales responses to individual and aggregat personal selling effort.

Summary of Size of Sales Force Determination

This section began by examining a simple profit equation as a functio of sales effort. Given this equation, three measurement techniques asso ciated with determining the sales response to sales effort were discussed The three approaches were historical data analysis, experimentation, an simulation. Published examples of each of the techniques were pre sented. These techniques were associated with models oriented towar solving the size of sales force problems, but the models were very simple They did not consider the multivariate effects of other marketing mi elements or the problems of competitive interdependencies. More com plex management models were not reported, because none exist in th area of sales force size determination. This void could be easily fille

[8] R. F. Hespos, "Simulation as an Aid in Staffing a Customer Service Function," *Management Technology*, III (Dec., 1963), pp. 160–66.

y a transference of the models that exist in the price and advertising ecision areas. Multivariate, dynamic, game theory, Bayesian, and daptive modeling techniques would be very appropriate and valuable n the determination of the optimal size of the sales force.

ALLOCATION OF SALES EFFORT

After the sales force size and budget have been determined, this esource commitment must be allocated over the potential sources of ales. The sources of sales can be characterized by the type of customer, he geographic location of the customer, and the time at which a sales timulus is presented to the customer. It is conceptually useful to think f three kinds of allocation:

1. Allocation to customers or types of customers
2. Allocation to sales territories
3. Allocation over time

deally, the allocation should simultaneously be made across all three limensions, but this problem has not yet been solved. In most firms lecision sequences based on the firm's perception of the market are used. These perceptions may be expressed in the firm's definition of the decision nit or control unit that it utilizes in its operation.

For example, the firm may perceive its market in terms of areas and lefine a geographic control unit. Counties might then be chosen as the mallest meaningful control unit for planning purposes in the firm because his is the finest level at which the firm is able to obtain measures of narket potential and response. The definition of a control unit may ffect the allocation sequence. If counties are control units, this speci- ication may have strong implications about the importance of sales effort llocation to geographic areas. The use of a geographic control unit vould lead directly to the territorial decision as the first dimension of ales allocation. The definition of consumer types as a control unit vould lead to allocation of effort to customers first.

After allocating over geographic areas or customers, the allocation over he other dimensions would be undertaken. In most cases the last limension would probably be time. This allocation specifies the call equence and route for a salesman to follow in completing the customer llocations in specific geographic areas.

In this chapter the dimensions will be examined sequentially: (1) ustomers, (2) territories, and (3) time. The discussion will indicate the interaction between these types of allocation and will close with consideration of the multidimensional allocation problem.   In each are examples will be cited to clarify the problems.   During the analysis of th examples and allocations, the high level of interaction between the budge and allocation decision will be obvious.   If the allocation procedure yield results that are consistent with the response assumptions of the budge decision, there may be no feedback and no revision of the size of sale force decision.   If allocation procedures produce unexpected response: the budget must be reviewed.   In fact, some firms possess so littl information about the responses that might be expected from a goo allocation that they give only the briefest consideration to the size c sales force before allocation.   They then return to the budget decisio after the allocation plan has been developed.   In this fashion a firn can utilize the feedback loops indicated in Fig. 6-1 to converge upon th best or at least good budget and allocation decisions.

Allocation to Customers

A number of management science modeling approaches are availabl for use in allocating selling effort across customers.   The first considere in this section is the deterministic modeling approach.   Then a stochasti formulation is presented.   Finally, models that attack the allocation o effort between new and old accounts and questions of new accoun acquisition are discussed.

Deterministic modeling of the customer allocation program

The basic question in allocating effort is the sales response tha various customer types will display.   With an estimate of the response o various groups, the effort can be carried out so that the marginal return to each customer type are equal and total returns are maximized.   Th most direct approach to this problem is to develop deterministic respons functions for each of the customer groups and then to allocate effor on this basis.

Buzzell has reported a deterministic study in which the firm sought t specify the extent to which it should go directly to customers versus th extent to which it should sell to wholesalers, who would then sell to fina customers.[9]   This application considered the question of allocatio

[9] R. D. Buzzell, *Mathematical Models & Marketing Management* (Boston: Harvar University Graduate School of Business Administration, Division of Research, 1964) pp. 136–56.

etween direct and wholesale accounts. The criterion used in this analysis was the maximization of profit subject to the requirement of a 10 per ent return on sales. The return on sales constraint represented a minimum profit expectation. In this analysis, all salesmen were assumed to be equal, all were assumed to sell the same mix of products, and no competitive effects were considered. Two allocation procedures were proposed. One ignores geographic aspects, whereas the other treats them as given (i.e., sales territories are specified).

The first solution method is based on maximizing profits. The profits were dependent upon the quantities sold to wholesalers and those sold directly to customers. The deterministic sales responses were assumed to be of the form:

$$Q_i = S(1 - e^{-a_i n_i}) \qquad (6\text{-}3)$$

where Q_i = quantity sold to customer type i,

S = saturation level of sales to either customer,

a_i = constant reflecting the sensitivity of sales to increase in n_i (Note that if a is large, sales will increase rapidly toward S as n_i is increased from zero. Conversely, the smaller the magnitude of a_i, the slower will be the response of sales as n_i is increased from zero.), $a_i > 0$,

n_i = number of salesmen serving customer type i,

$i = D$ = direct customers

$i = W$ = wholesale customers

Note that the saturation (asymptotic) sales level is assumed to be identical for both classes of customers. The sales response functions for $i = D$ and $i = W$ were based upon one empirical observation per customer class. The data point provided information for Q_D, Q_W, n_D, and n_W. This left the researchers with two equations and three unknown parameters: S, a_D, and a_W. In order to achieve a solution for a_D and a_W, they used a subjective estimate of the saturation level of sales, S. Values of $a_D = 0.01725$ and $a_W = 0.065$ were found from this solution. As would have been expected from the extended sales reach achieved through the use of wholesalers, a_W is greater than a_D. This indicates that sales respond more rapidly to the first few wholesale salesmen than to the first few direct salesmen. The empirical estimation procedure used for this model is subject to criticism. It is statistically unsatisfactory to estimate a two-parameter response function using only one data point. Such a statistically underidentified response function provides no information concerning the adequacy of the representation imbedded in the response function. A preferable approach would have been to examine historical records for other time periods in order to obtain more than one point for estimation purposes. To proceed with this revised approach, however, would require that the size of the respective sales forces had varied some what in the past.

With these parameter estimates the problem is to maximize profits sub ject to a profit return on sales constraint. The profit function in thi analysis was

$$Pr = m_D S(1 - e^{-a_D n_D})$$
$$+ m_W S(1 - e^{-a_W n_W}) - c(n_D + n_W) - FC \quad (6\text{-}4)$$

where Pr = profit,

m_D = profit margin per unit of direct sales,

m_W = profit margin per unit of wholesale sales,

c = cost of maintaining a salesman in the field,

FC = fixed cost.

It should be noted that the marginal profit contribution is taken to be constant over the entire range of sales for both wholesale and direct sales This contains the implicit assumption that there are no cost economies as sales increase and further that there is no need to use price cutting as a weapon to increase sales. In addition, it is assumed that field mainte nance costs are identical for both wholesale and direct salesmen. Equa tion (6-4) is a function of two variables, n_D and n_W, but for any given size of sales force n the problem becomes a one-variable problem, since $n_D = n - n_W$. The simplified one-variable problem can be solved by differ entiating the profit equation and using the usual calculus procedures.

The profit equation also allows the exploration of the profit effects of varying the sales force size. This information may lead to a reevaluation of the size of commitment the firm is willing to make to personal selling Thus the allocation decision has implications for the budget and size of sales force decisions that have been established.

The results of the analysis in Buzzell's example are shown in Fig. 6-3 The figure indicates the profit-maximizing allocation of salesmen to each of the two types of accounts for various sizes of sales forces. The opti mum allocations were based on Eq. (6-4).

The results of these analyses were some interesting recommendations for changes in sales strategy. The sales force of the company at the time of the study was composed of 42 salesmen: 40 direct, and two indirect. The results suggested that for a sales force of 42 salesmen the allocation should be 19 salesmen to final customers and 23 salesmen to distributors. Thus the analysis indicated that a considerable shift in emphasis in sales effort toward distributors was in order. Further results indicated that if the sales force size could be changed the best size would be 156 men of whom 110 would sell to final customers and 46 would sell to wholesalers. As indicated in Fig. 6-3, when the total size of the sales force increases, the *proportion* of men assigned to direct sales should be increased.

Analysis of the allocation of effort between the two customer groups was based on two aggregate deterministic response estimates. This response model treated geographic territories as external to the model and therefore was at a relatively high level of abstraction. To include territory considerations, the research team reformulated the allocation question. In the reformulation, territories were developed by applying a set of rules to the market. Each territory was to contain less than two million people, be smaller than 10,000 square miles, and be "reasonable" in the minds of the company executives. It was assumed that a direct

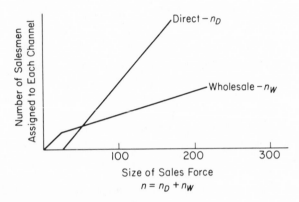

Figure 6-3: Allocation of sales effort to customers*

salesman could cover one such territory and a wholesale salesman could cover five territories defined in this manner. This five-to-one ratio reflects the relative sales response of the two sales systems. With this given set of territories, the market potential for each region was calculated on the assumption that the firm's market share would be 25 per cent whether the territory was covered by a direct or indirect salesman. With these territories arranged by sales potentials in a decreasing order, the lowest potential that could justify a direct salesman was found. In this lowest territory, the direct salesman would just break even, or the profit in the area would be zero. Customers in all territories above this would receive direct sales effort. Customers in territories below the break-even territory would receive no direct sales effort; rather, the wholesalers in these areas would receive sales effort.

This analysis indicated that the best allocation of the current 42 salesmen would be 20 salesmen assigned to direct sales and 22 to distributor sales. This is reasonably consistent with the first model's results. In

* Buzzell, *ibid.*, p. 153.

the second model geographic influences were considered, but the response functions were much simpler. The relative sales response was a simple ratio, rather than the more sophisticated response function used in the first model. The second model assumed a constant 25 per cent share of market regardless of the allocation between direct and indirect customers. Recognizing that the analysis was subject to errors in its market share and market potential assumptions, the research team explored the sensitivity of the policy recommendations to substantial changes in the assumptions. This sensitivity analysis indicated that the policy recommendations of the second model were basically sound even if there were substantial errors in the estimates of market share and potential. Sales were increased and selling costs were decreased during the first few months after the new policy suggested by the analysis was implemented.

Recommendations from such sales allocation analyses can at times be difficult to implement. For example, the recommended almost fourfold increase in sales force size is an action that can only be implemented slowly, because of inherent problems in recruiting, selecting, and training such a substantial increase in the sales force. In addition, problems may occur when personnel must relocate or change their job patterns. It may also be difficult to implement the direct-indirect customer allocations in the specified territories, since it may be difficult or impossible to locate competent distributors in the appropriate areas.

The two deterministic models present good examples of the factors to be considered in sales force allocation. The analyses began with a given sales force size, but proceeded to the size decision and recommended a new number of salesmen. This represents the feedback between the size of sales force and allocation decisions indicated in Fig. 6-1. In attacking the allocation problem the researchers began by analyzing the customer dimension, but they were led to consider geographic effects. They did not directly attack territorial design, but rather used some simple rules to define territories and then considered them as given in the customer allocation analysis. Although this second analysis was made under some strict assumptions, the sensitivity of the results to those assumptions was examined. This is a good methodology for all management science models where strong assumptions are necessary.

Stochastic modeling of the allocation of sales effort

The deterministic approach to allocation is a useful one, but it assumes that customer response can be described reasonably by a deterministic function. The discussion of the stochastic aspects of consumer behavior resented in the models of market response chapter of this book indiated that consumer behavior is sufficiently complex that probabilistic esponses might often be more valid and useful. This section will prent an example of a stochastic sales effort allocation model that was eveloped by Magee.[10]

Magee attacked the problem of the allocation of missionary sales effort) retailers on the part of the manufacturer of a food product. Although holesalers served the inventory needs of the retailers, the objectives of he missionary salesmen were to obtain favorable shelf space and locaons, as well as to assist the retailers with displays and point-of-sale romotion for the product. The question was, "What is the optimal vel and allocation of this missionary sales effort?"

The firm's policy prior to the study was to make calls on the top 0 per cent of the retailers as measured by the last two months' sales. he present study was designed to answer the questions of: "How good s this present allocation procedure?" and "What is the optimum level f sales effort in terms of the proportion of retailers who should receive ales calls?" The proportion of dealers who receive promotion under ormal (nonexperimental) circumstances will be denoted by a. The roblem is to determine the sales response to a particular promotional olicy and subsequently to specify an optimal policy (a).

In order to answer these questions, Magee first developed a probailistic model of the market. He assumed that the distribution of the umber of cases of the product sold to a given dealer in a unit of time i.e., one month in this case) could be described by a Poisson distriution, given as

$$P(n) = \frac{e^{-c}c^n}{n!} \tag{6-5}$$

where $P(n)$ = the probability that the dealer will order n cases in a month,

c = the expected or average number of cases ordered per month by this dealer.

Magee further assumed that different values of the Poisson parameter c vere distributed among the dealers, i.e., that dealers are heterogeneous vith respect to their mean purchase rates c. If dealers are arrayed in rder of decreasing c, a distribution $Y(c)$ will result. The distribution $Y(c)$ is taken to be the probability density function for c in the population f dealers when all dealers receive normal promotion—i.e., when the roportion of dealers receiving promotion is a.

---

[10] J. F. Magee, "The Effect of Promotional Effort," *Journal of the Operations Research Society of America*, I (Feb., 1953), pp. 64–74.

Experiments indicated the distribution $Y(c)$ was of the form

$$Y(c) = \frac{1}{s} e^{-c/s} \tag{6-6}$$

where $s =$ the average number of cases ordered per dealer per month in the entire population of dealers.

Using Eqs. (6-5) and (6-6), it is found that the fraction of dealers order‍ing n cases in a given month is given by

$$f(n) = \int_0^\infty \frac{e^{-c} c^n}{n!} \cdot Y(c) dc = \frac{s^n}{(s+1)^{n+1}} \tag{6-7}$$

Magee, however, was interested in evaluating the effect of the the‍ current promotional allocation rule. In order to make this evaluation, h‍ needed to know the probability density function of the mean purchas‍ rate c for groups of dealers when they receive missionary sales effort‍ Experimental data were used to make this assessment. The total popu‍ lation of dealers in the experiment was divided into two groups—thos‍ who were ordinarily eligible for promotion (the top 40 per cent based upo‍ the previous two months' sales) and those who ordinarily were not eli‍ gible for promotion (the lower 60 per cent).

Trial and error curve-fitting procedures, using the criterion of bes‍ prediction of $f(n)$, were used to obtain the following distributions:

$$Y_p(c) = \frac{(1 - e^{-g(c/s)})e^{-c/s}}{s} \tag{6-8}$$

$$f_p(n) = s^n \left(\frac{1}{(s+1)^{n+1}} - \frac{1}{(s+g+1)^{n+1}} \right) \tag{6-9}$$

$$Y_{np}(c) = \frac{e^{-[(g+1)/s]c}}{s} \tag{6-10}$$

and $\qquad f_{np}(n) = \dfrac{s^n}{(s+g+1)^{n+1}} \tag{6-11}$

The quantity $Y(c)$ denotes the distribution of average monthly pur‍ chase rates, and $f(n)$ denotes the fraction of dealers purchasing n units i‍ one month. The parameter s is defined in Eq. (6-6); recall that $a =$ th‍ fraction of dealers normally promoted; and $g = a/(1 - a)$. The sub‍ script p denotes the group that would be promoted under the usua‍ allocation rule a and np denotes the group that would ordinarily not hav‍ been promoted. These distributions were developed from experimenta‍ data in which *all* dealers received promotion.

The final estimate necessary to establish the stochastic sales respons‍

or the behavior of the lower 60 per cent of the dealers was their response
f they did not receive missionary sales effort. This will be denoted by
$\overline{f_{np}(n)}$. Data from a nonexperimental period were used to estimate
$\overline{f_{np}(n)}$, the fraction of normally unpromoted dealers purchasing n units,
under conditions of no promotion. The result for this ordinarily non-
promoted group was

$$\overline{f_{np}(n)} = \frac{(0.7)(0.71s)^n}{(0.71s + g + 1)^n} \qquad \text{for } n \geq 1 \qquad (6\text{-}12)$$

$$\text{and} \quad \overline{f_{np}(n = 0)} = (1 - a)\left(1 - \sum_{n=1}^{\infty} \overline{f_{np}(n)}\right) \qquad \text{for } n = 0 \quad (6\text{-}13)$$

(where s, a, and g are as previously defined).

The impact of promotion on dealers who are ordinarily not promoted
may be assessed by comparing Eqs. (6-11), (6-12), and (6-13). Such a
comparison yields Magee's conclusion that promotion has a dual impact
on sales. In the first place, if a dealer is given no promotion, there is a
probability of $1 - 0.7 = 0.3$ that he will act as though his average order
size is zero. That is, there is at least a 30 per cent chance that he will
not order. Moreover, in the remaining 70 per cent of the time, when
he does order, he will act as if his average order size c is only 0.71 of
what it would be if he were promoted. The net effect is about a 50
per cent reduction in business to an unpromoted dealer. In other
words, the dealers who were normally bypassed would on average buy
twice as much if they received promotional effort. This finding represents the potential sales effect of personal selling to the dealers not
normally receiving promotion.

The empirical relations developed above may be used to link sales
effort to sales and profit. The sales in the market are given by

$$Q(a) = N\left[a \int_0^\infty cY_p(c)\,dc + K(1 - a)\int_0^\infty cY_{np}(c)\,dc\right]$$

$$= \frac{Ns}{2}(1 + 2a - a^2) \qquad (6\text{-}14)$$

in this example, where

$Q(a)$ = quantity sold if a per cent of the customers received
promotion,

K = proportionate loss in sales if a customer does not
receive a sales call (Recall that in this case it was
found to be 0.5.),

N = number of possible dealers,

with other notation as previously defined. The profit equation is then given by

$$Pr = p \cdot Q(a) - TC(Q) - C(a) - FC \qquad (6\text{-}15)$$

where Pr = profit,

p = unit price,

$TC(Q)$ = total costs of selling quantity Q, except personal selling costs,

$C(a)$ = cost of extending personal selling effect to fraction a of the total number of dealers,

FC = fixed costs.

If Eq. (6-14) is substituted into Eq. (6-15) a single variable function will be produced and calculus procedures can be followed to obtain a solution. The solution will be the optimum proportion (a) of dealers to receive missionary sales calls. This model may thus be used to answer the question of how to allocate sales effort over customer types when customers are characterized by size of order.

Magee has also discussed some of the limitations of this stochastic approach. First, it is a static analysis and does not incorporate the possibility of carry-over effects of the promotional activity. In the present case Magee regarded this as minor, but in general this is a consideration in stochastic modeling. The dynamic stochastic models developed in the second chapter of this book could be utilized to overcome this limitation. Second, the model does not explain the "why" of the response. It is more an empirical than a theoretical approach. If improvements in the quality of promotion are to be considered as a decision alternative, the "why" question will require examination. A statistical limitation of Magee's model and many other model applications should be emphasized. The distributions of the model were empirically determined by trial and error procedures. They were developed as a result of considerable "data massaging." This procedure limits the generalizability of the results, and spurious relationships may be generated. One approach to overcoming this problem would be to save some data for validation of the empirically determined functions. Unfortunately, many practical applications do not have sufficient data available to enable the model builder to take this approach, but a good operating rule would be to save some data for validation whenever it is practically feasible.

The stochastic modeling approach to allocation appears to have great potential. This is especially true since the stochastic models developed to describe basic consumer response would seem to have application in the sales allocation problem. Magee's model seems to be an excellent starting point, since it specifies a basic stochastic mechanism and indicates how to measure the factors needed in determining the best level of effort.

Dynamic Modeling of Sales Effort Allocation to Customers

Both of the examples in the deterministic and stochastic sections of this chapter were static models. In this section dynamic deterministic and stochastic modeling approaches will be discussed.

The study by Brown, Hulswit, and Kettelle[11] cited earlier in this chapter represents an attempt to estimate the dynamic response functions of new and old customers and determines an optimal allocation between these two customer classes. The optimal allocation was then used to determine how many current and potential accounts should be assigned to each salesman. Once the sales program has been specified for the individual salesman and its effectiveness has been evaluated, the firm is then in a position to examine how many salesmen it should maintain in the field. This again represents a feedback between the allocation and size of sales force decision.

The application began with the determination of the sales response to selling effort for each type of account (current and potential). In contrast to the historical data approach employed in the case reported by Buzzell, the present study measured sales response to selling effort via field experimentation.

In order to provide a sound basis for their experimental design, a market survey was conducted. The survey indicated that over 88 per cent of all customers tended to concentrate their business with a single supplier (i.e., gave over one-half of their business to one firm). This finding suggested a change in strategy. Previously, the firm had concentrated upon winning a particular job. This survey result suggested that a policy of striving to become the favored printer might be better. The survey also revealed that industry sales tended to be concentrated among the largest customers. Further analysis revealed that the 3500 customers the firm was then calling upon (about 27 per cent of the total number of customers) accounted for about 88 per cent of total market sales. This suggested that the firm would probably be in a better position by striving for more effective sales results from the customers upon whom it presently called than it would be in trying to reach the remaining 12 per cent of the total market sales.

[11] A. A. Brown, F. T. Hulswit, and J. D. Kettelle, *op. cit.*

These two findings, concentration of industry sales in a small percentage of all customers and a tendency for customers to concentrate purchases with one supplier, provided the study team with a criterion for classifying customers as current or potential accounts. A current account was defined as any customer who already concentrated his purchases (i.e., purchased at least one-half of his total product need) with the firm. Potential accounts were defined as those which did not so concentrate their business with the firm.

An experiment was initiated to examine the increment in sales that would result from various increments of sales effort (measured in time per month spent with the customer). This experiment exemplified the difficulties of field experimentation in personal selling in particular, and marketing in general. To reiterate the previous discussion, the experimental design was not satisfactory. Increases in effort were not randomly assigned to customers. In order to avoid lost sales opportunities during the experiment, the greatest increment in effort went to the largest customers. This, of course, violates the randomization assumptions necessary for good statistical results. Furthermore, the salesmen were allowed to choose which firms would receive what increment in selling effort. This introduces the chance of bias, since the salesman's most favored accounts would probably receive the incremental effort. The joint effect of these will be to overstate the average effectiveness of large increases in sales effort. Difficulties also occurred in maintaining appropriate levels of the control variable (sales time). Actual sales effort applied to a customer during the experiment often differed from what was called for in the experimental plan.

The experimental results, although not unbiased, indicated that the most productive sales calls were those made on the largest customers. Although large customers were somewhat less likely to respond, this was more than compensated by the magnitude of their response when they did respond.

The classification of customers into new and old accounts led the research team to consider two types of effort—conversion and holding. The former represents effort applied to new accounts, whereas the latter represents effort allocated to old accounts. Conversion effort was described by a conversion curve derived from the experimental data, which related the sales effort per month x expended upon a customer to his probability of exhibiting a substantial increase in purchases $C(x)$. The criterion used for specifying the best level of sales effort to expend upon new customers X_C^* was to maximize the expected conversions per hour of sales effort, which is given by the point x for which $C(x)/x$ is a maximum.

Holding effort was described by a holding function relating the sales effort per month x expended upon a customer to his probability of not decreasing his purchases significantly during the month $H(x)$. The best rate of holding effort X_H^* was determined by the principle of expending holding effort up to the point of equal incremental profitability for conversion and holding effort. Recall that the best level of conversion effort has already been determined, so that the holding effort rate is based on the outcome of that analysis.

The analysis then proceeded to the assignment of accounts to salesmen. The first relation in this analysis was established by using the effort rates determined above as

$$X_C^* N_C + X_H^* N_H = T \qquad (6\text{-}16)$$

where T = total monthly sales time available to a salesman,

X_C^* = optimal monthly sales effort to allocate per conversion customer,

X_H^* = optimal monthly sales effort to allocate per holding customer,

N_C = number of new (conversion) accounts assigned per salesman,

N_H = number of old (holding) accounts assigned per salesman.

Equation (6-16) is an equation in two unknowns, N_c and N_H. Another relation is required for solution. The system will be in equilibrium whenever the expected conversions per month balance the expected relapses per month. This second relation is given by

$$N_C Pr(C) = Pr(H) N_H \qquad (6\text{-}17)$$

where $Pr(C)$ = probability of conversion with optimal sales effort X_C^* (obtained from conversion response function),

$Pr(H)$ = probability of holding with optimal sales effort X_H^* (obtained from holding response function).

Equations (6-16) and (6-17) may be solved to yield N_H and N_C, the number of old and new accounts to assign per salesman. The use of Eqs. (6-16) and (6-17) along with the costs of adding additional salesmen could be used to make calculations of the profit implications of adding an additional salesman. The results of the allocation analysis, therefore, yield response information that can be used in a review of the total sales force resource commitment. The analysis assumes that the criterion is to establish an equilibrium sales level. It would be useful to extend Eq. (6-17) to allow for growth. Then the allocation necessary for increasing sales could be examined. This would yield valuable information for determining the growth pattern for the sales force. Once again, this illustrates the considerable interaction which often occurs between the size and allocation decisions in personal selling.

The modeling of the allocation between new and old accounts is sensi tive to the dynamic process by which new accounts are developed. The new account acquisition process is often worthwhile to model separately so that the allocation of effort over classes of potential accounts can be determined. Two new account models will be presented. The first classifies new accounts by the number of sales calls they have received while the second describes potential new accounts by the level of interest they display in the firm's product offerings. Both models are stochastic models that utilize absorbing state Markov chain theory.

The first new account effort allocation model has been developed by Shuchman.[12] In his model, effort is defined as the number of calls made on a prospect. The model yields information for controlling sales effort as well as for the determination of the number of times to call upon a prospect before dropping the prospect. This is termed the *call frequency policy*.

Each prospect is classified by the number of calls that the salesman has made upon him in the past. This description is the state of the prospect in a Markov model. There are two mechanisms whereby a prospect may leave the prospect class: (1) he purchases from the salesman and thereby enters the established customer class, and (2) he is dropped as a prospect by the salesman. The Markov transition matrix for prospects is given in Fig. 6-4. The elements in this matrix represent the probability of the prospect's going from state i to state j between times t and $t + 1$. Implicit in this representation is the assumption that each prospect is called upon once and only once during each interval of time. Under Shuchman's assumptions, one of three things must happen to a prospect in state i who is called upon between times t and $t + 1$. He either enters the prospect state $i + 1$ with a probability $P_{i,i+1}$, is sold with probability $P_{i,s}$, or is dropped with probability $P_{i,d}$. In this model, n represents the maximum number of calls that will be made upon a prospect before that prospect is either sold or dropped. This value is a policy value which can be studied via the model.

Results from the theory of absorbing state Markov chains can now be used to yield analytic estimates of:

1. The expectation and variance of the number of calls that will be made upon a prospect starting in any nonabsorbing state before he is either sold or dropped
2. The expectation and variance of the proportion of prospects sold and dropped for any initial state distribution of prospects.

[12] A. Shuchman, "The Planning and Control of Personal Selling Effort Directed at New Account Acquisition," in Lee Preston, ed., *New Research in Marketing* (Berkeley: University of California, 1965), pp. 45–56.

If it is further assumed that the salesmen add to their prospect lists at each time period a number of prospects equal to those that have been absorbed into either state s or state d, a steady-state age distribution of prospects will result. The mean and variance of this distribution may be obtained as may the mean and variance of the number of prospects sold and dropped once the steady state is reached.

			Time $t+1$					
		s	d	0	1	i	$i+1$	n
	s	1.0	0	0	$0 \cdots 0$		$0 \quad \cdots 0$	
	d	0	1.0	0	$0 \cdots 0$		$0 \quad \cdots 0$	
	0	P_{0s}	P_{0d}	0	$P_{01} \cdots 0$		$0 \quad \cdots 0$	
	.	.	.	.	.	.	.	.
	.	.	.	.	.	.	.	.
Time t	.	.	.	.	.	.	.	.
	i	P_{is}	P_{id}	0	$0 \cdots 0$		$P_{i,i+1} \cdots 0$	
	.	.	.	.	.	.	.	.
	.	.	.	.	.	.	.	.
	.	.	.	.	.	.	.	.
	$n-1$	$P_{n-1,s}$	$P_{n-1,d}$	0	$0 \cdots 0$		$0 \quad \cdots P_{n-1,n}$	
	n	P_{ns}	P_{nd}	0	$0 \cdots 0$		$0 \quad \cdots 0$	

State Definitions

State s = the prospect is sold by the salesman and leaves the prospect class for a customer class,

State d = the prospect is dropped by the salesman,

State i = $0, 1, \ldots, n$ denotes that the prospect has been called upon $0, 1, \ldots, n$ times, where n is the maximum number of times a prospect may be called upon.

Figure 6-4: Absorbing state Markov model for determining prospect call policy*

The means and variances are associated with some specified policy regarding the maximum number of sales calls n per prospect. The Markov analysis can then be used to generate the expectation and variance of the number of sales per period that will result in the steady state for alternative values of n. If the firm then relates the profitability of these sales to the cost implications of the alternative n, it has sufficient information to establish the best maximum call policy n.

The results of the model may also be used for control purposes. The model yields the mean and variance of several statistics of interest, such as the total number of prospects who will be sold in a given period. This type of information may serve as a base line in an exception reporting system. Salesmen's performance can be monitored and compared to

* Shuchman, *ibid.*, p. 52.

these base line results. Since both the mean and variance are available, control chart procedures may be used to indicate cases of exceptionally good or very poor results. This information may then serve as the impetus for further study of these exceptional situations and perhaps ultimately may serve as the basis for reward or corrective action, depending upon the direction of the deviation.

This model incorporates a number of assumptions, and these are pointed out by Shuchman. For instance, it assumes that the transition probabilities are stationary (or constant) in time and that they are independent of the initial age distribution of prospects. The latter assumption seems reasonable. In view of the dynamic characteristics of most markets, the assumptions of stationarity of the transition probabilities will not hold except perhaps in the short run. Seasonal and cyclical fluctuations also pose problems. Nevertheless, if short run stationarity holds, the model can be estimated and subsequently used to make conditional predictions concerning what will occur if no change takes place.[13] A further assumption is that prospects are of equal value. This, of course, is unrealistic. However, prospects may be stratified into relatively homogeneous value groups, and the analysis may be run separately for each of these groups. An implicit assumption is that all prospects in the analysis are identical in terms of their transition probabilities. An interesting research topic would be the incorporation of heterogeneity of transition probabilities for a class of prospects.[14]

An alternative formulation of an absorbing state Markov chain model for new account sales allocation has been presented by Thompson and McNeal.[15] Their model involved two absorbing states and four transient or nonabsorbing states. These states were defined as:

$S_1 =$ an absorbing state indicating that a sale was made on the most recent call,

$S_2 =$ an absorbing state that indicates that the customer was deleted from the prospect list as of the most recent call,

$S_3 =$ a transient state indicating that a new prospect had no history of sales calls,

$S_4 =$ a transient state that indicates that the prospect expressed a *low* degree of interest on the most recent sales call,

---

[13] See the discussion of conditional prediction in Chap. 2.

[14] Recall the discussion of Morrison's work with heterogeneous Markov models of consumer behavior in Chap. 2. His results, however, were for ergodic rather than absorbing Markov chains.

[15] W. W. Thompson and J. U. McNeal, "Sales Planning and Control Using Absorbing Markov Chains," *Journal of Marketing Research*, IV (Feb., 1967), pp. 62–66. This paper is reproduced in D. B. Montgomery and G. L. Urban, eds., *Applications of Management Science in Marketing* (Englewood Cliffs, N. J.: Prentice-Hall, Inc., 1969).

S_5 = a transient state indicating that the prospect expressed a *medium* degree of interest during the most recent sales call,

S_6 = a transient state indicating that the prospect expressed *high* interest during the most recent sales call.

The state definitions are related to interest level and are not related to real time effects, as were the Shuchman state definitions. The absorbing chain transition matrix appears in Fig. 6-5. Note that the entire column of transition probabilities under S_3 (the new prospect state) is zero. This reflects the fact that a new prospect must enter one of the other five states once one sales call has been made.

		Prospect's state after new sales call					
		S_1	S_2	S_3	S_4	S_5	S_6
	S_1	1	0	0	0	0	0
Prospect's state before	S_2	0	1	0	0	0	0
new sales call	S_3	P_{31}	P_{32}	0	P_{34}	P_{35}	P_{36}
	S_4	P_{41}	P_{42}	0	P_{44}	P_{45}	P_{46}
	S_5	P_{51}	P_{52}	0	P_{54}	P_{55}	P_{56}
	S_6	P_{61}	P_{62}	0	P_{64}	P_{65}	P_{66}

Notation: P_{ij} = the probability that a prospect that was in state i after the last sales call will be in state j after the next sales call.

Figure 6-5: An alternative absorbing chain call policy model*

Absorbing state Markov chain theory will yield the expected number of sales calls that will be made upon a prospect before he enters one of the two absorbing states (i.e., is sold or is deleted from the prospect list). This value is available for a customer presently in any of the four transient states. If it is assumed that there is a constant cost per sales call, the expected cost of calling upon a prospect presently in state i (i = 3, 4, 5, 6) may be computed. The theory also yields an analytic expression for the probability that a prospect currently in state i (i = 3, 4, 5, 6) will ultimately be sold (i.e., be absorbed into state 1). If a constant (or expected) profit contribution per sale (excluding the cost of sales calls) can be ascertained, the expected revenue that will result from a prospect currently in state i (i = 3, 4, 5, 6) may be obtained. The value of a customer in each state i may then be determined by the difference between the expected profit contribution and the expected sales call costs. The relative values of prospects in each of these states then provides useful information for allocating sales time. A salesman should

* Thompson and McNeal, *ibid.*, p. 64.

first call upon the accounts that are in the state having the highest expected profit. He should continue to allocate one call per account in this state until one of two conditions occurs:

1. He exhausts the time he has available during the call planning period.
2. He exhausts the set of prospects available in this class or state.

When condition 1 occurs, he is finished for the period. When 2 occurs, he should then go to the next most attractive set of prospects (classified by their current state). Naturally, a class of accounts (i.e., accounts in a given current state) will receive calls only if the expected profit from calling upon them is positive.

As was true in Shuchman's model, the present model can be used to establish certain base lines for sales performance. Exception reporting schemes may then be implemented. In order to accomplish this, however, it will be helpful to utilize the variance of certain measures that are available from Markov theory, as Shuchman recommended.

A dynamic, stochastic model for determining optimal sales call policies for both new and current accounts has been proposed by Lodish, Montgomery, and Webster.[16] The model focuses upon the number of sales calls to allocate to a given customer. The central elements in the model are two probabilities—the probability that the customer will order and the conditional probability associated with the size of his order, given that he orders from the firm. These probabilities are discussed below.

Before outlining the nature of these probabilities, it is useful to specify two salient characteristics of the customer which will influence the success of sales calls in the current period. The first of these represents an exponentially smoothed history of sales to this customer and is given by

$$H_{t+1} = \alpha \left(\frac{X_{t-1}}{\pi} \right) + (1 - \alpha)H_t \qquad (6\text{-}18)$$

where H_t = smoothed history of sales to the customer entering period t,
  X_t = sales to this customer in period t,
  π = sales potential of this customer,
  α = smoothing constant ($0 < \alpha \leq 1$).

[16] L. M. Lodish, D. B. Montgomery and F. E. Webster, Jr., "A Dynamic Sales Call Policy Model," Working Paper 329–68, Sloan School of Management, M.I.T. This paper was presented at the joint meeting of ORSA and TIMS in San Francisco, May 1–3, 1968.

The second characteristic is the customer's remembered sales effort, which is given by

$$E_t = \gamma[E_{t-1} + S_{t-1}] \qquad (6\text{-}19)$$

where E_t = sales effort remembered at the start of period t
$\quad S_{t-1}$ = sales effort in period $t - 1$,
$\quad \gamma$ = proportion of sales effort remembered from period to period.

This remembering of sales effort allows for carry-over effects.

In formulating the probability that a customer will order, current customers are modeled differently from potential customers. For a current customer, the probability of his ordering in the current period is taken to be a function of his sales history, remembered sales effort, and the sales effort allocated to him during the current period. The probability that the customer will order is then given by

$$P_0(H_t, E_t, S_t) = C(1 - e^{-GH_t}) + (1 - C)(1 - e^{-D(E_t+S_t)}) \qquad (6\text{-}20)$$

where $\quad C$ = constant representing the relative impact on the order probability of a recent sales history vs. remembered sales effort. $0 \le C \le 1$,
$\quad G, D$ = constants representing diminishing returns to sales history and remembered sales effort. $G \ge 0$. $D \ge 0$.

The order probability for a prospective customer is given by

$$P_{tn} = Pmax(n, E_t)[1 - e^{-Q(E_t+S_t)}]$$
$$= [e^{-knE_t}][1 - e^{-Q(E_t+S_t)}] \qquad (6\text{-}21)$$

where $\qquad n$ = the number of previous periods in which the prospect has been called upon and in which he has not ordered. $n = 0, 1, \ldots, N$,
$\quad P_{tn}$ = the probability that a prospect who has been called on and yet has not ordered for n periods will order in period t. Note that t corresponds to $n + 1$,
$\quad Pmax(n, E_t)$ = the maximum order probability for a prospect having a remembered sales effort of E_t and having been called upon for n previous periods without buying, $(0 \le Pmax(n, E_t) \le 1.0)$,
$\quad k$ = parameter reflecting the reduction in the maximum probability of an order as n and/ or E_t increase, and
$\quad Q$ = parameter reflecting diminishing returns to current and remembered sales effort.

Notice that Eq. (6-21) introduces the concept of a prospect's age as measured by n. It is postulated that the longer a prospect is called upon and yet remains a prospect, the lower the likelihood that he will order from the firm. Furthermore, the older the prospect is in this sense (i.e., the larger his n) and the more intensively he has been called upon with no success (i.e. the higher his E_t), the greater the diminution in the firm's prospects for winning him as a customer. Consequently, in Eq. (6-21) the maximum probability of winning the prospect as a customer in period t has been represented as an exponentially declining function of nE_t.

However, remembered sales effort should also have some positive effect upon the prospect's order probability in period t. The fraction of $Pmax(n, E_t)$ that will be realized in period t is taken to be a positive function of both current and remembered sales effort. The function also exhibits diminishing returns.

The conditional probability $P_{X_t|0}$ that the customer will order X_t in period t, if he orders, is viewed as an increasing function of his smoothed sales history H_t, his remembered sales effort E_t, and current period sales effort S_t. The magnitude of the sales to the customer X_t is taken to be a random variable having a Poisson distribution with mean sales rate λ_t. The random variable X_t depends upon H_t, E_t, and S_t as reflected in λ_t, which is given by

$$\lambda_t(H_t, E_t, S_t) = \pi(1 - e^{-[AB(E_t+S_t)+(1-A)FH_t]}) \qquad (6\text{-}22)$$

where A = constant representing the relative importance of remembered sales effort and smoothed sales history, $0 \leq A \leq 1$,

B = constant representing diminishing returns to remembered sales effort, $B \geq 0$,

F = constant representing diminishing returns to smoothed sales history, $F \geq 0$.

One interesting aspect of this formulation is that sales history and remembered sales effort are viewed as partial substitutes in determining the expected sales rate to this customer.

The probability that the customer will order some specific amount $X_t = 0, 1, 2, \ldots$ may be developed in terms of Eqs. (6-20) and (6-22). The probability that $X_t = 0$ is given by

$$P(X_t = 0|H_t, E_t, S_t)$$
$$= 1 - P_0(H_t, E_t, S_t) + P_0(H_t, E_t, S_t)e^{-\lambda_t(H_t, E_t, S_t)} \qquad (6\text{-}23)$$

while the probability that the customer will order an amount $X_t > 0$ is

$$P(X_t|H_t, E_t, S_t) = P_0(H_t, E_t, S_t) \frac{[\lambda_t(H_t, E_t, S_t)]^{X_t}}{X_t!} e^{-\lambda_t(H_t, E_t, S_t)}$$

$$\text{for } X_t = 1, 2, \ldots \quad (6\text{-}24)$$

Equation (6-23) is the probability that he does not order plus the product of the probability that he orders and the Poisson probability that the order size is zero. Equation (6-24) is the product of the probability that he orders and the Poisson probability that he orders an amount X_t. Similar results hold for prospects using Eqs. (6-21) and (6-22).

If a current period sales effort S_t is expended with the resultant sales of X_t units to the customer, there will be an associated profit (or loss). The profit will be given by

$$\text{Profit} = RE \cdot X_t - CA \cdot S_t \quad (6\text{-}25)$$

where RE = gross profit per unit of sales,
CA = cost per sales call.

Now the firm is viewed as having a single control variable S_t, current period sales calls to this customer. This level of sales effort to a customer having some particular H_t and E_t will result in some level of sales X_t whose distribution is given in Eqs. (6-23) and (6-24). The profit for a specific time period is defined as the expected profit that would result from the expected sales level determined by this distribution. The criterion for optimization is chosen as the maximization of discounted expected profits. Thus current period sales effort may not only help current period sales, but may have longer term effects in creating a favorable sales history and remembered sales effort in future periods.

This model is amenable to a determination of optimal sales effort S_t by means of dynamic programming on a Markov process.[17] Since a presentation of the dynamic programming recursion would require considerably more elaboration, the reader is referred to the reference for the details. Suffice it here to note that the model yields an optimal sales call policy for a customer having any sales history and remembered sales effort. Efficient use of the model would require that current customers and prospects be stratified on dimensions related to the parameters. It should also be noted that the optimization method does not depend upon the functional form of the order probabilities and the conditional probability of order quantity, given an order. Any discrete distribution may be used to

---

[17] See R. A. Howard, *Dynamic Programming and Markov Processes* (Cambridge, Mass.: The M.I.T. Press, 1960).

represent these probabilities. The functions used above were merely for illustrative purposes and would involve measurement difficulties, particularly Eq. (6-22).

Summary of allocation to customer types

In summary, the modeling approaches of Buzzell, Brown, et al., Magee, Shuchman, Thompson and McNeal and Lodish, Montgomery, and Webster described in this section indicate a number of interesting and rather sophisticated attacks on the problem of the allocation of sales efforts to customer types. These applications represent the starting point for more intensive management science modeling in the area. The models developed to describe basic consumer response and solve advertising problems would also seem to have a high degree of applicability to the sales allocation problem. The models discussed in this section have dealt with one dimension of the total allocation problem. The existing models attack the allocation of effort between customers, given a geographic plan or treating territories as exogeneous and without consideration of scheduling effects.

Allocation to Geographic Areas

Although units of sales potential can be identified by the type of customers in that unit, it is also possible to characterize these units geographically. This is a useful dimension for allocation and may take place before or after customer allocation. In this section a number of efforts to analyze the geographic allocation of sales effort will be outlined. These examples analyze area effects, assuming a given customer and time allocation or assuming customer class and time effects to be exogeneous. Two approaches to geographic allocation will be considered. The first is the allocation of sales effort to given territories, and the second is the use of territorial design to allocate sales effort.

Allocation to given territories

The simplest approach to area allocation is to maximize the total returns of allocating a given sales effort to a specified set of territories. In general, the necessary condition for an optimum will be that the marginal returns in each geographic area are equal.

Nordin has described this marginal approach for allocating sales effort between two geographic areas.[18] Nordin's objective was to maximize total sales subject to a budget constraint on the total cost of the sales effort. His problem may be stated as maximize:

$$\text{Total sales} = X_1 + X_2 \tag{6-26}$$

subject to

$$TC_1 + TC_2 = K$$

where X_1 = unit sales in area 1,
$\quad X_2$ = unit sales in area 2,
$\quad K$ = the available sales expense budget,
$\quad TC_1$ = the total sales costs of selling X_1 units in area 1,
$\quad TC_2$ = the total sales costs of selling X_2 units in area 2.

Sales expense in each territory is taken to be a function of the number of units sold in that territory. In particular, Nordin assumed that the incremental cost y of selling the Xth unit in an area was of the form

$$y_i = a_i X_i^\alpha, \qquad i = 1, 2 \tag{6-27}$$

where a_i, α are constants.

Thus the total cost of selling X_i units in area i will be given by

$$TC_i = a_i \int_0^{X_i} X_i^\alpha \, dX_i = \frac{a_i(X_i)^{\alpha+1}}{\alpha + 1}, \qquad i = 1, 2 \tag{6-28}$$

The maximization problem in (6-26) can be restated as a Lagrangian expression, and the necessary condition for a sales maximizing allocation is given by the simultaneous set of partial derivatives that result from the Lagrangian form.[19] The necessary condition for an optimal allocation occurs when effort is allocated such that the incremental cost of selling the X_ith unit in each area is equal for all areas. That is,

$$y_1 = a_1(X_1)^\alpha = a_2(X_2)^\alpha = y_2 \tag{6-29}$$

This marginal condition for sales maximization subject to a budget constraint also holds for any number of territories.[20] The generalization

---

[18] J. A. Nordin, "Spatial Allocation of Selling Expenses," *Journal of Marketing*, II (Jan., 1943), pp. 210–19.

[19] See the "Pricing Decision" chapter of this book for a discussion of the use of Lagrangian expressions. The sufficient or second-order conditions for a maximizing allocation will pose no problem so long as incremental selling expenses always are positive (i.e., as long as $y > 0$ for all territories).

[20] See John A. Howard, *Marketing Management* (Homewood, Illinois: Irwin, 1963), pp. 475–79, for details of this extension.

of the sales-maximizing condition for n territories is given by

$$y_1 = y_2 = \cdots = y_n \qquad (6\text{-}30)$$

A more direct approach to allocation problems is to treat personal selling as a demand creation element rather than as a cost. This is more logically consistent with the functions visualized for personal selling. Zentler and Ryde have proposed a model using this approach.[21] The problem is to maximize

$$\sum_{r=1}^{n} N_r R_r(X_r)$$

subject to

$$\sum_{r=1}^{n} N_r X_r = S$$

where X_r = sales effort to expend in area r (i.e., the control variable),

N_r = sales potential of area r,

$R_r(X_r)$ = sales response function of area r to selling effort X_r,

S = sales effort budget.

Zentler and Ryde assume that $R_r(X_r)$ varies between territories, but that the general form of response will be an S curve for all areas. The response is also made dependent upon past sales effort. The lagged relationships and the assumed S response form produce an $R_r(X_r)$ that is very complex. This complexity precludes the direct use of calculus, since the partial equations describing the necessary conditions for a maximum response are not directly solvable. Zentler and Ryde propose a graphical heuristic approach to solve this maximizing problem. The heuristic is based on equating the marginal returns up to the budget constraint. Although the model is not analytically tractable, the consideration of the dynamic lagged effects compensates for this inconvenience. In general, it is better to compromise the technique rather than the essential characteristics of management's definition of the problem.

The competitive effects of sales effort could be encompassed in the game theory promotional allocation model developed by Friedman.[22] Friedman's model is directed at the geographic allocation of advertising

---

[21] A. P. Zentler and D. Ryde, "An Optimum Geographic Distribution of Publicity Expenditure in a Private Organization," *Management Science*, II (July, 1956), pp. 337–52.

[22] Lawrence Friedman, "Game-Theory Models in the Allocation of Advertising Expenditures," *Operations Research*, VI (Sept.–Oct., 1958), pp. 699–709. See the discussion in Chap. 3, "Advertising Decisions."

expenditure, but the promotional variable could be construed as sales effort. The model is a two-person zero sum game where the decision alternatives are allocation plans which specify the amount of promotional effort each area is to receive. The payoffs for the strategies are proportional to the firm's share of total industry promotional expenditure in the areas and the potential of the areas. Under the assumption of a zero sum game, the maximin equilibrium is achieved when each firm allocates its promotional expenditures in proportion to the sales potential of each area. The greatest limitation of this formulation is the zero sum assumption of the game, but it does represent an attempt to build competitive effects into geographic allocation. The nonzero sum game concepts developed by Shakun, Krishnan and Gupta and Baligh and Richartz that have been discussed in earlier chapters would make this approach more feasible.

Territorial design to allocate sales effort

A second approach to area allocation is to treat territorial definitions as a variable and assume that one salesman will be assigned to a given area. This is the converse of the approach outlined in the last section, which treated territories as given and assigned an amount of sales effort (implicitly a number of salesmen) to each area.

The most elementary approach to territorial design is to divide the market into geographic areas of equal sales potential. By forming N such areas, where $N =$ number of salesmen, each salesman would be assigned to an area of equal potential. The disadvantage of this approach is that it does not include consideration of customer allocation or the routing and scheduling aspects of sales allocation.

A more sophisticated territorial design method is to design territories so that each salesman has an equal work load. This design procedure is based on a given allocation of sales effort to customer types. The work load equalization procedure accepts the customer allocation in the form of the call frequency on each class of customers. With this desired level of effort, each territory is defined so that each salesman has a full work load based on the assigned number of calls to each account in his territory.

Talley has outlined this approach.[23] Given call frequencies for each account, territories are assigned in a heuristic manner so that the salesman's travel and sales call time provides him with a full work load. Talley has indicated that territories might be assigned not only on the

---

[23] Walter J. Talley, Jr., "How to Design Sales Territories," *Journal of Marketing,* XXV (Jan., 1961), pp. 7–13.

basis of existing customers, but also on the basis of consideration of potential calls. The potential calls would be an estimate of the number of customers and calling frequencies in the future. These future call potentials may be combined with existing requirements to design work loads and territories. An estimate of the number of salesmen needed could be obtained by dividing the total number of calls required to accomplish the given call frequency requirements by the average number of calls a salesman could make.

$$N = \frac{\sum_{i=1}^{n} f_i C_i}{F} \qquad (6\text{-}31)$$

where N = number of salesmen,
f_i = given call frequency on customer type i,
C_i = number of customers of type i,
F = average number of calls an average salesman can make during the planning period.

These considerations of sales force size may lead to reevaluation of the sales force size decision.

The most detailed statement of the work study approach is given by J. O'Shaughnessy.[24] O'Shaughnessy establishes the time requirements for selling, travel, and administrative activities for each customer type by means of work study. Then, given a call frequency requirement for each class of customer, he groups accounts so as to give each salesman a full work load. This grouping is done on a trial and error basis. The groupings that produce the best work load patterns of the alternatives explored are specified as the respective salesmen's territories.

Summary of territorial allocation

In summary, the allocation of sales effort to geographic areas has centered around two approaches. The first is to allocate effort to a given set of territories. This approach is implemented by defining response functions for each area and resorting to calculus or other procedures to obtain solutions. The second approach is to assume that customer sales effort allocation is given by call frequency requirements and to design territories to give each salesman a full work load. Both approaches attack the area allocation assuming a given customer allocation or

[24] J. O'Shaughnessy, *Work Study Applied to a Sales Force* (London: British Institute of Management, 1965).

reating customer classes as outside the analysis and assuming that the
calling schedule and routes are given.

Allocation of Sales Effort Over Time: Scheduling and Routing

The final dimension of sales allocation is the specification of the manner
n which sales effort will be applied within a given unit of time. The
dimension is measured in time or by the geographic position of a salesman
at a specified time. Given effort allocations by customers in each geographic area, the solution to the time allocation problem would be the
optimum sequence for calling on the customer. The sequence would
include specification of the best route to follow and the schedule of calls
to be made.

The routing aspects of time allocation have received a large amount of
attention from management scientists. The work has been concerned
with the special case of routing when one call is to be made on each of a
given number of customers in various geographic locations. This has
been called the "traveling salesman problem." Explicitly, the problem
is to find the best route to follow in visiting each customer location once
and returning to the starting point. The best route has alternately been
defined as the shortest length route, the route requiring the least travel
time, or the lowest cost route. Although this problem has been called
the traveling salesman problem, it should be pointed out that it is not a
general formulation of the intraperiod time allocation problem of selling.

In fact, technical interest has centered upon the traveling salesman
problem as a general formulation of a certain class of scheduling problems.
For example, it has been applicable to production and traffic flow problems. Thus the "traveling salesman problem" is not really an attempt
to represent a sales problem in a realistic and meaningful fashion.[25] It
abstracts from the scheduling aspects of the calling sequence by assuming
that one call will be made on each account each period. Therefore, a
one-period cycle is specified. If some accounts were to receive more than
one call per period, the time between these calls would affect the best
route.

Solving the traveling salesman problem is a difficult task. The problem could be solved by examining each route, but since there are $(n - 1)!$
possible routes, this is usually impossible. Many management science

---

[25] The name is perhaps unfortunate in that it has served skeptics of the management science approach as an example of the utter artificiality of analytic approaches
and thus has contributed to a premature rejection of this developing field in certain
circles.

techniques have been developed to solve the problem. The techniques of linear programming,[26] integer programming,[27] dynamic programming,[28] heuristic programming,[29] and branch and bound methods[30] have been proposed. It is not within the scope of this book to discuss these techniques in detail. All of them are capable of yielding solutions to the problem. The choice between them depends on the size of the problem, the degree of approach to optimality desired, and the computation costs. The use of any of these techniques to solve the sales call scheduling problem is valid only if each customer is to be called upon once during the travel period. This may be a reasonable approach if the list of customers to be called upon is specified for each routing period and is modified each period to reflect a given allocation of effort among specific customer types in each geographic area.

Multidimensional Allocation

Each of the modeling attempts outlined in the last three sections have attacked one of the dimensions of sales effort allocation. Each analysis has examined either customer, area, or time allocation and treated the remaining dimensions as given or exogenous to the analysis. It would be desirable to have practical management science models that would simultaneously attack the allocation along more than one dimension.

Only one reported management science research effort has been directed toward this end. This is based on an interesting modification of the traveling salesman problem that simultaneously considers allocation to customer types. It has been developed by Cloonan.[31] Cloonan attacks the sequencing of sales calls and the development of a call policy. Beginning with a traveling salesman problem solution (a routing to minimize the travel time to visit each account and return home), he examines the effects of deviating from this minimum cost route to increase

[26] G. B. Dantzig, R. Fulkerson, and S. M. Johnson, "Solution of a Large-Scale Traveling Salesman Problem," *Operations Research*, II (Nov., 1954), pp. 393–410.

[27] M. M. Flood, "The Traveling Salesman Problem," *Operations Research*, IV (Feb., 1956), pp. 61–75.

[28] M. Held and R. M. Karp, "A Dynamic Programming Approach to Sequencing Problems," *Journal of the Society of Industrial and Applied Mathematics*, X (March, 1962), pp. 196–210.

[29] R. L. Karg and G. L. Thompson, "A Heuristic Approach to Solving Traveling Salesman Problems," *Management Science*, X (1964), pp. 225; and S. M. Roberts and Benito Flores, "An Engineering Approach to the Traveling Salesman Problem," *Management Science*, XIII (Nov., 1966), pp. 269–88.

[30] J. D. C. Little, K. G. Murty, and Dura Sweeney, "An Algorithm for the Traveling Salesman Problem," *Operations Research*, VI (Nov.–Dec., 1963), pp. 972–89.

[31] J. B. Cloonan, "An Analysis of Sales Tours," in D. B. Montgomery and G. L. Urban, eds, *Applications of Management Science in Marketing* (Englewood Cliffs, N.J.: Prentice-Hall, Inc., 1969).

he effectiveness of the sales effort. The effectiveness of the effort is related to the time at which the call is made. Cloonan proposes that the value of a call is parabolically related to the time since the last call:

$$V_{iT} = (at - bt^2 + c)V_{im} \qquad (6\text{-}32)$$

where V_{iT} = value of call on customer i at time T,
t = time since last call on customer i,
V_{im} = maximum value of a call on customer i,
a, b, c = positive constants.

This relationship indicates that scheduling of the calls on customers as well as the route of salesmen are important to the return to sales effort. The minimum cost route could be departed from whenever the value of a call is greater than the costs of deviating from the minimum cost route. To find the best schedule of calls, Cloonan proposes a heuristic programming model. The model utilizes the concept of opportunity cost in calculating the cost of making a call other than the one specified in the minimum cost route. The opportunity cost of leaving the route is the difference between the total time required to leave the network, to make a call, and to return to the next customer, less the time necessary to transverse the next link in the lowest cost route. For example, if the time to travel the next link of the minimum cost route is five hours (point Z), the time to the alternate prospect is four hours (point Y), and the time from the alternate customer to point Z is four hours, the opportunity cost is $3 = (4 + 4) - 5$. The total time for the deviation from the route is the opportunity cost plus the time spent in the actual sales call. If the value of the call prescribed by Eq. (6-32) is greater than the cost of deviating from the route by a prescribed margin, the deviation is taken. By analyzing the minimum cost route in this way, the heuristic procedure attempts to generate a good sequence of calls that considers both the costs of routing and the increases in sales value associated with changing the calling schedule. In this heuristic program, customers could be visited more than once and therefore the program could be used to generate a call policy. The call policy would reflect the allocation of sales effort to various customers. The heuristic has been tested on several small problems on which it performed quite well. This preliminary model indicates a productive avenue for future research in the area of multidimensional sales force allocation.

Summary of allocation of sales effect

The discussion of the allocation of sales effort has been developed by examining the three dimensions of allocation: customers, areas, and time.

In each area the allocation problems were defined and existing management science applications in these areas were described. Deterministic, stochastic, and dynamic modeling techniques have been applied to allocation between classes of customers, but the potential for transferring other models developed for use in advertising and pricing decisions was emphasized. Geographic allocation has been attacked by allotting sales effort to given areas and by designing geographic sales territories so that each represents a reasonable work load for one salesman. Friedman's game theory allocation model was cited as an example of the potential for the utilization of existing advertising models in geographic allocation of sales effort. Other techniques such as mathematical programming would appear to be applicable to this problem. The last dimension of allocation discussed was the problem of routing, a special case of which has become called "the traveling salesman problem." It was emphasized that the traveling salesman problem is of interest in management science because it represents a class of theoretically interesting combinatorial problems and that it represents only a small portion of the total sales allocation problem. The final comments on the allocation of sales effort were directed at the desirability of developing multidimension allocation models. A heuristic programming model that represents an attempt simultaneously to allocate across more than one dimension was presented to indicate the research potential in this area.

The allocation decision represents an attractive area for future model building effort. In this research, the usage of models developed in the pricing and advertising area will probably be feasible, but the researcher must not lose sight of the basic human aspects of selling. Salesmen are men and are therefore heterogeneous with respect to their behavior patterns. Good models should encompass this heterogeneity in their analyses of the problem of allocating sales effort.

ORGANIZATIONAL ASPECTS OF PERSONAL SELLING

After the size of the sales force has been determined and the available sales effort has been allocated to sales units, a number of organizational questions must be analyzed. It is not within the scope of this book to analyze all of the organizational aspects of personal selling. Only those aspects which seem most amenable to management science modeling will be discussed in this section. First, the question of span of control will be considered. Specifically, the definition of control units and the question how many sales offices to establish will be considered. The next topic ll be salesman compensation. After considering this motivational estion, attention will be directed toward the assignment of salesmen to rritories and the implications of such assignment for the hiring of sales- en. Finally, sales control procedures and their interaction with infor- ation system design concepts will be outlined.

Span of Control in the Sales Organization

The definition of the control unit to be used in sales force decisions is ecessary if organizational control procedures are to be efficiently imple- ented. The definition of the microcontrol unit is the beginning of a escription of a hierarchy of control units characterized by an increasing vel of aggregation. For example, counties may be the microcontrol its, but these microunits may be combined into states for use as district ntrol units, and these district control units may then be combined to ecify regional units. Thus there generally is a hierarchy of control its representing different levels of aggregation of primary sales units.

The design of the span of control of this hierarchy can be modeled. he best span of control is the one that would generate the best over-all rofits for the firm. If the revenue of the firm is not affected by the span control, the best design is the one that minimizes costs. Stern has eveloped a model that attacks a part of this span-of-control problem.[32] is model determines the optimal number of sales offices. The approach as to find the minimum cost number of branch offices for a given level of les. Three major categories of costs were distinguished: overhead, avel, and direct customer costs. Overhead costs were composed of the ase salary of the salesmen, the branch manager's salary, and the capital nd administrative costs associated with a branch office. Travel costs cluded direct transportation, related costs, salesmen's personal expenses hile traveling, and communication with the branch office while on a usiness trip. Direct costs involved salesmen's commissions, entertain- ent of customers, and extra discounts and services. For a fixed level of les, the postulated relation between the cost components and the umber of branch offices is given in Fig. 6-6.

Direct selling expense is unrelated to the number of offices and there- ore does not affect the cost minimizing number of branch offices. Thus could have been omitted entirely from this analysis. Overhead costs crease with the number of offices, since there will be more managers and

[32] M. E. Stern, *Marketing Planning: A Systems Approach* (New York: McGraw- ill, 1966), pp. 65–69.

administrative expenses involved for a fixed level of sales. The shape of the curve reflects an assumption of economies of scale in the size of branch offices. Travel costs to customers from the branch offices will tend to decline as the number increases, since the salesmen will have shorter distances to travel as well as fewer nights to spend on the road at company expense. In Fig. 6-6, the cost-minimizing number of branch offices denoted by n^*. Notice the relative insensitivity of total cost to moderate departures from n^* in this example.

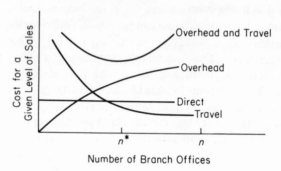

Figure 6-6: Cost versus number of
branch offices

Stern's formulation would seem to have three major types of value to management. In the first place, the model forces the firm to consider how the various elements of sales costs vary with the level of sales. This is important input to the planning of the span of control. Second, it provides a measure of the adequacy of the present sales organization. For the present level of sales, the model will yield the optimal number of branch offices. This number may then be compared to the present number of branch offices in order to evaluate how far from the best span of control the present organization is. The model may also be used to evaluate the increased costs resulting from a current nonoptimal number of offices. Finally, the model can be used for planning purposes. It can be used to explore the optimal number of branch offices (n^*) for various anticipated future sales levels. If a probability distribution can be ascribed to these future sales levels, the expected optimal number of branches called for in the future may be determined. The potential of management science in organizational problems displayed by this elementary model should be exploited by further research.

Compensation of Salesmen

The motivational considerations of the method of compensation represent an area of organization decision making where management science

an be of use. A model that would include the motivational effects of
ompensation plans and the profit implications of the costs and revenues
enerated by such a plan could be an aid in finding the best level and
method of rewarding salesmen.

Modeling effort has been expended in this direction by Farley.[33] He
as shown that under certain conditions an optimal policy is one of paying
qual commission rates for each product, where the commissions are based
n the gross margins of each product in a firm's line. It is optimal in the
ense that if a salesman maximizes his total income under this scheme,
his behavior will result in a maximum profit contribution to the firm.
The motivational assumption here is that salesmen attempt to maximize
heir dollar earnings. This is a simple mechanism, and modeling efforts
hould be directed at including social and psychological rewards and
motivations. These attempts should also be directed at evaluating the
mplications of salary, salary plus bonus, or straight commission plans in
erms of the motivational effects on the salesman and their resultant
ffects on company sales and profits.

Assignment of Salesmen

All the models presented in this chapter have assumed that salesmen
re identical. But salesmen are not homogeneous. Although other
models do not consider heterogeneity, differences in sales ability can be
onsidered in models designed to assign salesmen to territories. It is
resumed that the number of salesmen has been determined and that
sales territories have been defined. The problem is to assign n heterogeneous salesmen to n heterogeneous sales territories in such a manner
hat profits will be maximized. The problem can be stated verbally as:
Maximize the total profit subject to the constraint that each area is
overed by one and only one salesman. This is a linear programming
problem. In fact it is a special type of linear programming problem
hat occurs in so many fields that it has been called the "assignment"
problem and special computationally efficient algorithms have been
devised to solve it.[34] Given a matrix that describes the profit resulting
rom assigning a particular salesman i to a particular territory j, the
determination of the optimal assignment is a routine process of applying

---

[33] J. U. Farley, "An Optimal Plan for Salesmen's Compensation," *Journal of Marketing Research*, I (May, 1964), pp. 39–43. This paper is reproduced in D. B. Montgomery and G. L. Urban, eds., *Applications of Management Science in Marketing* Englewood Cliffs, N.J.: Prentice-Hall, Inc., 1969).

[34] See D. Teichroew, *Introduction to Management Science: Deterministic Models* New York: John Wiley & Sons, Inc., 1964), pp. 520–25 for an exploration of the algorithm and a sales assignment example.

the algorithm.   The marketing aspects of the problem are contained in finding the profit matrix.   An example will clarify the issues involved.

Assume that not only do salesmen differ in their effectiveness with different types of customers or territories, but that sales territories also differ with respect to the distribution of the customer characteristics which are relevant to the salesman-customer interaction.[35]   Suppose, for example, that there is only one relevant variable, customer size (profit potential) and that it is measured at three levels.   Then the distribution of customer size for two territories, I and II, might be given as in Table 6-1.   The firm must now specify the profit potential of an account in each

TABLE 6-1: Customer Size Distribution by Sales Territory

		Customer Size Group*		
	D_{jk}	$k = 1$ *Small*	$k = 2$ *Medium*	$k = 3$ *Large*
Territory	$j = \mathrm{I}$	100**	10	10
	$j = \mathrm{II}$	10	20	50

* Measured as dollar profit potential.
** Number of accounts in this cell.

size group.   These will be denoted as P_s, P_m, and P_l for small, medium, and large accounts, respectively.   Note that territory I has a concentration of small accounts, whereas territory II has fewer total accounts but a preponderance of large accounts.

The next input required is a description of the salesmen in terms of their effectiveness with accounts of various sizes.   The measure of effectiveness to be used will be the proportion of potential profit the salesman has been able to obtain for each class of accounts.   If historical experience is not available, judgmental input would be required.   A set of sample values appears in Table 6-2.   Notice that salesman 1 is especially effective

TABLE 6-2: Sales Effectiveness by Customer Size*

		Customer Size Group*		
	SE_{ik}	$k = 1$ *Small*	$k = 2$ *Medium*	$k = 3$ *Large*
Salesmen	$i = 1$	0.8**	0.5	0.1
	$i = 2$	0.1	0.2	0.6

* Measured as dollar profit potential.
** The proportion of total potential profits realized in this cell.

[35] This application follows M. Stern, *op. cit.*, pp. 69–74.

with small accounts, whereas salesman 2 is relatively more effective with large accounts.

Using the data from Table 6-1 and Table 6-2 along with P_s, P_m, and P_l, one may obtain the expected profitability of each salesman in each territory by the formula

$$V_{ij} = \sum_k D_{jk} SE_{ik} P_k \qquad (6\text{-}33)$$

where D_{jk} = number of customers of size k in territory j (see Table 6-1),

SE_{ik} = sales effectiveness for salesman i for each customer size group k (see Table 6-2),

P_k = profit potential of each customer in group k,

V_{ij} = expected profitability of assigning salesman i to territory j.

This profitability data can then be arrayed in a table such as Table 6-3.

TABLE 6-3: Assignment of Sales- men to Territories

		Territory	
	V_{ij}	$j = I$	$j = II$
Salesmen	$i = 1$	$V_{1,I}$	$V_{1,II}$
	$i = 2$	$V_{2,I}$	$V_{2,II}$

While the solution of the two salesman-two territory problem is obvious, the generalized n salesmen and n territories problem can be solved by the straightforward application of the assignment problem algorithm.

This simple model has been extended by King so that the selection of salesmen from a potential set of employees can be examined.[36] His extension is based upon the use of probabilities of sales success given that a salesman is assigned to a particular territory. This is an alternate interpretation of the entries in Table 6-2.

When the SE_{ik} are interpreted as the probabilities of success, the P_k used in Eq. (6-33) are the sales that a successful salesman would obtain in area k. King proposes the use of discriminant analysis to estimate the probabilities of successful performance SE_{ik}. The discriminant analysis would be performed on past salesman-territory data. Each past salesman would be represented by a set of characteristics such as personality or ability test scores. The output of the analysis would be the

---

[36] W. R. King, "A Stochastic Personnel-Assignment Model," *Operations Research*, XIII (Jan.–Feb., 1965), pp. 67–81.

probability of success in each territory for a salesman with a particula set of characteristics.

This information and a set of scores for a group of potential salesmer along with an assignment model can be used to select the men to hire With the new scores and the discriminant analysis output, the probability of each new salesman's succeeding in each area could be determined Since the degree of sales difficulty may vary in each area, managemen probably would assign different prior probabilities of success to each o the territories. These two probabilities can be combined by Bayes theorem to yield an estimate of the conditional probabilities of succes for each proposed salesman, given that he is assigned to a particula territory. These are the desired SE_{ik} values and can be used with P_k i Eq. (6-33) to generate a reward matrix.

This revised matrix can be used to make hiring decisions if all the potential candidates are represented in the matrix.[37] Since the assign ment algorithm requires a square matrix, column vectors representing fictitious territories could be added to the matrix until the number of rows and columns were equal. All the values in these vectors would be zero The straightforward application of the assignment algorithm to this profit matrix would yield the best specification of salesmen to territories. Salesmen that were assigned to fictitious territories would not be hired, while all those assigned to real territories would be employed.

King's extensions to the simple model represent a healthy type of modeling. He combined the sales recruitment and selection problem with the assignment problem in an integrated model while still maintain ing the essential behavioral heterogeneity of selection and assignment.

Control of the Selling Process

After salesmen have been assigned to territories or sales tasks, the selling process should be monitored to ascertain whether the plans were well designed, to identify any underlying changes that are taking place in the market which will require strategy changes, and to control the per formance of salesmen in their many tasks. This control procedure should monitor sales information and submit this information to the data bank section of the firm's information system.

For example, detailed call reports containing the name of the party called upon, the sales presentation appeals, the aids used, a report of competitive activities, and the results of the encounter would be useful. In particular, this information would provide an effective historical data

---

[37] W. R. King, *Quantitative Analysis for Marketing Management* (New York: McGraw-Hill Book Company, 1967), pp. 469–73.

ase for analyzing various aspects of the firm's personal selling effort.   In tuations where sales are large and infrequent it would often appear esirable to establish a system that will monitor the effectiveness of sales alls in terms of awareness and attitudes.[38]

At this level of control the sales data should be stored in disaggregated orm.   That is, if a sales report is submitted, all the information on the eport should be stored in disaggregated form.   With this disaggregated ata the sales response to selling effort could be monitored.   The new stimates could be used to update the sales budget or allocation decisions. `he firm might give consideration to implementing an adaptive model hat includes continuous experimentation and updating of decisions. `his type of model has been proposed in the advertising area and may e applicable to sales analysis as well.[39]

The use of an information system in the selling area must be carefully nstituted, since second-order motivational effects may result. Asking a alesman to fill out a lengthy call report so that a control procedure will e efficient may result in lost sales because of a loss of selling time and a eduction in the salesman's morale.   The system input requirements nust be carefully designed to balance the total costs of obtaining the nformation and the profit improvements this information would allow.

SUMMARY OF MANAGEMENT SCIENCE AND PERSONAL SELLING DECISIONS

In this chapter personal selling decisions in the areas of size of sales force, allocation of sales effort, and organization have been considered. Although these decisions were discussed sequentially, the feedbacks between them were emphasized. The discussion of the models in these areas was often more detailed than in previous chapters so that the peculiar nature of selling decisions could be understood and so that the potential for additional modeling would be apparent.

The discussion of sales budgeting models concentrated upon the advantages and disadvantages of using historical data, experimentation, and simulation in estimating sales response. This emphasis was utilized since the modeling techniques applicable to the problem had previously been indicated in this book. The lack of complex models in the area of

---

[38] See G. D. Hughes, "A New Tool for Sales Managers," *Journal of Marketing Research* (Feb., 1964), pp. 32–38 for an approach to this problem.

[39] J. D. C. Little, "A Model of Adaptive Control of Promotional Spending," *Operations Research*, XIV (Nov.–Dec., 1966), pp. 175–97.

size of sales force determination could be overcome if the management science models developed in the price and advertising areas were transferred to the selling area and used as the basis of the development of comprehensive sales models.

The allocation of sales effort was discussed in each of the dimension of customer type, geographic areas, and scheduling-routing. Example of deterministic, stochastic, dynamic, and game theory models were presented to clarify the allocation problem and the potential of management science in improving allocation. Although each dimension was individually analyzed, the need for multidimensional allocation models that include the effects of salesmen's heterogeneity was indicated.

The human basis of sales operations was emphasized in a discussion of some selected organizational aspects of selling decisions. After describing the need for defining control units and a span of control for the selling organization, the motivational aspects of compensation were examined. The need for the development of mathematical models that include the behavioral science aspects of motivation was suggested. The behavioral heterogeneity of salesmen was examined in the context of assigning salesmen to territories. The extension of the basic assignment model to salesman selection was cited as a good example of the potential of the modeling approach in organizational decision making. The final organizational topic discussed was that of control. The use of information systems, carefully designed to consider the human aspects of control, was suggested as a productive approach.

The discussion of sales decisions was intended to demonstrate that personal selling is an important, interesting, and challenging area for management science. Although it has been neglected in the past, the potential rewards for research in this area should result in a surge of model building and an improvement in the quality of sales management decisions.

7

New Product
Decisions

INTRODUCTION

In the preceding chapters of this book, various marketing mix elements such as price, advertising, personal selling, and channels of distribution have been analyzed and discussed. In this chapter these elements will be integrated with product characteristics and competitive strategies in the consideration of product decisions. The emphasis in this chapter will be upon new product decisions. This approach is taken for two reasons. First, the new product decision has become increasingly important to many firms. Some industries find that over half their current sales are composed of products developed during the past ten years. For many firms, product innovation has been the road to enhanced profits and improved competitive posture. But product innovation has been a two-edged sword since the risk of failure is great. The tendency toward product innovation in the United States economy, coupled with the inherently high risks in this area, makes the new product decision process a particularly fruitful area for management science developments. Second, new product decisions must consider both competitive reaction and total marketing mix aspects of marketing management. Thus it is a useful framework for discussing the entire marketing posture of the firm. The transfer of these approaches to decision problems other than new product ones should not be particularly difficult.

Modern corporations have come to recognize the importance of new products to their continued growth, profitability, and long-run competitive success. Industries such as the chemical industry find that the majority of their products were unheard of a decade ago. Although innovation requires financial risk to the firm, it may prove even more dangerous not to innovate in this era of rapid technological change. Consequently, modern firms try to generate a stream of successful new products that will produce profitable growth rates.

The selection of new products for introduction to the market is an extremely difficult and risky decision. The estimates of new product failure rates vary widely. In some industries rates of failure as high as 80 per cent have been reported. The most conservative figures have been reported by Booz, Allen, and Hamilton.[1] On the basis of a 1964 study of 366 products introduced by 54 "prominent" companies, they reported that 33 per cent of the new products introduced to the market were not successful.[2] This failure rate reflects the complexities and difficulties associated with new product decisions.

The new product decision may be viewed as a four-stage process: generation of new product ideas, screening these ideas to identify the most promising ones, detailed analysis of the resulting product proposals, and implementation of acceptable new products. These stages are outlined in Fig. 7-1.

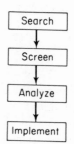

Figure 7-1: New product planning system

The process begins with a search procedure designed to generate a large number of new product ideas. These ideas are then screened to remove suggestions that are obviously unsuitable or are not compatible with the goals of the firm. The new product proposals that pass through the screening step are then analyzed. This analysis takes place in an information network (see Fig. 7-2). At each step in the process, the product can be adopted (GO decision), rejected (NO decision), or

[1] *Management of New Products*, 4th ed. (New York: Booz, Allen, and Hamilton, Inc., 1965).

[2] *Ibid.*, page 11. Ten per cent were clear-cut failures and 23 per cent were doubtful.

nvestigated further (ON decision). If an ON decision is reached, the
evaluation analysis is repeated and the sequence continues until either
a GO or NO exit is made. If a GO decision is reached, the firm has
committed itself to the product, and implementation of the new product
marketing plan is begun.

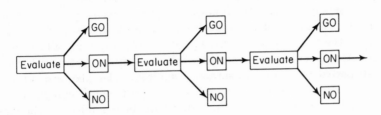

**Figure 7-2: Analysis stage in the
new product planning system**

The purpose of the search stage is to expand the set of available alternatives, whereas the purpose of the next two stages is to narrow the
feasible set down to a few of the most promising product alternatives.
The study by Booz, Allen, and Hamilton found that about 20 per cent
of the new product ideas developed during the search phase survived the
screening stage.[3] About 3.5 per cent of the initially generated ideas survive the analysis stage and become commercially available. Only about
30 per cent of the financial resources invested in the new product area
were found to be associated with successful new products.[4] Thus the
potential for improvement in this decision area seems clear.

In the remainder of this chapter, the four steps in the new product
decision process will be considered in some detail. These discussions
will be followed by a note on the similarity of product line and new
product decisions. The chapter will close with a summary statement of
management science approaches to new product decisions.

SEARCH FOR NEW PRODUCT IDEAS

The first step in the new product planning process is to generate new
product ideas. These ideas may come from internal sources such as
salesmen, research and development personnel, and company records.

[3] *Ibid.*, p. 9.
[4] *Ibid.*, p. 11.

Alternatively, new product ideas may come from external sources such as customers, competitors, industry associations and research groups and government-sponsored research. In any case, the firm would like to generate a meaningful set of potential new product proposals.

In order to implement a policy of new product development, the firm generally budgets funds for use in the search for new product possibilities. Since there are many potential sources of new product ideas, the problem is to determine an appropriate allocation of these search funds to the various areas in which search may be fruitfully conducted. The firm wants to obtain the set of relevant new product ideas that will yield the largest potential return subject to budget and risk constraints.

A Programming Approach to the Allocation of Search Effort

The problem of maximizing the expected return to new product search, subject to a budget constraint, can be expressed in terms of a general mathematical programming problem. In this case the firm wants to maximize

$$ER = \sum_i S_i(X_i) \qquad (7\text{-}1)$$

subject to

$$\sum_i X_i \leq SB$$

$$X_i \geq 0$$

where $ER =$ expected return from the allocation of the search budget,

$X_i =$ number of dollars spent on search in area i,

$i =$ index of areas to search. For example:

$i = 1$ may be surveying customers on future needs,

$i = 2$ may be monitoring of competitor's new products,

$i = 3$ may be a search of the firm's past and present research and development efforts,

$i = 4$ may be a survey of the company's salesmen,

$i = 5$ may be a search of existing patents,

$i = 6$ may be forming a brainstorming committee of the firm's managers,

$i = 7$ other sources of new product ideas,[5]

---

[5] For examples, see G. A. Larson, "Locating Ideas for New Products," in T. L. Berg and A. Shuchman, *Product Strategy and Management* (New York: Holt, Rinehart, and Winston, Inc., 1963), pp. 420–30.

$S_i(X_i)$ = a general function representing the expected return from new ideas generated by searching in area i with a search budget of X_i,

SB = total search budget available.

Most potential areas of search probably have a response function $S_i(X_i)$ that is similar to the function in Fig. 7-3. This type of function reflects

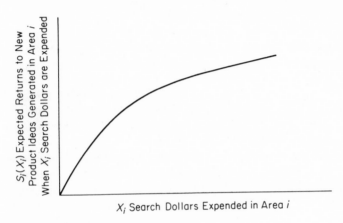

X_i Search Dollars Expended in Area i

Figure 7-3: Relation of new product ideas to search expenditures

diminishing returns to search effort. Such a response means that the firm is faced with a nonlinear programming problem. The discussion of mathematical programming and nonlinearities in the advertising chapter of this book is relevant. In particular, piecewise approximations to this type of function would be applicable.

The firm may also want to specify additional constraints on the search process. It may wish to implement a policy of having at least some minimum amount of search in certain areas. These policies may reflect threshold effects in the specified search areas. For example, the firm may want to devote at least some minimum amount of resources to monitoring competitive product developments. Such information may also have considerable value to management in assessing its relative market position, even if no new product ideas result. In addition, there may be practical upper limits to search in certain areas. For instance, there probably is some limit to the amount of time the firm's managers will be willing and able to devote to brainstorming sessions.

It would be interesting to examine changes in the level of the budget constraint. The determination of the search budget level is based on an estimate of the amount of search needed to produce an attractive set of new product ideas. Changes in the budget are made by balancing the costs required to generate additional new ideas with the possibility of discovering a highly desirable new product idea. When a sufficient set of attractive proposals is identified, additional resources may be better spent in evaluating the existing proposals rather than searching for new ideas. A search policy will be optimal when the increase in the value of the set of ideas due to locating new proposals equals the incremental cost of search.[6]

A Simulation Approach to New Product Search Decisions

A simulation model to aid managers in the generation of new product ideas has been developed by Pessemier.[7] His simulation model seeks to provide the firm with recommendations concerning the areas to search and the search effort to expend in each area.[8] This model will be described with the aid of the flow diagram given in Fig. 7-4. The discussion will consider the inputs required, the use that is made of them, the output of the model, and the utility of this output for decision purposes.

The first step of the simulation is the generation of the inputs needed by the model. Expert opinion and knowledgeable management judgment must be used to generate these inputs. A firm that decides to use this approach will probably want to accumulate information in its data bank which will be useful in providing these inputs in the future. Five basic types of input are needed:

1. Identification of the areas to be considered for search
2. Identification of the search policy alternatives to be considered
3. Determination of the minimum expected rate of return required before a new product proposal will be sent to the analysis stage
4. Estimates of the nature of the universe of potential product proposals that might result from search activity in each area
5. Specification of the arrival frequency of new product proposals that will be generated per time period when each area is searched with a specified search policy

[6] The determination of the "value" of the set is troublesome. One approach is the expected value of the profit generated by the products accepted. See J. B. MacQueen, "Optimal Policies for a Class of Search and Evaluation Problems," *Management Science*, (July, 1964), pp. 746–60, for an approach to this problem.

[7] E. A. Pessemier, *New Product Decisions: An Analytical Approach* (New York: McGraw-Hill Book Company, 1966), Chap. 2.

[8] Although Pessemier confines attention to *product* search areas, his approach need not be limited to product areas but may include such areas as monitoring new patent applications.

Input

Policy decisions on:
1. The areas to be considered for search
2. The cutoff rate of return for acceptance of a proposal
3. Search strategies to be considered

Estimates of:
1. The nature of the universe of potential product proposals in each area
2. The response to specified search strategies in each search area in terms of the rate of generation of new product proposals

Monté Carlo Simulation

Using the input data, a Monté Carlo simulation generates a distribution of return on investment to searching in each area i with search policy j and cutoff return criterion k. The simulation is run a sufficient number of times to yield a good idea of the distribution.

Repeat Simulation

The simulation is repeated for each combination of search areas, search strategies, and cutoff rate s of return management wants to consider.

Select Search Strategies and Areas for Search

Select the best combination of search area, strategy, and cutoff return on the basis of expected return on investment and risk as measured by the standard deviation of return for the area-strategy-cutoff combination. Additional combinations may be added to the total search policy as funds are available, or the search budget may be increased if the risk-expected return possibilities appear sufficiently attractive.

Final Output

The final output is the best search and preliminary evaluation policy for the firm, given the inputs to the model.

Figure 7-4: Simulation model for new product search procedures

The first three input items are policy inputs that serve to define the scope of the system. For examples of some potential search areas, see the discussion of Eq. (7-1). Search strategies will generally relate to search intensity (i.e., to the magnitude of resource commitment to search in an area). Note that these search intensities were denoted by the X_i's in the previous model. The appropriate cutoff rate of return is the firm's opportunity cost of capital in this model.

The description of the universe of potential new product proposals in each search area is somewhat more complex. The universe of such proposals (for a given area) is divided into cells that are homogeneous with respect to required investment, economic life, and the time pattern of investment and earnings cash flows. In order to define these cells, management is first asked to specify the maximum investment required and the maximum economic life that may be expected for a proposal identified in this search area. These upper bounds should be established at levels which only a very small proportion of proposals would be expected to exceed. Management next must specify the smallest increments in capital investment and economic life for which meaningful distinctions can be drawn. Pessemier suggests that the investment increment be at least $100,000 and that the economic life increment be at least one year. For each of the investment-economic life cells defined by these increments and upper bounds, the time pattern of investment and earnings cash flows must be specified. If the time pattern of these flows is expected to vary widely between proposals in this investment-economic life cell, it will be necessary to subdivide the cell by alternative flow patterns.

A flow pattern of earnings and investment represents the proportion of total earnings and total investment that will accrue during each year under consideration. As an example, consider a proposed new product, which has an economic life of three years and a total required investment of $200,000. The investment flow pattern might be 75 per cent of the total investment in the first year with the remaining 25 per cent in the second year. Thus the firm would have to invest $(0.75)(\$200,000) = \$150,000$ the first year and $(0.25)(\$200,000) = \$50,000$ the second year. Similarly, the flow pattern of earnings over the economic life is described by a probability distribution, which is discussed below.

Thus, in Pessemier's simulation model, the universe of potential product proposals in each search area is described by a set of cells defined as containing potential proposals that are homogeneous with respect to investment, economic life, and time pattern of cash flows.

Within each of the cells described above, it is also necessary to specify the total earnings cash flow which the proposal would generate over its entire economic life. Recall that the *pattern* of cash flow entered into the definition of the cell. Now management is required to supply a mutually exclusive and exhaustive set of ranges for total earnings and the probability that a proposal in this cell will exhibit total earnings within each of these ranges. For example, the distribution of total earnings over the economic life of projects in some cell might be taken to be as follows: fifty per cent of the proposals in this economic life, total investment, and cash flow pattern cell will yield a total return between $0 and $100,000, 30 per cent will yield from $100,000 to $200,000, and 20 per cent will yield $200,000 to $300,000. This frequency distribution, coupled with the total investment and time pattern of earnings and investment cash flows that define the cell, serves as the basis for computing the distribution of return on investment yielded by projects in this cell.

The final information required to describe the universe of proposals in this search area is the probability that a proposal which is generated will have the characteristics defining each of the cells. For example, management must specify the probability that a proposal generated in this search area will have some particular economic life, investment requirement, and cash flow pattern.

Finally, management must specify the relationship between the generation (or arrival) of proposals in search area i and the search strategy j. For instance, the generation of projects might be viewed as a Poisson process, in which case the time between the generation of successive new ideas would be exponentially distributed. The generation of proposals might then be linked to the search strategy or search intensity j by making the single parameter of their exponential interarrival distribution a function of the strategy. If the strategy j refers to search intensity, the relation would probably indicate that the time between proposals decreases as search effort increases.

The second stage of the model, Monté Carlo simulation, uses these inputs to generate the distribution of return on investment produced when area i is searched with search policy j and a cutoff return k. The procedure of the Monté Carlo analysis begins by sampling from the distribution that describes the results of applying the search policy to area i. (This is input 5.) This distribution describes the arrival rate of new product proposals from area i under search strategy j. As a simulated proposal appears, it is assigned to a cell by a random selection procedure based on the proportion of the search area's potential projects that may lie in that cell (input 4). Recall that the cell defines the total investment, economic life, and investment and earnings flow pattern for the proposal. It then remains to determine the total earnings generated by the proposal. The total earnings are obtained by a random draw from the distribution of total earnings defined for the cell.[9] This then yields a total description

---

[9] This sampling from the cell is analogous to I. Gross' approach to creating advertising appeals. See Chap. 3. Gross' approach would also seem to have the potential to yield information relevant to establishing a budget for search activities.

of the economic impact of the proposal. If the return exceeds the cutoff that has been established, the investment, earnings, and return to the project are recorded. Proposals continue to be generated over the planning horizon. The total cash flows and investment for all the projects selected by the plan during the planning horizon are then added and a rate of return to the search strategy is found.

This process is repeated until a sample distribution of rate of return to the plan (i, j, k) over the planning horizon is established. This distribution of return to the plan (i, j, k) represents the output of the second stage of the model.

The third stage of the model repeats the Monté Carlo simulation for each of the search strategies' cutoff returns and areas to be evaluated. The output of this stage is a series of rate of return distributions that represent the outcomes of applying particular search strategies j using cutoffs k to particular areas i.

In the final stage of the model, a choice between the level of search activity (i.e., the search strategy) for each area and the areas to be searched must be made. Pessemier proposes that each distribution of return on investment be described by its expected value and standard deviation. When these values for each search intensity and area are plotted on the same graph, the best search plan can be selected. An example of this plot is shown in Fig. 7-5. The line in the figure represents the firm's risk-return constraint. It implies a subjective balancing of risk and return by the managers. All search points (i, j, k) above and to the

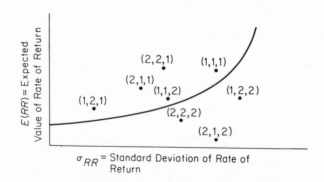

where (i, j, k) = search area i and search strategy j using cutoff return k.

Figure 7-5: Risk-return search plot*

* Note that each point in the figure is actually the projection of the hyperplane $(i, \;, k)$ in the risk-return plane. (From Pessemier, *op. cit.*, p. 66.

left of this line would have an acceptable risk-return balance and should be subjected to search.   If an area is represented by more than one point in the region, Pessemier suggests that the point with the greatest expected rate of return be selected.   The output of this model is a specification of the areas i appropriate for search, the intensity of search j, and the cutoff return k to use in preliminary screening of projects.

Pessemier's procedure promises to yield interesting insights into the nature of the search for new product ideas and has been presented in some detail to encourage further research in the area of search.   It does, however, have certain limitations.   In the first place, management is asked to supply a considerable amount of information in the form of estimates. This is not only time-consuming but also fraught with the danger that the estimates will be poor.   In any practical application the firm may wish to explore the sensitivity of the proposed solution to errors in management's inputs.   The second limitation is that the computational burden to the model may be large.   The model is simulation-based, and "what if" questions must be asked about every strategy, cutoff, and area to be tested.   Each of these tests requires an execution of the Monté Carlo simulation.   These limitations may become less significant as firms develop historical data banks that can be utilized to generate the needed distributions and as improved computers become available.[10]

Two models for planning search efforts directed at generating new product proposals have been suggested in this chapter.   Although both of the models are relatively complex, the payoffs they may produce in terms of efficiently generating new product ideas may be great.

The output of the search step is a listing of potentially desirable new product ideas.   These reflect the identification of market needs and technological developments the firm may find profitable to exploit.

SCREENING NEW PRODUCT POSSIBILITIES

After a set of potential products has been identified, the next step in the analysis is to screen out the obviously unsuitable ideas.   This screening is intended to identify those ideas that are not compatible with the company's goals, do not match the company's capabilities, or do not appear to have enough market potential.

These criteria are elimination criteria for the product idea.   For example, if the company has decided to restrict itself to durable consumer

[10] See Chap. 1 of this book.

products, all nondurable consumer products would be removed from the set of ideas because of incompatibility with the firm's goal structure, even though they might show great profit potential. The next elimination factor reflects the technical, financial, and managerial capabilities of the firm. If the firm cannot produce the product or does not have the technical or managerial abilities necessary for the product, the idea would be rejected. Similarly, the product must have sufficient market potential to justify further investment of the firm's resources.

After the products have passed through these rough elimination screens, the remaining ideas are ranked to determine the most suitable ideas. This ranking reflects an initial consideration of all the relevant factors associated with the proposed idea. This second phase of the new product proposal screening process is somewhat more detailed than the rough compatibility screens noted above, but not as detailed as those of the analysis stage discussed in the next section. The purpose of the more detailed phase of the screening process is to reduce the total set of product proposals to a set that will be manageable at the more costly and time-consuming analysis stage. The output of the more detailed screening should be the set that contains the product ideas which display the most potential for the firm.

The basic factors and subfactors relating to the suitability of a new product idea are listed in Fig. 7-6.[11] The first factor, marketability, is concerned with the relation of the new product to the firm's present product line and its distribution channels. It also relates to the compatibility of the product with the firm's merchandising strengths, its quantity-price comparison to competing products, and the inventory and production cost implications of the number of sizes and grades that will be necessary. The durability factor relates to the extent: (1) to which there is a broad, lasting demand for the product, (2) to which the product's design is protected, and (3) to which the product is resistant to seasonal and cyclical fluctuations which might prove costly and increase the risk inherent in the product. The productive ability factor is concerned that the firm has sufficient production knowledge, personnel, and equipment to produce the product and that there is a viable source of the necessary raw materials. The final factor, growth potential, raises the issues of the expected growth of uses, the growth of competition, and the product's over-all place in the market.

Now that many of the relevant considerations in the screening of new products have been outlined, it seems appropriate to focus attention on alternative approaches that have been taken to the screening of new products. Three alternatives can be identified: break-even analysis, pre-

[11] Other factor listings could, of course, be proposed.

liminary financial return analysis, and product profile procedures. Break-even concepts were considered in Chap. 4 and will not be repeated here. Pessemier's use of a cutoff rate of return in his simulation approach to the allocation of search resources illustrates the use of financial return analysis.[13] This type of analysis generally sets a cutoff rate of return

I. Marketability
   A. Relation to present distribution channels
   B. Relation to present product lines
   C. Quality-price relationship
   D. Number of sizes and grades
   E. Merchandisability
   F. Effects on sales of present products
II. Durability
   A. Stability
   B. Breadth of market
   C. Resistance to cyclical fluctuations
   D. Resistance to seasonal fluctuations
   E. Exclusiveness of design
III. Productive Ability
   A. Equipment necessary
   B. Production knowledge and personnel necessary
   C. Raw materials availability
IV. Growth Potential
   A. Place in market
   B. Expected competitive situation—value added
   C. Expected availability of end users

Figure 7-6: Factors and subfactors in new product desirability[12]

on investment for a new product. If the estimated return is greater than the cutoff (which is usually the firm's opportunity cost of capital), the product then proceeds to the analysis stage. The third approach, product profile procedures, is discussed in some detail in this section.

In product profile analysis, knowledgeable managers and experts are asked to rate the new product in terms of how well it is expected to perform on each of a number of dimensions. For example, they might be asked to rate a new product in terms of its compatibility with the present

[12] This outline is based upon J. T. O'Meara, "Selecting Profitable Products," *Harvard Business Review* (Jan.–Feb., 1961), pp. 83–89.

[13] For further elaboration of this approach, see Pessemier, *op. cit.*, and P. Kotler, "Computer Simulation in the Analysis of New Product Decisions," in F. Bass, C. King, E. Pessemier, eds., *Applications of the Sciences in Marketing* (New York: John Wiley & Sons, Inc., 1968).

product line on a scale such as:

Very Good	Good	Average	Poor	Very Poor
(5)	(4)	(3)	(2)	(1)

In this case the score of the product on the product line factor F_j will be a number between 1 and 5. If more than one person has ranked each factor, the factor score for the product F_j could be determined by an average of the score each person gives the product for that factor. An alternate averaging procedure would be to weight each person's score by the confidence he has in that score. The firm may also want to maintain information on the performance of each individual rater in order to be able to detect the tendencies of some individuals to consistently under- or overestimate the factor scores of potential new products.[14] This information could be stored in a data bank and be utilized to apply correction factors to individual ratings.

The individuals called upon to rate a new product will generally find their task somewhat easier if the scale categories of very good to very poor are defined somewhat more explicitly for each dimension. O'Meara has provided such definitions for the subfactors. His definitions are reproduced in Fig. 7-7 (on pages 308–310) as an example of how the score on each factor may be further specified.

In order to facilitate the comparison of potential new products, the firm generally finds it convenient to develop a system for combining a product's scores on each subfactor into a single index of the proposed product's quality. For example, the firm may form a score for product proposal i as

$$S_i = \sum_{j=1}^{f} W_j F_{ji} \qquad (7\text{-}2)$$

where S_i = product i's total score,

W_j = weight associated with subfactor j where $0 \leq W_j \leq 1$

and $\sum_{j=1}^{f} W_j = 1$,

F_{ji} = product i's score (e.g., from 1 to 5) on subfactor j.

The score S_i of each potential product serves as a rough index of its relative desirability. The establishment of a lower cutoff value for the index will help to eliminate the apparently unsuitable projects. The

[14] See Pessemier, *op. cit.*, Chap. 3, for a discussion of an approach to such corrections.

projects that survive this screening are then sent to the analysis stage for a detailed profitability analysis.

Use of the scoring procedure described in Eq. (7-2) requires that the firm establish appropriate weights W_j for the various subfactors. These weights represent the relative importance of the subfactors. Dean has suggested a method for determining these weights in which the members of the firm's new product review board independently rank the factors under consideration.[15] This ordering proceeds from the most important factor to the least important factor. The rank ordering could be converted into numeric values if the increment of importance between successive ranks were assumed to be equal. One criticism which might be made of this procedure is that it treats ordinal rankings as intervally scaled data. It might be better to use paired comparisons of the factors and Thurstone's "law of comparative judgment" to get the scaled data.[16] If it is assumed that this translation of rankings to numeric values is appropriate, the factor weights are averaged across individual raters to obtain a composite weight for each factor W_j. In a sensitivity analysis of actual rating situations, Dean found the final ranking of proposals to be relatively insensitive with respect to small changes or errors in the factor weights used.

The above approaches to determining factor weights and factor scores have certain limitations. Green, for example, has criticized this analysis on the grounds that:

1. The factor weights may not be independent of a product's scores on the various factors.
2. The factors themselves may not be independent, as has been implicitly assumed above.
3. The procedure assumes more knowledge on the rater's part about product characteristics than might be apparent at first glance.[17]

With respect to the last issue, Green contends that if the rater's knowledge is sufficient to provide meaningful evaluations, this knowledge might better be turned to a more direct linking between the product characteristics and economic indices of its likely market performance.

[15] B. V. Dean, "Quantitative Methods in New Product Planning," paper presented to the 1964 joint national meeting of TIMS and ORSA, October, 1964. Also see B. V. Dean and M. J. Miskey, "Scoring and Profitability Models for Evaluating and Selecting Engineering Projects," *Operations Research*, XIII (July–Aug., 1965), pp. 550–69.

[16] See P. Green and D. Tull, *Research for Marketing Decisions* (Englewood Cliffs, N.J.: Prentice-Hall, Inc., 1966), Chap. 7, and W. Torgerson, *Theory and Methods of Scaling* (New York: John Wiley & Sons, Inc., 1958).

[17] For further comment on Green's criticisms, see W. Alderson and P. Green, *Planning and Problem Solving in Marketing* (Homewood, Illinois: R. D. Irwin, 1964), pp. 205–206.

	Very Good	Good	Average	Poor	Very Poor
I. MARKETABILITY					
A. *Relation to present distribution channels*	Can reach major markets by distributing through present channels.	Can reach major markets mostly by distributing through present channels, partly through new channels.	Will have to distribute equally between new and present channels, in order to reach major markets.	Will have to distribute mostly through new channels in order to reach major markets.	Will have to distribute entirely through new channels in order to reach major markets.
B. *Relation to present product lines*	Complements a present line which needs more products to fill it.	Complements a present line that does not need, but can handle, another product.	Can be fitted into a present line.	Can be fitted into a present line but does not fit entirely.	Does not fit in with any present product line.
C. *Quality/price relationship*	Priced below all competing products of similar quality.	Priced below most competing products of similar quality.	Approximately the same price as competing products of similar quality.	Priced above many competing products of similar quality.	Priced above all competing products of similar quality.
D. *Number of sizes and grades*	Few staple sizes and grades.	Several sizes and grades, but customers will be satisfied with few staples.	Several sizes and grades, but can satisfy customer wants with small inventory of nonstaples.	Several sizes and grades, each of which will have to be stocked in equal amounts.	Many sizes and grades which will necessitate heavy inventories.
E. *Merchandisability*	Has product characteristics over and above those of competing products that lend themselves to the kind of promotion, advertising, and display that the given company does best.	Has promotable characteristics that will compare favorably with the characteristics of competing products.	Has promotable characteristics that are equal to those of other products.	Has a few characteristics that are promotable, but generally does not measure up to characteristics of competing products.	Has no characteristics at all that are equal to competitors' or that lend themselves to imaginative promotion.
F. *Effects on sales of present products*	Should aid in sales of present products.	May help sales of present products; definitely will not be harmful to present sales.	Should have no effect on present sales.	May hinder present sales some; definitely will not aid present sales.	Will reduce sales of presently profitable products.

II. DURABILITY A. *Stability*	Basic product which can always expect to have uses.	Product which will have uses long enough to earn back initial investment, plus at least 10 years of additional profits.	Product which will have uses long enough to earn back initial investment, plus several (from 5 to 10) years of additional profits.	Product which will have uses long enough to earn back initial investment, plus 1 to 5 years of additional profits.	Product which will probably be obsolete in near future.
B. *Breadth of market*	A national market, a wide variety of consumers, and a potential foreign market.	A national market and a wide variety of consumers.	Either a national market or a wide variety of consumers.	A regional market and a restricted variety of consumers.	A specialized market in a small marketing area.
C. *Resistance to cyclical fluctuations*	Will sell readily in inflation or depression.	Effects of cyclical changes will be *moderate*, and will be felt *after* changes in economic outlook.	Sales will rise and fall with the economy.	Effects of cyclical changes will be *heavy*, and will be felt *before* changes in economic outlook.	Cyclical changes will cause extreme fluctuations in demand.
D. *Resistance to seasonal fluctuations*	Steady sales throughout the year.	Steady sales—except under unusual circumstances.	Seasonal fluctuations, but inventory and personnel problems can be absorbed.	Heavy seasonal fluctuations that will cause considerable inventory and personnel problems.	Severe seasonal fluctuations that will necessitate layoffs and heavy inventories.
E. *Exclusiveness of design*	Can be protected by a patent with no loopholes.	Can be patented, but the patent might be circumvented.	Cannot be patented, but has certain salient characteristics that cannot be copied very well.	Cannot be patented, and can be copied by larger, more knowledgeable companies.	Cannot be patented, and can be copied by anyone.
III. PRODUCTIVE ABILITY A. *Equipment necessary*	Can be produced with equipment that is presently idle.	Can be produced with present equipment, but production will have to be scheduled with other products.	Can be produced largely with present equipment, but the company will have to purchase some additional equipment.	Company will have to buy a good deal of new equipment, but some present equipment can be used.	Company will have to buy all new equipment.
B. *Production knowledge and personnel necessary*	Present knowledge and personnel will be able to produce new product.	With very few minor exceptions, present knowledge and personnel will be able to produce new product.	With some exceptions, present knowledge and personnel will be able to produce new product.	A ratio of approximately 50–50 will prevail between the needs for new knowledge and personnel and for present knowledge and personnel.	Mostly new knowledge and personnel are needed to produce the new product.

Figure 7-7:—Caption on page 310.

	Very Good	*Good*	*Average*	*Poor*	*Very Poor*
C. *Raw materials' availability*	Company can purchase raw materials from its best supplier(s) exclusively.	Company can purchase major portion of raw materials from its best supplier(s), and remainder from any one of a number of companies.	Company can purchase approximately half of raw materials from its best supplier(s), and other half from any one of a number of companies.	Company must purchase most of raw materials from any one of a number of companies other than its best supplier(s).	Company must purchase most or all of raw materials from a certain few companies other than its best supplier(s).
IV. GROWTH POTENTIAL A. *Place in market*	New type of product that will fill a need presently not being filled.	Product that will substantially improve on products presently on the market.	Product that will have certain new characteristics that will appeal to a substantial segment of the market.	Product that will have minor improvements over products presently on the market.	Product similar to those presently on the market and which adds nothing new.
B. *Expected competitive situation—value added*	Very high value added so as to substantially restrict number of competitors.	High enough value added so that, unless product is extremely well suited to other firms, they will not want to invest in additional facilities.	High enough value added so that, unless other companies are as strong in market as this firm, it will not be profitable for them to compete.	Lower value added so as to allow large, medium, and some smaller companies to compete.	Very low value added so that all companies can profitably enter market.
C. *Expected availability of end users*	Number of end users will increase substantially.	Number of end users will increase moderately.	Number of end users will increase slightly, if at all.	Number of end users will decrease moderately.	Number of end users will decrease substantially.

Figure 7-7: Factor and subfactor ratings for a new product*

* O'Meara, *op. cit.*, pp. 84-85.

Freimer and Simon have attacked the weakness represented in the second of Green's criticisms by suggesting an approach that encompasses interactions between the factors.[18] Using O'Meara's 17 subfactors (given in Figs. 7-6 and 7-7), they require as input a description of the distribution of two populations of product proposals (successful and unsuccessful) in terms of this seventeen-dimensional space of subfactors. These distributions may be determined by a historical analysis of successful and unsuccessful product proposals, by subjective estimates of these distributions, or both. If the historical results approach is to be taken, the firm will be required systematically to accumulate information for such analysis.

Their procedure for developing factor weights and determining appropriate cutoff scores uses two-way multiple discriminant analysis and its associated classification rules to estimate whether any given new product with a set of subfactor scores will be a success or a failure. They use the most general form of the classification rules which incorporates the cost of misclassifying a good proposal as a failure and vice versa, and which accounts for the prior probability of the occurrence of successful and unsuccessful products.

They carry their analysis further. Recognizing that the assigned subfactor scores for a proposal will be subject to error or uncertainty, they go on to analyze the implications of this variation in terms of the decision to market or to drop the product.

Freimer and Simon have provided interesting generalizations of past approaches to product profile analysis. However, one may question the utility of dichotomizing product proposals into successful and unsuccessful categories. It would seem that information on the degree of success should be incorporated. Perhaps the Freimer and Simon approach could be generalized to an N-way discriminant approach where the categories represent degrees of success or failure. Such an approach would, of course, magnify the problems of analysis and data input. If this increment to screening cost and complexity appears worthwhile, it would seem to be a fruitful area for future research. However, it must be kept in mind that the purpose of the screening stage is to provide an economic framework for reducing the number of proposals that are to be sent to the more costly and time-consuming analysis stage. Given any new product planning situation, there is likely to be some bound to the increment in screening complexity which will be economically justifiable.

The output of the screening stage of the new product decision process

[18] M. Freimer and L. Simon, "The Evaluation of Potential New Product Alternatives," *Management Science*, XIII (Feb., 1967), pp. B-279–B-292. This paper is reproduced in D. B. Montgomery and G. L. Urban, eds., *Applications of Management Science in Marketing* (Englewood Cliffs, N.J.: Prentice Hall, Inc. 1969).

is a set of new product proposals that display the most potential and should be further subjected to detailed analysis.

ANALYSIS OF NEW PRODUCT PROPOSALS

At the analysis stage, the projects that have passed through the screening network are subjected to a detailed evaluation. After this evaluation three alternatives are present: (1) the project may be rejected (NO decision), (2) the project may be accepted (GO decision), or (3) more information may be sought concerning the project (ON decision). Note that a decision to delay further consideration of the project is one of the feasible alternatives when an ON decision is made. The analysis step in the new product decision process can be visualized as a networking problem[19] (see Fig. 7-8 for a network example). At each ON decision, a number of studies could be carried out to lead to the next evaluation.

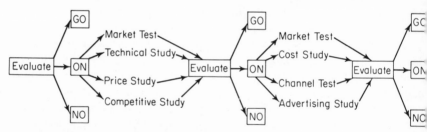

Figure 7-8: Analysis information network

With this formulation in mind, the analysis of new products can be visualized in two stages. The first stage is an optimization of the controllable parameters associated with the project at the present evaluation node. This analysis might be designed to maximize the profit associated with the product subject to the financial, managerial, and technical constraints on the problem. After this best state of the project has been defined at the evaluation node, the GO, ON, or NO decision is made. If an ON decision is made, the second-stage analysis is undertaken.

[19] This networking approach was first presented by A. Charnes, W. W. Cooper, J. K. DeVoe, and D. B. Learner, *DEMON: Decision Mapping Via Optimum GO-NO Networks—A Model for Marketing New Products* (a report presented at the Tenth International Meeting of the Institute of Management Science, Tokyo, Japan, August 24, 1963), p. 3.

This stage is directed at the determination of the optimum route to follow through the remaining nodes of the information network. It is designed to define the best sequence of studies to be carried out to reach a GO or NO decision. Both of these stages of analysis may be repeated at each evaluation node. The ultimate output of the analysis is a GO or NO decision for the product. If a NO decision is reached, the project is rejected. If a GO decision is reached, the optimum marketing mix and production variables are specified. Since the second stage specifies the most efficient path to a terminal GO or NO decision, the final decision is reached in such a way that the long-run return on the analysis funds is maximized.

First-stage Analysis

The first-stage maximization is based on an analytical consideration of the factors considered in the screening stage. These factors are represented in Fig. 7-9 and are grouped into structural classes of demand, cost, profit, and decision.

The over-all considerations relate to the profit to be generated by the new product, the investment required to obtain this profit, and the risk associated with the proposed product.

The profit generated by the new product will depend upon both the demand and cost associated with the product. The demand for the new product will probably change over time; the product will grow, reach maturity, and decline over its life cycle. The quantity sold in any one year will not only depend upon the stage of the life cycle, but will also depend upon the price level, the amount of advertising expenditure, the quality level, and the intensity of the distribution and sales effort in each year. These factors together constitute the marketing mix for the new product. The sales of the product will depend upon not only the level of each factor in the mix, but also upon their combined effectiveness. The competitive environment surrounding the new product will also affect the firm's sales of the product. The competitive effects will depend upon the competitors' strategies and the counterstrategy employed by the introductory firm. The total sales of the firm will depend upon the resultant effects of the competitive and marketing mix factors.

The costs of production will depend on the plant size, the technological level of plant facilities, and utilization of the plant. The new product decision will also be affected by future technological developments. A firm may be less likely to invest in a large productive plant if developments in the future may significantly lower production costs. If this happens, the competition could enter at these lower costs and force the originating firm to an unprofitable price level.

The combination of the demand and costs will determine profits for the new product. These profits will be received in future years, so the timing of this cash inflow will affect the return on investment. Thus the time value of the inflow should be considered.

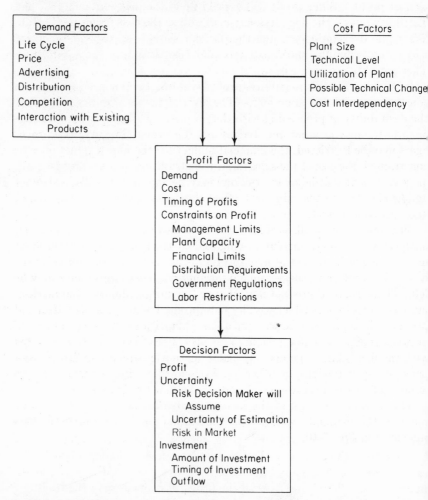

Figure 7-9: Factors affecting new product decision*

The investment required for the product will be an important parameter in the decision. The amount and timing of the investment outflow must be combined with profit considerations to see if the return on investment is satisfactory. The determination of the satisfactory level of

* Glen L. Urban, "Sprinter: A Tool for New Product Decision Makers," *Industrial Management Review*, VIII (Spring 1967), p. 45.

return will not only depend upon the level of profits and investment, but also upon the amount of uncertainty the decision maker will assume. The total uncertainty will depend upon the risks inherent in the market and the uncertainties of estimation. This uncertainty will be balanced against profit. Since profit will depend upon the price, advertising, and distribution level the firm designates, as well as the cost structure it establishes, the decision concerning the product should be made at the point where the optimum marketing mix and cost structure are established. There, profits are greatest.

In striving for this maximum profit level for the new product, certain constraints will have to be met. The level of the constraints may affect the desirability of proceeding with the project. The production facilities open to the new product may be limited, the availability of trained managers may be restricted, the financial budget for the new product may be constrained, the size of the sales force or distribution system may be fixed, or government and labor restrictions may be significant. The existence and level of these constraints will affect the demand creation, investment, and cost aspects of the new product proposal.

The new product will probably not be offered as an entity independent of the other products currently being sold by the firm. The new product may reduce or increase the sales of other existing products offered by the firm. In addition to these demand interactions, cost interactions may be felt. The proposed product may change the unit production and marketing costs of other products. The new product will certainly affect old products if common resources such as advertising funds are allocated between them. The new product may also affect the total risk associated with the firm's line of goods. Its sales fluctuations may amplify or compensate for variations in other products. These interactions may be important to the advisability of adding the new product.

The integration of all of the factors can be discussed by the development of the demand, cost, profit, uncertainty, and decision submodels indicated in Fig. 7-10.

Demand Model

The demand model attempts to relate a product's marketing variables (i.e., its marketing mix) in a quantitative expression that can be used to predict the sales effects of marketing strategies. The starting point for the demand model will probably be an estimate of the sales of the product in each year, given a specific set of the firm's decision variables and a forecast of the market and competitive environment. For example, it may be estimated that the product's sales will show an S-shaped pattern.

That is, sales may grow slowly at first, then increase rapidly, and finally tend to level off. This curve will depend upon the success in the market-place, the diffusion rate of the new product, and competitive behavior. The kinds of diffusion models that might be appropriate to describe new product growth will be discussed in the implementation section of this chapter. At this point, it is sufficient to say that the reference forecast

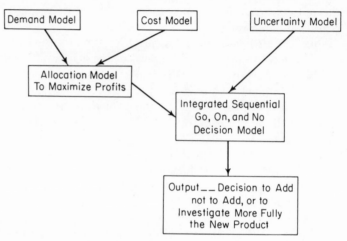

Figure 7-10: First-stage analysis model

will reflect the diffusion rate, the firm's marketing mix, customer accept-ance, and competitive behavior. This forecast of sales over time may be called the life cycle, but it should be clearly understood that this is not an innate phenomenon. It is controllable. For example, it is possible to have either a very short life cycle at a high price or a long life cycle at a low price for the same product.

When the reference forecast of sales in each year has been developed, the demand model should describe how the level of sales would change if the marketing mix were changed. For example, the demand for the prod-uct may be expressed in functional form as:

$$X_{ijt} = f(P_{ijt}, A_{ijt}, D_{ijt}, PS_{ijt}, Q_{ijt}, K_{ijt}, Pd_{ijt}, \bar{X}_{It}, X_{ij,t-1}) \quad (7\text{-}3)$$

where X_{ijt} = quantity of product j sold by firm i during period t,

P_{ijt} = firm i's price for product j during period t,

A_{ijt} = firm i's advertising for product j during period t,

D_{ijt} = firm i's distribution effort for product j during period t,

PS_{ijt} = firm i's personal selling effort for product j during period t,

Q_{ijt} = quality of product j sold by firm i during period t,

K_{ijt} = competitive conditions in the market for product j sold by firm i during period t,

Pd_{ijt} = demand characteristics of other products offered by firm i and other firms during period t as they relate to the demand for firm i's product j in period t,

$\bar{X}_{It}$ = reference forecast of industry sales in period t.

The problem is how to relate explicitly these controllable variables to the quantity of the new product to be sold. Several approaches can be taken to the problem of relating the controllable marketing variable to sales. The modeling and measurement problems for individual marketing variables have been dealt with in previous chapters. In this section the emphasis will be on the combined effects of the marketing variables.

One way to formulate the marketing mix effects is by postulating a specific model structure to relate sales and the other variables. For example, it may be felt that advertising affects awareness and that awareness along with promotion and distribution determine the trial rate for this product. The trial rate, competition, and price might then be hypothesized as determining the sales of the product. A new product model called DEMON has postulated that advertising dollars affect gross rating points, which affect reach and frequency, which specify advertising awareness, which along with promotion and distribution determines the trial rate.[20] The trial rate determines the usage rate which along with price determines sales. With this description of the relationships between the factors, the nature of the linking between them can be investigated. For example, empirical research may indicate that the awareness-trial link is a linear function. Although it is doubtful that a general relationship for all product types can be developed, the use of linking relationships and appropriate measurement techniques can provide a method of specifying a demand model for a product.

An extension of this sort of modeling would lead to the process type of models used by Amstutz. His microanalytical models encompassed the functional effects in Eq. (7-3) for each segment in the market.[21] When the demand in each segment is summed over all segments, the total demand is determined. The disadvantage of this approach is that the complexity of the representation is so great that computational limits would restrict consideration to only a few alternative marketing strategies.

Another approach to describing a demand model is to consider all the

[20] See D. B. Learner, "DEMON New Product Planning: A Case History," in F. E. Webster, Jr., ed., *New Directions in Marketing* (Chicago: American Marketing Association, 1965).

[21] A. E. Amstutz, *Computer Simulation of Competitive Market Response* (Cambridge, Mass.: The M.I.T. Press, 1967).

variables of demand to be independent variables in an aggregate equation. The simplest equation of this form would be (for firm 1 and product 1)

$$X_{11t} = k\bar{X}_{11t}p_t P_{11t}a_t A_{11t}d_t D_{11t}s_t PS_{11t}q_t Q_{11t} \qquad (7\text{-}4)$$

where $\quad X_{11t}$ = quantity of product 1 sold by firm 1 in period t,

$\bar{X}_{11t}$ = reference sales forecast for firm 1's product 1 in period y,

P_{11t} = price of firm 1's product 1 in period t,

A_{11t} = advertising for firm 1's product 1 in period t,

D_{11t} = distribution effort by firm 1 for product 1 in period t,

PS_{11t} = personal selling effort by firm 1 for product 1 in period t,

Q_{11t} = quality of firm 1's product 1 during period t,

k = scale factor (constant),

p, a, d, s, q = proportionality constants.

The constants $p, a, d, s,$ and q represent the magnitude of the sales effect that unit changes in the respective variables produce. For example, p represents the dollar change in sales as the result of changing price by one unit. This formulation does have the limitation of assuming that each of the variables is linearly related to the quantity sold when all other variables are held constant. The relationships can be made nonlinear by using factors of the form Y^{EY} in place of the yY form used above where

$$EY = \frac{\delta X/X}{\delta Y/Y}$$

(i.e., demand elasticities of marketing variables) and the EY must be constant. This implies that the effect of each variable is one of the specific forms in Fig. 7-11. These nonlinear relationships are more general than the linear relationships, but they still may constrain the specification of the sales response to particular variables.

General nonlinear or discontinuous functions have been formulated in a model called SPRINTER.[22] They are admitted by describing "response functions" which measure the proportionate changes in the quantity sold (i.e., $X/\bar{X}$) as a result of an absolute change in the level of a variable. For example, if the sales of a product were estimated by the graph in Fig. 7-12, the price response function PR would be

$$PR = \frac{268}{P - 104.5} - 0.843 \qquad (7\text{-}5)$$

---

[22] See G. L. Urban, "SPRINTER: A Tool for New Product Decision-Making," *Industrial Management Review*, VIII (Spring, 1967), pp. 43–55.

That is, if the reference price $\bar{p}$ of 250 were established, PR would be 1. If a price of 200 were established, the value of PR would be almost 2. This means that if the price were dropped $50, sales would be about twice the reference forecasted value. After the price response value has been

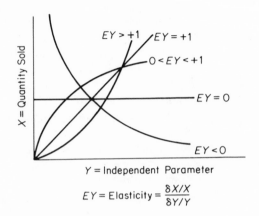

$$EY = \text{Elasticity} = \frac{\delta X/X}{\delta Y/Y}$$

Figure 7-11: Constant elasticity curves

determined, sales are specified by multiplying the reference forecast $\bar{X}_t$ times PR. This response function approach could be extended to other variables, and the quantity sold would be the reference forecast value times the response function values. In Eq. (7-4) this would mean that each yY term would be replaced by its response function which represents the proportionate change in sales for an absolute change in the level of the variable.

Another method for describing intricate market responses is by using a series of equations to describe a variable's effect. For example, Kuehn and Weiss have described the value of distribution D_t by a series of equa-

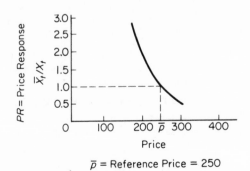

$\bar{p}$ = Reference Price = 250

Figure 7-12: Price response function

tions.[23] The D_t value reflects the brand's market share in period $t - 1$, the efforts of the sales force, advertising, and any retail allowance offered the retailer. This form not only allows a richness in the description of response, but also considers more complex interrelationships between the variables.

In order to build in the lagged effects of marketing variables, the values used to specify the marketing variables can be represented by a smoothing of the past values of the variables. Palda used this technique in analyzing advertising response.[24] Another dynamic phenomenon might be the effect of initial marketing programs on the diffusion of the innovation. This can be visualized as a shift in the occurrence of life cycle sales levels. For example, Urban has used a time shift function which depends upon the early pricing of a product.[25]

A description of the new product's sales as a function of each of the firm's marketing variables does not complete the demand model. Competitive effects must be included. The simplest approach to this problem is to include competitive effects in the response estimates by assuming a particular strategy for competitors. This does not, however, capture the interdependent nature of competition and competitive strategy outlined earlier in this chapter. To fully comprehend competitive interdependencies, it is useful to separate industry and competitive effects. The industry effects are measured by the total industry sales produced by the industry's over-all marketing program. These price, advertising, and distribution effects can be modeled by the procedures outlined in the last paragraph. If this industry sales prediction were multiplied by a term that reflects the firm's market share, the firm's sales could be estimated. A number of competitive formulations have been developed earlier in this book in Chaps. 3 and 4. The most common form is based on one firm's marketing response relative to the sum of all firms' responses. For example, Kotler has formulated the competitive effects as:[26]

$$MS_i = \frac{P_i^{EP} A_i^{EA} D_i^{ED}}{\sum_{i=1}^{n} P_i^{EP} A_i^{EA} D_i^{ED}} \qquad (7\text{-}6)$$

[23] A. A. Kuehn and D. L. Weiss, "Marketing Analysis Training Exercise," *Behavioral Science*, X (Jan., 1965), pp. 65–67.

[24] See Chap. 3.

[25] G. L. Urban, "A New Product Analysis and Decision Model," *Management Science* (April, 1968) pp. B490–B517, and reproduced in D. B. Montgomery and G. L. Urban, eds., *Application of Management Science in Marketing* (Englewood Cliffs, N.J.: Prentice-Hall, Inc., 1969).

[26] P. Kotler, "Competitive Strategies for New Product Marketing Over the Life Cycle," *Management Science*, XII (Dec., 1965), pp. 104–19. This article is also reprinted in D. B. Montgomery and G. L. Urban, eds., *Applications of Management Science in Marketing* (Englewood Cliffs, N.J.: Prentice-Hall, Inc., 1969).

where MS_i = market share for firm i,
    P_i = price of product from firm i,
    A_i = advertising for product by firm i,
    D_i = distribution effort for product by firm i,
    EP = price sensitivity of market share,
    EA = advertising sensitivity of market share,
    ED = distribution sensitivity of market share,
    n = number of firms in industry.

The exponents in Eq. (7-6) are sensitivities that reflect the change in market share produced by changing a marketing variable, if it is assumed that competitors do not change their variables. Urban has empirically estimated sensitivities for a similar market share term.[27] The resulting expression was

$$MS_1 = \frac{P_1^{-0.855}F_1^{1.13}}{P_1^{-0.855}F_1^{1.13} + P_2^{-1.245}F_2^{1.20}} \tag{7-7}$$

where MS_i = market share for firm i,
    P_i = price established by firm i,
    F_i = number of shelf facings for firm i.

In this expression each firm has a different sensitivity, and the number of shelf facings F_i is used to represent promotion and distribution effects. The estimation was carried out by an on-line trial and error search routine that minimized the squared error between the predicted market share and actual market shares. The data base was 100 store audits. Equation (7-7) explained 54 per cent of the variance in the data.

The competitive market share formulation may be modified to include product characteristics as well as price, advertising, and distribution.[28] Suppose there are two product characteristics of relevance in the market under consideration. Let C_{1i} be the value of product characteristic 1 for the product offered by firm i. A similar definition holds for C_{2i}. The market share term might now be expressed as:

$$MS_i = \frac{P_i^{EP}A_i^{EA}D_i^{ED}C_{1i}C_{2i}}{\sum_{i=1}^{n} P_i^{EP}A_i^{EA}D_i^{ED}C_{1i}C_{2i}} \tag{7-8}$$

The value of the product characteristics might represent a transformation

[27] G. L. Urban, "An On-line Technique for Estimating and Analyzing Complex Models," in R. Moyer, ed., *Changing Marketing Systems* (Chicago, Ill.: American Marketing Association, 1967), pp. 322–27.

[28] For an application of this modification in a large-scale model, see A. Kuehn and D. Weiss, "Marketing Analysis Training Exercise," *Behavioral Science*, X (Jan., 1965), pp. 51–67.

of the actual product's characteristics. For example, the following relation might describe C_{1i}:

$$C_{1i} = (1 - a_1) \, exp \, (C_i^{(1)} - \hat{C}_1) + 1.0 \qquad (7\text{-}9)$$

where C_{1i} = value of product characteristic 1 for firm i's product,
    $\hat{C}_1$ = reference level of product characteristic 1,
    $C_i^{(1)}$ = amount of product characteristic 1 present in firm i's product,
    a_1 = consumer discrimination parameter for characteristic 1, $0 \leq a_1 \leq 1$.

The parameter a_1 reflects the customer's ability to recognize the product characteristic. If $a_1 = 1$, the customer can not discriminate between products with respect to this characteristic. As a_1 approaches zero, the consumer is better at discriminating between products on the basis of the relevant product characteristic.

Another modification to the competitive term can be made to reflect the dynamic effects produced by one firm having a competitive time lead in the new product market. This can be done by exponentially smoothing past market share values or by summing both the numerator of the competitive expression over some time period and establishing heavier weights for the most recent periods.

The final consideration in the demand model relates to interdependencies between the new product and existing products in the firm's line. These interactions may be measured through any of the marketing variables associated with other products. For example, it may be felt that the price level set for another product would affect the new product sales. In this situation, the price of the other product could be included in the equation as an independent variable. It could then be assigned a proportionality coefficient or sensitivity exponent. In the case of the marketing variables of other products in the line, the exponent is the cross sensitivity of the demand for the new product with respect to the marketing variable of the other product in the line. In Chap. 4 some empirical experience with this form of product interdependency was described. If the constant elasticity form is inappropriate, cross response functions which describe the proportional sales effects of a change in another product's variable could be formulated.[29] The effects of product interdependency can also be encompassed in the market share term. Shakun's expression for market share included coupling coefficients and was discussed in Chap. 4 of this book.

The final demand model would be a mathematical expression describ-

---

[29] See G. L. Urban, "A New Product Analysis and Decision Model," *op. cit.*

ng the quantity of the new product the firm can expect to sell as an explicit function of the firm's marketing variables, competition, and product line interdependencies.

Cost Model

The cost model attempts to describe the cost of producing specified quantities of the product (see Fig. 7-10). The cost function associated with the new product would be most simply represented by a function:

$$TC_{1t} = FC_{1t} + TVC_{1t} \qquad (7\text{-}10)$$

$$TVC_{1t} = (AVC_{1t})(X_{1t})$$

where TC_{1t} = total cost for product 1 in year t,
TVC_{1t} = total variable cost for product 1 in year t,
FC_{1t} = fixed cost for product 1 in year t,
AVC_{1t} = average variable cost for product 1 in year t,
X_{1t} = quantity of product 1 produced in year t.

If AVC = constant in the equation, there are no changes in the variable unit cost of the product as quantities are changed. If AVC is a function of the quantity of the good produced, a single (probably nonlinear) equation could describe the cost relationship. If the product has costs interdependencies with other products, the cost function would be more complex. These interdependencies might arise because the products share the same production resources or compete in the same input factor markets. It would be possible to use the sensitivity exponent or response function form to comprehend the interdependencies as was done in the demand equation. Another approach is to build a mathematical programming model that minimizes the cost of producing specified quantities of goods in the firm's offering. In addition to direct cost interdependencies, system interdependencies effects (such as delivery delay and quality) upon sales of products may deserve consideration. Industrial dynamics would be an appropriate tool when these effects are significant.[30]

Profit Model

Given the demand and cost models, the total profit produced by the new product can be calculated, but this may not be the appropriate profit to credit to the new product. The new product may affect the

[30] J. Forrester, *Industrial Dynamics* (Cambridge, Mass.: The M.I.T. Press, 1961).

profit of other products in the firm's offerings. The new product is actually responsible for only the change in the firm's total profits. This over-all change may be called the "differential profit." The differential profit in any year is the difference between the profit generated by the new line less the estimated profits of the line if the new product had not been introduced.

$$DP_t = \text{PROFIT}_{\text{NEW},t} - \text{PROFIT}_{\text{OLD},t} \qquad (7\text{-}11)$$

where DP_t = differential profit in year t,
$\text{PROFIT}_{\text{NEW},t}$ = total new line profit in year t,
$\text{PROFIT}_{\text{OLD},t}$ = estimated old line profit for year t.

The new line profit is the sum of the profit of the products in the line after adding the new product.

$$\text{PROFIT}_{\text{NEW},t} = \sum_{j=1}^{m} P_{jt}X_{jt} - \sum_{j=1}^{m} TVC_{jt} \qquad (7\text{-}12)$$

where m = number of products offered by the firm,
P_{jt} = price of product j in period t.

When this is summed over a specified planning period PP and discounted at the firm's target rate of return on investment RR, the discounted differential profit DDP can be calculated.

$$DDP = \sum_{t=1}^{PP} \frac{DP_t}{(1 + RR)^t}$$

This profit model can be used as the objective function for the first-stage maximization. The problem is to maximize the new product's discounted differential profit as a function of the marketing variables, but subject to the production, distribution, and financial constraints on the firm.

As the previous discussion indicates, the profit expression is a very complex function of many variables. It is dependent upon the demand and cost of the product and perhaps other products in the line. The demand in turn is dependent upon the levels established for each of the variables in the marketing mix (P, A, D, PS, Q) and the competitive environment. The function is further complicated since the levels of these variables may be changed in each time period and dynamic lagged effects may be produced. The first-stage optimization attempts to locate the dynamic marketing program for the new product that produces the greatest discounted differential profit over a planning period while satisfying the financial, production, distribution, and managerial constraints in each time period.

This maximization is difficult, because the nature of the profit function

ısually precludes the use of analytic solution procedures. The function
ıs usually not linear and the number of variables is large. Calculus and
ıonlinear programming may be applicable in some simple cases, but the
ɔroblem must usually be solved by an iterative search routine. For these
ᵣeasons, most new product decision frameworks do not attempt to reach
ı maximum but rather select the best of a number of trials specified on a
'what if" basis or from a restricted set of alternative situations.[31]

On-line iterative computer search routines that utilize the marketing
manager and his business judgment may provide a method of generating
ɡood solutions.[32] This type of search routine can also be used to evaluate
ɪhe effects of alternate competitive strategies and could be used to generate a payoff matrix that could be analyzed by the Bayesian or game theory
ɪechniques described in Chaps. 3 and 4 of this book. The first-stage analysis should include consideration of the best level for each of the market-
ᵢng variables in each year.

The first-stage maximization is a significant one, since the initially proposed level of variables may be far from the optimum marketing program.
During this first-stage optimization, it is also valuable to examine the
effects of changing the level of the constraints on the problem. The selection of better constraint levels may increase the profitability appreciably.

Uncertainty Model

The result of the profit and allocation considerations is the maximum
level of profit and the optimal marketing program over the planning
period for the new product. This return must now be balanced against
the uncertainty and the investment associated with the project to reach
a GO, ON, or NO decision. The decision would be relatively simple if
the estimates of demand, cost, and interdependency were known with
certainty. This is not usually the case in new product decisions. Great
uncertainties exist about the product, because by its nature it is new and
very little previous experience that is directly relevant to the product has
been accumulated.

The uncertainty associated with the project can be determined by
estimating the over-all probabilities associated with levels of total profit
other than the one predicted by the first-stage maximization. This

---

[31] See A. Charnes, W. W. Cooper, J. K. DeVoe, D. B. Learner, "DEMON: A
Management Model for Marketing New Products," Carnegie Institute of Technology,
1965 (Management Sciences Research Report No. 52), and W. Alderson and P. Green,
Planning and Problem Solving in Marketing (Homewood, Illinois: Irwin, 1964), pp.
216–33, for examples of such first-stage procedures.

[32] See G. L. Urban, "An On-Line Technique for Estimating and Analyzing Complex Models," *op. cit.*

would generate a distribution about the best estimate of profit. The standard error. of this distribution would be a measure of uncertainty. Another approach would be to establish probability levels for deviations from each of the subfactors in the problem. These estimates would generate distributions that would then be aggregated to produce a total profit distribution. Two basic methods are available for carrying out the aggregation. The first is Monté Carlo simulation. This is essentially a statistical sampling procedure. Given the distributions about all the variables, a sample of a number of points is randomly drawn. One value is selected from each of the component distributions, and the profit associated with each of the sets of sample points is calculated. These profit calculations are used to describe an over-all distribution of profit results.[33] The second procedure is based on an analytical combination of the variances of each of the distributions to specify the variance of the total profit distribution. If the resulting distribution can be assumed to be a standard distribution, such as a normal distribution, the desired uncertainty and probability measures may be found.[34]

In estimating the uncertainties, it is again important to realize that the product may not be independent of other products. Fluctuations in the new product might amplify or compensate for fluctuations in the sales and profits of existing products. A useful way of defining the uncertainty attributed to the new product is by the concept of "differential uncertainty." The differential uncertainty is the change in the total uncertainty of the product line as the result of adding the new product and could be measured by the standard deviation of the distribution of differential profit:

$$DU^2 = V' + V - 2 \operatorname{cov}(Pr', Pr) \tag{7-13}$$

where
DU = differential uncertainty,
V' = variance of new line profits,
V = variance of old line profits,
$\operatorname{cov}(Pr', Pr)$ = covariance of new and old line profits,
Pr' = new line profits,
Pr = old line profits.

Since the new line will generally include all or most of the old line products, the covariance term will tend to be high.

Since there are likely to be product interdependencies within a given line

---

[33] See Pessemier, *op. cit.*, for additional considerations of Monté Carlo analysis and new product decisions.

[34] See G. L. Urban, "A New Product Analysis and Decision Model," *Management Science* (April, 1968) pp. B490–B517, and reprinted in D. B. Montgomery and G. L. Urban, eds., *Applications of Management Science in Marketing* (Englewood Cliffs, N.J.: Prentice-Hall, Inc., 1969).

(old or new), the covariance terms will also be important in determining the variance in profits for the product line (i.e., V or V'). For example,

$$V = \sum_{i=1}^{m} \sum_{j=1}^{m} \sigma_{ij}$$

where m = number of products in the line,

$\sigma_{ii} = \sigma_i^2$ = variance of product i's profits,

σ_{ij} = covariance of the profits of product i and product j.

Decision Model

The output of the uncertainty model is an estimate of the distribution of profit levels about the best estimate produced in the first stage maximization.[35] The GO, ON, and NO decision must be made by balancing the return from the new product against this uncertainty. The balancing of the risk and return may be achieved by dividing the return and uncertainty quadrant into three appropriate areas. This division could be accomplished by determining the firm's utility function relative to uncertainty and return.[36] Constant utility lines would be sloped upward and to the right. By specifying the minimum level of utility for a GO decision and the maximum utility level to allow a NO decision, the risk and return coordinate for the proposed project could be plotted and a decision reached (see Fig. 7-13, where I = investment).

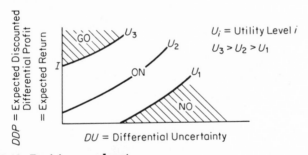

Figure 7-13: Decision quadrant

In this figure, return is measured by the expected value of the new product's differential profit. The uncertainty is measured by the standard error of the total differential profit distribution (i.e., the differential uncertainty). The utility approach is troublesome to implement, since the determination of the utility for a corporation is most difficult.

[35] See G. L. Urban, *op. cit.*, for the effects of changing uncertainties during optimization.

[36] See P. C. Fishburn, "Methods of Estimating Additive Utilities," *Management Science*, XIII (March, 1967), pp. 435–53.

An alternate and more easily specified decision structure has been proposed in the DEMON model for new product decisions.[37]   This model divides the GO, ON, and NO areas on the basis of the probability of making a specified payback and specified level of expected profit. The GO decision is specified when the expected value of profits is greater than a specified value and when the probability of a particular payback requirement is greater than the GO criterion level specified by management.   The NO alternative is taken when the expected value of profit is less than a specified level or the probability of achieving a particular payback requirement is less than the NO criterion level.   The remaining area is for the ON decision.

The GO, ON, and NO areas could be divided on the basis of the probability of achieving the target rate of return on investment rather than the probability of recovering investment in a specific payback period. Suppose the following constraints are chosen to divide GO, ON, and NO areas:

1. For a GO decision the probability of obtaining at least a target rate of return must be greater than a specified level.
2. For a NO decision the probability of obtaining a given discounted rate of return must be less than a specified level.

These constraints can be derived in terms of the differential profit and differential uncertainty. For the GO decision the constraint is

$$P(TDDP \geq I) \geq A_G \qquad (7\text{-}14)$$

where A_G = minimum probability for a GO decision,
          P = probability,
          I = total investment in new product,
     $TDDP$ = total differential profit discounted at the target rate of return.

When the total differential profit, discounted at the target rate of return, is just equal to the investment, the rate of return generated by the product is exactly equal to the target rate of return.   Equation (7-14) states that this equation must be achieved or exceeded with a probability of at least A_G.

Equation (7-14) can be expressed as

$$P \left[\frac{TDDP - E(TDDP)}{DU} \geq \frac{I - E(TDDP)}{DU} \right] \geq A_G$$

where DU = differential uncertainty.

[37] See A. Charnes, W. W. Cooper, J. K. DeVoe, and D. B. Learner, "DEMON: Mark II Extremal Equations Approach to New Product Marketing," *Management Science*, XIV (May, 1968), pp. 513–24.

If it is assumed that $TDDP$ is normally distributed, $[TDDP - E(TDDP)]/DU$ is normally distributed with a mean of 0 and a variance of 1. The equation can be restated in an equivalent form as

$$\frac{I - E(TDDP)}{DU} \leq t_{GO} \tag{7-15}$$

where t_{GO} is the fractile of $[TDDP - E(TDDP)]/DU$ associated with A_G. In Fig. 7-14, the shaded area represents the probability required

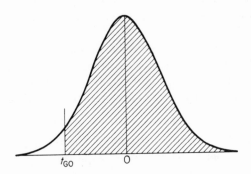

Figure 7-14: GO decision fractile

for a GO decision A_G. Equation (7-15), when solved for the expected total discounted differential profit, is

$$E(TDDP) \geq -t_{GO}DU + I \tag{7-16}$$

where $A_G > 0.5$, $t_{GO} < 0$, and it is convenient to express Eq. (7-16) as

$$E(TDDP) \geq |t_{GO}|DU + I$$

This is the equation for the GO constraint level of probability of achieving the specified rate of return.

For a NO decision the constraint is

$$P(TDDP \geq I) \leq A_N \tag{7-17}$$

where A_N is the maximum probability for a NO decision. This constraint can be rewritten by the procedure used to transform Eq. (7-15) to Eq. (7-16). It is then

$$E(TDDP) \leq |t_{NO}|DU + I, \quad \text{if } A_N > 0.5$$

where A_N = maximum probability for NO decision.

t_{NO} = fractile corresponding to A_N.

If $A_N < 0.5$, $t_{NO} > 0$, the equation for the NO decision is

$$E(TDDP) \leq -|t_{NO}|DU + I$$

GO and NO constraints can be plotted as straight lines on the risk return plane, and the decision areas can be specified (see Fig. 7-15).

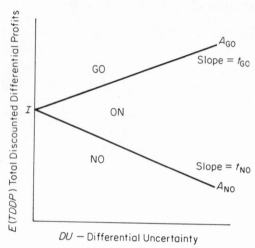

Figure 7-15: Decision quadrant

Given some system of utility or decision rules to divide the uncertainty-return quadrant, the new product decision can be specified.   If the profit and uncertainty coordinates of the proposed project fall in the NO area, it is rejected.   If they fall in the GO area, the firm makes a commitment to market the product and begins the implementation step of the new product process.   If the project falls in the ON area, the second-stage analysis is undertaken.

Second-stage Analysis

If an ON decision is specified, the link leading to the next evaluation node must be chosen.   The study to be selected should be optimal in terms of the total path to be followed through the information network. The path to be followed is determined by selecting the sequence of studies, the size of each study, and the total number of studies to be undertaken. The procedure is to select a path that appears to be the best one, given the data available at that ON node.   After the first link is traversed, the GO, ON, or NO decision is again made.   If an ON decision is specified, a new optimal path through the remainder of the information network is determined.   Thus the project proceeds step by step down the information network, but each ON step is made by looking ahead through

*Urban, *op. cit.*, p. 48.

the network. For example, if there were only one good test market for the product, this information link probably should not be used very early in the network. It would be more valuable to save it for use later. This foresight at the ON node assures that the first ON study does not eliminate the possibilities of more advantageous use of that study link at other ON nodes. This networking approach is a heterogeneous sequential testing procedure. Each test is different and each test is selected by considering the optimum size, number, and sequence of tests to be carried out.

The first problem in the second-stage optimization is the definition of "optimum." One approach to this problem is to use Bayesian analysis. The optimal route through the network would then be the one with the greatest expected value of utility.[38] For this analysis, it will be assumed that the utility function is linear with respect to profit so that maximum utility is equivalent to maximum profit. The set of possible sequences is indicated in Fig. 7-16 when there are three studies available. After

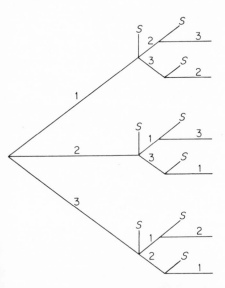

1 = Market Test
2 = Product Cost Study
3 = Study of Potential Competition
S = Stop by GO or NO Decision

Figure 7-16: Possible sequences of three study links

each study there is also the option to terminate the network. The expected value of profit would have to be calculated for each possible sequence. This would be computed in the usual Bayesian decision tree

[38] See Alderson and Green, *op. cit.*, pp. 216–37, for a Bayesian case study of this problem.

fashion.[39]   If we assume (1) states of nature S_i $(i = 1, \ldots, I)$ and prior probabilities for each state $P(S_i)$, (2) possible results from the sequence of tests Z_j $(j = 1, \ldots, J)$ with associated reliabilities $P(Z_j|S_i)$ for the sequence, (3) a payoff matrix R_{ki} associated with the decisions $A_1(\text{GO})$ and $A_2(\text{NO})$ and states of nature S_i, the expected value could be calculated for each possible sequence.

The expected value of the sequence EV_{SQ} is the expected value of the returns of the decisions that result from each Z_j less the costs of carrying out the sequence.   The costs are the out-of-pocket costs of the study sequence and the opportunity costs that may be occasioned by competitive losses because of delay in introducing the product.

The value of the sequence

$$EV_{SQ} = \sum_j [P(Z_j) \cdot EV_j] - \text{COSTS}$$

where

$$P(Z_j) = \sum_i P(Z_j|S_i) \cdot P(S_i)$$

and where EV_j is the expected reward if Z_j occurs and the best decision is made.   It is the greatest of

$$\sum_i P(S_i|Z_j) \cdot R_{1i} \quad \text{and} \quad \sum_i P(S_i|Z_j) \cdot R_{2i}$$

where

$$P(S_i|Z_j) = \frac{P(Z_j|S_i) \cdot P(S_i)}{\sum_i P(Z_j|S_i) \cdot P(S_i)}$$

See Fig. 7-17 for a typical EV_j branch.   The sequence to be selected would be the one which has the highest expected value of profits.

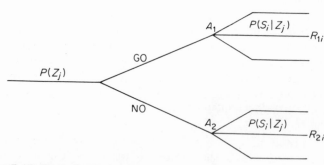

Figure 7-17: Typical EV_j **branch**

[39] See R. Schlaifer, *Probability and Statistics for Business Decisions* (New York: McGraw-Hill, 1959), and F. Bass, "Marketing Research Expenditures: A Decision Model," *Journal of Business* (Jan., 1963), pp. 77–90.

The computational burden of this Bayesian approach is large. Even with only four available studies, 64 sequences $(4 + 4 \cdot 3 + 4 \cdot 3 \cdot 2 + 4 \cdot 3 \cdot 2 \cdot 1)$ would have to be evaluated. The number of study sequences is

$$\sum_{i=1}^{n} {}_nP_i$$

where ${}_nP_i$ = the permutation of n things taken i at a time,
n = the number of ON branches.

This expands rapidly as the number and kinds of studies are increased and various sizes for each type of study are allowed.

The Bayesian approach described above is the fixed mode of analysis. The sequential mode of Bayesian analysis could also be used. In the sequential mode each test result Z_j is described and then the GO, ON, and NO alternatives are examined for each test result. The ON rewards are not known until the final study has been carried out, so each Z_j branches to a new test which produces new test results, each of which branches to another test. The number of decision alternatives that must be evaluated is

$$\sum_{i=1}^{n} T^i {}_nP_i$$

where n = the number of tests,
T = number of possible test results to be considered.

Although the computational burden of this approach is heavy, it is capable of considering tests on different aspects of the product such as cost, sales, and advertising response. The fixed mode of analysis would be ineffective in dealing with such heterogeneous tests, since the states of nature S_i and aggregate test result Z_j could not be meaningfully defined. The computational burden of the sequential analysis can be reduced by heuristics directed at narrowing the decision tree, controlling the number of tests to consider at a point in the network, and by reducing the number of test results by equivalence measures.[40]

The Bayesian method is not the only way to attack the network problem. An alternate approach to the second-stage optimization prob-

---

[40] See G. A. Gorry and G. O. Barnett, "Sequential Diagnosis by Computer," *Working Paper* 299-67 (Sloan School of Management, Massachusetts Institute of Technology, 1967), and G. L. Urban, "New Product Decisions: Information Discounting and Product Selection," *Working Paper* 292-67 (Sloan School of Management, Massachusetts Institute of Technology, 1967).

lem is by the use of matrix algebra to represent the networking problem.[41] A network can be represented by a matrix of unitary coefficients and zeros. These are called x_{ij}, where $x_{ij} = 0$ or 1. "One" indicates selection of link ij. A zero value for x_{ij} indicates that the link ij is not utilized. At the first node, the alternatives are GO (x_{1G}), ON (x_1), and NO (x_{1N}). One of these must be taken, so the sum of the first coefficients must equal 1.

$$x_{1G} + x_{1N} + x_1 = 1$$

If $x_{1G} = 1$, then x_{1N} and $x_1 = 0$, since the sum of the x's are required to be equal to positive 1. The second branch can be represented by removing the ON evaluation from the last step (x_1) and adding the study alternatives. With three alternatives, the branching requirement is

$$-x_1 + x_{21} + x_{22} + x_{23} = 0$$

where x_{2j} are the j tests available after the ON decision if step ON is reached. If $x_1 = 1$, this means one of the x_{2j}'s must be chosen. If $x_1 = 0$, all x_{2j}'s must be zero, which is the desired result if the network has been exited by a GO or NO decision at the previous stage. By continuing in this manner, a set of equations describing the necessary conditions for movement through the links can be established as follows for three evaluation nodes:

$$
\begin{aligned}
x_{1G} + x_{1N} + x_1 \qquad\qquad\qquad\qquad\qquad &= 0 \\
-x_1 + x_{21} + x_{22} + x_{23} \qquad\qquad\quad &= 0 \\
-x_{21} - x_{22} - x_{23} + x_{3G} + x_{3N} &= 0
\end{aligned}
$$

To find the best route through the network, reward values must be established for each route and a solution method must be applied.

This function will depend upon the information secured via the selected path. The authors of DEMON suggest that the updated estimate of sales generated by transversal of an information link be used as a measure of value.[42] They go on to suggest that this objective might be represented by a linear function, but this will not encompass the complexities that usually exist in new product networks. To optimize their objective function, recourse is made to linear algebra. The generalized inverse of the network conditions with certainty equivalents for the GO and NO

[41] The following comments are based on: A. Charnes, W. W. Cooper, J. K. DeVoe, and D. B. Learner, "DEMON: Decision Mapping Via Optimum GO-NO Networks— A Model for Marketing New Products," *Management Science* (July, 1966), pp. 865–87.

[42] *Ibid.*, p. 873

reward function can be theoretically used to locate the best information path.[43]

The networking concepts and GO and NO conditions developed in the model were utilized in a revised formulation of the model called DEMON: Mark II.[44] This model builds on the theoretical base of the earlier model and attempts to develop numerical solution procedures for particular estimation and distribution functions. In the revised model, chance constrained programming is proposed to solve the networking problem.[45] The problem is formulated by defining the return at the evaluation node by a partitioned equation. One portion describes the GO rewards, one the NO rewards, and one the ON rewards. The ON rewards depend upon the remainder of the information network and are fully represented only after writing additional partitioned equations for each of the succeeding nodes. These equations become very complex when the number of nodes is greater than two. The complexity is further increased when it is realized that the available set of alternatives at succeeding ON nodes may be different from previous ones. After the additional equations have been formulated, they must be combined into one overall equation so that chance constrained programming can be implemented. This combination can be obtained after a special solution form has been posited for the equation set.[46] Although the equations can be reduced to a single equation system, the compounding complexity produced by the number of nodes and choices of studies makes the DEMON: Mark II model computationally feasible for only very simple networks (perhaps three or fewer ON nodes).[47]

Although attractive theoretical formulations for carrying out the network optimization have been proposed, computationally feasible models do not seem to exist for carrying out the second-stage sequential optimization. This inability to specify the complete network may not be too significant, since in any event an evaluation will be conducted after each study. The analysis may proceed in a stepwise fashion down the network, but without the second-stage optimization, it does so only in a myopic way. It sees only the next study rather than considering the best total information network available at that point in time.

---

[43] *Ibid.*, p. 884, and C. R. Rao, *Linear Statistical Inference and Its Applications* (New York: John Wiley and Sons, 1965), pp. 24–26.

[44] A. Charnes, W. W. Cooper, J. K. DeVoe, and D. B. Learner, *op. cit.*

[45] See A. Charnes and W. W. Cooper, "Chance Constrained Programming," *Management Science*, VI (March, 1962), pp. 134–48, and G. H. Symonds, "Deterministic Solutions for a Class of Chance Constrained Programming Problems," *Operations Research*, XV (May–June, 1967), pp. 495–511.

[46] A. Charnes, W. W. Cooper, J. K. DeVoe, and D. B. Learner, "DEMON: Mark II Extremal Equations Solution and Approximations," *Management Science*, XIV (July, 1968), pp. 682–91.

[47] *Ibid.*, p. 690.

New Product Selection at the Analysis Stage

The two-step maximization approach presented above must be modified in some respects when the problem is not one of evaluating a new product proposal but rather one of selecting from a group of new product proposals. This new problem is further complicated by the fact that each project may be at different nodes in the information network. Some projects may have more information and less uncertainty associated with them than others. The ease of gaining additional information might also vary with each project. The project selection problem could be approached by using an information evaluation scheme to bring all of the projects to their best informational position. The procedure of imputing the value of future information can be called "information discounting."[48] The second-stage optimization approaches indicated in the last section can serve this purpose, since they give an estimate of the optimum level of information and profit for a project facing the remainder of its information network. With this new estimate for the return and uncertainty associated with the project, the addition of combinations of the new product ideas could be proposed and tested by the procedures developed in the single-product first-stage optimization. The computational burden of this testing could be great if the number of potential new products were large. The number of trials necessary would be C_n^i, where C_n^i is the number of combinations of n items taken i at a time, n is the number of projects to be evaluated, and i is the number of projects to be selected. Heuristic search procedures can be useful in carrying out this evaluation. D. Rice has developed a search procedure, called discrete optimizing, for use in evaluating such complex combinatorial questions.[49] His procedure is a heuristic program that stops searching when a given probability of being a fixed distance away from the optimum is determined.

The computational burden of product selection is even greater if the proposed projects are interrelated. In this situation, the optimum marketing program will depend upon the combination of products added, and the total first-stage profit-maximizing search routine would have to be run for each combination that satisfies the firm's technical, managerial, and financial constraints. The models developed in finance to analyze capital budgeting and portfolio selection problems are relevant here, since they include considerations of interdependency and selection of a best

[48] Urban, *op. cit.*

[49] D. B. Rice, "Product Line Selection and Discrete Optimizing," Institute Paper No. 66 (Jan., 1964), Institute for Quantitative Research in Economics and Management, Krannert Graduate School of Industrial Administration, Purdue University.

subset under constraints. The best combination would then proceed down the decision network. Each product would be subjected to a GO, ON, or NO decision and the group combination would be reevaluated in the light of new information if an ON decision were reached. The computational problems of project selection deserve a good deal of research effort.

Inputs to Analysis Stage

The input demands for the analysis models described in this chapter are great. The models have been developed on a theoretical level, and not enough attention has been directed toward the questions surrounding the generation of input for them.

The required demand, cost, and information network inputs could be estimated on a subjective basis that reflects the decision maker's best judgment. This approach might be justified because the decision must be made, and if the model is not used, a much simpler and perhaps less accurate decision procedure would be used. Subjective inputs, however, should be used only after all empirical information relating to the problem has been considered.

The relationships between the demand and the controllable marketing variables might be approximated by statistical regressions of empirical data. A data bank would include existing products, and statistical regressions would be feasible. If a proposed new product is expected to behave in a way related to an existing product or if test market data were available, a regression of the data might shed light on its demand responses. If this is not the case, resort must be made to subjective inputs with their associated confidence intervals. The best estimates would be used to calculate return and the confidence intervals to determine the uncertainty. If historical data relevant to the product is available, the industry elasticities and cross elasticities could be estimated from a regression of industry sales on past industry price and nonprice variables.[50] The competitive input would be based on a formalization of the reaction functions of the competing firms. These forecasts of future competitive response might be obtained by examining the past competitive responses to price and nonprice changes.

The cost function and cost interaction could be approximated by examining the cost records of the firm for various quantity mixes or by formulating a linear programming model to minimize the cost of producing specified quantities of the firm's products. Successive runs of

---

[50] See the discussion of this approach in Chap. 4 of this book.

the cost minimization model and a regression procedure could yield estimates of the cost interaction.

The examination of past data could be supplemented by directed studies to measure the perceived interrelationships between products. Such a procedure has been developed by Stefflre.[51]

The information network input demands are especially difficult. It seems reasonable to estimate the outcomes of various studies between the existing ON node and the next evaluation node. This input would be in the form of the most likely results of the study and the distribution about this estimate. Given the past estimate, it would supply a basis for determining the conditional distribution of the new estimate. The difficulty is confronted when attempts are made to forecast the results of a number of future studies. This input is needed to find the optimum path through the information network at the second-stage optimization of the new product analysis. The estimation of future conditional distributions requires estimates of second and more remote studies before earlier studies are carried out. These problems of higher degree estimation are an additional restriction on full optimization down the network, but they do not preclude effective step-by-step transversal of the network based on determination of only the next best study.

The problems of generating meaningful input deserve additional research effort. This would be especially true in the area of generating procedures for subjective estimation. Subjective estimates reflecting good business judgment must be relied upon frequently in new product decisions, since in many cases little past data exist that are relevant to the new product innovation. In addition to directing attention to subjective inputs, the statistical analysis of data bank information for estimation deserves additional consideration. New product information systems should be developed so that test market and relevant past data can be integrated with subjective estimates to produce the best possible inputs for the analysis models.

IMPLEMENTATION OF NEW PRODUCTS

Exit from the analysis stage of the information network is made by either a GO or a NO decision. If a NO decision is reached, the product is

[51] V. Stefflre, "Market Structure Studies: New Products for Old Markets and New Markets (Foreign) for Old Products," in F. Bass, C. King, and E. Pessemier, eds., *Applications of the Sciences in Marketing Management* (New York: John Wiley & Sons, Inc., 1968).

rejected and the decision process is terminated for that product. If a GO decision is made, implementation of the marketing plan for the product is begun. Management science approaches are useful in at least two major aspects of the implementation of a new product: (1) planning the implementation process, and (2) monitoring the performance of the new product in test or in full-scale markets.

Planning the Implementation Process

Useful frameworks for the coordination, planning, and control of a new product introduction are the PERT (Project Evaluation and Control Technique) and CP (Critical Path) approaches, which have found widespread use in project management.[52] The PERT/CP framework may be used explicitly to map interrelationships between the various steps of the implementation process. In this way PERT/CP is used to identify potential bottlenecks in the implementation process. This should help reduce the risks involved in marketing the new product. The PERT/CP approach may also be used to minimize the time or costs associated with placing the new product on the market.

Monitoring New Product Implementation

The GO decision reflects the accumulation of enough information about the project to make a commitment of the firm's resources to the product. This does not imply, however, that the firm will blindly proceed with the final marketing of the product. The firm must be careful to ascertain that early estimates of the demand parameters are not erroneous and that the parameters underlying the decision to market the product do not change significantly. An information system should be set up to assure that the relationships assumed or estimated in the model remain correct.

This sensing or monitoring system may be implemented even before full-scale introduction is begun. For example, a market study might be undertaken to monitor changes that are taking place in the market. If changes or errors in the decision premises are detected, the project may be recycled through the analysis state to reoptimize the marketing program for the project and to assure that the GO decision remains appropriate. The test market study may indicate new market response relationships,

---

[52] For a discussion of the use of PERT/CP in new product planning and implementation, see Pessemier, *op. cit.*, Chap. 1, and F. K. Levy, G. L. Thompson, and J. D. Wiest, "The ABC's of Critical Path Scheduling," *Harvard Business Review*, XXXXI (Sept.–Oct., 1963), pp. 98–108.

new parameter values in the original relationships, or changes in the uncertainty associated with current parameter estimates.

At the core of any monitoring system is a model of how the market will respond to the new product. The purpose of such a model is to diagnose the progress of the new product and predict its ultimate performance under current market conditions, using only early market returns as input. If the projected performance is unsatisfactory, the firm is then faced with the question of whether to alter its marketing strategy in an effort to salvage the product or to abandon the product in order to minimize its losses. The question may be resolved by returning to the analysis stage of the new product decision process.

A simple model that might be used to monitor product performance might be one that predicts a sales growth curve of the form:

$$X_t = L(1 - a^t)$$

where X_t = sales in period t,
L = limiting value of sales as $t \to \infty$,
a = constant, where $0 < a < 1$.

This equation may be used to monitor either test market results or full-scale market introduction. Early sales data by time period would be used to estimate a and L. The parameter a measures the rate at which the product is expected to achieve its full market potential, while L represents the ultimate sales level that may be anticipated. If early results indicate that either a or L is likely to be too low, the project should be reexamined, and the product and its accompanying marketing plan should either be modified or dropped.

More complex growth curves are possible. For example, if a Gompertz curve or S-shaped growth curve were hypothesized for the market, early data could be used to approximate its parameters:[53]

$$X_t = A^{B^t} \text{ is a Gompertz relationship}$$

where X_t = sales in period t,
A, B = constants.

On the basis of the early sales results, estimates of A and B can be obtained by plotting the sales levels for each period in a $\ln \ln X$ versus time graph. The equation is then linear ($\ln \ln x = t \ln B + \ln \ln A$), and graphical extrapolation or linear regression procedures may be used to

[53] A logistic function would be another candidate function to represent an S shaped market response function.

generate estimates of A, B, and future sales levels. If the estimated future sales are not favorable, the project would be recycled to the evaluation stage of the decision process. These examples serve to indicate how sales growth models may be used in monitoring new product introductions. The objective of these models is to transform raw market data into a form useful for diagnostic and predictive purposes.

The models of consumer behavior discussed in Chap. 2 of this book could also be utilized at the implementation stage of the new product decision. For example, the linear-learning model proposed by Haines could be used during implementation to estimate market response relationships and to predict the asymptotic level of demand.[54] Markov models might also be useful for prediction, since early data can be used to estimate the transition matrix. If stationarity is assumed, the sales levels for future periods can be predicted. If the firm were to depend upon these predictions as long-term forecasts, then clearly, the nonstationarity that the transition matrices are likely to exhibit would greatly reduce the utility of these forecasts. But long-range forecasting is not the purpose of the monitoring model. The purpose of applying such a model is to diagnose the market trends under *current* conditions. In fact, the firm itself is likely to take steps to alter the transition matrix in the future in the light of what it discovers from the current matrix. The fact that the current values will not be true forever in no way obviates the diagnostic utility of a Markovian monitoring model.

Much of the work on models for monitoring new product introductions has been done in the context of frequently purchased, low-price products. The stochastic consumer models mentioned above are examples of the restriction to these product markets.[55] Another model of this type has been proposed by Fourt and Woodlock.[56] Their approach focuses upon two significant aspects of a new product's performance: (1) its ability to attract new customers—i.e., its penetration—and (2) its ability to hold customers—i.e., its repeat purchase performance. Their method of predicting sales performance from early data is based upon an analysis of repeat buying ratios and first trial penetration. Repeat buying ratios are estimated from the observed number of households that purchase the product on the $(n + 1)$st occasion after having purchased it on the nth occasion. Penetration is estimated by an exponential growth model which has the property that increments in penetration for equal time

[54] G. H. Haines, Jr., "A Theory of Market Behavior After Innovation," *Management Science*, X (July, 1964), pp. 634–58.

[55] This is a general feature of consumer modeling, as was pointed out in Chap. 2.

[56] L. A. Fourt and J. W. Woodlock, "Early Prediction of Market Success for New Grocery Products," *Journal of Marketing*, XXV (Oct., 1960), pp. 31–38.

periods are proportional to the difference between the present penetration level and the asymptotic penetration level for the product. The form of this relation was chosen on the basis of empirical observations of numerous new products in this type of market. Assuming that:

1. The product and package remain the same.
2. Prices remain relatively stable.
3. Competitive activity does not change markedly.
4. Promotional expenditures remain about constant.
5. Distribution does not shift greatly.

Fourt and Woodlock were able to combine the penetration estimate with the repeat ratios and some measure of standard purchase size to obtain an ultimate sales performance estimate based upon these early data.[57]

Building upon the penetration and repeat purchasing notions of Fourt and Woodlock and incorporating the prescribed properties for stochastic models discussed in Chap. 2, Massy has developed an intricate stochastic adoption model for monitoring the introduction of a new product.[58] The model considers the time between successive purchases to be stochastic. A primary model links interpurchase time to the probability that a household will purchase the product in any particular time interval. Secondary models relate the purchase probabilities to time-varying phenomena (which may be the result of such factors as forgetting and word-of-mouth product recommendations) and provide for each household to have its own idiosyncratic response characteristics. The population of consumers is divided into several depth-of-trial classes, depending upon their number of past purchases of the product. The parameters of the model are allowed to vary between these depth-of-trial classes. Once the parameters of the model have been estimated from early market data, forecasts may be developed via a Monté Carlo simulation using these estimated parameter values. Although this model is still in an early stage of development and application, it seems to hold considerable promise in the analysis of test market results and monitoring new product performance.

---

[57] For a detailed example of their approach, see Fourt and Woodlock, *op. cit.*, or R. Kelly, "Estimating Ultimate Performance Levels of New Retail Outlets," *Journal of Marketing Research* (Feb., 1967), pp. 13–20.

[58] See W. F. Massy, "A Stochastic Evolutionary Model for Evaluating New Products," *Working Paper* (Carnegie Institute of Technology, 1967) and "Stochastic Models for Monitoring New Product Introductions," in F. M. Bass, C. W. King, and E. A. Pessemier, eds., *Application of the Sciences in Marketing Management* (New York: J. Wiley and Sons, Inc., 1968). For greater detail see W. F. Massy, D. B. Montgomery, and D. G. Morrison, *Stochastic Models of Consumer Behavior* (Cambridge, Massachusetts: The M.I.T. Press, forthcoming in 1969).

A NOTE ON PRODUCT LINE
DECISIONS

After a new product has been fully introduced to the market, it becomes a part of the firm's product line. This group of products behaves as an interdependent, profit-generating team. Each may be a demand complement of or substitute for other products in the line. Cost interdependencies reflecting production economies or diseconomies of joint production may be present. All the products in the line are interrelated by the allocation of fixed financial and managerial resources. Risk interdependencies may appear, because the fluctuation of any given product may amplify or compensate for fluctuations in other products. The product line problem is to determine the number of products and the marketing mix for each product that will maximize the total profit for the firm.

The number of products offered by the firm can be varied by adding new products or by dropping existing products. The first method is the new product problem discussed in the last sections. The second can be approached by using the models developed for analyzing new products. The decision to drop a product must be based on the change in total line profit and the change in the total risk associated with the line. Thus comparison of the change in total profit and uncertainty can be accomplished by the decision framework described in the analysis stage of the new product decision procedure. The decision to drop a product may also proceed through an information network until it is decided to retain or drop the product. The first-stage optimization might suggest a change in the marketing program of the old product, a decision to keep the product, and an increase in differential profit.

The specification of the optimum product line width could be directly attacked if the demand function facing the firm could be linked to the number of products offered by the firm. Baumol and Ide have structured this approach for the retail market. In their model the demand for the retail firm is a function of the number of products offered N. The single variable calculus model could be applied to specify the optimum product line width N if the equation is differentiable, if the equation for the first derivative is solvable, and if the sufficiency condition can be satisfied.[59]

A more complex approach has been developed by Holdren.[60] Holdren

[59] W. J. Baumol and E. A. Ide, "Variety in Retailing," in F. M. Bass, et al., eds., *Mathematical Models and Methods in Marketing* (Homewood, Illinois: R. D. Irwin, 1961), pp. 121–38.

[60] B. R. Holdren, *The Structure of a Retail Market and the Market Behavior of Retail Units* (Englewood Cliffs, N.J.: Prentice-Hall, Inc., 1960).

divides products into groups defined as transfer effect (i.e., complementary) commodities, without transfer effects commodities, and fixed price commodities. These product definitions are used to investigate the marginal effects of adding or dropping a product from the line. Holdren approaches the product line problem by first assuming that all the products with a transfer effect are included in the line. With this assumption first-order calculus conditions are developed, and products are added to the line on the basis of their contribution to profit until the firm's financial or physical constraints are met. Holdren's marginal approach to the product line decision does not consider the problem of how many complementary or substitute products should be added. The interdependent nature of the product line decision should be considered in determining the products to be included in the product line.

The considerations of interdependency that surround the determination and specification of the optimum size of the product line are similar to those of the new product selection problem. The first-stage maximization of profit would become a function of the variables of all the products, and the output would be the best marketing mix for each product. To find the best number of products to offer, the maximization would be repeated for each relevant combination of new and old products.

The computational problems of this approach are significant. The number of variables at each search would be n times the number considered in the new product case, where n = number of products in the line. The number of combinations to test would also be large as n increases. There are some compensating factors to ease the computational burden of the product line problem. Some of the parameters may be fixed by the market structure, and other parameters may be variable within only narrow ranges. In addition, the number of combinations to test could be reduced by dividing the line into interdependent groups and then treating each group as independent of the others by fixing separate fixed resource allocations for each one. Then the total profit would be the sum of the profit of the group and optimization would be carried out only on each smaller group. Another compensating factor in product line decisions is the availability of data. Existing products have amassed a backlog of experience that can be used to estimate response functions and the other inputs necessary for optimization. The existing products are usually at about the same information level so that the information discounting problem of new product selection is not present. Even with these compensating factors, the computational burden of the product line solution procedures is large. In most cases, simplifying assumptions will have to be made to make the determinations of the optimum product line width and product line marketing program a practical reality.

MANAGEMENT SCIENCE AND
NEW PRODUCT DECISIONS

This chapter has formulated, analyzed, and discussed problems associated with product planning decisions and competitive strategies. Par-
icular attention was given to new product decisions in view of their
ncreasing importance and in view of the fact that new products provide
a convenient framework for discussing topics of relevance to all product
decisions. Recall the discussion of the determination of the optimum
marketing mix that was embedded in the analysis stage of the new product
planning process. The new product problem was viewed through a
four-step process of (1) generating new ideas, (2) screening proposals, (3)
analyzing the projects, and (4) implementing the new product. In each
of the steps of the process, management science models were found useful.

In the generation of new product ideas, allocation and probabilistic
models were found useful in determining the areas of search and the level
of resources to be committed to each area. In the future, these models
probably should be more closely integrated with notions of information
systems and the behavioral phenomena that characterize creativity.

The screening step of the decision sequence has received more management science attention, and useful models have been proposed to aid in
the determination of the relevant set of projects to submit to detailed
analysis. In fact, the screening models have become so comprehensive
that a cost-benefit analysis might be helpful in determining the best
degree of sophistication for a preliminary screening model.

The projects that pass through the screening stage are subjected to
a detailed analysis. This attempts to bring the product to its most
attractive position by the specification of the best marketing mix for the
product for each year in the firm's planning horizon. Model building
efforts should be directed at formulating explicit functions that reflect
the interdependent nature of the variables in the firm's marketing mix.
Effort should also be directed at empirical verification and estimation of
response relationships. The development of empirically verified relationships will begin to give management useful base lines which may then
be judgmentally altered to fit particular situations. Once the model has
been developed, the specification of the optimum marketing mix will
generally require some form of iterative search procedure. Recent years
have witnessed increasing efforts on this front by management scientists.
It would be appropriate for management scientists concerned with marketing problems to give particular attention and assistance to these devel-

opments, since they are powerful tools that can be applied to problems without losing the marketing content.

After the best marketing program for the product has been determined the GO, ON, NO decision must be made. This aspect of the decision modeling should be refined to reflect more complex and realistic decision rules. If an ON decision is made, the second stage of the analysis is undertaken. The determination of the optimum path through the deci sion network needs additional research efforts. Present models are severely limited in their ability to comprehend the information network effects and derive optimal results. The input problems at this stage are particularly difficult, and procedures for estimating the effects of decisions further than one node down the network are needed.

If a GO decision is reached at the analysis stage, implementation of the proposal is begun. PERT models are useful in planning and implement ing the product introduction. Before introduction, models are valuable in assessing the effects of changes in the decision parameters. During testing and introduction of the product, monitoring models are helpful in diagnosing market trends and in assessing their impact on the product's success. Additional research in this stage should be directed at building more detailed models of market response. The consumer models out lined in Chap. 2 should provide a basis of future development of models for the implementation stage of the new product decision process.

The results of utilizing the proposed new product decision system are the decision to accept or reject each proposed product and a specification of the optimum marketing program and implementation plan for each accepted product. If a new product is introduced, it becomes part of the firm's product line. The product line problem is the determination of the best set of parameters for each product in the line and the number of products to be in the line. The similarities between this problem and the new product selection problem were noted, and the associated computa tional problems were outlined. In both new product and product line decisions, a synthesis of all the marketing elements discussed in previous chapters was required for an effective marketing management decision.

8

Implementation of
Management Science
In Marketing

INTRODUCTION

The approach to marketing problems developed in the first eight chapters of this book stands in marked contrast to the usual conceptualization and solution of marketing problems. Traditionally, solutions to marketing problems have been based almost entirely on "common sense." This book has sought to understand the elements in management's "common sense" approach and to structure them in models that can be used in an analytical attack on the problems. In most existing marketing decision environments common sense is reflected in simple "rules of thumb" or "heuristics" that represent policies which seemed to be satisfactory in the past. One of the objectives of this book has been to develop analytical approaches that expand the scope and depth of the considerations given to specific decisions and thereby improve the quality of these decisions. It should be emphasized that this analytical approach does not imply that management judgment will be replaced. Rather, the management science approaches discussed in the earlier chapters will enable management more effectively to use its business judgment.

The transition from the intuitive to the more analytical approach of management science will not be easy, nor is it a perfectly certain event. The nature of barriers to and considerations in the successful implementation of this approach will be discussed in this chapter. The objective is to stimulate further analysis and research in this vital area of implementing management science solutions in actual problem situations.

347

PROBLEMS IN IMPLEMENTING THE MANAGEMENT SCIENCE APPROACH IN MARKETING

Marketing, as a management decision area, has been a substantial laggard in the application of management science. While production and finance grew to maturity in terms of management science approaches to problem solving during the 1950's and early 1960's, marketing only now seems on the verge of very rapid and significant development. In fact, marketing might well be described as a "new frontier" for the application of management science. Many problems remain to be structured, and there is considerable need for creative new technical approaches. Many examples of these needs have been introduced in the preceding chapters of this book.

If marketing is ever to achieve a mature posture in the application of management science methodology to real problems, it is important that increasing attention be given to problems that arise in implementing management science solutions. In this section consideration will be given to characteristics of marketing decision problems, marketing managers, management scientists, and the manager-management scientist interface that give rise to significant implementation problems in this area. To be sure, most of the problems discussed below arise in the implementation of management science solutions in all decision areas of the firm; however, it would seem that marketing suffers under the most acute set of implementation barriers.

The Nature of Marketing Problems

In the first chapter of this book several factors characterizing the nature of marketing decision problems were outlined as major contributors to the lag of management science applications in marketing relative to achievements in production and finance. To reiterate, these factors were

1. Complexity of marketing phenomena
2. High level of interaction between marketing policy variables
3. Competitive reactions
4. Measurement difficulties
5. Instability of marketing relationships

Marketing, existing as it does at the interface of the firm with its environment and consisting virtually entirely of behavioral phenomena, is especially susceptible to the problems outlined above.

A further impediment to progress has been the lack of a free interchange of experience relating to management science applications in marketing. Firms are generally unwilling to discuss successful applications for fear of aiding their competitors. Although these fears have no doubt impeded progress in all areas of management science applications, marketing again would seem to represent an extreme case. This fear is, perhaps, understandable, since marketing is the management decision area that interfaces directly with competitive activity. Furthermore, most firms are unwilling to discuss model failures because of the obvious embarrassment of admitting a mistake. It would seem that progress would be enhanced if by some means better communication could be established concerning both successes and failures.

The Marketing Manager

In this section several tendencies of marketing managers are identified as important reasons for slow progress in applying management science in marketing.[1] All marketing managers do not exhibit these tendencies, and these tendencies do not completely describe the important characteristics of marketing managers, but they seem to have functioned as constraints on management science progress in marketing.

The first tendency of marketing managers is to be oriented toward immediate and observable results. The intrafirm pressure on the marketing manager to achieve yearly sales, market share, and profit goals requires his careful attention to current operations. For example, competition and the firm's adaptation to it usually require careful monitoring and quick reaction. Consequently, although the marketing manager might prefer to do more planning and analysis, he may only be able to do this by directing less attention to current problems and thereby may incur a cost in terms of present results.

Second, by training and career experience the marketing manager is not given to analysis and generalization based on analysis. In many instances the marketing manager lacks a sufficient background in quantitative methods and the behavioral sciences to be a good user of management science, which by its nature depends upon these foundation disciplines. Thus, in order to utilize these tools the marketing manager

---

[1] For further elaboration of these concepts in the context of sales management, see D. B. Montgomery and F. E. Webster, Jr., "Application of Operations Research to Personal Selling Strategy," *Journal of Marketing*, XXXII (Jan., 1968), pp. 50–57.

would often have to yield significant decision control to a technician. H has not been willing to do this and, consequently, there has been a lag in the development of management science in marketing. In addition, marketing managers have a tendency to focus on the idiosyncrasies of each situation. They tend to perceive each situation as a very unique convergence of circumstances and to distrust attempts at generalization Although some scepticism of generalizations is necessary and healthy, in excessive doses it creates strong barriers to the use of management science which seeks to represent complex phenomena in terms of their essential relationships. Hence, the tendency for marketing managers to see each decision situation as a unique phenomenon has contributed to marketing's slow management science development.

The Management Scientist

In many respects the perspective of the management scientist is almost directly opposite to that of the marketing manager. By background and training the management scientist is oriented toward analysis and generalization. He attempts to structure the key relationships in a problem situation in such a way that new decision insights may be gained. Furthermore, his analytic approach often has as its object the establishment of a more general set of policies that may be applied under changing market conditions.

In order to facilitate the structuring and analysis of a market situation, the management scientist must resort to simplifying assumptions and generalizations concerning key variables and their interrelationships. He abstracts the essential aspects from the real world situation and incorporates these into a model that may be manipulated to achieve problem insights and marketing policies.

Although this abstraction and simplification of the key relationships and variables is essential to the management science approach, it very often can and has gone too far.[2] The management scientist's abstractions must appear reasonable to management if the policy implications of the management scientist's work are to be implemented by operating managers. Too often in the past, management scientists have sacrificed reasonable representations of a marketing decision problem for the sake of analytic tractability. Too many so-called applications of management science to marketing have had the appearance of a technique looking for

---

[2] For a delightful parody on this problem see Harold Peterson, "The Wizard Who Oversimplified," *Quarterly Journal of Economics*, LXXIX (May, 1965), pp. 209–11. This paper is reproduced in D. B. Montgomery and G. L. Urban, eds., *Applications of Management Science in Marketing* (Englewood Cliffs, N.J.: Prentice-Hall, Inc., 1969).

a problem. One suspects that the incidence of this "Have model, will travel" approach has contributed to the erection of implementation barriers in marketing. As management science technology enhances its capacity to solve more complex and realistic problems, this implementation problem will hopefully diminish in importance.

The Manager-Management Scientist Interface

The marketing manager's perspective has been characterized by an orientation toward present results, a perception of the complexity and uniqueness of each decision situation, and an incompatibility with analytic approaches. In contrast, the management scientist is oriented to analysis and generalization and utilizes simplifying assumptions to achieve structure and solution capability. Thus it is not surprising that the two often do not mix well. The problem of how to mix these divergent perspectives in a manner profitable to the firm is the basis of the implementation problem. In this section consideration will be given to several viewpoints concerning how this interface should be achieved.

In 1965 Churchman and Schainblatt published what has come to be a much discussed classification of positions to describe the management scientist-manager interface.[3] These four positions are the separate-function position, the communication position, the persuasion position, and the mutual understanding position. These positions are outlined below. In spite of certain design weaknesses, the Dyckman study represents interesting and insightful information bearing on attitudes toward the management scientist-manager interface.

The separate-function position conceives of management and research as separate functions in the implementation of management science. The technical design and solution is taken to be the purview of the researcher, while implementation of the solution is entirely in the hands of the manager. In other words, the researcher is charged with the generation of a theoretical solution, while the manager must see to it that an operational solution is implemented. This separate-function view precludes the need for the researcher and manager to understand each other. Each has a

---

[3] C. W. Churchman and A. H. Schainblatt, "The Researcher and the Manager: A Dialectic of Implementation," *Management Science*, XI (Feb., 1965), pp. B-69–B-87. The entire October, 1965 issue of *Management Science* was devoted to commentary on this paper. Other discussions appear in A. Charnes and W. W. Cooper, "Management Science and Management—Some Requirements for Further Development," *Management Science*, XIII (Oct., 1966) pp. C-3–C-9, and Thomas R. Dyckman, "Management Implementation of Scientific Research: An Attitudinal Study," *Management Science*, XIII (June, 1967), pp. B-612–B-620.

well-specified, separate role to play, and there is no adaptation to one another.

The communication position holds that it is vital for the manager to understand the researcher. Although the scientist must appreciate the need for communicating his solutions so that they can be operationalized, this position sees no great need for the researcher to understand the manager.

The persuasion position is the converse of the communication position. It holds that the researcher must understand the manager in order to overcome managerial resistance to change, to alter managerial attitudes, and to persuade managers to accept recommendations. In this view there is no need for busy managers to understand the researcher.

The mutual understanding position emphasizes the need for both management scientists and managers to understand each other and themselves. A condition of mutual understanding is deemed necessary if both the manager and the management scientist are to respond effectively to the stimuli provided by the other. Thus it is seen as the key to effective implementation.

In their categorization of these manager-management scientist interface positions Churchman and Schainblatt had in mind a very precise definition of the term "understand." In their words:

> the assertion 'the manager understands the researcher' means that the manager reacts to what the researcher is trying to do in a manner that improves the manager's chances of attaining a purpose empirically assigned to him.[4]

A similar definition holds for the assertion "the researcher understands the manager."

The four positions outlined above are displayed in matrix form in Table 8-1.

The question then arises as to the extent to which managers and management scientists hold the various Churchman and Schainblatt positions on the manager-management scientist interface. Dyckman surveyed 45 managers in a Cornell executive program and 45 practicing management scientists in an effort to examine this question.[5] Each of the four positions was represented by a statement. All four position statements were presented simultaneously, and each respondent was asked to indicate whether he agreed, disagreed, or was neutral on each of the statements.

---

[4] *Ibid.*, p. B-70.

[5] Dyckman, *op. cit.* It should also be noted that Ladd published a more limited survey on students in an operations research class in D. E. Ladd, "Report on a Group's Reaction to: 'The Researcher and the Manager: A Dialectic of Implementation,' " *Management Science*, XII, No. 2 (Oct., 1965), pp. B-24–B-25.

TABLE 8-1: Churchman and Schainblatt's Four Positions on the Manager-Management Scientist Interface

		Management Scientist	
		Understands the Manager	*Does Not Understand the Manager*
Manager	*Understands the Management Scientist*	Mutual Understanding	Communication
	Does Not Understand the Management Scientist	Persuasion	Separate-function

Source: Op. cit., p. B-86.

Dyckman's results may be summarized as:

1. Both managers and management scientists made restrained use of the neutral response. Thus both groups appear to have definite views on these issues.
2. The positions are not viewed as mutually exclusive. More than double the number of "agree" responses was observed than would occur under the mutually exclusive condition.
3. Managers and management scientists responded differently to the questions. For example, management scientists disagreed with the separate-function position by a margin of about 5 to 1, whereas managers were about evenly divided. Furthermore, managers gave the greatest number of "agree" responses to the communications position (the one indicating that managers should understand researchers better), whereas researchers gave the greatest number of "agree" responses to the persuasion position (the one in which the researcher should understand the manager better).
4. Both groups exhibited a strong belief in the need for some type of understanding (communication, persuasion, or mutual understanding) but the mutual understanding position did not receive as much agreement as the communication and persuasion positions.

It is not clear from Dyckman's study whether result 2 represents a defect in the design of the questionnaire or whether the respondents really did not see the positions as mutually exclusive. The former seems more likely. Result 3 is interesting, and perhaps even encouraging in that both the managers and the researchers seemed to feel responsibility to shoulder the greater burden at the manager-management scientist interface. With respect to the fourth point, Dyckman found that when the experimental statements were made more clear, simpler, and more general, the mutual understanding position became the position that had the greatest number of agree responses.

In a critique of the Churchman and Schainblatt paper Bennis has argued that understanding of unconscious motives (as implied by the mutual understanding position) is not requisite to the establishment of viable and good relationships.[6] What is needed (and probably most difficult to achieve) in the future is evidence as to which position or combination of positions will yield the best implementation results in what kinds of situations. The task of research on implementation of management science has just begun. It is a critical task for management science in general and especially for marketing, which exhibits many implementation problems in the extreme. The Dyckman research has been described in some detail in the hope that this will encourage additional research into the behavioral aspects of implementation.

CONSIDERATIONS IN IMPLEMENTING MANAGEMENT SCIENCE IN MARKETING

The problems discussed in the previous section suggest that there may be considerable difficulties in implementing the models and approaches discussed in this text in solving real world problems. The problem to be addressed in this section is what considerations and methods may be useful in implementing the management science approach in marketing.

To understand the impact of the approach on an organization, the underlying nature of an organization should be investigated. First thoughts of an organization suggest a formal organization chart, but this is to a large extent a sterile method of considering how to implement management science procedures. The organization is the sum of a large number of individuals. Furthermore, these individuals are grouped into formal and informal groups. These human elements lead to a social structure for the organization that is not dissimilar to social structures in the large. It is characterized by group interaction, power relationships, roles, and political factions with vested interests. The organization also develops communication networks that are based on personal interaction resulting from friendship patterns and formal information channels. The organization is a complex behavioral nebula that is influenced by the individual psychological needs of its members and by the sociological

[6] W. G. Bennis, "Commentary," *Management Science*, XII (Oct., 1965), pp. B-13–B-16.

requirements of its subgroups. These comments suggest that problem solving may not always be the dominant consideration in an organization and that the organization may not always attempt to make optimum decisions.[7] The recognition and understanding of these personal and organizational conditions by both management and management scientists is precisely the mutual understanding position advocated by Churchman and Schainblatt.

The problem is to determine how an innovation such as the mathematical models outlined in this book can be inserted and utilized in an organization. The first limit on the diffusion of the innovations of management science in a firm is the prerequisite personnel capabilities in mathematics and scientific methodology. These abilities are not prevalent in most organizations; usually only a few individuals possess such skills. The organization may procure these skills by hiring capable employees, training existing personnel, or by enlisting outside consultants. If it is assumed that some individuals can be obtained with these skills, the second problem is one of compatibility. Can the person with these skills function usefully in the social, political, psychological milieu of the organization?

Since qualified personnel with the requisite skills are relatively scarce, the possibility of utilizing the personnel possessing the technology of management science in a "staff" capacity is apparent. This staff group would act to train managers in analytical techniques and serve as a consulting group to help solve "line" problems. These groups become part of the sociological structure of the company and must operate realizing that their existence is dependent upon their effectiveness in serving other groups.

The success of the management science group will depend upon (1) their ability to communicate with other segments of the company in understanding and defining realistic and important problems, (2) the group's ability to solve these problems, (3) the group's ability to encourage implementation of their solutions. Studies of business organizations have identified a number of factors that are important in the effective operation of management science groups. On the basis of the study of 66 large companies, Rubenstein, *et al.* have identified ten factors of importance.[8]

---

[7] See R. C. Ferber, "The Role of the Subconscious in Executive Decision Making," *Management Science*, XIII (April, 1967), pp. B-519–B-527, and critiques by G. Fish and K. A. Longman, *ibid.*, pp. B-527–B-529 and B-529–B-533, respectively, for a discussion of psychological aspects of decision making.

[8] A. H. Rubenstein, M. Radnor, N. R. Baker, and D. R. Heiman, "Some Organizational Factors Related to the Effectiveness of Management Science Groups in Industry," *Management Science*, XIII (April, 1967), pp. 508–18.

These factors are grouped under the three headings outlined below:

1. Ability to generate and define important and realistic problems
   a. Receptivity of "line" group to management science group
   b. Level of managerial support
   c. Organizational location of activity
   d. Reputation of management science group in organization
2. Ability to solve problems
   a. Technical capability of management science personnel and group
   b. Adequacy of resources allocated to management science activities
3. Ability to encourage utilization of solutions
   a. Relevance of problem selection for solution
   b. Influence that MS group and its leaders have in the organization
   c. Level of opposition to MS group within the organization
   d. General perception of level of success

Each topic in this outline, along with some additional considerations, will be discussed with reference to marketing.

The ability of the management science group to generate and define important and realistic marketing problems will depend upon the empathy that exists between the marketing and management science group. If the management science group (abbreviated as MS) is organizationally located under the marketing vice president, the mutual understanding is likely to be high. If the MS group is located in the production or engineering areas of the company, the empathy needed to generate and define important marketing problems will probably be relatively small. The higher the level of top management support for the MS group, the less likely this will be.

This top level support will partly depend upon the ability of the MS group to define and attack relevant problems. It is hoped that the understanding of marketing problems by MS groups has been aided by this book. The last seven chapters have attempted to structure and describe over-all marketing problems. This development should help MS groups understand marketing and help marketing personnel to realize the possible contributions of management science in this area. The mutual understanding of marketing problems should help lead to a reasonable definition of any problem to be solved. In the definition of this problem, care should be taken not to oversimplify the problem so that analytic techniques can be applied. Oversimplification is dangerous, since it can yield meaningless and irrelevant results that will be detrimental to future MS efforts. *The problem should be defined, and then a technique should be found to solve it. The problem should dominate the technique.*

In searching for a technique to solve a particular problem it should be remembered that the results of applying the technique will be judged by their effectiveness during implementation rather than the theoretical sophistication involved in the solution method. The competence of the MS group should not be measured only by their command of management science techniques, but also by their ability to apply them to a given problem with a minimum loss of realism in the problem and resulting solution. The resources available for use in the solution of the problem will also affect the capability of the MS group to solve marketing problems. The concept of the model bank developed in this book should be helpful in this respect. The model bank should include a number of models that yield varying degrees of accuracy at varying levels of cost.[9] With this range of model capabilities, a costs/benefits tradeoff may be made for model usage on any given problem. Hence effort could be allocated to solve problems so as to yield the most effective use of the firm's management science resources.

After a problem solution has been found, the job of the management science group is not finished. If the approach is to yield rewards for the firm, the solutions must be implemented. If the problem selected was mutually designated as important, defined in a relevant manner, and properly solved, the chances of acceptance and implementation will be enhanced. At the implementation stage, empathy is again important. The marketing group must be convinced of the usefulness of the solution and must find the implementation compatible with its social and political position in the company. This conviction should be based on their involvement with the model and the quality of the solution rather than merely the result of persuasion by the MS group.

The conditions necessary for successful implementation can be greatly aided if the manager who is to use the solution is involved in the derivation of that solution. The information system concepts outlined in the first chapter and developed throughout the text may provide a practical mechanism for gaining acceptance and implementation of management science findings. The notion of a user-designed system that serves to answer managers' questions is highly desirable. The use of an on-line interactive computer system in conjunction with a marketing model bank allows the "man" to be put into the management science solution procedure. By interacting with a model that is designed to solve his problems, he can explore his subjective feelings and generate solutions. This high involvement by the marketing manager in the problem solution should lead to a greater willingness to implement the solutions yielded by management science techniques.

---

[9] The developers and users of the model bank should be aware that a "Have model, will travel" approach could result from inappropriate use of the models in the model bank. In each case, an appropriate modeling approach should first be determined. If the existing models in the model bank do not meet the needs of the particular problem in terms of a costs/benefits tradeoff, then a new model must be developed to solve the problem.

In initial attempts to involve the "man" or the marketing manager in the MS system, it may be wise to forego the sophisticated models that could be applied to the problem. A descriptive model of how the manager makes this decision may be the best starting point for involvement of the man in the system. With this descriptive model and a retrieval system, the manager may see ways to improve his decisions. This involvement might then provide the basis for an evolution of the decision maker's model to a more normative level, which eventually results in confidence and involvement in a sophisticated management science model. The use of an *evolutionary* approach to the design of the model bank and information system may yield the greatest long-term rewards for the firm, since it will lead to utilization of management science technology to solve relevant problems and to implementation of the ensuing MS recommendations. The potential involvement in solutions may aid in more than the utilization of the outcome. This man-system involvement may lead to a higher level of support for the MS group and may reduce the isolation of the MS group during utilization of its recommendations.

The problems of the MS group and its relationships to marketing could be overcome if each marketing executive was a manager scientist, but this would not be healthy. Many of the activities of marketing people, such as motivating salesmen, developing advertising appeals, generating new product ideas, and handling organizational problems, are not directly within the realm of management science. The marketing organization will probably be characterized by specialists. The management science modeling will probably be done by specialists, so the management scientist-marketing manager considerations outlined above will be important.

The future will contain MS specialists, but it can be expected that marketing managers will progress through three stages of development if the management science approach is to be productively implemented in marketing organizations.

The first stage is a realization that management science techniques are not to be feared and that they are designed to aid a user (marketing manager) solve his problems. The second stage is the ability to overcome the naive confidence that management science techniques can solve all problems. The manager will always have a vital role in the model design, input, and implementation. The final stage of development will be a mature attitude toward management science. This maturity will be reflected in a realization of the limitations of the management science approach in marketing and the potentialities of the approach in the understanding, exploration, and solution of problems. If this maturing occurs, the place of management science in marketing will be correctly specified and the model building approaches outlined in this text will be correctly used.

SUMMARY

In this chapter marketing was depicted as a functional management area exhibiting great barriers to the application of management science. Factors in the nature of marketing problems and in the tendencies of marketing managers and management scientists were identified as causes of the lag in applications of management science in marketing. The sharp contrast between the approach and perspective of the management scientist and the marketing manager identifies the manager-management scientist interface as a key focus in implementation. Four basic positions on this interface were identified and some attitudinal results on each position were presented. Finally, factors that should lead to successful implementations were discussed.

The basic premise underlying this chapter was that management science in marketing will stand or fall on its ability to implement solutions to real problems. Unfortunately, little research has been done in this area. It is vital that a concerted attack be launched on these problems if the full benefits of the management science approach to marketing are to be realized.

9

The Future of
Management Science
In Marketing

In this chapter certain salient aspects of the future of management science in marketing will be considered. Attention first will focus on the expected impact of marketing information systems upon management science in marketing. Then the model bank component of the marketing decision-information system will be examined. This component of the decision-information system has been the focus of Chaps. 2 through 7. In this final chapter, emerging model structures and methodologies will be emphasized. Finally, certain important areas of future research opportunity for management science in marketing will be outlined.

FUTURE DEVELOPMENTS IN
MARKETING INFORMATION
SYSTEMS

Models and Information Systems of the Future

As marketing information systems and their associated data banks develop, they will greatly expand the information base for management decisions. Management will be able to collect, store, retrieve, and manipulate vast quantities of data much more readily and at lower cost than at present. There may be some danger in these developments, however. As more data are generated, the manager will experience a greater need for and difficulty in assimilating this information in such a way that it will prove useful in the decision processes of the firm. Although the manifold expansion of the manager's data resources and data-handling capabilities would seem to promise considerable rewards in decision making, there is the possibility that the manager will suffer from an information overload. That is, the manager may be swamped with data to such an extent that he cannot make effective use of the data even with the data manipulation capabilities that the information system will provide him.

Faced with an almost bewildering array of data, the manager seems likely to turn to the management scientist for assistance in putting the powerful new information system tools to good use in the decision processes of the firm. The management scientist may assist the manager by developing models that may be used to transform data into understandable and meaningful measures for management's use. These models may also generate recommended decision solutions or help to identify classes of information which are lacking and which the firm should incorporate within its marketing information system. The evolution of marketing information systems may be expected to generate a management need and desire for management science applications in marketing.

While the data explosion encouraged by information systems will make the necessity for models more apparent, the enlarged data bases will also provide the model builder with a richer source of data to use in formulating, estimating, and testing marketing models. The data bank and the system's statistical bank will combine to give the management scientist new leverage in the development of realistic marketing models that can be used to solve significant management problems.

Computer Developments and Their Impact on Information Systems

A particularly promising development in information systems hardware and software has been the advent of the time-shared computer. A time-shared computer is one that may be used virtually simultaneously by several users, each communicating with the computer from remote consoles. The time-shared computer has made possible the development of the computer utility. A computer utility is an operation which maintains a time-shared computer on which individuals and organizations may purchase computing time according to their needs. The utility handles all maintenance aspects of the necessary hardware and software. The user need only be concerned about his own programs. Thus the user need not commit himself to a significant investment in hardware, software, and personnel if he is to take advantage of the computer's capabilities. With a computer utility, he buys only what he needs. The development of central utilities will also make the economies of scale of a large third-generation computer available to users of all sizes. This means small users will be able to access high-speed machines having very large memory capacities and they will be better able to develop and utilize complex models efficiently. Thus the time-shared computer utilty has altered the economics of computer usage. Relatively small businesses now find the computer well within their financial capabilities. This should make the development of models and information systems more feasible for smaller businesses.

A derivative development from the computer utility is beginning to appear. It might be termed the "model utility." The model utility provides a model and solution capability for a general type of problem, such as media selection and scheduling. The model is then made available to clients via the framework of the computer utility. That is, the model is maintained within the central computer system of a computer utility. Clients are then permitted access to the model via remote terminals. Just as in the case of the computer utility, the model utility changes the economics of the application of management science to marketing. A firm no longer has to sustain a costly management science staff in order to begin to use management science in its marketing decisions. Again, relatively small firms will find it feasible to take advantage of such model developments. At least one such model utility does exist. The MEDIAC media selection model developed by Little and Lodish and discussed in Chap. 3 has been commercially implemented as a model utility. The computer and model utilities should greatly enlarge the population of firms which may usefully and economically take advantage of the computer and marketing models.

Along with the development of better computer hardware, new software is also emerging. One of the most important developments has been an improvement in the input and output capabilities in time shared systems. The most significant trend is toward graphical input and output. This is important because graphical display is meaningful to managers. It is easier for most managers to think in terms of graphics rather than in mathematical symbols and numbers.

An example of the application of graphic input/output to a problem of sales management will make the potential communication contribution clear. For this example, consider the problem of sales territory definition. A map of the area that is to be partitioned into sales territories could be projected on a graphical display device. The graphical device could be connected to a computer, which would contain the relevant information about the area. For example, the computer might have information regarding the distribution of present and potential customers in the area. The sales manager would then be provided with a light pen which he could use to partition the graphic display of the area into sales territories. Once he had arrived at a territory definition that he would like to consider, he would then call upon the computer to take the graphic input and evaluate the sales and other marketing implications of the proposed territorial definitions. The evaluation would be performed by a sales model or models that would utilize the area information that had been stored in the data bank. If the manager approves of the implications of his current territorial definition, he might decide to adopt the current definition. Probably he would like to explore several alternatives in an effort to achieve a satisfactory (even if not globally optimal) definition of sales territories. This method of user-machine interaction should enable the manager to utilize effectively his business judgment in creating alternatives. The computer, as an enthusiastic clerk, would then assist him in evaluating each alternative. This brief example illustrates the fact that future hardware and software developments promise to open up new areas of marketing decision for the management scientist by improving the computer's ability to communicate effectively with the manager.

Another development in computer software will be the creation of programs for use in retrieving and displaying information from the data bank. It can be expected that the major computer manufacturers will make available prepackaged programs to carry out the data bank organization and retrieval functions (see Chap. 1 for a discussion of these functions). For example, IBM is developing a comprehensive language for this task that is called GIS (Generalized Information System). In the utilization of these programs the manager and model builder will have considerable flexibility in exploring relevant data. A likely mode for this exploration is what might be called "data browsing." In this mode the management scientist or manager may use the display, retrieval, and manipulation capabilities of the decision information system to explore relationships in the data stored in the data bank. Such exploration or browsing may yield new insights into relationships between variables, may indicate fruitful opportunities, or may diagnose previously undetected problems in the firm's marketing system.

In summary, the developments cited in this section are examples of the expanding capabilities that the computer will offer managers in designing and utilizing information systems. These developments will make more sophisticated systems a practical reality and will extend the advantages of such systems to medium and small, as well as large, companies.

The Role of the Management Scientist in the Evolution of Information Systems

One final point should be emphasized in examining the future of information systems. This is the role of the management scientist in the evolution of such systems. Although marketing information systems have great potential as sources of better data for formulating, estimating, and testing marketing models, full realization of this potential will require management scientists actively to participate in the design and development of these systems. Failure by management scientists to participate in this process will likely result in information systems that will not adequately meet the needs of future model-building activities.

For example, involvement of the management scientist in the design of the marketing information system will place him in a position to help assure that the system will maintain information that will be required in future development, estimation, and validation of marketing models. Without the participation of the management scientist, such information might not be maintained in appropriate form within the system.

MODELS AND THE MODEL BANK

The primary focus of this book has been a consideration of the models that might be placed in the firm's marketing model bank. The purpose of this section is to indicate certain directions in which marketing model development seems to be advancing.

The most valuable trend in marketing models is toward realism. Marketing models can be expected to become more realistic by the incorporation of more of the relevant market phenomena. Forthcoming models will consider multiple marketing policy variables and will probably include a dynamic consideration of these variables. In particular, the multiproduct aspects of promotion, pricing, and distribution will need to be considered if realism is to be gained.

Another major factor in increasing the realism of marketing models will be the incorporation of behavioral science theories in mathematical models. The microanalytical market simulation approach developed by Amstutz (see Chap. 2) provides an excellent example of the possibilities in this area. This initial approach to integrating behavioral material should be developed and applied to other models that may be characterized by higher levels of aggregation.

Since additional behavioral realism can generally be obtained by disaggregation, an important issue in the future will be the level of detail (or aggregation) to use in any given problem. As an example of different levels of detail or aggregation in a marketing model, consider the level of detail used in representing market response to distribution effort. In Chap. 7 on new product decisions, market response was simply made a function of a distribution index D. This approach treats distribution effort in a very aggregative manner. A more disaggregative approach was taken by Kuehn and Weiss. They were concerned with how the manufacturer's marketing effort would cause the retail outlets to present the consuming public with a given quality of distribution.[1] The index of distribution quality presented to the consumers by the retailer was taken to be a function of the product's percentage of distribution, shelf space, and shelf position. The retailer's performance of these activities on behalf of the product was in turn taken to be a function of the product's sales record in the outlet, the manufacturer's consumer level advertising, the manufacturer's special promotions, and detailing effort directed at the retailer by the manufacturer's salesmen. Thus the Kuehn and Weiss approach encompasses greater detail and consequently is less aggregative than the new product models. Finally, there is the very disaggregative microanalytic approach in which the retailer's attitudes toward the product and its associated marketing activities are modeled in considerable detail, as are other aspects of the retailer's offering to the consumers. In deciding upon an appropriate level of aggregation, the manager or management scientist must make (at least implicitly) a costs/benefits tradeoff.

Although a definitive solution to the costs/benefits question regarding level of aggregation has not yet been achieved, there are. at least a few observations that can be made at the present state of the art. In the first place, it would seem that, in general, the greater the detail (or disaggregation) in a model, the greater is the number of behavioral phenomena that may be incorporated in the model. This tends to enhance the realism of the model and thereby its plausibility to the manager. The enhanced plausibility to the manager proves, in turn, to be a considerable asset when it comes to implementing the model. However, greater disaggregation also has its costs. As disaggregation increases, so, in general, do the costs. These costs include the time and financial costs of model development, input generation, operation, and maintenance, and they increase very rapidly, perhaps exponentially, as the level of detail increases. For example, experience has shown that the firm that wishes to utilize the microanalytic simulation approach will probably have to commit hundreds of thousands of dollars' worth of internal manpower and financial resources. The more aggregative models, such as those discussed in Chap. 7, may be formulated, operated, and maintained for much less. Finally, the more aggregative models have the advantage that a reasonably large number of alternative marketing mixes may be tested. In fact, using numerical optimization techniques,

---

[1] A. Kuehn and D. Weiss, "Marketing Analysis Training Exercise," *Behavioral Science*, X (Jan., 1965), pp. 51–67.

the manager or management scientist will often find it feasible to locate an optimal marketing mix in the context of these models. The time and cost constraints that are operative in the case of the more detailed models generally preclude consideration of more than a few alternatives. Thus, there are advantages and disadvantages to each level of model aggregation.

There is a need for further theoretical and practical empirical work on this question of the appropriate level of aggregation for any given problem. One concept is clearly relevant, however. It is the model bank concept. The model bank could contain several models for each of the relevant problems, but they would represent different levels of aggregation and operation cost. In a given problem the model with the best cost/benefit characteristics for a particular decision situation would be used. The model bank concept also suggests that models may be compatibly used to solve problems. For example, an aggregate model may be used to determine which marketing mix alternative should be selected, and then this mix may be presented to a microanalytical simulation to determine the detailed behavioral responses associated with the strategy. In this way the detail of disaggregation can be combined at a reasonable cost with the capability for examining many alternatives.

In considering the model bank composition, two model types deserve special mention at this point in terms of their future promise in management science applications to marketing. The first of these is what might be termed manager-model interactive formulations. The purpose of these models is to provide the manager with a direct communication link with the model so that he may use the model as a tool for applying his business judgment to a given problem. This manager-model interaction is different from a mere on-line capability. The manager-model interaction would be designed to be effective in communicating with a manager rather than a management scientist or programmer. The development of computer graphics indicated in the previous section should make this kind of modeling more feasible, since graphics are generally an effective means of communication for managers. The interactive mode of operation offers particular advantages. In the first place, it enables the manager to gain confidence in the model by allowing him to explore how the model responds to different conditions. This involvement with the model may result in a better model, since upon direct interaction with the model, the manager may find the model unsatisfactory in terms of structure or level of detail and call for its revision and improvement. The interactive mode may also improve the model by allowing the manager immediately to explore his intuitive insights. In batch processing model operations, the manager can not immediately follow all his intuitive leads. Rather, it is necessary for him to work sporadically on the model over several days or weeks of calendar time. It would seem that model involvement in the interactive mode would better enable the manager to explore his problem insights in a more efficient manner. The level of managerial involvement encouraged by manager-model interaction should also smooth the path to implementation of the model.

The second model type is the adaptive model. Since marketing phenomena are notoriously dynamic, models that enable management to track changes in the market seem to offer significant advantages. Although this model type has just begun to be explored in marketing, preliminary results indicate considerable future promise for this class of models in marketing. Model banks of the future will probably contain adaptive models and interactive models of various levels of aggregation for use in solving specific problems.

RESEARCH OPPORTUNITIES FOR MANAGEMENT SCIENCE IN MARKETING

Previous chapters as well as the preceding sections of this chapter have indicated a number of potential research opportunities in the application of management science to marketing. Rather than present an itemized review of these opportunities, this final section will outline some of the most promising and important areas for research.

In reviewing the existing management science research in marketing, it is clear that the most attention has been given to two topics: advertising decisions and stochastic models of consumer behavior. While these topics will continue to be important foci for research, there remains a significant untapped potential in other areas of marketing. Personal selling is perhaps the prime example. In spite of its significance in the marketing mix of many firms, it has been slow to yield to management science efforts. The potential rewards for successful applications in this area would seem to justify a more intensive management science effort. A similar case may be made for distribution channel decisions. Greater efforts are required to generate models that encompass the demand creation aspects of channels and consider multichannel systems. The increasing importance of new products in the growth and profitability of the modern corporation would also seem to justify more intensive efforts at all levels of the new product decision—search, screening, analysis, and implementation. Although all problem areas deserve research, these areas would seem, perhaps, to have the greatest marginal rewards to the management science effort.

While modeling work is necessary in some previously neglected problem areas, research is also needed at the basic marketing response level. Market response functions are common to all the problem areas and although additional theoretical work will be useful, empirical testing and comparison of response functions would seem to be especially important. Since response functions represent the building blocks from which models are formulated, increased empirical research in this area would seem to be vital to the growth of management science applications in marketing.

Empirical research on market response functions is dependent upon measurement techniques. The problems of data-based measurement present many opportunities for research. For example, most data-based measurement in the past has been performed upon models that were linear or linearizable in the parameters. Yet most interesting marketing response functions are not intrinsically linear but exhibit threshold effects, increasing returns over some range, decreasing returns over another range, and perhaps even negative returns as the market becomes offended by overzealous marketing effort. As a consequence, methods for estimation of nonlinear market response functions will become increasingly important.[2]

Along with the need for work on data-based measurement, judgment measurement procedures deserve additional consideration. Many of the models discussed in earlier chapters require management judgment concerning relationships, parameters, and variables. These factor inputs must somehow be quantified in such a way that they accurately reflect the manager's judgment. Some interesting theoretical work has recently been reported,[3] but experience must also be gained in the use of these methods with marketing managers. The theory and practice of quantifying management judgment is especially important to the success of management science in marketing and therefore should receive accelerated research attention.

The final and perhaps most important area for research concerns implementation of management science in marketing. Research on the implementation of management science in general has not received a level of research effort commensurate with its obvious importance. With respect to research on the implementation of management science in marketing, the picture is even worse. The participation of behavioral

---

[2] For some results relating to nonlinear regression, see N. Draper and H. Smith, *Applied Regression Analysis* (New York: John Wiley & Sons, Inc., 1966), pp. 263–304, and E. Malinvaud, *Statistical Methods of Econometrics* (Chicago: Rand McNally, 1966), pp. 277–318.

[3] See R. L. Winkler, "The Quantification of Judgment: Some Methodological Suggestions," *Journal of the American Statistical Association*, LXII (Dec., 1967), pp. 1105–20, and "The Assessment of Prior Distributions in Bayesian Analysis," *Journal of the American Statistical Association*, LXII (Sept., 1967), pp. 776–800.

scientists in such research must be encouraged. It would seem that procedures must be developed to overcome management's fear of quantitative techniques and lead to mature usage of the management science technology. One positive trend that can be seen is that business schools are supplying their students with basic quantitative capabilities. As these young managers move into influential positions, they should supply a positive force toward effective utilization of management science models in marketing.

POSTSCRIPT

Although marketing has been somewhat tardy in the development of management science applications, it now seems that with the development of more realistic models and better computer capabilities, marketing is on the threshold of accelerated progress which holds many challenging opportunities for the manager and management scientist. It is the hope of the authors that this book may contribute to the development of useful marketing models and information systems.

Index

CONCEPT AND TECHNIQUE INDEX